THE CHURCH'S CONFESSION OF FAITH

A Catholic Catechism for Adults

A CATHOLIC CATECHISM FOR ADULTS

The Church's Confession of Faith

Originally published by the
German Bishops' Conference

Translated by Stephen Wentworth Arndt
Edited by Mark Jordan

COMMUNIO BOOKS

IGNATIUS PRESS   SAN FRANCISCO

Title of the German original:
Katholischer Erwachsenen Katechismus:
Das Glaubensbekenntnis der Kirche
© 1985 Verband der Diözesen Deutschlands, Bonn

Cover by Roxanne Mei Lum

With ecclesiastical approval
© 1987 Ignatius Press, San Francisco
ISBN 0–89870–162–7
Library of Congress catalogue number 87–80530
Printed in the United States of America

About Communio Books

With *The Church's Confession of Faith*, the North American edition of *Communio: International Catholic Review* begins a series of *Communio Books*. The international *Communio* was founded in the early 1970s by Hans Urs von Balthasar, Joseph Ratzinger, and other theologians in Europe. Its purpose can be stated simply: to express and promote the reality carried in its name, the reality which is the essence of the Church. The *communio*-unity which defines the Church is modelled upon and rooted in the trinitarian unity of God; and it is specifically Catholic in that such unity is understood fundamentally, though not exclusively, as unity and hierarchical *communio* with the office of Peter. There are many ways of expressing and promoting this reality of the Church. What is distinctive about the way of *Communio*?

The international *Communio* seeks above all to provide theological discernment with respect to the major issues facing Catholics in our time. A discernment proper to *communio* attaches to certain principles. Above all, such discernment presupposes prayerfulness, understood in all its ontological depth: the loving listening to our Lord which is the way of our transformation into him. Only one who is truly united with Christ can discern in the name of Christ. This loving listening to our Lord involves in turn a loving listening to the Church, which is his Body. Only one who is truly united with the Church can discern in the name of the Church.

These fundamental principles indicate why *Communio*, in its effort to provide theological discernment, is concerned to retrieve the central and enduring doctrines of the Church tradition: for understanding these doctrines is the way into the mind of Christ, and the mind—the truth—of Christ is the measure of *communio*. These principles also indicate why *Communio* is concerned to overcome polarization wherever it exists: criticizing where necessary, but always in charity, for the love of Christ is the measure of *communio*.

Publishing is a natural forum for carrying on this work of theological discernment, and so the international *Communio* has directed its energies toward the publication of journals, first in Germany and Italy, and now in federated editions in ten additional countries: France, North America, Yugoslavia, Spain, Portugal, Poland, the Netherlands, Brazil, Chile, and Lebanon. But the intention of *Communio* from the outset was, where feasible, to link the publication of journals with the development of groups of associates, the planning of conferences, and the publication of books. Beginning with the present work, therefore, the North American *Communio* now adds a series of books to its journal (*Communio: International Catholic Review*), and to its many conferences (on the work of Hans Urs von Balthasar; on religion and politics; on women in the Church; on dissent and development in the Church; on theoretical physics and the problem of mechanism). These books will reflect the purpose and practice of the journal: to seek out writings which meet the highest standards of scholarship, but in a form which distills the fruits of scholarship for the end of discernment from the perspective of the Catholic tradition.

The book we have chosen to publish first is a catechism for adults, authored largely by Walter Kasper under the aegis of the German Bishops' Conference. Such a work of course represents but one of many different possible kinds of writing appropriate for our series. The series is intended to include titles in theology, philosophy, spirituality, history, and the like, works by contemporary authors as well as reprints or translations of not easily accessible classical authors. Nonetheless, the choice of the catechism as the first book in the series is intentional: *The Church's Confession of Faith* is a sure and faithful distillation of the central doctrines and principles of the Catholic tradition, a distillation which takes account of the fruits of modern scholarship even as it exercises discernment with respect to such scholarship.

David L. Schindler
General Editor
Communio Books

CONTENTS

PART TWO
JESUS CHRIST

PART THREE
THE WORK OF THE HOLY SPIRIT

CONTENTS

The Nicene Creed

We believe in one God,
  the Father, the Almighty,
  maker of heaven and earth,
  of all that is seen and unseen.

We believe in one Lord, Jesus Christ,
  the only Son of God, eternally begotten of the Father,
  God from God, Light from Light,
  true God from true God,
  begotten, not made, one in Being with the Father.
  Through him all things were made.
  For us men and for our salvation
    he came down from heaven:
  by the power of the Holy Spirit
    he was born of the Virgin Mary, and became man.

For our sake he was crucified under Pontius Pilate;
  he suffered, died, and was buried.
  On the third day he rose again
    in fulfillment of the Scriptures;
  he ascended into heaven
    and is seated at the right hand of the Father.
  He will come again in glory to judge the living and the dead,
    and his kingdom will have no end.

We believe in the Holy Spirit, the Lord, the giver of life,
  who proceeds from the Father and the Son.
  With the Father and the Son he is worshipped and glorified.
  He has spoken through the Prophets.

We believe in one holy catholic and apostolic Church.
We acknowledge one baptism for the forgiveness of sins.
We look for the resurrection of the dead,
  and the life of the world to come. Amen.

FOREWORD

"Catechesis was always considered by the Church as one of her most important tasks." With these words Pope John Paul II begins his apostolic letter *Catechesi Tradendae*, which he published as the fruit of the Bishops' Synod of 1977. The great importance of catechetical instruction can be seen in the commission of the Risen Lord: "Go, therefore, and make disciples of all the nations. Baptize them in the name 'of the Father and of the Son and of the Holy Spirit'. Teach them to carry out everything I have commanded you" (Mt 18:19–20).

The Church fulfills the Lord's commission in evangelization, through which men are led to faith, and in catechesis, through which incipient faith is strengthened and matures. The disciples of Christ are led by catechesis to a deepened insight into the mystery of the person of Jesus Christ and of his message.

As successors to the Apostles, we bishops bear a particular responsibility for the proclamation of the word of God. Our times, in which many have become unsure in their faith or no longer know it properly, challenge us to increased efforts in instruction in the faith. In order to do justice to this task, the German Bishops' Conference is publishing the present catechism, which reliably presents the Catholic faith and is supported by the Conference's authority.

On the basis of the Great Confession of Faith, the Nicene Creed, which is common to Christians of the East and the West, this catechism unfolds the mystery of Christ in a way accessible to the men of our time. Its use should strengthen faith within our dioceses, deepen the living union of the faithful with Jesus Christ and help the faithful in living as Christians in the world.

The German Bishops' Conference resolved at its Spring Meeting of March 12–15, 1985, in Altötting to publish the present text, which presents the Church's teaching of faith, according to canon 775, § 2, of the *CIC* as a Catholic Adult Catechism (Part I). The moral teaching of the Church is to be presented in a second part. The Apostolic See approved, by a Letter of the Congregation for the Clergy dated December 22, 1984, the publication and dissemination of the catechism *Katholischer erwachsenen Katechismus* (*The Church's Confession of Faith*), by the German Bishops' Conference (again pursuant to canon 775, § 2).

I wish to thank the Catechism Commission which compiled the text and to give my special thanks to Professor Walter Kasper, who bore the main burden of drafting this text.

The German Bishops now present this catechism to the public, especially to those who are commissioned in the service of the Church with the proclamation of the word of God and instruction in the faith. May this new catechism effect a renewal of catechesis, and thereby a renewal of the Church, and contribute to a blossoming of faith in our dioceses.

At Cologne, on the solemn feast of the Resurrection of Jesus Christ, 1985.

+ Joseph Cardinal Höffner
President, German Bishops' Conference

PART ONE

GOD THE FATHER

I

I BELIEVE—HELP MY UNBELIEF

1. Man: A Mystery

The Church's confession of faith begins with the two small words "I believe". Just two small words, and yet they are exceedingly rich in content. *The two words "I believe" are decisive for our whole life*. For who am I? From what, why, and for what purpose am I? Can I really believe? That is, can I trust? What should I believe, and whom may I believe and trust? Perhaps I should like to believe, but is there not better reason to be distrustful? Does not anxiety overcome us often enough? Do we not have occasion for sceptical reserve? Can I commit myself in faith to a definite religion or confession? Can I say the first words of the Church's great confession of faith, the Niceo-Constantinopolitan Creed—the words   39–40
"We believe"?

Our lives flow along, day by day, week by week. Normally everything has its place and its order, until one day the question arises: What really is the purpose of it all? Adam, where are you?

Even a small child just awakening to consciousness will ask adults question after question. What is that? Why is that so? What is that for? Even the parents often do not have a good answer and feel that many things that earlier seemed self-evident to them are really not so. In adolescence, people begin to discover their own identities. From then on, they want to shape their lives for themselves. They protest and question the adult world. In the criticisms of their maturing children, many parents feel themselves called into question. Every generation, and even more so every historical epoch, has its own manner of seeing things and develops its own way of life. We are experiencing this upheaval today in an especially clear way. What remains? What can we pass on? By what can we orient ourselves? Where can we find a foothold, some ultimate meaning for our lives?

The *question about the meaning of life* is posed differently for each of us. It   327–328
can arise as the question about happiness. We experience happiness in so many different ways: when our work turns out well, when we are

15

successful; we experience it in being with a person we love, in a good deed and in service of others, in sport and play, in art and science. We know we cannot make happiness and that it can fade away very quickly. Bitter disappointments can set in. What then? What meaning does life have then? What is true human happiness anyway? The question about the meaning of existence is posed even more intensely in the experience of suffering, whether my own suffering or that of another—whether incurable disease, sorrow, loneliness, or need. What meaning is there in the suffering of so many innocent people? Why is there so much hunger, misery, and injustice in the world? Why so much hatred, envy, deceit, and violence? Finally, there is the experience of death, when a friend, an acquaintance, or a relative is suddenly no longer among us or when we are confronted with the thought of our own death. What comes after death? Where have I come from? Where am I going? What will remain of what I have struggled for?

Our answers to these questions are never fully satisfactory. *Man ultimately remains a question and a deep mystery to himself.* This is his greatness and his burden. His greatness, because the question about himself distinguishes man both from inanimate objects, which are simply present at hand, and from the animals, which through their instincts are closely adapted to their environment. Questioning constitutes human dignity: we are conscious of ourselves and know that we are free to give a direction to our lives. But this greatness is also the burden of being human. For us, life is both a gift and a task; we ourselves must shape it and take it in hand. The meaning of being human is not immediately given with our being. Being human is a journey, then, into the wide open and the unforeseeable.

We can repress the question about meaning, run away from it, or dismiss it as unanswerable. There are many ways to do this: a flight into work, activity, consumption, sex, pleasure, alcohol, or drugs. In fleeing, we deceive only ourselves; we run away from ourselves. The meaning of being human is a question which belongs to our dignity precisely as humans. If we no longer posed the question about ourselves, we would regress to the level of clever animals. So the question is posed unavoidably for us: What is it to be human? Where have we come from? Where are we going? This is the old catechism question, old and yet always new: For what purpose are we on earth?

2. Preliminary Answers

2.1 Science

Many expect modern science to answer their questions. No one can deny the advances made by the sciences. The sciences offer knowledge secured by proofs, methodically established, and made logically coherent. The sciences have settled many questions for which earlier centuries had only imperfect answers or none at all. We know today infinitely more, for instance, about the world's development, the origin of life, the laws that determine the reality of nature and of man and that regulate our relationships with one another. This knowledge, with the help of modern technology, was needed to make human life more pleasant in many ways than it was in earlier times. For instance, we have lightened our work load with machines, eliminated many diseases or found cures for them, and considerably raised the average life expectancy. In the last two hundred years, humanity has witnessed more changes wrought by science and technology than in all the preceding millennia.

These advantages and advances are incontestable. More and more, though, the other side of progress is revealing itself as well. Science and technology not only help us to solve problems, they also create new problems: the destruction of our environment, the stunting and dehumanization of interpersonal relationships, and the breath-taking pace at which we live, with its increasingly excessive demands on body and soul. Progress is ambivalent. It expands not only the possibilities for good but also for the destruction, even the extinguishing, of all life on earth. Our modern possibilities for dominating nature also place in our hands the means to dominate and manipulate one another, whether through brute violence, subtler methods of propaganda, or the one-sided selection of information.

So the question becomes clearer and clearer: *Should* we do everything we can do? Obviously not. We must use our scientific and technological expertise for humane goals. But what are humane goals? With all we know today, do we know what is really worth knowing, or is the magnitude of our knowledge and the multiplication of its kinds finally confusing?

We come back to our original question: What is man? The modern sciences related to man (the human sciences) can teach us much that is helpful on specific aspects of this question. Modern psychology and sociology can help remove numerous disturbances in the life of the individual and of the community and can help us shape a more meaningful and fulfilling life. But the answer to the question about the ultimate meaning of man exceeds the possibilities of even these sciences.

The modern sciences, with the help of their exact methods, can indeed clarify many individual aspects in a quite general way. These very methods, however, have their own limitations. There are domains of reality that these methods cannot reach. Above all, they cannot say anything about the ultimate meaning and ground of reality as a whole.

Faced, then, with the positive possibilities as well as with the limits and dangers that the modern sciences have brought us, we must ask more urgently than ever before: What is man?

2.2 World Views

As distinguished from the modern sciences, the world views seek to give us a comprehensive picture, a total view of reality. They usually claim that their synoptic view corresponds to the state of scientific knowledge and surpasses the "antiquated" notions of the Christian faith. In this way, they answer our need to understand ourselves and our world. For that reason, the world views derive everything from a single principle: either from matter (materialism) or from spirit, which pervades all and symbolizes itself in all (spiritualism, as in anthroposophy). Their claim to provide a unitary view makes them pluck out even the most diverse elements of the religions, including Christianity, and mix them with one another (syncretism, a mixture of religions).

Such a monolithic vision, of course, does justice neither to the multiplicity of the phenomena nor to the unfathomableness of man and the world. Whoever wishes to derive everything from a single principle easily becomes totalitarian and intolerant. The claim that such world views are truly scientific must be denied, since science can always answer only individual questions and can systematically handle only individual departments of knowledge. It never attains a finished picture of the world but must continually hold itself open for new insights and questions. The Christian faith does indeed contain essential elements of a world view, but it is not a world view in the strict sense. It is aware that in this life we can know things only in a fragmentary and sketchy way (1 Cor 13:12). At bottom, the world views seek to achieve too much and so achieve too little.

Of special importance today are *political world views*. What is at issue in all the questions about meaning that we have mentioned is the meaning not only of our individual lives but also of our communal life. No one lives for himself alone; we live with others, for others, and from others. Each is dependent on each; the fate of each hinges on all. So the answer to the question about the meaning of our individual lives is closely connected with achieving a just political order for everyone—an order based on the principles of freedom. Withdrawal into one's private happiness would be an illusion. Political responsibility and political involvement are required of each. So the question becomes: How can we organize and shape our communal life in a human way? How can we achieve a state of affairs in our society where human dignity, truth, freedom, justice, and peace reign in place of the might of the stronger, naked violence, envy, and hate? How can the differing interests of individuals, of peoples, of races and classes be reconciled?

The concern of the political world views and the importance of political 208–209 involvement for the improvement of human living conditions are incontestable. They fail, of course, when they claim to give an ultimate answer. We can no more make society our absolute than we can matter or spirit. The question about personal happiness and about personal death cannot be postponed until that "some day" when a perfect and just order exists. In this world, at any rate, perfect justice cannot be realized; the only possibility is to *approach* it. But as long as the individual's well-being is not secured, there can be no perfect society. Hate, envy, and conflict of interests will still be there. Even if all political problems were solved, the question about the meaning of one's own life, about personal guilt, about the death that each must undergo individually, would remain. A tension will thus always exist between the individual and the whole. The individual with his needs, cares, joys, and troubles can never find in the social process the answers he seeks. On the contrary, the individual person is not the outcome of social processes but their root and goal. Social life must then orient itself by man. So the question arises once again in the political domain as well: What is man?

We realize that the sciences and political world views give us important answers to our questions in their respective domains. But they cannot answer the question about the meaning of human life itself. Without such an answer, though, they themselves lose their orientation. This lack of orientation is *the crisis of our time*. The common notions of values and goals 96 according to which past centuries lived have become questionable for many. We lack stirring ideas and grand perspectives for the future—ideas and perspectives about which we can become enthusiastic and for which we can make sacrifices. Scepticism and resignation are spreading. Young people particularly feel a terrible emptiness. Production, consumption, and affluence alone do not begin to solve all problems. We do indeed need bread to live, and it is a scandal that many have no bread or not enough to

survive, whereas others have problems with the consequences of their abundance. But "man does not live by bread alone", nor by work, pleasure, or protest alone. We are more. We need love, meaning, hope. We want not only to have more but to be more. So our situation compels us to reflect once again, more creatively and more deeply, on the ground and goal of being human.

3. Religions and the Critique of Religion

3.1 The Answer of the Religions

For millennia the religions gave us an answer to the question about the meaning of our lives. This answer is not primarily a theory. It expresses itself in life as a whole, in rites and practices, in prayers and songs, in stories, symbols, images, feasts, works of art, and religious ministries. It takes effect in the entire formation of life, in the morality and law of a people, and it accompanies the entire life of the individual from birth to death. There are many *different religions*. Besides the archaic tribal religions, such as we find even today in Africa, for instance, there were the high religions (Hinduism, Buddhism, Confucianism) that complex cultures have brought forth. They arose in Asia above all, perhaps contemporaneously with the Old Testament, and are alive there even today. Other high religions, such as that of the Incas in South America, were destroyed. The only great post-Christian religion is Islam, which we encounter especially in North Africa and the Near East. Because of immigration and cultural exchange, the various religions are also represented in our country.

34–35;
53–54;
64–65;
116

However much these religions may differ, they agree in one *common concern*: they take seriously the fact that we are a question for ourselves— a question to which we can give no answer. In religion, rather, we experience ourselves as moved and sustained by a higher and more comprehensive reality, the reality of the holy and the divine. We encounter it with reverence and awe, but we also trust it and are drawn toward it. We owe it everything. It gives us security, it allows us to be festive and to celebrate. We and the visible world around us are thus not the only reality for the religions. We and the world belong in a more comprehensive context of reality. The visible world is real only through participation in the invisible world of the holy and the divine. Religious stories and symbolic actions are intended to render present this sheltering ground of all existence. The religions, of course, have often falsified the image of God and given God the mask of the demonic. Instead of joy and hope, they have often instilled anxiety into us and fettered us. Nevertheless, we have for millennia found in religious rites the strength to find meaning in joy and suffering, good and evil, life and death; and even today the religions give millions of people meaning and support, a ground and goal for their lives.

3.2 The Modern Critique of Religion

Even in the past there were always those who questioned belief in the gods and criticized religious practice. Since the Enlightenment in the eighteenth century, the critique of religion has become increasingly acute. Only since the end of the last century, though, has that critique managed to make *atheism a popular phenomenon* and attempted to construct social life on a religiously neutral or even atheistic foundation. This atheism of the masses is among the most serious conditions today. And we find atheism even in our own hearts. If we are honest, we Christians must also admit that the experience of God's absence oppresses us, that we often perceive only his silence, that we are scarcely able to experience God in the secularity of our everyday lives. We too live for the most part as if God did not exist. Practically speaking, is not God often dead for us too?

Many *causes* have led to this situation. In the first place, there is the 79–81 *collapse of the world view of antiquity and of the Middle Ages*, the view also presupposed in the Bible. Since Copernicus and Kepler, we know that the earth is not the center around which the cosmos revolves. In the last century, Darwin developed the doctrine of the evolution of life, including human life. For many, this shook the earlier notion of the immediate creation of man by God. Freud discovered the unconscious. He posed more sharply the question about our freedom and responsibility. More and more, the modern sciences believed themselves able to explain the world without God. God seemed to have become dispensable, and religion was seen as a level of human consciousness since surpassed. We believed we had *come of age* and so were able to explain and shape the world on our own terms.

Having come of age, we imagined ourselves able to explain God away by the critique of religion: God was a merely human wish-image and a wish-fulfillment (Feuerbach, Freud), an expression and justification of an evil world and an empty consolation and opium for the people (Marx), or a sign of resentment against life (Nietzsche). Understood in this way, God is not only dispensable but is also a hindrance to our free self-realization and to the assertion of our responsibility in the world. So Nietzsche declared God dead not only in the name of the sciences, but also in the name of man and his freedom.

Modern atheism has many faces. There is still *militant atheism* that would like to eradicate religion. In trying to do so, it often uses not only intellectual arguments but also the means of oppression, discrimination, and persecution. In our Western societies, on the other hand, we encounter *indifferent atheism*. It has become tired and apathetic to a large extent and no longer combats religion, at least not openly. This atheism considers belief in God to be antiquated; it holds that the last remains of religion will die out on their own. Then there is *pedestrian atheism* that accepts only what one can perceive with the senses or prove with reason. In addition, there is the *atheism of human freedom and liberation* from dependencies of every kind, 209–210   including liberation from an all-powerful God who overpowers us and from a religious "system" that restricts freedom and oppresses life. Most 106–107   important is the atheism that is affected by the *experience of evil* in the world and protests against a God who is supposed to be all-knowing, all-powerful, and good and yet permits all this senseless pain. The question "Why do I suffer?" is considered by many as the foundation of atheism (Büchner). Finally, there is *sceptical and critical atheism*, which suspends judgment when confronted with ultimate answers. For it, religious questions are unanswerable and therefore meaningless. According 28   to it, one can only be silent about God. (On the question of modern atheism, see GS 19–20.)

3.3 Religious Renewal

What should we say to all this? First of all, modern atheism must be an occasion for a careful *examination of conscience* for the religions. This is especially true for Christianity, since mass atheism originated partly in 53   Christendom. Atheism is a critical reaction to a misleading image of God and to a deficient realization of faith in God in moral and social life. People have often used the name of God to oppose the findings of science, to instigate wars, to defend unjust conditions, to deny freedom through compulsory measures, or to subjugate others. So atheism can also have a purifying function for the religions. Very much will depend on whether in the future religions can make people believe that religion and scientific progress, or faith in God and human freedom, are not antitheses—that they can coexist.

On the other hand, the crisis of the modern sciences and the political world views must also become a question of conscience for the atheists.

They were often protesting only against forms of religion that were conditioned by the times and that are today antiquated; in some cases, they even protested against misunderstandings and abuses of religion rather than against religion itself. But are not science and politics often abused in horrible ways as well? And could they really answer the question of meaning in the individual and social domains? And are they not fundamentally disoriented if they do not integrate themselves into a more comprehensive context of meaning—the kind of context that only the religions can provide? Is there then a realistic alternative?

We can now see *a reawakening of religious questions* throughout the world. In situations of oppression and persecution, religion is often the last stronghold of freedom. Where there is no religion, people often create substitute religions for themselves. Today the religions are anything but dying. *Religion obviously belongs to man, who is a question for himself to which* 24; 28 *he himself can give no answers.* So the answer of the religions should not be dismissed too quickly. It requires thought now as much as ever. Having passed through the cleansing fires of atheism, religion could become the one and only thing necessary, the one thing able to meet the needs of our present crisis.

4. Ways of Knowing God

4.1 The Way Is Man

Religions have often distorted and falsified both the image of God and the 20–21; image of man. But there is also a profound truth in the religions of our 34–35; history. They tell us something always true about our being human. They 65; take *our finitude* seriously. This finitude shows itself in the fact that we can 116–117 never come to an end of all our questions. Every answer calls forth new 16 questions. We have to change our views again and again. At any given time, our ignorance is greater than our knowledge. Even in our search for happiness we can never be wholly fulfilled. There are indeed moments in which we feel wholly fulfilled and want to say, with Goethe's Faust: "Stay, you are so beautiful!" But quickly enough it becomes clear that these moments too are unfulfillable promises. Nothing in this world can be our all. For all that we encounter is finite and limited, imperfect and transitory. Even the Bible records this experience. In the Old Testament Book of "Qoheleth", the preacher, we read:

> Vanity of vanities, says Qoheleth, vanity of vanities! All things are vanity! What profit has man from all the labor which he toils at under the sun? One generation passes and another comes . . . (Qo 1:2–4).

> There is an appointed time for everything, and a time for everything under the heavens. A time to be born, and a time to die; a time to plant, and a time to uproot the plant. . . . A time to weep, and a time to laugh; a time to mourn, and a time to dance (Qo 3:1–2, 4).

> For the lot of man and of beast is one lot; the one dies as well as the other . . . both were made from the dust, and to the dust they both return (Qo 3:19–20).

Next to the experience of his finitude, man also has the *experience of something unconditional*. In spite of the experience of our finitude, we do not cease working, striving, and pursuing happiness. In doing so, we obviously intend something more than the transitory experiences of earthly happiness. Our striving goes further; it aims at something that can be our all. It drives at the whole. Thus we strive to reach beyond all that we can experience or attain; we are continually underway, never finished; we always hunger and thirst for more truth, more justice, more happiness. Man cannot himself fulfill this insatiable longing for something ultimate, for consummate justice, for unerring truth. It would be vain for him even to want to attempt it, for he would then fail to realize that he himself is finite, weak, imperfect. In this sense, man infinitely surpasses man, as Pascal says.

The life of man is a way, a way into mystery. It is the fundamental conviction of all religions, as well as of the Bible, that *the mystery of man borders on a still deeper and still greater mystery that they call God*. But how can we experience and know this God?

4.2 Ways of Knowing God in Human History

20–21; 48; 65 Religious men of all millennia believed that they discovered signs and vestiges of the divine in the world. They recognized divine mystery in extraordinary phenomena of nature that excite fear and wonder—in thunder and lightning or in the inexhaustible fertility of nature, for instance, but also in the fascination of the encounter between man and woman or in the voice of conscience. Later on, it was no longer the extraordinary experiences that excited wonderment so much as the pervasive order of nature, its beauty and splendor, its regularity and harmony. How else could one explain it than through a divine spirit ordering all? So the religious tradition served early on as an occasion for great thinkers to reflect more deeply on reality, to ask about the origin and ground of the world, and thereby to stumble onto God.

From about the sixth century before Christ, thinkers in our Western tradition reflected critically on religious experience and tradition and sought to know God *by way of thought*. Plato spoke of the idea of the Good, Aristotle of the Unmoved Mover, Plotinus of the One and what is beyond the One. At approximately the same time, great religio-philosophical systems of thought arose in Asia. Even many modern philosophers have sought to comprehend God in terms of thought.

The God of the philosophers is, of course, not immediately the living and personal God to whom the Bible bears witness. God is rather a ground of the world, something unconditioned and absolute, to be designated not with a personal name but only with abstract concepts. One cannot pray to the God of the philosophers. Still, the philosophical consideration of God as the ultimate ground of reality is important. For it can open up approaches to understanding faith and can show that faith in God, however much it surpasses mere thought, is not unreasonable.

4.3 Knowing God in the Bible

The Bible nowhere conducts a proof for the existence of God. It knows God from his *historical revelations* to Abraham, Isaac, and Jacob; from his   53–54
action through Moses at the Exodus from Egypt and during the wandering in the wilderness; and from his speaking through the prophets—all of which God brought to a close and recapitulated in Jesus Christ, who is the image of God for us. The Bible thus speaks of a living and personal God   63–66
who is benevolently close to us, to whom we can cry out in every need, but who also calls and summons us. *By its faith in the God of men, though, the*   83
Bible also sees vestiges of God in the world. It recognizes in the whole world a reflection of the glory of God:

> O Lord, our Lord,
>   How glorious is your name over all the earth!
> You have exalted your majesty above the heavens (Ps 8:2).
>
> The heavens declare the glory of God,
> and the firmament proclaims his handiwork (Ps 19:2).

For the Bible, man is created according to the image of God in a special way (Gen 1:27). Even externally man is distinguished by his upright   97–101
form, which is raised over other beings. Above all, we are the reflection of the glory and sovereignty of God through our freedom and responsibility. Because man is the likeness of God, inviolable dignity attaches to him.

Naturally, the Bible recognizes the *possibility of denying God*. It calls this folly.

> The fool says in his heart,
>   "There is no God" (Ps 53:2).

The fool here is not a stupid person, but an insolent and evil one. He does not trouble himself about God, does not wish to know him, and does not fear his judgment. He speaks and acts as if there were no God, as if he himself were God. The fool is haughty; he disdains the truth and tramples justice under foot. He does whatever he pleases. Such a practical atheism is foolish. No one can flee from God; no one can escape from him.

> O Lord, you have probed me and you know me;
>   you know when I sit and when I stand;
>   you understand my thoughts from afar. . . .
> Behind me and before, you hem me in
>   and rest your hand upon me.
> Where can I go from your spirit?
>   from your presence where can I flee? (Ps 139:1–2, 5, 7).

The Bible can analyze this denying of God, this acting as if he did not exist, as a dreadful closing of the self and as the expression of a perverted heart. The Bible sees that we are able to be so foolish only because we are "blind".

31–32   In the later writings of the Old Testament we find detailed *considerations on the possibility of knowing God* and on the folly of denying him:

> For all men were by nature foolish who were in ignorance of God,
>   and who from the good things seen did not succeed in knowing
>   him who is,
>   and from studying the works did not discern the artisan. . . .
> Or if they were struck by their might and energy,
>   let them from these things realize how much more powerful is he
>   who made them.
> For from the greatness and the beauty of created things
>   their original author, by analogy, is seen (Wis 13:1, 4–5).

The *New Testament* takes up these thoughts, but with a missionary concern. When the young Church turned to the pagans, it could no longer so easily begin with the historical revelation in the Old Covenant. It had to start instead with the pagans' knowledge of God from nature, history, and conscience. We read in Paul's speech to the sages at the Areopagus in Athens:

"They were to seek God, yes to grope for him and perhaps eventually
to find him—though he is not really far from any one of us. 'In him
we live and move and have our being' " (Acts 17:27–28; cf. 14:17).

In the Letter to the Romans, Paul is critical of the pagans' knowledge of
God; indeed, he indicts them. As with the Old Testament wisdom
literature, he attributes to all men the ability to know God from his created
works. Because they suppressed the truth they knew and, in spite of their
knowledge of God, did not honor God appropriately, he calls them to
account and holds them inexcusable.

> In fact, whatever can be known about God is clear to them; he himself
> made it so. Since the creation of the world, invisible realities, God's
> eternal power and divinity, have become visible through the things
> he has made. Therefore these men are inexcusable (Rom 1:19–20).

Paul is thinking not only of external nature, but also of the inner voice of
conscience (Rom 2:14–15). If the pagans could in no way know anything
of God, and if they did not give testimony of God even in their perversions,
the Christian proclamation would have to be wholly unintelligible to
them. The preaching of God's action in Jesus Christ would then be a flood
of words without any intelligible meaning, and the Christian faith would
be something totally foreign and unrealizable. The Christian witness to
God can reach man effectively only because man is created with an
orientation to God.

98–101;
101–103

4.4 The Church's Teaching on Our Natural Knowledge of God

The *First Vatican Council* (1869–1870) summarized the biblical testimony
about the knowability of God as follows:

> God, the origin and goal of all things, can with the natural light of
> human reason be known from created things with certainty (DS 3004;
> NR 27).

83

Even the Council was aware of the difficulties in knowing God in the
present human situation. For that reason, it does not teach that all men
know God with certainty; indeed, it does not even say that there ever were
men who knew God with ultimate certainty except by revelation. The
Council declares only that man can know God from the world by reason.
*The Council wanted to maintain that every man can receive the message about
God, so that the Christian faith is not something irrational or anti-rational.*
Believing and thinking are not antitheses, because by our faith in revelation

we encounter the same God whom we meet as creator of the world when considering the world. The believer may thus be confident that his or her faith will be confirmed in human experience and in thought.

The *Second Vatican Council* (1962–1965) took up the teaching of the First Vatican Council, making it concrete and continuing it in critical dialogue 21–23 with modern atheism. The Council proceeds from the fact that man can be understood only in terms of his origin and goal in God:

> The Church holds that to acknowledge God is in no way to oppose the dignity of man, since such dignity is grounded and brought to perfection in God. . . . When, on the other hand, man is left without this divine support and without hope of eternal life his dignity is deeply wounded, as may so often be seen today. The problems of life and death, of guilt and suffering, remain unsolved, so that men are not rarely cast into despair (GS 21).

Atheism ultimately misses not only the truth of God but also that of man. For that reason, it is categorically condemned by the Council. *Only through the mystery of God does the mystery of our being human receive an answer that does not destroy it, but accepts and deepens it. Only he who knows God also knows man* (Guardini).

4.5 Proofs for the Existence of God?

In order to show the reasonableness of faith in God, theology developed the so-called proofs for the existence of God. Certainly these are not *proofs such as those familiar to us in natural science and mathematics*. God is not a set of facts that stands open to general examination. Still, there are "proofs" that invite us to accompany the speaker along a way of thought. Thomas Aquinas, one of the greatest theologians of the Middle Ages, who especially elaborated these proofs for the existence of God, speaks of these proofs as *"ways"* for a reason. We must travel along a way in order for a landscape to show itself, but we must also look at it. So too upon these ways to knowing God, we must lay prejudices aside and open ourselves to the mystery of God. Then it can become clear that faith in God is not unreasonable but thoroughly corresponds to the mystery that intimates itself in our reason.

We could not ask about God, of course, if we had never heard anything about him, if we had not been touched within by his reality, if we had had no share in any experience of him. The proofs for the existence of God are thus not intended to replace faith with knowledge. On the contrary, they invite us directly to faith, they strengthen us in faith and give *an account of faith*. They answer the scriptural exhortation: "Should anyone ask you for the reason of this hope of yours, be ever ready to reply . . ." (1 Pet 3:15).

The first, older form of the proof for the existence of God begins from the *reality of the world*. The world is in constant movement and in perpetual flux. Everything that is moved is moved by another. Still, at the same time, order reigns throughout the world. Where does everything come from? Where, in particular, does this order come from? The questions can be pushed farther and farther back. One cause moves another; everything is conditioned by something else. But the questions cannot regress to infinity. Somewhere there must be a first cause, a beginning of movement and change. Is this perhaps a proto-atom or a proto-cell? Yet that would not suffice. What causes this beginning? What provides the enormous energy to release the entire further development from out of itself? It is a question not only of explaining *how* the world came about. Today's science can say very much about that. It is also a question of explaining the fact *that* it came about.   83

To posit a proto-matter here explains nothing. Does proto-matter explain itself? It is subject to change and so highly imperfect. The ultimate ground, however, can only be something that of itself is perfect and complete, something that exists of itself as the purest fullness of being and life. That something is what we mean when we speak of God. *In God alone the reality of the world has its ground. Without him it would be groundless and thus meaningless. Without him nothing would be.* Since, though, reality does exist and does exhibit a meaningful order, it is reasonable to believe that God, as the ground of its being and order, also exists.   79–81

The decision for God means a *decision against the primacy of matter*. Belief in God means that spirit does not first emerge at the end of a long material development, but stands already at the beginning. Spirit is the power that brings about all, sustains all, determines all, and has ordered all according to measure, number, and weight (Wis 11:20). Thus the person who decides for God decides for the meaningful character of the world. The scientist encounters these structures of meaning at every step. How could a scientist understand reality if it were not spiritually intelligible? And how could it be spiritually intelligible if it were not fashioned by a spirit and did not exhibit spiritual structures? So our thinking about the world is ultimately possible only as one that patterns itself after the thoughts of God. *Faith in God is thus anything but an antithesis to thought; it is rather the ultimate foundation of thought and a persistent encouragement to thought.*

The second, more modern form of the proof for the existence of God refers not immediately to the world but to the *reality of man*. He is a finite being through and through, dependent on and threatened by the nature that surrounds him, held in bondage to death. In man, something   23–24

27;
98–101;
102–103

unconditioned and absolute also makes itself felt—in the *voice of conscience*, for instance, which speaks in us over and over again through exhortation, reproach, and recognition. Certainly, many moral norms are historically conditioned. But the fundamental demand to do good and avoid evil is unconditional. We would not be ourselves if we did not protest against injustices that cry out to heaven, such as the malicious killing of an innocent child. We cannot cease hoping that a murderer will not finally triumph over his innocent victims. Even if we do not find complete justice anywhere in the world and cannot count at all on ever being able to achieve it, we should not give up demanding it. Beyond the voice of conscience, the unconditioned and absolute also encounters us in *interpersonal love*. In the beloved, everything can suddenly become new. In one blessed moment, all time vanishes; in the midst of time, we touch eternity. Is all this to count for nothing in the end?

In these ways, we live always in the tension between our own finitude and imperfection and our longing for the infinite, absolute, and perfect. This tension causes the restlessness and dissatisfaction that sweep over us again and again. Is this longing meaningless? Must we make ourselves content by forgetting it? In that way, we would give up the mystery of our being human. *If being human is not to be ultimately meaningless and absurd, the reality of the absolute must correspond to our hope for the absolute. Our questioning and seeking must echo and respond to the call of God, which makes itself felt in our conscience.* To attempt to salvage an absolute meaning without God would be futile (Horkheimer). God alone is the answer to the greatness and misery of man. Whoever believes in him can do justice to the greatness of man without having to deny his misery. Whoever believes in God can be wholly realistic.

The decision for God thus shows itself to be a *decision for man*. Only if God exists, and only if God is the absolute freedom that encompasses and guides all, is there a place for human freedom in this world. The decision for God means a decision for the freedom and the unconditional dignity of man. Only if God exists can man be more than a marginal being in a

86–90

cosmos that is insensitive to his questions and needs. But if God does exist, then abstract or impersonal laws, blind chance, and anonymous fate do not rule the world. Faith in God allows, indeed demands, that we accept ourselves and all others unconditionally because we have been unconditionally accepted. Faith makes possible a fundamental trust in reality; without it, no one can live, love, or work. *Faith in God does not suppress human freedom. On the contrary, it grounds the conviction of freedom's unconditional value and obligates us to have unconditional respect for every person and to commit ourselves to a just order among men based on the principles of freedom*. If God were dead, it would necessarily mean the death of man. Human hope exists not because God is dead, but because he lives.

5. God: A Mystery

5.1 The Hidden God

How far do all these considerations take us? It is obvious that God is not a ready-made answer to our questions. *God is a deep mystery*. He is not an object to be seized like other objects. There is no God in the way that there are things or even men in the world. He is not somewhere "up there". His mystery encompasses us everywhere. But then neither is God a stopgap that only comes into view at the limits of human knowledge. The Bible calls him the hidden God (Is 45:15) who dwells in unapproachable light (1 Tim 6:16). As finite beings, we can never comprehend the infinite One, the One encompassing all.

60–66

> Such a knowledge is too wonderful for me;
> too lofty for me to attain (Ps 139:6).

So we cannot derive this mystery of God from the mystery of our being. God is not a construct of man, not a homemade idol, not the wish-fulfillment of our longings. God is truly divine only when his mystery is deeper and greater than the mystery of man. Paul confesses:

> How deep are the riches and the wisdom and the knowledge of God! How inscrutable his judgments, how unsearchable his ways! For "who has known the mind of the Lord? Or who has been his counselor? Who has given him anything so as to deserve return?" For from him and through him and for him all things are. To him be glory forever. Amen (Rom 11:33–36).

Our human notions of God must be broken again and again by the mystery of God. We must set out anew and deepen our faith again and again.

> Your presence, O Lord, I seek.
> Hide not your face from me . . . (Ps 27:8–9).

The more we embark upon the search for God, the more all previous answers will prove unsatisfactory. The most impressive example of this in the Bible is the figure of Job. The heaviest blows of fate strike him, and he loses everything—his possessions, his family, his health. He can no longer understand God and quarrels with him. Yet in the end he must recognize that no one can dispute with God, no one can fathom him. So Job falls silent and confesses:

> "I have dealt with great things that I do not understand;
>   things too wonderful for me, which I cannot know" (Job 42:3).

The great mystics speak of the dark night into which the experience of God leads us. This night is the brilliant light of God that blinds us because our eyes are too weak for it.

26   *Because God is a great mystery man can also deny him.* He can give other names to this mystery at the center of the mystery of his own life. He can call it all-encompassing nature or matter that is only becoming, fermenting, giving birth; or nameless and meaningless nothing, so that his life sinks into a bottomless emptiness and ends in a wilderness of non-being. God is both an answer and a question for us. He asks us how we wish to understand the mystery of our life: Is it hope in a future perfection wrought by ourselves? Is it the whim of fate, the fleeting, gentle breeze of nothing? Or is it the gift that comes from the fullness of being and strives back toward this fullness? The believer is convinced that only the mystery of God corresponds to the mystery of man, and he believes himself able to adduce the reasons for his belief. He holds at least that none of the reasons against believing in God is sound and that all can be rationally refuted. Still, in view of the always-greater mystery of God, all the reasons and counter-reasons are nothing more than a well-grounded invitation to faith.

36–39   What does it mean then to know God? Obviously it is more than taking cognizance from a distance of the fact that God exists. In knowing God, we ourselves, the meaning of our being human, and the meaning of our world are also at stake. *We know God, therefore, not only with the reason but with the heart, with the involvement of our entire person.* To know God also means to acknowledge him as the ground and goal of life; it means to affirm him as one and all. Whoever knows God knows that he owes God everything. Knowledge of God expresses itself not only in thinking but also in thanking, extolling, and praising. One must *do the truth* in order really to know it (Jn 3:21). The life of the one who really knows God and believes in him will be transformed. Such a person knows himself to be utterly accepted; he can and should therefore accept both himself and others. Precisely because he knows of an ultimate support and meaning of life, he can and should advocate life against all powers that destroy life.

The believer, who believes with his whole person, knows more only in the sense that he knows the limitless mystery of God and of man and for that reason questions every attempt at merely human ultimate solutions. The one who believes in God does not need to hide the many questions that remain open, nor to harmonize the often shrill dissonances in human life. He is able to endure them because the answer he gives is not a finished solution but a still deeper mystery. Faith in the hidden God will always be a seeking, questioning, adventuresome faith.

5.2 Only Images and Parables

The believer is convinced that the mystery of God is the only possible answer to the mystery of man. *Yet all that we can say about the mystery of God is nothing more than images and parables.* Through them we touch on the mystery of God only as if from afar. The words of the Apostle Paul apply here: "Now we see indistinctly, as in a mirror" (1 Cor 13:12). "Mirror" and "parable" mean that our images and concepts can predicate "something" of God. Jesus speaks in parables and uses everyday events in order to acquaint us with the action of God. We cannot speak of God at all other than in the language of the world. But *God is infinitely greater than our images and concepts.* He is that than which nothing greater can be thought, even greater than anything that can be thought (Anselm of Canterbury). At bottom, all our concepts and images can only say what God is not, rather than what God is (Thomas Aquinas). God fits into no system and grounds no self-contained world view. On the contrary, faith in God cracks the shell of every world view in order to make place for the always-greater mystery of God and of man. Thus the Fourth Lateran Council (1215) declared: "For no similarity can be predicated of Creator and creature without its including a greater dissimilarity between the two" (DS 806; NR 280).

So *everything that we can say and think about God holds only in a quite unique, infinitely perfect sense.* All our concepts and images of God are at best like arrows pointing in his direction. In none of them do we capture God. Rather, each sends us on the way toward God. They are initiations into a mystery that can be approached only in worship. They prepare us to listen again to what God says to us through his word and through his deeds in history. Only in Jesus Christ are the mystery of God and the mystery of man definitively disclosed to us. In Jesus Christ, God reveals his mystery to us as the mystery of his unfathomable love. Yet even in his revelation, and precisely in it, he remains the hidden God whose love we can grasp only in human images and parables.

62–63; 73–74

6. The Self-Revelation of God And the Response of Faith

6.1 Revelation: The Way of God to Man

Even in the human domain the innermost part of man is largely hidden from us. A man must reveal to us how he is disposed toward us, not only through what he says but even more through what he does. When someone says to us, "I love you", we can ultimately affirm only by a human faith that this is true. This holds all the more for God, who is an unfathomable mystery to us.

The Old and New Testaments bear witness to this on every page: God, who is hidden from men and who dwells in unapproachable light, has stepped out of his hiddenness and has revealed his mystery "hidden for many ages" (Rom 16:25; compare Eph 1:9). So man does not grope blindly in his search for God. God comes to meet him. God is not enthroned in unattainable distance; he has drawn close to us and makes himself known to us through word and deed. God reveals to us not only *that* he is but also *who* he is: Yahweh (Ex 3:14), Immanuel, God with us, who invites us and takes us up into communion with him. He is not ashamed to be called "our God" (Heb 11:16). He is "the God of hope" (Rom 15:13).

23–31

19–21;
53–54;
64–65

God has revealed himself since the beginning of the world through his creation, especially through the conscience of man and his guidance in history. There is thus a *general history of God's revelation*. The Bible tells in various places of "holy pagans" who are witnesses to the living God: Abel, Enoch, Melchizedek, Job, and others. God "wants all men to be saved and come to know the truth" (1 Tim 2:4). For that reason, the Second Vatican Council teaches:

> Throughout history even to the present day, there is found among different peoples a certain awareness of a hidden power, which lies behind the course of nature and the events of human life. At times there is present even a recognition of a supreme being, or even more of a Father. . . . The Catholic Church rejects nothing of what is true and holy in these religions. She has a high regard for the manner of life and conduct, the precepts and doctrines which, although differing in many ways from her own teaching, nevertheless often reflect a ray of that truth which enlightens all men (NA 2).

Yet God wills to reveal himself to men not only as individuals independent of all reciprocal bonds, but also as social and historical beings. He wants to gather men into a people and to make that people a light for the nations (Is 42:6). So precisely in view of the general history of God with men, there is also a *special history of God's revelation*. In it God makes himself known at given times and places to particular men in a special way. The revelation is not made only privately to individuals, but is made for the sake of a mission to proclaim the word of God openly and publicly to all men. Special revelation begins with the call of Abraham and the patriarchs. With the gathering of Israel and its deliverance from Egypt, it enters a new period. Through the prophets, Israel becomes more deeply acquainted with God and is prepared at the same time for the definitive revelation of God in Jesus Christ.

> In times past, God spoke in fragmentary and varied ways to our fathers through the prophets; in this, the final age, he has spoken to us through his Son . . . (Heb 1:1–2).

The special history of revelation is not primarily a series of individual revelations communicating truths and commandments that man cannot know on his own strength. Revelation is an event that occurs from person   63–66
to person. Through it, God discloses in word and deed not some *thing*, but *himself* and his *salvific will* for men. *The revelation of the personal mystery of God also discloses to man his own deepest mystery and the meaning of his*   103–105
being human. This is communion and friendship with God. By revealing himself, God also reveals man to man. The high point of this revelation is   65–70;
the God-Man Jesus Christ. In him God is definitively disclosed as our   134–137
salvation and our hope.

The Second Vatican Council explains the revelation of God in the following way:

> It pleased God in his goodness and wisdom, to reveal himself and to make known the mystery of his will (cf. Eph 1:9). . . . By this revelation, then, the invisible God (cf. Col 1:15; 1 Tim 1:17), from the fullness of his love, addresses men as his friends (cf. Ex 33:11; Jn 15:14–15), and moves among them (cf. Bar 3:38), in order to invite and receive them into his company. This economy of Revelation is realized by deeds and words, which are intrinsically bound up with each other. . . . The most intimate truth which this revelation gives us about God and the salvation of man shines forth in Christ, who is himself both the mediator and the sum total of Revelation (DV 2).

When we ask, "Who is God, anyway?", we do not need complicated speculations or appeals to vague feelings. Even less is our faith in God a projection of our wishes and desires. It is the response to God's history with men. So we can answer this question only by recounting the history of God with men and saying: Look, there is our God! He led Abraham,

54-55 delivered Israel, raised Jesus Christ from the dead, and he calls us into communion with him and is coming to redeem us (Lk 21:28). *Faith in God lives on the remembrance and re-presentation of this history that has happened once for all (Rom 6:10). It is the source and the norm of our speaking about God and the ground of our hope.* In remembering God's word and action in history, we both renew and surpass the primeval memory of God implanted in man from creation, the created image of God in man.

6.2 Faith: The Way of Man to God

Ordinarily when we say, "I believe that . . .", we mean to describe a hesitant or uncertain knowledge. Accordingly, many people think that Christian faith means considering as true propositions that cannot be proven. So faith appears to many as an infantile, childish attitude, a subjection to authority that shows a lack of courage to think for oneself. On the other hand, we know that in relationships with others we depend on fidelity and faith. In the end, we *believe* that someone is well disposed toward us, that he even loves us.

We see the biblical sense of faith especially in Abraham, with whom the special history of God and men begins. Holy Scripture names Abraham as the father of believers (Rom 4:12). At the beginning, Abraham lives in Ur in Chaldea and honors the gods of his tribe. One day the call of God comes to him:

> "Go from the land of your kinsfolk and from your father's house to a land that I will show you. I will make of you a great nation. . . . All the communities of the earth will find blessing in you" (Gen 12:1–3).

> Abraham put his faith in the Lord, who credited it to him as an act of righteousness (Gen 15:6).

Abraham believes. He takes his stand on God's word and sets out according to the divine instructions. In doing so, he risks home and homeland, everything. He becomes homeless for God's sake (Heb 11:8–14). He gambles on an uncertain future; he wagers on God and God's word. Against all hope, he is full of hope (Rom 4:18). In this way he becomes the father of believers.

The way of Abraham is brought to completion in the way of Jesus, whom every believer must imitate. Just as Jesus has no home, no place to lay his head (Mt 8:20), so his disciples must "leave everything" to follow him (Mk 10:28). Jesus' obedience to the Father leads him to the cross, where in the darkest night of abandonment by God he cries out: "My God, my God, why have you forsaken me?" (Mk 15:34). Yet even in death he is sustained by God and is awakened to new life. So Jesus, who "learned obedience from what he suffered" (Heb 5:8), is the one who "inspires and perfects our faith" (Heb 12:2). "Faith" in the New Testament is therefore another word for imitation.

Faith is a way. One must travel this way in the light of hope in order to recognize one's goal. Faith is a venture, a letting-go of all security, and a reversal of the customary ways of seeing and doing things. All this is possible only because faith responds to a call. The believer begins to have confidence in the word and places his *trust* in God and God's word. The first word of faith is not "I believe *that* . . .", but "I believe *you*". In this trusting venture with God, a *light* dawns on the believer. He recognizes in the external words and deeds of revelation the God who reveals himself. Faith thus bestows new *knowledge*. Still the believer does not believe because he knows; he knows because he believes. He can respond to the known love of God only with more love. 206–208

Faith is to a certain degree a declaration of love to God. God's speaking to us leads us to speak to God, to pray. *Prayer* is faith's most important form of expression. Because the believer knows himself to be accepted by God, he can also accept himself, others, and the world. Faith becomes a deed that transforms one's life and the world.

In sum, faith is an *all-encompassing project of life and an attitude toward the whole of existence*. The believer is incorporated into the basic, innermost attitude of Jesus. The Hebrew Bible primarily employs the word "aman" for our word "believe", which is found even today in the liturgical assent of "Amen". The basic meaning of "aman" is "to be firm or constant". Believing means making-oneself-firm in God, trusting and building on him, grounding one's existence and finding one's foothold and stability in him (Is 7:9). Faith is the trust I have, with my gaze fixed on Jesus Christ, that God will keep faith with me in every situation of my life and that he will form the support and substance of my life. *Believing is saying "amen" to God, with all the consequences of this.* It requires the most deep-reaching transformation of man, his self-understanding, and his life. Through faith, we are a new creation in Christ (Gal 6:15; 2 Cor 5:17). 351–352

The Second Vatican Council describes faith summarily in the following words:

> By faith man freely commits his entire self to God, making "the full submission of his intellect and will to God who reveals" and willingly assenting to the Revelation given by him (DV 5).

This declaration suggests these points.

1. Faith is *man's response to the self-revelation of God*. It is not a vague feeling without content. It has a *content*, but that content is fundamentally God himself, God as he has revealed himself in history with men.

2. The response of faith is possible only if God comes to man first and lets the light of his truth enlighten him; God must illuminate the "eyes of his heart" (Eph 1:18). So faith is a *gift of the illuminating grace of God*. Conviction comes not from external reasons or from one's own inner insights, but from God himself, who makes his truth evident.

3. Nonetheless, faith remains a *free and responsible human act*. Neither reason alone nor the will alone nor feeling alone is sufficient. In faith, the entire man, with all his questions, hopes, and disappointments, is at stake. So the faithful response must come from one's entire existence and one's entire life. According to Augustine, three elements belong to the act of faith: the assent of reason, the consent of the will, and then the decision to proceed to God and with God. First, I believe that God exists and that he has revealed himself. Second, I believe God—I trust him and come to depend wholly on him. Finally, as a consequence, I set out toward God and with him.

4. Since faith is both wholly the act of God and wholly the act of man, it re-enacts God's history with men here and now. Faith is *encounter, communion, and friendship with God*. Thus it is the fulfillment of the meaning of human life, the becoming-whole of the entire man. That is what it means to say that he who believes is saved.

The believer has this salvation, of course, not as a secure possession but as a certainty only in the light of hope. Faith is the initial anticipation of the eternal vision of God face to face (1 Cor 13:12). Faith has always been a questioning, seeking, challenged faith that is "on the way". Often enough, the reality in which we live speaks a language entirely different from the word of God. Quite different standards often apply, standards that may seem to the believer more plausible than the declarations of the gospel, which can then strike one as other-worldly and harsh. So too the absurdities of life, unjust suffering, and cruel death can seem to make a mockery of the message of God's love. The believer should not and cannot avoid such questions; but neither may he capitulate to them. Confronted with these questions, which have taken differing forms in every age, he must fortify and deepen his faith. We must believe and believe anew against "the world". Like the father in the Gospel who seeks help for his sick child, we must say, "I do believe! Help my unbelief!" (Mk 9:24).

7. We Believe

7.1 The Church: Community and Teacher of the Faith

211–230;
253–261

The ancient Church's formulations in the confessions of faith differ. We read "I believe" in the Apostles' Creed, but the Nicene Creed, which dates back to the first two ecumenical councils, says, "We believe". The two formulations do not contradict each other; their difference gives expression to a tension inherent in the essence of faith itself. "I believe" expresses the fact that faith is the free, responsible, untransferrable decision of the individual. No one may be compelled to faith against his will or conscience. "We believe" says that no one can believe by himself alone. No one has given the faith to himself; everyone has received it from those who believed before him. Nor can anyone keep the faith for himself alone; he must pass it on to others. Each person is thus a link in the chain of believers. Each believer depends on being carried along by others who believe with him. For that reason, "*One* Christian alone is *no* Christian" (Tertullian). Each Christian depends on the community of believers.

The "*community of believers*" is one of the most ancient names that the Church gives herself. Many see in the Church more of an organization, an institution, a "system", characterized by influence and power. Or the Church seems a preacher of morality, urging men to do good, but often enough nagging them in the process. The form and face of the Church 211–212;
234–236 have certainly been distorted in both the past and present by the guilt of her members, even of her official representatives. The greatness of the Church, however, is that she has carried faith in Jesus Christ down through the ages, from the days of the Apostles until today, and so has always given men support and substance for their lives. She is truly the community of believers spanning the centuries. Through her we stand in 253–255 communion with the blood witnesses (the martyrs) of the first centuries, with the great Fathers of the Church, and with the saints, both known and unknown, of all ages. Through her we stand today in a worldwide community that is concretized in the local congregation to which we 221–223 belong. In this community of believers extending over time and space there are varying ministries and tasks (which we will later treat in detail), 243–246;
257–261 including those of shepherds and teachers (Eph 4:11). But all Christians, 224–225;
239–243 each in his own way, are called to give witness to the faith through word and deed (Rom 12:3–8; 1 Cor 12:4–31a). The Church is not *only* the pope and the bishops; all we who believe are the Church—a great community in faith. The injunction "Help carry one another's burdens" (Gal 6:2) applies to all. The whole community of believers is the We of faith, comprising all the faithful individually.

The Church has often been compared to a *ship* shaken by the waves and storms of history that still, because Jesus is with her, brings the faith and the faithful safely to the other shore of new life (Mk 4:35–41). Even more important is the image of "Mother Church". She it is indeed to whom we owe our life of faith; she gives us nourishment and security in the faith (Gal 4:26). As our mother, she is at the same time our "teacher in the faith". We call her *"mater et magistra"* (mother and teacher) because we learn the language of faith from her. We must test and prove this language in our own experiences, but these experiences must be measured against what the first witnesses and those of later centuries, the whole community of believers, have handed down. The entire Church is, because of the promise of Jesus Christ, "the pillar and bulwark of the truth" (1 Tim 3:15).

Therefore, "I believe" can be seen to mean "I join in that which we believe." *This joining in the common faith is the confession of faith.* The confession of faith, which binds all together and is binding on all, is not possible without a common language of faith. Formulations of the common faith binding on all are already handed down to us in many

49   passages of the New Testament (Rom 10:9; 1 Cor 15:3–5, among others). The Church's confession of faith developed from them. It is both a *summary of the central content of the Holy Scriptures and their binding interpretation*.

68–69;   The most important confession is the Nicene Creed, established by the first two 70–71   ecumenical councils of Nicea (325) and Constantinople (381) on the basis of even more ancient forms used in the local congregations. Today it is still common to all the major churches of the East and the West. It is "catholic" in the original sense of the word: all-encompassing, spanning the whole world; it is an ecumenical confession. It is also the official liturgical confession at the celebration of the Eucharist. The shorter Apostles' Creed dates as far back as the Roman baptismal confession of the third and fourth centuries. Today it is common to all churches of the Western tradition (the Roman Catholic, the Old Catholic, the Anglican; the case is different in those free churches that have no binding confession of faith). This confession is called "apostolic", not because it was formulated by the Apostles themselves (despite a pious legend attested to around 400), but because it faithfully bears witness to the faith of the Apostles. Almost all its declarations hark back even literally to declarations in the New Testament. Later confessions and dogmas seek to expound these two confessions, to secure them against errors and misunderstandings, and to develop them in view of contemporary challenges. Both confessions are thus *summaries of the whole faith* and *signs of recognition among the faithful*. For that reason, they form the basis of this catechism.

Not a few Christians today have *difficulties* with the confession of faith recited in common. Sentences such as "begotten, not made, one in being with the Father", "born of the Virgin Mary", or "descended into hell" are foreign and unintelligible to them. They think that such declarations no longer answer today's questions, that they are more or less vacuous. They therefore want to recite the common confession only insofar as they can understand it and "affirm it personally"; sometimes they also attempt to formulate new confessions. Their difficulties must be taken seriously.

But it must also be pointed out that there can never be a new faith or another gospel (Gal 1:7–8), something other than what was handed down from the very beginning and to which the Church of all centuries bears common witness. *The Church must always expound and deepen this faith, which remains one and the same.* It is given to us both as an inheritance and as a task. A mindless recitation of the old formulas will not do. In any case, the brief formulations only summarize the fullness of the faith. They always contain more than a particular time or an individual Christian can grasp. So the confessions must be unfolded and interpreted. But they cannot be given up, or we would break off community with those who have believed before us in great unanimity. Both the Church and the individual Christian would then lose their identity.

49–50

7.2 Holy Scripture as the Original Record And Soul of the Proclamation of Faith

The Church can bear witness to and confess no other faith than the one handed on to it once for all (Jude 3). It stands *"on the foundation of the apostles and prophets"* (Eph 2:20). The prophets are those interpreters of the apostolic proclamation, awakened by the Holy Spirit and appearing in the early Church, who make known the will of God to the local congregation in specific situations. The Apostles are the first and original witnesses to the gospel; they received it immediately from Jesus Christ and were sent out by him into the entire world (Mt 28:18–20). The Church stands permanently on the foundation and under the rule of the apostolic faith (DV 7–8). Especially in the pastoral letters, Timothy and Titus, the disciples of the Apostles, are exhorted to hold fast to the sound teaching. They are told: Guard what has been committed to you! Do not let yourselves be confused! Remain faithful to what you have learned! (1 Tim 4:16; 6:20; 2 Tim 1:13–14; Tit 2:2).

The Apostles' original witness takes concrete form in the writings of the apostolic period that were collected very early in the New Testament. Since the New Testament understands itself as the fulfillment of the Old Testament, one cannot separate the two Testaments. They must be interpreted in the light of each other; together they form *the one Holy*

Scripture of the Old and the New Covenant. Scripture is the *original record of our faith* from which every proclamation of the Church must nourish itself and by which it must orient itself; it must be, as it were, the soul of the Church's proclamation (DV 21, 24). "Not knowing the Scriptures means not knowing Christ" (Jerome). Reading and expounding Holy Scripture is an essential element of the Church's liturgy. It is also the basic mission of the Church's hierarchy and the fundamental task of theology. Without regular personal reading of Scripture, no serious Christian life is possible. That is also why this catechism takes up as far as possible the language and the declarations of Holy Scripture in its exposition of the Church's confession of faith.

Since God's revelation is accessible to us only through the witness of the messengers of the Old and New Testament and its written deposit in Holy Scripture, the origin of Holy Scripture itself belongs to the event of revelation. In and through Holy Scripture, God himself speaks to us. It not only contains and bears witness to the word of God; it truly is *God's word*. Written under the inspiration of the Holy Spirit (2 Tim 3:16; 2 Pet 1:19–21; 3:15–16), it has God himself as author (DV 11; 24). "In the sacred books the Father who is in heaven comes lovingly to meet his children, and talks with them" (DV 21). To express God's presence in Jesus Christ through the word of Holy Scripture, the book of the Gospels is solemnly carried in and honored at the festive celebration of the liturgy.

The word of God does not fall down from heaven; it reaches us only through human words. To say that God is the author of Holy Scripture does not exclude the fact that the individual books of Holy Scripture have *men as their writers*. These writers express the word of God in the language of their time, according to the conditions of their culture, with the help of their familiar literary genres. To expound Holy Scripture correctly, the exegete must pay attention to what the biblical writers intended to say. This means we must attempt to understand what God wished to make known to us through them. "Due attention must be paid both to the customary and characteristic patterns of perception, speech and narrative which prevailed at the age of the sacred writer and to the conventions the people of his time followed in their dealings with one another" (DV 12). This *human and historical character of Holy Scripture* belongs to the "humbling" of God that reached its high point in the Incarnation of Jesus Christ.

The human and historical character of Holy Scripture is seen in the way the individual writings of the New Testament arose in and for the early Church, or rather for the early local congregations. These writings have their context in early Christian proclamation, liturgy, catechesis, apologetics, and in the concrete problems about proper order in the local congregations. The early Church collected the various writings of the New Testament and declared them canonical, together with those of the

Old Testament. Thus Holy Scripture is a *book of the Church*. It can be understood correctly only if it is interpreted in the context of the life, the spirit, and the faith of the Church in which it arose. To listen to Holy Scripture is to hear the witness of faith from every century. Holy Scripture is not given into the hands of the individual expositor of Scripture, but is bestowed on the Church as a whole. The Church as a whole is the encompassing We of faith.   39

In the sixteenth century, there arose a *controversy with the Reformers* about the   46–48; relation of Scripture and the Church. They put forth the thesis that "Scripture   193–195 alone" is the "judge, rule, and guide" of the faith. Luther was of the opinion that Scripture is clear by itself and interprets itself when it is read in terms of its center, Jesus Christ. The Church, as the "creation of the Word", does not stand above Scripture. Luther did not mean, of course, just the dead letters of Scripture, but Scripture proclaimed in a living way, the living word of God, which by the power of the Holy Spirit always gains a new hearing in the Church. For that reason, even according to Luther, the word of God cannot be without the people of God.

The *Council of Trent* (1545–1563) taught that the gospel in the Church is the "source of all saving truth and moral order" (DS 1501; NR 87). But the Council refused to make Scripture a self-interpreting juridical authority in the Church. Who interprets Scripture validly at any given time? The Council taught:

> No one trusting in his own cleverness should dare in matters of faith and morals, which belong to the core of Christian doctrine, to twist Holy Scripture according to his own meaning against the meaning that Holy Mother Church has held and holds—she is entitled to the judgment on the true meaning and the explanation of Holy Scripture —or even to interpret Holy Scripture against the unanimous mind of the Fathers . . . (DS 1507; NR 93).

Since then, there has been a considerable rapprochement on this question. The *Second Vatican Council* did indeed hold fast to the doctrine of Trent: "But the task of giving an authentic interpretation of the word of God, whether in written form or in the form of Tradition, has been entrusted to the living teaching office of the Church alone. Its authority in this matter is exercised in the name of Jesus Christ" (DV 10). But the Council added that the Church must first hear the word of God with full reverence before it can announce it with full confidence (DV 1). "Yet the Magisterium is not superior to the word of God, but is its servant" (DV 10). Thus, in the dialogue with Evangelical Christians, Holy Scripture is "a precious instrument in the mighty hand of God for attaining to that unity which the Savior holds out to all men" (UR 21).

Both the Catholic and the Evangelical churches want in principle to hold fast to the solidarity that exists between the word of God and the Church as well as to the superordination of the word of God. The problem that has divided the churches until today concerns whether and to what degree there are magisterial authorities within the Church that interpret the word of God in a binding and, if need be, infallible way. The problem is not Scripture or its position, but rather its binding

46–48;
204;
257–261
122–124
145–148

interpretation. How does the authority of Scripture become concretely effective? We will go into this question later in more detail.

New problems have arisen with the *historical-critical interpretation of the Bible* in the eighteenth and nineteenth centuries. On the one hand, criticism has disclosed the riches of Scripture anew and has contributed to the renewal of the Church and her faith. On the other hand, criticism pushed both individual passages and Scripture as a whole into a changed relation with Tradition. Many of the faithful see here not only a questioning of their faith but also of the authority of Scripture itself. *Two extremes* stand opposed. Some consider Holy Scripture as entirely the word of God and wish, in disregard of the historical character of Scripture, to understand every statement in a purely literal way (fundamentalism). Others consider the Bible as a purely human book just like any other. The differences and contradictions established by them between individual writings and between literary strata lead to a relativization of scriptural authority and further tensions with the traditional interpretation of the Church.

The *scriptural interpretation of the Church today* takes the only responsible middle road. For it, Holy Scripture is wholly the word of God and wholly the word of man. It is thus imperative to hear the word of God in and through its human-historical form. Inerrant authority attaches to Scripture in view of the truth alone "which God, for the sake of our salvation, wished to see confided to the sacred Scriptures" (DV 11). What is binding in this connection is the witness of Scripture as a whole in the unity of Old and New Testaments. The individual passages of Scripture must thus be interpreted in the light of one another (DV 12). The essential thing is to hear the one symphony in the polyphony of Scripture (Irenaeus of Lyons). In order to grasp this embracing meaning in Holy Scripture, we must proceed from the Church's consciousness of the faith today, above all from the Church's confession of faith. We must then interpret this confession in the mirror of the original witnesses of Scripture and then translate it again into the present context of the Church. The Church interprets Scripture, but essential points for the interpretation of the Church's teaching and practice come from Scripture. As long as the historical-critical exposition of Scripture is integrated into the larger process of interpretation and does not assert itself as the sole and supreme judge of the meaning of Scripture, its critical inquiries and new perspectives may have a fruitful effect on the Church's understanding of the faith.

The next question arises quickly: What is the faith of the Church? Where do we find it? The Church seems to be no less a polyphonic choir than the Bible is. To what can one adhere?

7.3 Tradition and Traditions

Whoever says "I believe" and so joins in the great "We believe" enters into a context of Tradition that extends from the Apostles down to today. But what is Tradition? Ordinarily when we speak of tradition, we think of long-standing individual forms and customs that we may regard either as venerable or as stuffy, depending on our attitude. Tradition often has only a nostalgic or a folkloric value for us. But there is a growing conviction that without a tie to tradition one loses one's orientation in the present and for the future. That does not make everything old into something good. Tradition too falls under the Pauline injunction: "Test everything, retain what is good" (1 Th 5:21). Many traditions were conditioned by the circumstances of the times, just as much that is fashionable today will be outmoded tomorrow. Even in the Church there are manifold traditions that can change quickly, as we have certainly experienced in this century. The question returns: What remains? On what can one depend?

Jesus himself was critical of the "tradition of our ancestors" (Mk 7:3, 5); he saw that the Jews had put "human tradition" in the place of God's commandments (Mk 7:8). But he was not an iconoclast who wanted to overthrow everything. In many respects he adhered to the tradition of his people; indeed, he drew richly from the Old Testament. He replaced rabbinical interpretation with his own interpretation, of course: "What I say to you is . . ." (Mt 5:22, among others). This means "I am telling you what real and true Tradition is." Even more: "I *am* Tradition, living and life-giving transmission." This understanding is confirmed for us by the Apostle *Paul*. He passes on what he himself received from the earlier Christians and their local congregations (1 Cor 15:3). For him, behind this chain of Tradition stands Jesus Christ. "I received from the Lord what I handed on to you" (1 Cor 11:23). For Paul, then, Jesus Christ is the one and only authority by which everything else must be measured. *At the beginning of theology, the Tradition is Jesus Christ himself as the Lord, permanently and effectively present in the Church.* He is at the same time the criterion for all individual traditions.

We must proceed from this *one* *Tradition*. So the Second Vatican Council intends when it speaks of the life-giving presence of this Tradition.

> Thus God, who spoke in the past, continues to converse with the spouse of his beloved son. And the Holy Spirit, through whom the living voice of the Gospel rings out in the Church—and through her in the world—leads believers to the full truth, and makes the word of Christ dwell in them in all its richness (cf. Col 3:16) (DV 8).

Jesus Christ did not create the Church and the hierarchy at the beginning in order then to depart from this world, having provided for the faith until the end of time. Rather, Christ is efficaciously present in the Church: his word lives on in the Church. "*Tradition is the word living continuously in the hearts of the faithful*" (J. A. Möhler).

The one Tradition expresses and embodies itself in *manifold traditions*.

176–177; 255–257

In this way the Church in her doctrine, life, and worship, perpetuates
and transmits to every generation all that she herself is, all that she
believes (DV 8).

The way in which the faith is transmitted can take almost any form in the
Church: the sign of the cross that a mother traces on the forehead of her
child; teaching the basic prayers of Christianity, especially the "Our
Father", in the home and in religious instruction; living, praying, and
singing in the local congregation, into which the young person grows;
Christian example in everyday life and Christian action even to the point
of martyrdom; the witness given by Christian music (especially hymns
and chorales), by architecture and the plastic arts (especially representations
of the cross, which is considered a privileged Christian symbol); and, not
least, by the liturgy of the Church. The different ways in which the
Church's Magisterium expresses itself also belong in a special way to the
257–261   forms of Tradition (addresses and sermons, pastoral letters and encyclicals,
up to the infrequent solemn doctrinal promulgations of the Councils and
the infallible decisions of the pope). In principle, one can say: *Tradition
occurs in the Church's proclamation, her liturgy, and the service she renders.*

Since the Church of all times and places is the We of faith, the witnesses
of Tradition from the past are of permanent significance. These include
the ancient liturgies, the declarations of the Councils, the writings of the
Fathers and doctors of the Church, the witnesses of piety, and the
archeological and artistic witness of the past (the inscriptions in the
catacombs, for instance, or the historically changing representations of
Christ). Not least are the great saints. In this catechism, we will always
endeavor to give these witnesses of the faith a hearing. Of course, not
every one of these manifold figures and witnesses to Tradition can be
equally important. Too many differences become apparent as soon as one
occupies oneself with them in greater detail. The question about which
criteria to use for grasping the one Tradition in the multiplicity of
traditions must still be asked.

We have already named a *first criterion*: Jesus Christ, above all as he is
attested to in Holy Scripture, the original record of the faith. Holy
Scripture bears witness to everything necessary for salvation, especially to
the center of our faith—God's salvation in Jesus Christ through the Holy
Spirit. All other propositions of the faith interpret, secure, and delimit this
one truth. The original witness of Holy Scripture is the most important
criterion for evaluating the witnesses of Tradition. A *second criterion* is a
principle: any single witness of Tradition is probative only insofar as it
gives expression to the common faith of the entire We of the Church of its
age and of every age. In the fifth century, Vincent of Lerins wrote:

"Likewise in the Catholic Church one must see to it that we hold fast to that which was believed everywhere, always, and by all; for that is catholic in the true and proper sense." It may well be only in the course of history that the Church will recognize the fullness of the truth of faith originally handed down to her. But this must happen, as Vincent of Lerins said and as the First Vatican Council repeated, "in the same sense and in the same understanding" (DS 3020; NR 44). The truth of the gospel is always one and the same despite the manifold cultural and historical forms of its expression.

The relation between Holy Scripture and Tradition was also the object of sharp disputes in the sixteenth century. In the late Middle Ages, many fundamental statements of the gospel were obscured by human traditions. Against these foreign accretions the Reformers set forth the principle "Scripture alone". "God's Word should set the articles of faith and no one else, not even an angel" (Smalcaldian Articles). 43–45; 194–197

The *Council of Trent* (1545–1563) took up the justified concern of the Reformers. According to the Council, there can be no binding tradition that contradicts Scripture. The Council declared only those traditions to be binding on faith which the Apostles received from Jesus Christ and which have come down to us from the Apostles. All purely human or only particular traditions were excluded. This allowed the Council of Trent to introduce a great reform and renewal of the Catholic Church. But at the same time the Council added to the Reformers' principle of "Scripture alone". The one gospel, according to the Council, is contained "in written books and unwritten Traditions". Both are to be recognized and honored "with the same pious willingness and reverence" (DS 1501; NR 87–88). This addition need not mean that the truth of the gospel would be contained partially in Holy Scripture and partially in the Tradition. The conciliar declaration can be understood as agreeing with the Fathers of the Church and the great theologians of the high Middle Ages in this way: Holy Scripture contains the whole faith in substance, but the faith can be grasped in its totality and fullness only in the light of Tradition. So the Second Vatican Council teaches: "The Church does not draw her certainty about all revealed truths from the holy Scriptures alone" (DV 9).

Given the *ecumenical rapprochement* in our century, the controversy has lost much of its former sharpness. Tradition has been seen as older than Scripture, while Scripture itself has been recognized as a product of the primitive Church's Tradition. At the same time, the many negative results of modern historical-critical interpretation have created a crisis for the purely scriptural principle. Still, the insight that the Bible is the basis of Church teaching and Church practice has gained acceptance by all churches in our century. Many ecumenical documents, especially the declaration of the Fourth World Conference for the Faith and the Constitution of the Church on "Scripture, Tradition, and Traditions" (Montreal, 1963), indicate the high degree of agreement now attained. Nevertheless, important material questions remain open, above all the question of an ecclesiastical 203–204; 257–261 teaching office. Today, the fundamental position of Scripture and the meaning of Tradition are really no longer ecumenical problems. But there are problems with the distinction between correct and mistaken scriptural interpretation, or between a commonly binding Tradition and the manifold traditions, which bear witness to a legitimate wealth of differing forms of expression. Our question now is: How does the Church, which appeals to Holy Scripture, speak in a binding way? This is the question about the Church's dogma.

7.4 Do We Need Dogmas?

Today many people pride themselves on approaching problems "non-dogmatically" and "pragmatically". The word "dogma" has negative connotations for many because it suggests the idea of what is immobile, narrow-minded, enslaving; it evokes memories of the Inquisition, religious wars, and moral constraint, among other things. Today the Church stands with those who rightly consider good freedom of thought, speech, research, conscience, and religion. Many think the time has come for a nondogmatic, practically oriented Christianity.

But freedom can avoid becoming caprice only if it remains oriented by the truth. Indeed, the truth alone makes us really free (Jn 8:32). Today, as at all times, *Jesus' exhortation* to unambiguous and fearless confession holds:

> "Whoever acknowledges me before men I will acknowledge before my Father in heaven. Whoever disowns me before men I will disown before my Father in heaven" (Mt 10:32–33).

All Christians are bound to this unambiguous confession. For the sake of avoiding ambiguity in confession, unity of confession is also necessary. There were divisions and factions in the Church from the beginning, of course (Acts 6:1; 1 Cor 1:11–13). For that reason, we hear *exhortations to unity* at many points in the New Testament:

> Agree in what you say. Let there be no factions; rather, be united in mind and judgment (1 Cor 1:10).

> Make every effort to preserve the unity which has the Spirit as its origin and peace as its binding force. There is but one body and one Spirit, just as there is but one hope given all of you by your call. There is one Lord, one faith, one baptism; one God and Father of all, who is over all, and works through all, and is in all (Eph 4:3–6).

229–233   The unity of the Church in faith, especially in an ecumenical perspective, certainly cannot be uniformity; it can be a unity only in the multiplicity of ways of proclamation, liturgical forms, theologies, and Church orders. But must it not also be first of all a unity in the truth? *Legitimate multiplicity is to be distinguished from a plurality of contradictory propositions about the faith.* A wild, unrestricted pluralism would make the search for unity meaningless. Christians could no longer gather for the liturgy and recite the confession of faith in common. If Christian truth no longer possessed any unambiguous clarity, the faith would lose its credibility in the eyes of the world. We can be thankful, then, for the *blessing* that God bestows on us by leading his Church, through the Holy Spirit, despite confusing and destructive unclarities, ever deeper into the truth. He does this through men and in a human way.

What, then, is a dogma? It is not an addition to the original gospel or even a new revelation. A dogma is an official exposition of the revelation, 34–36 issued once for all, that is binding on the whole Church. It is usually a definition formulated against erroneous, reductive, and falsifying interpretations. So dogma has a double aspect: it must refer to the original, common truth of revelation, and it must be presented officially, definitively, and in a way binding on all. When the Church proclaims a dogma, she 259–261 trusts in the abiding presence of Jesus Christ and the assistance of the Holy Spirit promised to her, who leads her into the fullness of truth (Jn 16:13).

For the sake of the unity and unambiguousness of the faith, the *primitive Church* itself had to formulate such definitions. The most important and most painful demarcation was necessary with regard to the Jewish synagogue. The Apostolic Council in Jerusalem proclaimed freedom from the Jewish law against those Christians who had fallen back into Judaism (Acts 15). The word "dogma" is used already here (Acts 16:4). In the same context, Paul formulates the first "anathema" of Church history (Gal 1:8–9; cf. 1 Cor 16:22). In many other places in the New 40 Testament, we already find fixed and binding formulas of confession (Rom 10:9; 1 Cor 12:3; 15:3–5, among others). These were further developed through the 40–41 ecumenical councils of the ancient Church, especially in the Nicene Creed. These definitions were now no longer intended for Christians who had fallen back into Judaism, but for those who had not completely cast off pagan notions and had thereby falsified the Christian faith. Disputes were frequently necessary in later times as well: in the *Middle Ages*, with movements such as the Waldensians and Albigensians (especially at the Fourth Lateran Council); in the sixteenth century, 196–203; with the *Reformers* (the Council of Trent, 1545–1563); and in the modern period, 215–216; with the errors stemming from the Enlightenment (summarized by the *First* 249–251 *Vatican Council*, 1869–1870). The situation was different with the *Marian dogmas* of 149–152 1854 ("Mary was conceived without original sin") and of 1950 ("Mary was assumed body and soul into heavenly glory"). They had their origin less in a definition provoked by errors than in the deepened insight into the position of Mary in salvation history.

The dogmatic development of doctrine led above all to greater *precision in the*

Church's way of speaking and to a *deepening of her insight into the faith*. Sometimes, of course, narrowings resulted from a dogmatic proclamation; the polemic often led some to adhere to the opposite of the combated error and prevented them from seeing the justified concern that stood behind its one-sided formulations. That was one of the reasons why the Second Vatican Council (1962–1965), while not retracting a single dogma of the past or setting forth a new one, decided for a positive exposition of the truth. The positive, *"pastoral" way of speaking* should not, of course, be misunderstood. The Church performs her pastoral ministry precisely by announcing the truth.

216

The definitiveness with which dogmas are presented does not deny that they speak in the language of their time. Their meaning depends on the expressiveness of the language employed at a particular time and under particular circumstances. We must distinguish, then, between the truths of faith and their manner of expression (GS 62). This *historical character of dogmas* also explains why dogmas sometimes express the truth, not falsely, but in the limited historical or linguistic perspective according to which the question was formulated. No single proposition, not even a dogma, can exhaust the fullness of the gospel. Each one enunciates the one infinite truth, the mystery of God and his salvation in Jesus Christ, in a finite and therefore imperfect way, a way capable of being improved, expanded, and deepened. This is different from saying that dogmatic expressions speak in a way variously approximating or indeterminately approaching the truth. Such a dogmatic relativism would contradict the central mystery of faith according to which God in Jesus Christ has entered definitively into human form and given it its determinate meaning. Even if dogmas are not a prolongation of the Incarnation, a certain similarity (or analogy) nonetheless exists. Dogmas are intended to re-present the Incarnation in an analogous way. For that reason, dogmatic truth in a particular form is also definitively binding (*Myst. Ecclesiae* 5).

40–41;
214–215;
225–226

Understood in this way, the concrete binding character of dogmas makes them *open formulas* at the same time—open into boundless mystery. They point beyond themselves not because they are false but precisely because they are true. They must therefore be interpreted and re-interpreted in a living way. Dogmatic Tradition is possible only through interpretation. Dogmas must be interpreted in view of Holy Scripture and the entire, usually more comprehensive, Tradition, as well as in view of the situation of their time and ours (the "signs of the times"). In interpreting, one must understand each individual dogma in the context of all other truths of faith and must pay attention to the *hierarchy of truths*, i.e., to the structural whole of the propositions of the faith (UR 11). One must weigh dogmas, not count them! Above all, the individual dogmas must be understood as the unfolding and securing of the one and all-encompassing content of the faith: God's salvation in Jesus Christ. This is the one dogma behind the many dogmas, the one word in the many words of the dogmatic Tradition.

Must a Catholic Christian be familiar with all dogmas? If he is, must he believe them all? To this one must simply answer: whoever believes like Abraham, who travels his way in the imitation of Christ, and who does this in and with the whole community of believers, implicitly believes not only a part but the whole faith, which does *not present an external sum of individual propositions but a whole* which the individual propositions expound and secure. The extent to which the individual Christian must be familiar with this unfolding depends on his task in the Church and on the degree of his general education. In the present situation, it is surely more important to concentrate on the one faith behind the many propositions instead of expounding the faith in more and more propositions. Today our faith must become simple again! That does not mean abridging and simplifying it. What has been said so far means that one cannot separate an individual dogma from the whole and deny it without destroying the structure of the whole.

We now return to our earlier statement: *faith* is an all-encompassing project of life and *an attitude toward one's whole existence*. This whole is not a proposition or a sum of propositions, but a trusting and building on God as he has disclosed himself to us in Jesus Christ. We do not believe in dogmas the way we believe in God, Jesus Christ, and the Holy Spirit. We believe *dogmas as concrete forms mediating* the one content of faith. The dogmas do not ground the truth of faith; the truth of faith grounds the dogmas. They are not true because they were proclaimed; they were proclaimed because they are true. We need them in order to be able to confess, in common and unambiguously, the one truth of faith. Thus the dogmas point beyond themselves to the truth that God is the almighty Father and the Father of Jesus Christ. Everything depends on this truth. We now turn to it.

GOD, THE FATHER, THE ALMIGHTY:
THE FATHER OF JESUS CHRIST

1. The Living God of History

1.1 God: Who Is He, Really?

"I believe in God." This first declaration of the confession of faith is the most important one. At bottom, the whole Creed is about God and nothing other than God; everything else enters only as it stands in relation to God. But who is God, really?

In the course of history, men have spoken very differently about God and to God. According to Martin Buber, "God" is

19–21;
22–23;
24–25;
34–35;
64–65

> the most highly charged of all human words. None has been so defiled, so mangled. . . . The generations of men have laid the burden of their anxious lives on this word and pressed it to the ground; it lies in the dust and bears the burden of them all. The generations of men have rent this word with their religious factions; they have killed and died for it; it bears the fingerprints of them all and the blood of all. . . . They draw grimaces and write "God" under them; they murder one another and say "in the name of God".

The name of God is also "deeply engraved in mankind's history of hope and suffering. In it this name encounters us, rising resplendent and obscured, venerated and denied, abused, profaned, and yet not forgotten" (*Gem. Synode, Unsere Hoffnung* I, 1).

Which God do we mean when we confess, "I believe in God"? Which God is meant when one cries, "God is dead!"? When we *as Christians* confess God, we are not talking about the God of whom the myths of primitive tribes tell. Nor are we talking only about the God who is experienced in mystical interiority or about the God of the philosophers. We mean the living God of history, the "God of Abraham, Isaac, and Jacob" (Ex 3:6; Mt 22:32), the God of Israel (Ps 72:18; Is 45:3; Mt 15:31), and not least the God who is "the Father of our Lord Jesus Christ" (2 Cor 1:3, among others). He is at the same time the God "who made heaven and earth" (Ps 121:2). For that reason, this God can take up what is true in other ways of speaking about God and bring them to fulfillment.

35–36   The question, Who is God?, becomes immediately the question, Where does God show himself that we may know him? *The Bible speaks of God by telling the history of God with men and by recounting the great deeds of God, who guides the history of his people. Through this history we know who God is.*

1.2 The God of the Old Covenant

The special history of God with men begins with *the pre-history of the patriarchs, Abraham, Isaac, and Jacob*. The story of Joseph already forms the transition to the history of the covenant with Israel. Who is "God, the Father"? Not a local cult god but a nomadic God, a God who chooses a people in sovereign freedom and not for any merit of theirs, a God who guides them in a "land where one is a foreigner". He promises possession of the land and a numerous posterity, but he goes beyond every legal and cultic standard. Many times the history of his promise threatens to get lost in a thicket of quite disedifying human weaknesses; but God continues on through all the human confusion. The story of the patriarchs is only the pre-history of the covenant with Israel. Nevertheless, essential motifs of God's history with men already become apparent in it: God goes along the way, and so faith is a setting-out-on-the-way with God and making-oneself-firm in God (*aman*, Gen 15:6). This happens in the tension between the friendly, familiar nearness of God and his inscrutable hiddenness.

The history of the patriarchs also has a permanent importance, since the Moslems also honor the God of Abraham and worship him as the one, living God. Just as Abraham subjected himself to God, they endeavor to surrender to the hidden will of God. The three historical and monotheistic religions, Judaism, Christianity, and Islam, are connected with one another through their common origin in Abraham. For that reason, it is imperative to overcome the past disagreements and enmities between Christians, Jews, and Moslems and to endeavor to attain mutual understanding (NA 3).

God's history with us really begins with *Moses and God's covenant with the people Israel*. Israel then lived under the most severe affliction in Egypt. Then God revealed himself to Moses, who was fleeing from Pharaoh:

> "I am the God of your father, . . . the God of Abraham, the God of Isaac, the God of Jacob. . . . I have witnessed the affliction of my people in Egypt and have heard their cry of complaint against their

slave drivers, so I know well what they are suffering. Therefore I have come down to rescue them from the hands of the Egyptians and lead them out of that land into a good and spacious land, a land flowing with milk and honey . . ." (Ex 3:6–8).

At the passage through the Sea of Reeds and the wandering through the wilderness, at Sinai, at the entrance into the promised land and the creation of the Davidic kingship, the Israelites experience again and again that God is with them. His name is "I am [here]" (Ex 3:14). He bears his people "up on eagle's wings" (Ex 19:4) in order to form a covenant with them and to make them his special people among all peoples, one that belongs to him as "a kingdom of priests, a holy nation" (Ex 19:6). This covenant is not a contract of equal partners with equal rights and obligations; on the contrary, it is granted graciously and freely by God. He obligates Israel through the "law of the Covenant", the Ten Commandments, with their ethical and socio-ethical precepts (Ex 20:1–17; Dt 5:1–22); but he also promises the people life, land, and a future. The shortest summary of the covenant relation is this: "I will be your God and you shall be my people" (Jer 7:23). The God of Israel is not a God who sits untouched in blessed repose, enthroned above the destinies of men and the course of their history. He is a living God who sees the misery of men and hears their cries. He is a God who champions life, a God who delivers and leads forth, a God who intervenes in history and opens up a new history. He is a God of hope.

The history of the covenant takes an extremely dramatic form. Again and again Israel falls into need and affliction because it falls away from the one living God and from the fundamental precepts of divine law; it turns to the idols of the surrounding pagan peoples. Again and again God awakens men and women to help his people in their hour of need. God especially calls the *prophets*. Beyond the older prophets who left no writings behind (Elijah, Elisha, Samuel, and others), the Bible includes the "writing prophets": the four "major prophets" (Isaiah, Jeremiah, Ezekiel, Daniel) and the twelve "minor prophets" (Hosea, Joel, Amos, Obadiah, Jonah, Micah, Nahum, Habakkuk, Zephaniah, Haggai, Zechariah, and Malachi). The prophets are not fortune-tellers. God appoints them rather as his messengers, spokesmen, and heralds. Again and again we read: "Go and say to this people" (Is 6:9), "Thus says the Lord" (Am 1:3, 6, among others). The prophets are to call the people back to obedience and justice on behalf of God; they are to encourage and comfort them in the difficult time of the Exile. For that reason, they speak of God who delivered Israel out of Egypt; of God, who is Israel's father, king, shepherd, and beloved; of God, who is the defender and deliverer of the poor and the oppressed. At the same time, the prophets warn against false security. Because of the injustice and disobedience of the people, their election turns into judgment (Am 3:2). So the prophet Amos announces "the day of the Lord" as a day of judgment, of darkness and not of light (Am 5:18).

In the two catastrophes of 722 (the fall of the Northern Kingdom) and of 587 (the fall of the Southern Kingdom), the judgment becomes reality. Israel loses its independence as a people. It lives in foreign parts, in an occupied land, or in dispersion (the Diaspora). Yet this collapse is not the end, because God is not at an end. He is faithful to his covenant in spite of human infidelity.

> Can a mother forget her infant,
>   be without tenderness for the child of her womb?
> Even should she forget,
>   I will never forget you (Is 49:15).

God is a God who creates the new and bestows the future. The great deeds of the past—the Exodus, the formation of the covenant, the taking possession of the land, the building of the temple—will be repeated in the future in an intensified form. At the end of days, the God of Israel will rise up again and form a *new covenant*, one not written in stone as the Ten Commandments were, but in the heart (Jer 31:31–33). On that day all peoples, attracted by the splendor of the new Jerusalem, will come flocking and will recognize the God of Israel. There will be eternal peace and one world under the one God (Is 2:2–4).

The history of the covenant with Israel, the confession of the one and only God who reveals himself in this history, and the hope for the coming of God and his kingdom, are common *to Jews and to Christians*. The Christian proclamation of God cannot and may not be severed from this root in the Old Covenant. It bears witness not just to any general idea of God but to the concrete God who has made himself known historically through Abraham, Moses, and the prophets. Jesus himself was formed by this history and its witness in the Old Testament. To that extent, present-day Jews can recognize Jesus as their brother. The faith of Jesus unites Jews and Christians; the faith in Jesus also divides them. As distinguished from Jews, Christians believe that Jesus, our brother, is at the same time the Son of God, in whose cross and Resurrection God has fulfilled the promises given to Israel. The cross, to which the Jewish leaders of that time delivered Jesus, is for Christians the sign of salvation. As such, it is to be announced as the sign of the universal love of God (NA 4). So the Apostle Paul says that it is a mistake to designate the Jews as disinherited and accursed (Rom 11:1–2). God still loves his people for the sake of the patriarchs. "God's gifts and his call are irrevocable"

(Rom 11:29). For that reason, all hatred of the Jews and, even more, all persecution of the Jews, which has occurred so often and in such terrible proportions in Christian history, is to be condemned. The dialogue with Judaism begun again in our days is to be continued and deepened.

1.3 The God of Jesus Christ

Jesus' proclamation of God bears the imprint *of the language and the notions* 123–130 *of the Old Testament and of Judaism*. For most of his sayings, parallels can be found in the Old Testament writings and in the Jewish tradition. As in the Old Testament, God is for Jesus the Creator who creates, sustains, guides, and preserves all. For Jesus, God's fatherly care is seen in the entire creation, in the grass and in the flowers of the field (Mt 6:28–30) as well as in the birds of the sky (Mt 6:26; 10:29–31). "His sun rises on the bad and the good, he rains on the just and the unjust" (Mt 5:45). No hair falls from our head without his knowing and willing it (Mt 10:30). The parables show how we can discover vestiges of God and of his workings in all events of daily life. For that reason, Jesus says, Do not worry! (Mt 6:25, 31). Do not be afraid! (Mt 10:31). As in the Old Testament, God 86–90 is for Jesus *the Lord of history* who helps and heals, delivers and redeems, who does new things. All of this happens not only in the depths of our soul but in our body as well. Nothing shows this more clearly than the miracles of Jesus. Jesus does not understand them as spectacular feats of 129–131 strength but as God's deeds of power through him (Mt 12:28; Lk 17:21). He teaches his hearers to believe in the God for whom everything is possible and to petition him in faith. For faith nothing is unattainable; "Everything is possible to a man who trusts" (Mk 9:23). Faith sets God's effective omnipotence into motion, as it were, and so is able to move mountains (Mk 11:23; 1 Cor 13:2).

In spite of this closeness to the Old Testament and to Judaism, the whole of Jesus' proclamation of God is nevertheless set in a new key 123–129 and is to that extent *unmistakable and unique*. The central content of Jesus' proclamation is that the Kingdom of God hoped for by the people of the Old Testament has now drawn near (Mk 1:14–15). It is dawning in Jesus' words, deeds, and person. But Jesus does not see the dawning of the lordship of God as wrathful (as John the Baptist does), but as full of grace, mercy, and the forgiveness of God. His message about God is *good news*, especially as it is expressed in the beatitudes of the Sermon on the Mount (Mt 5:3–12). This joy is intended by Jesus not least for the sinners who change their ways and follow his call. They may be certain that God is for them a Father who awaits his lost son, forgives him, reinstates him in his

filial rights, and even holds a great feast of joy for him (Lk 15:11–32). This
message that God is boundless love is the very heart of what Jesus says
about God.

A summary expression of Jesus' good news of God comes when Jesus
addresses God *in a wholly unique way as Father*. He teaches us to say, "Our
Father"(Mt 6:9; Lk:11:2). Jesus even dares in his conversation with God
to use the intimate form of address, "*Abba*" (Mk 14:36). The primitive
community's conviction that Jesus' most personal linguistic usage is
recorded here made this word "Abba" so holy to them that they kept it in
Aramaic even in Greek texts (Gal 4:6; Rom 8:15). The conviction existed
in the Church from the very beginning that *what is properly and specifically
Christian is an intimate personal communion with God*, in knowing oneself to
be a child, a son or a daughter of God. At the same time, the Christian
should know that anyone who calls God "Father" has brothers and sisters;
he never stands alone and lonely before his Father. A new family is formed
by the one Father, a new people of God as the beginning of a new
humanity.

The familiar intimacy characteristic of Jesus' form of addressing the
Father should not be misunderstood as making light of things. Jesus does
not simply speak of the "good Lord". On the contrary, Jesus' form of
addressing the Father expresses God's divinity in an unprecedented way.
For the patriarchically ordered clans of Palestine, the father remains the
lord. So in Jesus' message of God there is also the threat of judgment on
everything evil that resists God and debases man. To the "blessed are
you", there also belongs the "woe to you!" (Lk 6:20–26; 11:42–52). God's
omnipotence proves itself equally in salvation and judgment. Only if God
is all-powerful can his love truly help in every situation and lead the
lordship of love against all evil powers and dominions. Only if God is the
omnipotence of love does his love not mean a naïve transfiguration of the
world, but questioning it and transforming it creatively. Only an all-
powerful love can be the ground of our hope.

God's omnipotence in love, as Jesus proclaimed it and lived it, proved
itself best in the *death and Resurrection of Jesus*. In Jesus' dying, God turned
most radically to the outcast and helpless One, "freed him from death's
bitter pangs . . . and raised him up again" (Acts 2:24). Through the death
and Resurrection of Jesus we know definitively who God is: he is the God
who restores the dead to life (Rom 4:17; 2 Cor 1:9). *The death and
Resurrection of Jesus is the final revelation of God, of his creative fidelity
and his omnipotence in love, which brings to a close and recapitulates all else.*
In the living, dying, and rising of Jesus, the goodness and love of
God for man has appeared (Tit 3:4). God has proved himself as love
(1 Jn 4:8, 16). Thus we may be certain that "neither death nor life, neither

66–67;
125–126

156–161;
170–175

angels nor principalities, neither the present nor the future, nor powers, neither height nor depth nor any other creature, will be able to separate us from the love of God that comes to us in Christ Jesus our Lord" (Rom 8:38–39).

The definitive revelation of God in Jesus Christ is the ground of our hope for the coming Kingdom of God, in which God will at last be all in all (1 Cor 15:28). The last book of Scripture bears witness to the message of the Old and New Testaments with these recapitulations:

> "I am the Alpha and the Omega, the One who is and who was and who is to come, the Almighty" (Rev 1:8).

> He shall dwell with them and they shall be his people and he shall be their God who is always with them. He shall wipe every tear from their eyes, and there shall be no more death or mourning, crying out or pain, for the former world has passed away.
> The One who sat on the throne said to me, "See, I make all things new" (Rev 21:3–5).

2. God, the Father, the Almighty

2.1 The Uniqueness and Singularity of God

God, the Father, the Almighty—this phrase of the Creed has shown itself as a summary expression of Jesus' message of God and as the ground of our hope. What, then, does this confession mean?

In many religions the supreme God is designated as father. The Greeks named Zeus the "father of gods and men". Later, philosophers spoke of God as the father of all men; they wished to express by this that something divine is in all men by nature, so that all men form something like a family, a single race. Such parallels do not detract from the uniqueness and singularity of the biblical understanding of God. According to the Bible, God is our common Father, not on the basis of a common nature, but on the basis of election (Hos 11:1; Jer 31:20). Jesus Christ teaches and empowers us to address God in this intimate way as Father (Mt 6:9; Lk 11:2). For that reason, we often introduce the recitation of the "Our Father" at the celebration of the Eucharist with this preamble: "Jesus taught us to call God our Father and so we have the courage to say: Our Father . . ." In order to express the uniqueness of the biblical Father-God, the confession of faith says: "We believe in one God, the Father, the

Almighty." With this *faith-in-one-God* (monotheism), the Old Testament dispute with the many gods of the pagans (polytheism) is well summarized. Already in the covenant-charter, the Ten Commandments, we find the lapidary command:

> "You shall not have other gods besides me" (Ex 20:3).

For that reason, every Jew at the time of Jesus recited every day this summary of the whole history of the covenant:

> "Hear, O Israel! The Lord is our God, the Lord alone! Therefore, you shall love the Lord, your God, with all your heart, and with all your soul, and with all your strength" (Dt 6:4–5).

Jesus confirmed this faith-in-one-God of the Old Testament particularly in the command to love God "with all your heart, with all your soul, with all your mind, and with all your strength" (Mk 12:30). The New Testament emphasized this anew against the pagan worship of many gods (1 Cor 8:4; Eph 4:6, among others).

The biblical texts make it clear that faith-in-one-God does not mean that we believe only in one God rather than in two or three. It means rather that we confess that our God has proved himself so unique and so singular that he can *in essence exist only once*. A God who was limited or even impeded by other gods would no longer be the almighty Father. "That which is to be considered as the supreme magnitude must exist alone and have no equal . . . if God is not one, he is not at all" (Tertullian).

The faith-in-one-God is by no means a merely abstract theory but *a confession of very practical importance*. It tells us that the reality of the world is ultimately not a chaotic confusion because it is grounded in the one God. The world has order, meaning, and coherence because of God. There is also only one absolutely dependable ground and one absolutely certain meaning on which we can and must stake all. This decision grounds Christian freedom with regard to the world and man. "To serve God is to reign" (as the liturgy says). Indeed, one can even say that the more we have our Lord in God alone, the less we are slaves dependent on men and things, the more we are free sons and daughters in the house of the one Father. The rejection of the worship of many gods is not at all antiquated today, although there are no longer any gods as they were in the history of religions. Gods and idols are anything that we put as ultimate values in place of God. Idols may be money, prestige, work, power, progress, pleasure, but also nation, race, class, state, and even world views, ideologies, and principles. Every good but finite value becomes an idol that enslaves us when we absolutize it and place it alongside or above God and his will. The faith-in-one-God urges us to turn to God alone as our ultimate ground and ultimate goal, to have in him our one and all, to make use of all else only insofar as it helps us to this goal and to leave it when it hinders us (Ignatius of Loyola). *In the confession of the one and only God, the fundamental decision of our lives is at stake.*

2.2 The Essence and Attributes of God

When Holy Scripture wants to say who God is, it does not use abstract and complicated concepts. The Bible speaks of God in all sorts of *images*, sometimes even in very human (anthropomorphic) expressions. So we read in the Psalms, for instance:

> I love you, O Lord, my strength,
>> O Lord, my rock, my fortress, my deliverer.
>
> My God, my rock of refuge,
>> my shield, the horn of my salvation, my stronghold (Ps 18:2–3).

Naturally, Holy Scripture also knows that man cannot and may not fashion an image of God (Ex 20:4; Dt 5:8), for God is *unique and incomparable*.

> To whom can you liken God?
> With what equal can you confront him? (Is 40:18).

In order to express the fact that God is beyond everything worldly and human, the Bible calls him in many places "the Lord" (in Hebrew, "*adonai*"). He is the *Lord-God*, the Lord of lords, the ruler over all the world.

> O Lord, our Lord,
>> How glorious is your name over all the earth!
>> You have exalted your majesty above the heavens (Ps 8:2).

The *essence of God* is holiness and glory, which prove themselves in his love made manifest in Jesus Christ.

> For I am God and not man,
>> the Holy One present among you (Hos 11:9).
>
> "Holy, holy, holy is the Lord of hosts! . . . All the earth is filled with his glory!" (Is 6:3).

Holiness means God's superiority over the world and sin and his separation from them. Separation from sin means God's resoluteness in the good, in truth and justice. By God's *glory* is meant his sovereign lordship, his power and dignity, his splendor and beauty. It signifies that God is independent of all other beings, that he exists without need in and of himself because he is, without any lack and without any change, *the fullness of life and being, absolute perfection*. Everything else has a share in this fullness. All reality is therefore a reflection of his glory. As the Holy One and Glorious One, God is also the hidden God (Is 45:15). No one can see his face and live (Ex 33:20). Only his sovereignly free, gracious gift can reveal his deepest essence to us, the *mystery of his love*. "God is love" (1 Jn 4:8, 16b; compare Hos 2:21; 11:8–9; 14:4; Jer 31:20).

We often express the incomparable glory of God by saying: God is *beyond the world*. That is not meant in a spatial sense. God is nowhere "up there" in some heaven imagined as a floor above the clouds. Our expression means rather that God surpasses the reality of the world. He is above everything. Moreover, God is wholly other than the reality of the world; he is greater, more powerful, more mysterious. God surpasses all creaturely distinctions. He has both masculine and feminine, both fatherly and motherly traits, but he is in fact neither masculine nor feminine, and he grounds neither a patriarchal nor a matriarchal order, but only a human one. God also exceeds all time and history. His eternity is not infinitely consecutive time, but a trans-temporality, that is, an absolute simultaneity. Finally, God surpasses all possibilities of our imagination, of our language, and of our knowledge. This is what we mean by the *transcendence of God*.

On the other hand, God is not alongside or above the world; he is *within the world*. He is near to us in all things. We can encounter him in both the ordinary and the extraordinary events of life. Above all, he encounters us through other men. He pervades, encompasses, and governs everything. He is boundless, infinite, and therefore omnipresent. "In him we live and move and have our being" (Acts 17:28). This is the *immanence of God*.

God's mystery can be missed, then, in two ways. One can either identify God and the world instead of distinguishing them (pantheism), or one can push God into an infinite distance, as if God and the world had nothing to do with each other (deism). *Only when one sees the nearness and the distance of God together does one do justice to the unfathomable mystery of God*. Both properties are expressed in the statement that *God is Spirit*. Spirit pervades all and yet stands over all. So the confession of God sharply contradicts every world view that holds for matter, the visible, the calculable, the producible, or the needs and interests of men as the original, the ultimately valid, or even the only reality (materialism). In this way too, the confession of God has far-reaching practical consequences.

The Bible itself tries repeatedly to predicate individual *attributes* of God on the basis of his historical revelation.

> "The Lord, the Lord, a gracious and merciful God, slow to anger and rich in kindness and fidelity . . ." (Ex 34:6).

The various attributes of God are the one essence of God's relation to the world considered under different points of view. Since God is Spirit, he

30–33

knows about each and all. Nothing can remain hidden from him; *God is all-knowing*. He also effects all in all; nothing and no one can escape his lordship; *God is all-powerful*. His omnipotence does not, however, want to oppress man. God wants to give him his rights, and so God's wrath burns against injustice and falsehood. *God is just*. He also accomplishes what he wills; he can be relied on unconditionally. *God is faithful and true*. He turns above all to the small, the poor, the oppressed; he forgives the sinner who is ready to change his ways. *God is good and merciful*. God's justice and God's love are not opposites. The love of God means that God accepts everyone unconditionally; he gives each one his due. In the biblical sense, the justice of God even refers to God's gracious gift by which the sinful man first becomes just. God's justice is a creative and a bountiful justice that has mercy on the sinner out of pure love.   191–194

A *summary* of these powerful declarations is found *in the confession of the one God, the almighty Father*. Many have difficulties with this essential declaration because they think that with the confession of God as almighty Father, God is determined one-sidedly as masculine and support is given to the supremacy of males. But "Father" must be understood as a symbolic word when applied to God, who is beyond sexual distinctions.   98–100; 316–317
It designates God as the ultimate, all-encompassing, and yet at the same time transcendent origin and creative source of life who has turned to man with protection, faithful care, love, and mercy. The confession of God, the almighty Father, names God as the almighty who creates, sustains, and guides all, who holds the world and history in his hand. It also affirms that this almighty God is not a despot or a tyrant, but a good Father. He cares about man even more than about the grass of the field and the birds of the air (Mt 6:26–30). Men are not his slaves; he makes them rather his sons and daughters (Gal 4:6), even his friends (Jn 15:15). If God in his coming lordship will one day be "all in all" (1 Cor 15:28), the kingdom of freedom and the glory of the children of God will dawn at the same time (Rom 8:21).

2.3 The Name and Person of God

We know a man very little when we know only his individual attributes. So we little grasp God's essence in faith by traveling the way of his individual attributes. Men make themselves known by telling their names. One's name says something about one's essence. The bearer of a name is not an It but an I and a Thou, a person who can speak and to whom one can speak, a person whom one does not simply have at one's disposal, but who rather has inviolable dignity. When we call someone by name we show that we know him and have a relationship to him. To have a name in public is not to be just anyone, someone anonymous, but to be known and important. The nameless are the unimportant, those not worth mentioning, who have no voice and no influence.

God too reveals himself by making his name known. The *revelation of God's name* happened with Moses at the burning thornbush.

> "But," said Moses to God, "when I go to the Israelites and say to them, 'The God of your fathers has sent me to you,' if they ask me, 'What is his name?' what am I to tell them?" God replied, "I am who am." Then he added, "This is what you shall tell the Israelites: I AM sent me to you" (Ex 3:13–14).

The revelation of God's name, YAHWEH, *is the center of the Old Testament revelation of God.* If God has a name, it means that God is not a thing, not an object that one has at one's disposal. One may not misuse his name for one's own purposes (Ex 20:7). God has a name; he is not *a* higher being or the supreme being in the sense in which the Enlightenment used the term. He is not an abstract principle, not an impersonal law of the world, not a blind cosmic origin, not an impersonal absolute and an impersonal unconditioned, not an impersonal being, not even the depths of such being. God has a name. *God is not an It but an I, a Thou.* His name is a promise and a pledge for men.

Because God has a name, he is able to call us, and we are able to call him. He is not a mute God, but a God *who speaks and who can be spoken to.* In biblical passages, God refers to himself as "I":

> "I, the Lord, am your God, who brought you out of the land of Egypt" (Ex 20:2; cf. Hos 12:10).

> "I am God, there is no other;
>   I am God, there is none like me.
> At the beginning I foretell the outcome;
>   in advance, things not yet done.
> I say that my plan shall stand,
>   I accomplish my every purpose" (Is 46:9–10).

Because God says "I" of himself, and because he turns to us and opens himself to us, we may say "Thou" to him. We not only talk about God; we talk with God. We can call his name in our every need and be certain that he hears:

> The Lord will hear me when I call upon him (Ps 4:4).

> I call upon you, for you will answer me, O God;
>   incline your ear to me; hear my word (Ps 17:6).

> Out of the depths I cry to you, O Lord;
>   Lord, hear my voice!
>   Let your ears be attentive to my voice of supplication (Ps 130:1–2).

Jesus shows most clearly that we can address God by using the term *"Abba"*. This term takes God seriously as God precisely by believing him capable of all. Jesus' personal petition is true praise of God; the prayer of supplication is the earnestness and essence of faith in God.

The revelation of God's name and Jesus' use of "*Abba*" in prayer entitle us, indeed require us, to say that *God is a personal being*. Only a person can say "I" and can let himself be addressed as "Thou". A person distinguishes himself from all other beings by standing entirely in himself, by being incommutable and unique. He is free to turn to others, to enter into relationship with them, and to disclose himself to them. To be sure, God is not a person in the limited way that we are persons. But he is no less a person than we; indeed, he is a person in an infinitely higher way.

The personal understanding of God distinguishes the Old and New Testaments' message of God from the image of God in the *high Eastern religions* (Hinduism, Buddhism, Confucianism, Taoism). While Christianity, Judaism, and Islam understand the relationship of God and man as personal encounter and communion, the Eastern religions seek to overcome the narrowness and limitedness of individuality and to find liberation in the sheltering universal One or, rather, in a *nirvana* beyond objects. They fear that a personal God may become a finite being in relation to man and that man may be strengthened in his egoism and self-glorification. The Eastern religions differ here most deeply from Christianity. In spite of all parallels in individual points, prayer and meditation have a different sense in Christianity than in the Eastern religions. In Christianity, prayer is friendly interaction with God; in the East it is fusion and unification with the whole. In spite of these obvious differences, "the Catholic Church rejects nothing of what is true and holy in these religions." Rather it exhorts them to dialogue and cooperation, "with prudence and charity" (NA 2). `19–21; 34–35; 53–54`

Today many Christians have similar *objections to a personal understanding of God*, and go so far as to conceive of Christianity without God. But the denial or concealing of the personality of God creates a new gospel, not the one to which Holy Scripture bears witness. This denial makes God into an It; it makes of the message of salvation, "I am with you", a general world view of use to no one. A person wants a person. Only if God is the absolute person are we absolutely accepted and affirmed as persons. The personal understanding of God does not detract from the unlimitedness and infinity of God. Both belong to the concept of a person who is utterly unique and at the same time infinitely open. The concept of personality is thus more comprehensive than that of individuality. So understood, the concept of a person as applied to God expresses how God is the One encompassing and comprehending all, the almighty, but in a quite unique way as the mystery of the all-encompassing, unfathomable love of the Father.

The personal being of God is the deepest reason for the personal dignity of man. It is a misunderstanding to hold that God is at bottom nothing other than an expression of good behavior toward our fellow man, a particular way of living our common humanity. It is true that God's love grounds our love for one another. Love of God is indissolubly bound up with love of `98–102` neighbor (Mk 12:30–31). God is never only a private matter of the heart; our faith in God has importance for others. How can we love one another unconditionally if we have not already experienced unconditional love and so been awakened and enabled to love? God must love us first. Only if God accepts us unconditionally can we also accept and affirm one another unconditionally. For that reason, the Christian faith is not exhausted in "horizontal" relations; the "vertical" direction also belongs to it essentially. Only if God is a personal being in himself are we able to address him together as "Our Father". Because God is the *Father of all men, all men are brothers and sisters*.

3. God, the Father of Jesus Christ

134–137;
173–174
3.1 Jesus Christ: The Son of God

The confession of the one God, the almighty Father, is common to Christians and Jews and, in some respects, to Moslems as well. But we now come to the *distinctively Christian understanding of God*, since we will speak of God, the Father of Jesus Christ, and that means God, the Father, the Son, and the Holy Spirit. This understanding distinguishes Christianity not only from the Eastern religions but also from Judaism and Islam. With Judaism and Islam, Christianity confesses the one and only God; but it also confesses the one God in three Persons: Father, Son, and Holy Spirit. Today many Christians have difficulties with this central article of faith. They think that this confession says nothing to them, considering it a mere speculation far removed from the world. They often add that it is far removed from the Bible and foreign to its thought. This article of confession is explicitly rejected by Jehovah's Witnesses.

To clarify this, we must recall our point of departure. A Christian orients himself wholly by Jesus Christ, in his thought and in his life, and confesses him. As Christians, it is only through Jesus Christ that we know definitively who God really is. Jesus spoke of God in a unique way. How was that possible? From where did Jesus derive the certainty to talk about God?

Obviously, Jesus was able to speak about God, to live from God, with God, and toward God, only because he himself stood in a *singular*
57–59;
125–126
relationship to God. According to the witness of the Gospels, Jesus stands in a different relationship to the Father than we do. The Gospels never show Jesus as one among many in the circle at prayer; he is always in a special

position by which he distinguishes himself while praying (Mk 1:35; 6:46; 14:32–42; Jn 17:1). His relationship to the Father is so unique and singular that he never stands on the same rung with the disciples. He never says "our Father" in the sense of joining together with other men. We read instead "my Father", "your Father", or "the Father". The Risen One says to Mary Magdalen:

> "Go to my brothers and tell them, 'I am ascending to my Father and your Father, to my God and your God' " (Jn 20:17).

Who is Jesus? What is the unique and singular character of Jesus' relationship to his God and Father? Is Jesus a prophet, perhaps the last and greatest of the prophets? In the history of Israel, those chosen and sent by God, such as Moses and the prophets, did indeed speak to the people on behalf of God and in his name. Jesus, though, stands above Moses and the prophets; he stands above the law and the temple. For that reason, he can say:

> "You have heard the commandment imposed on your forefathers. . . . What I say to you is . . ." (Mt 5:21–22, 27–28, among others).

> "But blest are your eyes because they see and blest are your ears because they hear. I assure you, many a prophet and many a saint longed to see what you see but did not see it, to hear what you hear but did not hear it" (Mt 13:16–17).

> "At the judgment, the citizens of Nineveh will rise with the present generation and be the ones to condemn it. At the preaching of Jonah they reformed their lives; but you have a greater than Jonah here. At the judgment, the queen of the South will rise with the present generation and be the one to condemn it. She came from the farthest corner of the earth to listen to the wisdom of Solomon; but you have a greater than Solomon here" (Mt 12:41–42).

Jesus is more than a prophet; he knows that he stands in the unique relationship of Son to Father. He is the one Son of the Father, to whom the Father has revealed and entrusted all so that he can make us sons and daughters.

> "Everything has been given over to me by my Father. No one knows the Son but the Father, and no one knows the Father but the Son—and anyone to whom the Son wishes to reveal him" (Mt 11:27).

The New Testament explains what is contained in this relationship of Sonship. It says that Jesus is "the Son" (Mk 1:11; 13:32; Rom 1:3; 8:3, among others) and "the Son of God" (Mk 1:1; Mt 16:16; Jn 1:34, among others). Conversely, the New Testament sees God as the Father of our Lord Jesus Christ (2 Cor 1:3, among others). For that reason, it holds that whoever sees Jesus sees the Father (Jn 14:10). *As Son, Jesus is the image, the icon of God the Father* (2 Cor 4:4; Col 1:15). In him God becomes visible as the God with a human countenance. In Jesus, God has become definitively and wholly manifest, so that no one can speak of God in a Christian way without taking Jesus Christ into account. From this we realize that the Father-Son relationship belongs to the eternal essence of God. Jesus Christ is *the eternal Son of the Father*, whom God has sent into the world (regarding his pre-existence, see Rom 8:3; Gal 4:4; Jn 3:17). He exists from all eternity in the form of God (Phil 2:6) and in the glory of God (Jn 17:5). He is the Word in which the Father expresses himself from all eternity. As Word and image of the Father, the Son is at the same time the prototype of creation. In him the mystery of God, as well as that of the world and of man, becomes manifest. The prologue of the Gospel of John summarizes all of this:

> In the beginning was the Word;
> the Word was in God's presence,
> and the Word was God.
> He was present to God in the beginning.
> Through him all things came into being . . . (Jn 1:1–3).

In his discussions with unbelieving Jews, Jesus says, "The Father and I are one" (Jn 10:30). Finally, at the end of the Fourth Gospel, Thomas confesses, "My Lord and my God!" (Jn 20:28).

72–73   These passages in Holy Scripture led in the first centuries to long and difficult *disputes*. Their doctrine was difficult for both the Jews and the Hellenists to understand. Is Jesus a second God subordinated to the Father? Or is he a particular form of appearance (mask) of the one divinity? Both opinions were held and rejected. Around 320, Arius spread the view that the Son is subordinated to the Father and not truly God, but rather God's first and most perfect creation, through whose mediation God created the world. Arius thereby affirmed the Son not to be God but a creature of God. He thereby conformed to the philosophical thought of his time, though not to revelation and the faith of the Church. As the sharpest opponent of the doctrine of Arius and as the most powerful intellectual champion of the Church's traditional faith, there stood St. Athanasius, bishop of Alexandria. His most important argument was that if Jesus were only a creature, however noble and sublime, he could not redeem us from the power of sin and death.

Such disputes were an occasion for the Church to confess solemnly and to define at the first general council (Nicea, 325), its faith in the divinity of the Son. For the Council Fathers, it was not a question of idle speculation, but of defending the witness of Holy Scripture against misinterpretations and of preserving the faith handed on in the Church. The faith of the

Council of Nicea has been handed on to us in the Nicene Creed. It still unites all churches of the East and West:

> We believe in one Lord, Jesus Christ,
> the only Son of God,
> eternally begotten of the Father,
> God from God, Light from Light,
> true God from true God,
> begotten, not made,
> one in being with the Father. . . .

This confession proclaims that Jesus Christ has made manifest once for all who God is and who man is. In Jesus Christ we see in time and in history that God is not a rigid, solitary being in dialogue only with itself and jealously intent on itself. Rather, *God is love from all eternity*, a love that bestows and communicates itself. From all eternity the Father communicates all that he is to the Son. The Father lives in relation to the Son by bestowing himself on the Son. The Son likewise lives in relation to the Father; by receiving himself from the Father and relating himself lovingly back to the Father, he is the Son. The Father is the origin and the source of the Son. The Son, though, possesses the same divine being as that bestowed by the Father. For that reason, he is one in being with the Father. He has not been brought forth out of nothing or been created like creatures, but is generated without temporal beginning in the eternal now of the eternity of God.

Of course, this is an impenetrable mystery—the mystery of an incomprehensible love pouring itself out. In the revelation of this love through Jesus Christ, God has also *revealed "man to man"* and disclosed his deepest mystery (GS 22). In Jesus Christ, man has been accepted, loved, and destined for love by God from all eternity. We are called to participate in the communion of love between Father and Son in the Holy Spirit.

3.2 The Spirit: The Lord and Giver of Life

In spite of the charismatic renewal movement, there is ordinarily little talk of the Holy Spirit in the Church and in the local congregations. Many people find such talk unintelligible. *What is Spirit?* Or Holy Spirit? Or even the Holy Spirit as divine person?

Originally, the Bible used "spirit" to mean wind, air, storm, then   183–187
breath as a sign of life. God's Spirit is thus the *storm and breath of life*; he creates, sustains, and preserves all. He it is above all who works in history

and creates new things. In the Old Testament the Spirit works above all through the prophets. In the Creed we confess "who has spoken through the prophets". The Old Testament expresses the hope that at the end of time the Spirit will work a great renewal through his general outpouring (Joel 3:1–2).

The New Testament sees this renewal at the end of time as having come in *Jesus Christ*. His appearance and ministry were accompanied by the work of the Spirit from the beginning: at the baptism by John (Mk 1:10), in his proclamation (Lk 4:18), in his fight against demons (Mt 4:1; 12:28), at his sacrifice on the cross (Heb 9:14), and at his Resurrection (Rom 1:4; 8:11). The name "Christ" was originally a title: Jesus is the Messiah, the One "anointed" by the Spirit. Jesus Christ is not, however, a bearer of the Spirit in the way that the prophets were. He possesses the Spirit of God in immeasurable fullness. As the Risen One, he is the source of the divine Spirit; he bestows the Spirit as God's gift on the Apostles, sending him at Pentecost to the Church (Acts 2:32–33).

The *mission of the Holy Spirit* is to remind us of all that Jesus said and did and so to guide us into all truth (Jn 14:26; 16:13–14). In him Jesus Christ is abidingly present in the Church and in the world (2 Cor 3:17). For that reason, the Holy Spirit is called the Spirit of Jesus (Rom 8:9; Phil 1:19) and the Spirit of the Son (Gal 4:6). He is also called the Spirit of faith (2 Cor 4:13). Through him we are able to confess Jesus Christ as Lord (1 Cor 12:3) and to pray, "Abba, Father" (Rom 8:15; Gal 4:6). The Holy Spirit is *the gift of new life*. The Father and the Son send him to us. By bestowing his Spirit on us, God bestows himself. Through the gift of the Spirit, we receive communion with God, take part in his life, and become children of God (Rom 8:14; Gal 4:6). That is possible only because the Spirit is not a created but a divine gift in whom God communicates himself to us.

> The love of God has been poured out in our hearts through the Holy
> Spirit who has been given to us (Rom 5:5).

The Spirit of God is not only the gift, but also the giver. He is not only a power with which someone can work, but himself One who works. He is not some thing but someone: he is a person. The Spirit distributes his gifts as he wills (1 Cor 12:11); he teaches and reminds (Jn 14:26); he speaks and intercedes (Rom 8:26–27). He can be saddened (Eph 4:30).

There were *disputes* over the role of the Spirit, especially in the fourth century. Many were of the opinion that the Holy Spirit was a servant subordinated to the Son, a kind of angelic being. The three great Greek Fathers of the Church, Basil, Gregory of Nazianzus, and Gregory of

Nyssa, objected strongly to this opinion. They argued that if the Holy Spirit were not of the divine essence like the Father and the Son, neither could he bestow on us communion with God and participation in the life of God. With this preparation, the Church was able to confess at the second general council, the *Council of Constantinople* (381), that the Holy Spirit is the Lord—that he is of divine nature, that he is not only a gift but the giver of life, and that together with the Father and the Son he is to be worshipped and glorified. This faith finds its expression in the Nicene Creed:

72–73

> We believe in the Holy Spirit,
> the Lord and giver of life,
> who proceeds from the Father and the Son;
> together with the Father and the Son he is worshipped and glorified.

The formulation "and the Son", the famous *Filioque*, was not contained in the original confession of faith at Constantinople. It arose as a teaching formula in Spain some time in the fifth to the seventh centuries, but was taken up into the confession of faith in the Roman Church only in the eleventh century. This added formula still represents a divergence from the Orthodox Churches. The Orthodox employ the formula "from the Father through the Son". They wish to emphasize that God the Father alone is origin and source. The Roman Church and the other Western churches wish to emphasize more clearly that the Son is consubstantial with the Father and on an equal level with him. In these fundamental concerns, East and West agree. But they use different theological concepts and models of thought. According to today's Roman Catholic understanding, a legitimate unity in multiplicity is present here.

The confession that unites East and West proclaims that the Holy Spirit is not just any gift of God, but that he is *God's* gift in person. Man's life and mystery first find their fulfillment by participation in the life and mystery of God. Yet the Holy Spirit is not only God as gift, but also the divine giver of this gift, the *giver of life*. As the Father is the origin and source of the Son and bestows all that he is upon the Son, so do the Father and the Son, or the Father through the Son, further bestow the fullness of divine life and being proper to them. Together they bring forth the Holy Spirit. As the Spirit is a pure receiving in relation to the Father and the Son, so the Spirit is a gushing spring, the giver of life in relation to us. He is the motive and creative force of new life and of the final transformation of man and world.

The well-known hymn "*Veni Creator Spiritus*", dating from the ninth century (Rabanus Maurus, 776–856; trans. John Dryden, 1631–1700), expresses beautifully what this life bestowed by the Holy Spirit means (as does the "*Veni Sancte Spiritus*", written around 1200):

> Creator Spirit by whose aid
> The world's foundations first were laid,
> Come, visit ev'ry humble mind;
> Come, pour thy joys on human kind.
> From sin and sorrow set us free
> And make thy temples worthy of Thee,
> And make thy temples worthy of Thee.

No council, no catechism, no theologian can express more beautifully than these hymns what we mean when we confess: "We believe in the Holy Spirit, the Lord, the giver of life."

3.3 God, the Father, the Son, and the Holy Spirit

The most difficult part and the deepest mystery of the Christian confession of God still stands before us: the confession of the triune or trinitarian God. Criticisms of this doctrine are familiar enough. Some say that it is the result of hair-splitting speculations by unworldly monks and theologians from times long past; that it is of no use for simple, immediate faith and for Christian life. Furthermore, this doctrine may seem simply unintelligible, even absurd and illogical. It would in fact be illogical if the confession were to say that three times one is one. But it says nothing of the sort, as we will show.

Unworldly speculations were not the *origin* of this confession. It grew rather out of the experience with Jesus Christ and his Spirit at work in the Church. The baptismal command of the resurrected Lord already summarizes the revelation of a triune God:

> "Go, therefore, and make disciples of all nations.
> Baptize them in the name
> 'of the Father,
> and of the Son,
> and of the Holy Spirit' " (Mt 28:19).

In baptism man receives a share in the life and communion of God. He is so united to the Son of God that, filled with his Holy Spirit, he becomes a child of God, the Father. For that reason, the Apostle Paul summarizes the triune mystery of God as a wish for blessing and grace. We are familiar with this summary as the greeting at the celebration of the Eucharist:

> The grace of the Lord Jesus Christ, and the love of God, and the fellowship of the Holy Spirit be with you all! (2 Cor 13:13).

Recognizing this origin shows us that the confession of the triune God is the *sum total of the Christian faith*. To be a Christian is to be initiated by being baptized "in the name of the Father and of the Son and of the Holy Spirit". This ancient formula is the one still used today. Every celebration of the Eucharist, the center of Christian and Church life, is begun and ended in the name of the triune God. 77–78

The doctrinal *unfolding* of the witness of Holy Scripture took place after long discussions through the first two general councils in Nicea (325) and Constantinople (381). Two erroneous doctrines had especially to be repudiated: that the Son and Spirit are subordinated to the Father, and that the one God only appears, as it were, behind three different masks as Father, Son, and Spirit. The Church replied that God is as he appears. God appears in Jesus Christ as the one he is; God is thus Father, Son, and Spirit. And yet there are not three Gods, but a single God in three persons. Ss. Basil, Gregory of Nazianzus, and Gregory of Nyssa were decisively involved in this clarification in the East; in the West, St. Augustine wrote several volumes "On the Triune God". 67–69; 70–71

The trinitarian confession is of the greatest *ecumenical importance*. It unites the Roman Catholic Church with the Orthodox churches; even the Reformers held fast to it. In the Smalcaldian Articles, Luther says explicitly that there is neither quarrel nor dispute over the high articles of divine majesty. Both the (Lutheran) Augsburg Confession and the (Reformed) Heidelberg Catechism confess the triune God. The World Council of Churches understands itself as "a communion of churches that confess the Lord Jesus Christ according to Holy Scripture as God and Savior and therefore aspire to fulfill that to which they are called, to the glory of God, the Father, the Son, and the Holy Spirit."

The *content* of this ecumenical confession of the triune God can be stated most succinctly as *one God in three persons*. The confession does not say that one person equals three persons, or that one God equals three Gods, which would be absurd. The so-called Athanasian Confession of Faith (which does not stem from St. Athanasius himself, but probably originated around 500) says it in this way:

> We honor the one God in the Trinity and the Trinity in the unity, without mixing of persons and without division of nature (DS 75; NR 915).

So we read in the preface for Trinity Sunday:

> You have revealed your glory as the glory also of your Son and of the Holy Spirit: three persons equal in majesty, undivided in splendor, yet one Lord, one God, ever to be adored in your ever-lasting glory.

This confession of the triune God is a deep *mystery* that no created spirit can discover of itself or ever comprehend. It is the mystery of an unfathomable and overflowing love: God is not a solitary being, but a God who bestows and communicates himself out of the abundance of his being, a God who lives in the communion of Father, Son, and Spirit, and who can therefore also bestow and ground community. Because he is life and love in himself, God is able to be life and love for us. We are included from all eternity in the mystery of God. From all eternity God has a place for us. *The confession of the triune God is ultimately an exposition of the single sentence "God is love"* (1 Jn 4:8, 16b). God in himself is life and love from all eternity, so that he grounds hope for us in the midst of a world of death and hate. We should know in faith that the ultimate and deepest reality is life and love and that a share in this reality is bestowed on us through Jesus Christ in the Holy Spirit.

189–191

185–187;
205–208

4. Prayer: Expression of Faith in God

4.1 What Is Prayer?

Our response to the word of God in which he reveals the innermost mystery of his love to us is not first of all one of thinking, but one of thanking. It is prayer. Believing in God means not only the conviction that God exists, but rather a personal turning toward God, the ultimate ground and goal, the support and substance of our lives. *Prayer is the most important and most essential expression of faith in God*; it is responsive faith, the earnestness of faith, so to speak.

36–39

So Scripture—especially in the words of *Jesus* himself—exhorts us urgently and often to persevere in prayer (Mk 11:24; Mt 7:7–11; 21:22; Lk 11:9–13). Holy Scripture gives us many examples of prayer. The Book of Psalms is a single book of prayer. Most importantly, we are told that Jesus himself prayed. On the Sabbath, he entered the synagogue "as he was in the habit of doing" (Lk 4:16). At each turning point of his work, he withdrew into solitude to pray to God, his Father (Lk 3:21; 5:16; 6:12; 9:28; 10:21; 11:1). His prayer was both thanks and praise (Mt 11:25–27; Lk 10:21–22), as well as lamentation, petition, and surrender to the will of the Father (Mk 14:33–36, par.; Heb 5:7–8). *No one can live as a Christian without praying.*

Of course, for many Christians prayer is the real difficulty of their faith. They know that they should pray, but do not know how. They also raise many *fundamental objections* to praying. Many fear that prayer could be a flight from responsibility and involvement in the world, an empty consolation that hobbles man's strength and imagination. Others consider prayer childish. Because man is not strong enough or mature enough to bear harsh reality, they say, he deceives himself and constructs a figure with whom he fancies himself secure. Still others suspect that God is somehow abused in prayer and so placed at the disposal of the purposes, interests, and needs of man.

No one can contest the fact that there are such distortions of prayer. But do these criticisms touch true prayer as presented to us in the Psalms, by Jesus, and by the great saints? What does it mean for them to pray?

One of the greatest theologians of Christianity, St. Thomas Aquinas, gives what is doubtless the most fitting answer. He defines prayer as *the expression of our longing for God*. So prayer is more than a turning inwards and reflection, more than a hygiene and culture of the soul, more than a mere psychological "charge". In prayer man considers himself and his situation before God, insofar as he comes from God and returns to him. In doing so, he experiences himself as a creature in need of help, powerless to give himself the fulfillment of his existence and of his hope. God alone, the ground and goal of man, is great enough to fill up the heart of man. Prayer is a setting-out toward God, *an elevation of the heart to God*, an encounter of man with God. The deepest longing of man is for unification with God, for communion and friendship with him. So the proper definition of prayer becomes this: prayer is a *conversation with God*, an exchange of friendship with him (Teresa of Avila).

All this shows that prayer is not a weak flight from reality. Rather, it is *the only way that man can do justice to reality*. Prayer means standing firm in hope without any illusions. For that reason, it helps us come to terms with ourselves, with others, and with the world. It purifies and refines our basic attitude and unmasks the illusions with which we fool ourselves and others. It gives us the strength to renounce deception and to recognize the truth about ourselves and our lives. True prayer is never without effect. It proves itself in turning us around and in turning us toward God and toward others. It gives us the certainty that the deeds of love can never be meaningless. So prayer also gives us courage and strength for involvement in the world. At the same time it expresses both humility and magnanimity. It teaches us composure without any resignation and helps us to accept ourselves, others, and the world, because we are unconditionally and absolutely accepted by God. Prayer bestows inner peace, joy, and consolation but is never mere empty comfort. Whenever all consolation is ridiculed as empty comfort, existence itself becomes disconsolate.

4.2 How Can We Pray? Forms of Prayer

Prayer is something most personal and therefore extremely varied. There are no recipes or techniques for praying. But we learn one thing for certain in the New Testament: a merely external repetition of formulas is worthless. Jesus explicitly rejects this. He tells us not to "rattle on like the pagans. They think they will win a hearing by the sheer multiplication of words" (Mt 6:7). Prayer can be very sober and unadorned. Prayer can consist in pouring out one's heart before God, in lamenting and asking "Why?" It can consist in petition for oneself and for others: "Lord, help me!" Praying can consist of *confession* of sin and guilt, in surrender to God's will, and in *promising* to fulfill it; but it also means *praise, thanks, and worship.* So we can distinguish the lamentation, the confession, and the

88–89 vow, but also the prayer of praise, the prayer of thanks, and the prayer of supplication.

The ways of prayer are distinguished according to both content and form. There is *oral prayer.* It can happen freely and spontaneously, but can also adhere to an established text. This oral prayer can take place secretly, in the quiet of one's room (Mt 6:6), or in community, whether in the family, in various other groups, or in the official liturgy. Oral prayer also includes the rhythmic repetition of special formulas, such as the Jesus prayer of the Eastern Church, the rosary, or the litanies. These can be genuine prayer and not at all mechanical repetitions. Their rhythm corresponds to the body-soul totality of man and can help us enter more deeply into a particular phrase. The most perfect oral prayer is the prayer that our Lord himself taught us, the "Our Father" (Lk 11:2–4; Mt 6:9–13). It unites glory and praise of God with petition for what we most need. We should recite this prayer frequently and make it the standard for our praying.

Beyond oral prayer is *meditative prayer,* the pondering of a text, especially one from Holy Scripture, of a religious image, or of a situation in life. Meditation is not clever thoughts, analyses, and pieces of information; "for knowing much does not satiate the soul and give it its fill, but feeling and tasting the things within" (Ignatius of Loyola).

Finally and quite importantly, there is *interior prayer.* This is also called contemplative prayer or, most aptly, the prayer of the heart. It means becoming immediately aware of the presence of God, knowing oneself to be immediately addressed, and responding with "Thou". It can also consist in dwelling in God's presence and in finding God in all things; it can thus take place in the midst of our everyday lives. For those especially blessed in prayer, interior prayer can lead to the closest mystical intimacy with God. But the crucial thing is not extraordinary experiences or sublime spiritual moods. The greatest saints tell us that interior prayer is very often connected with experiences of spiritual aridity and desolation, with the experience of a dark night in which the whole hiddenness and mystery of God breaks upon them.

All this shows that there are not only many ways of praying, but that every serious Christian life is a *journey in learning to pray* and that there are *stages in the experience of prayer*. However often prayer must be graciously bestowed on us, we must still prepare ourselves for it through inwardness and quiet, through relaxation, recollection, and self-discipline. It is also important to observe a certain *order of prayer*, especially particular times of prayer (morning and evening prayer, the table blessing, Sunday observance, the Church year, and days of recollection). Prayer is also helped by spiritual conversation and the exchange of spiritual experiences with other Christians, who likewise are striving to pray.

4.3 Prayer in the Name of Jesus

Jesus told us not only to pray as he taught, but to pray in his name (Jn 14:13–14, among others). We may thus appeal in our prayer to Jesus and to our communion with him, and be certain of a hearing. Jesus always intercedes for us before God (Rom 8:34; Heb 7:25; 1 Jn 2:1). He has made possible for us a new relationship to God as our Father; through the Holy Spirit we may participate in his relationship to the Father and so call out, "Abba, dear Father" (Rom 8:15; Gal 4:6). *According to the New Testament, our prayer has an ultimately trinitarian foundation.* "Give thanks to God the Father always and for everything in the name of our Lord Jesus Christ" (Eph 5:20). Especially in the liturgy, all prayers are made "in the fellowship of the Holy Spirit through Jesus Christ, our Lord" to God, the almighty Father. This order of praying is very well expressed in the final summary of the Eucharistic Prayer. There the Church praises the Father:

> Through him, with him, in him,
> in the unity of the Holy Spirit,
> all glory and honor is yours, Almighty Father,
> forever and ever.

Beyond this fundamental trinitarian order of Christian praying, we already encounter in the New Testament a prayer addressed to Jesus Christ himself. The primitive Christian congregations prayed, "Come, Lord Jesus!" (Rev 22:20; 1 Cor 16:22). At the celebration of the Eucharist we cry out, *"Kyrie eleison"*—"Lord, have mercy." The Church traditionally also offers prayers for the coming of the Holy Spirit: "Come, Creator Spirit."

According to the Nicene Creed the Holy Spirit "with the Father and the Son, is to be worshipped and glorified".

As his sons and daughters we pray *to the Father*. Our praise and thanksgiving, our plea for forgiveness and for all that belongs in the broadest sense to the realm of "our daily bread", is intended for him. As his disciples we pray *to Jesus Christ* for all that concerns his business here on earth: for the Church, for our ministry to the world and to men, for the missions, and for the proclamation of the faith. The New Testament prayer for his second coming fits here quite meaningfully. As heirs of Jesus Christ, we pray *to the Holy Spirit* that he may come and fill us, that he may make us members of Jesus Christ, that he may bestow an increase in faith, hope, and love upon us, that he may give us joy and strength both in suffering and in resistance to evil. Finally, the Church does not tire, either in her public liturgy or in private prayer, of extolling and praising the *triune God*:

> Glory be to the Father and to the Son and to the Holy Spirit, as it was in the beginning, is now, and ever shall be, world without end. Amen.

If the confession of the triune God means that "God is love", we may be certain of his assistance in every situation because we know that nothing can separate us from this love of God (Rom 8:39). At this point, of course, many questions and problems make themselves felt. Do we not often have the experience that God apparently does not hear, that he remains silent and does not intervene? May we hope at all that he will help and answer us concretely? Why does he permit evil and injustice? What then does faith in God, in the almighty Father and the Father of Jesus Christ, mean concretely in our lives? We must now reflect more exactly on these pressing questions by asking about the relationship between God and the world and by speaking about God as the Creator of heaven and earth.

III

GOD: THE MAKER OF HEAVEN AND EARTH

1. God, the Creator

1.1 The Dialogue between Natural Science and Theology

In the Creed we confess that God is "the maker of heaven and earth, of all that is seen and unseen". With this confession, faith tries to answer *the deepest human question: Where does everything come from and what is its purpose? Where does man come from and what is his purpose?*

Many people today expect to find the answer to this twofold question in the modern *natural sciences*. The sciences can tell us much about the genesis and age of the world, about the universe, its "wonders" and riddles. They have brought us insights that clarify wonders in the material world, both in the domain of the very small (the microcosm)—the atomic and subatomic, the genetic—and in the domain of the very large (the macrocosm) —the universe and the multiplicity of its galaxies. Indeed, the results of the modern natural sciences make us ask in amazement about the origin of this cosmic order.

16–18;
20–22;
129–130

Nevertheless, conflicts have often occurred between the world picture presented by the Bible and the Church's tradition and the new world picture based on experiment and mathematical calculation. In the case against Galileo (seventeenth century), who first clearly formulated the hypothesis that the sun does not revolve around the earth but the earth around the sun, the ancient and the modern world pictures collided. When Darwin in the nineteenth century put forth the theory that the different species of organisms are not immediately created by God but descend from one another, and when he went on to include man in the evolutionary process, there were again longlasting disputes. The question was often posed in terms of false alternatives: Does man descend from God, or from the apes?

These conflicts have eased in our century. First, the modern *natural sciences* recognize their own limits today more clearly than before. They are aware that they always know reality from only one point of view and can determine such fundamental phenomena as space and time only relatively to the position of the observer (the relativity theory of Einstein). In research on the smallest particles of matter, it became necessary to use complementary notions such as waves and corpuscles (the indeterminacy principle in the quantum theory of Bohr and Heisenberg). The classical concept of matter had to be given up, together with the possibility of an unambiguous and coherent new concept. In spite of all the great and impressive successes on individual points, today's natural sciences have become more modest about the total interpretation of reality.

Theology also pays sharper attention to its limits. It now knows that the Bible uses modes of expression and representation dependent on the world picture of its time; these are not binding on us. The Bible does not wish to instruct us on the empirically knowable genesis of the world or of the different species of organisms. It wishes to stress that God is the Creator of the world and is its salvation. It is therefore not a matter of faith that God created the world in six days, as the Bible graphically presents it, or that in the beginning he created everything such as we find it today.

28–29; 86; 96–98; 110–111; 327–329; 350–351

If we distinguish between the Bible's theological message in describing creation and the trappings conditioned by its world picture, we pose the decisive problem: the *relation between creation and evolution*. Most of today's natural scientists proceed from the hypothesis that all material being evolves into higher forms of being and life, all the way up to man, the goal of evolution. In their account, the universe would have arisen about twelve billion years ago and our earth about five to six billion years ago. About three billion years ago the first life would have appeared, while human life has existed only for about two million years.

29–30

How is this conception related to faith in creation? A materialistic doctrine of development that assumes an uncreated matter from which all organisms (even man) have arisen through purely mechanical development is to be rejected theologically. The doctrine of evolution is no longer understood in this ideological way by most scientists. Today, the opinion that creation and evolution are answers to quite different questions and so lie on different levels is gaining more and more acceptance. Evolution is an empirical concept that deals with the question about the "horizontal" *origin* and the spatio-temporal sequence of creatures. Creation, on the other hand, is a theological concept that asks about the "vertical" *reason* and *purpose* of reality. Evolution always presupposes "something" that changes and develops; creation shows why anything that can change and develop exists at all. In order to unite these two points of view, many theologians today say that God creates things in such a way that they are empowered to cooperate with their own development. "God makes things to make themselves" (Teilhard de Chardin). In doing so, God does not work only at the beginning of time, leaving later development to itself. He constantly holds reality in being, and he sustains and guides it in its becoming also. God is the all-encompassing creative power; he makes the autonomous activity of creatures possible and is present as he sustains it. Creatures are images of the creative God precisely in their creative force. *Faith in creation and evolutionary theory do not conflict in principle. They answer quite different questions; they lie on different levels and are assigned to different modes of knowing.*

Despite these necessary distinctions, natural science and theology are not two worlds that have nothing to do with each other. Rather, they consider one and the same reality under different aspects. For that reason, natural science and theology cannot ignore each other; they depend rather on *mutual dialogue*.

1.2 Origin, Center, and Goal of the World

The *fundamental declarations of the Christian faith in creation* are already found on the first pages of the Old Testament. The fact that the Old Testament contains not one but two creation stories is, of course, important. Those stories agree fully in their faith in God the Creator; but they express this faith with differing notions. They make clear once again that the Bible is not concerned with the empirically knowable genesis of the world, but with the faith that the world has its ground in God.

The *first, but later account of creation* begins very succinctly:

> In the beginning, when God created the heavens and the earth, the earth was a formless wasteland, and darkness covered the abyss, while a mighty wind swept over the waters.
>   Then God said, "Let there be light", and there was light. God saw how good the light was (Gen 1:1-4).

This account of creation then describes how God brings forth the individual works of creation in the rhythm of seven days. The creation of man on the sixth day forms the high point. At the end, we read this summary: "God looked at everything he had made, and he found it very good" (Gen 1:31). It is otherwise with the *second, earlier creation narrative*. For it, man is not the high point but the middle point of creation. For that reason, the creation of the world is indicated only succinctly and briefly; the creation of man, though, is told in a detailed and vivid way:

> At the time when the Lord God made the earth and the heavens . . .
> the Lord God formed man out of the clay of the ground and blew into his nostrils the breath of life, and so man became a living being (Gen 2:4b, 7).

Both creation stories speak the language of their time and use the prevailing cultural notions. Still they express a content that does not stem from the historical world picture but that resulted from God's way with the people Israel. This content represents a *truth of revelation and of faith*. In its history, Israel experienced again and again the unlimited lordship of God. God is not only the Lord of Israel but the Lord of all peoples, of the whole world. He is able to help Israel and the individual believer only if he is the almighty Father of all reality. So Israel repeated, "Our help is in the name of the Lord, who made heaven and earth" (Ps 124:8), a Psalm verse we often encounter in the Church's liturgy. Faith in creation is the farthest extension of God's history with his people. Creation is the prehistory, the introductory act, and the presupposition of the rest of history. *Creation is the first of God's revelatory deeds.* It is the permanent foundation of our relationship to God and of our understanding of God.

Creation is a beginning ordered to completion. The first account of creation expresses this graphically by having God rest on the seventh day, after he had accomplished his work (Gen 2:2). This does not mean that God had grown tired; it tells us, rather, that the goal of creation is the Sabbath, the glorification of God. So Paul writes that the whole creation is waiting with longing and birth pangs for the revelation of the sons of God, for the glory of the consummated Kingdom of God (Rom 8:19–24). The first creation is ordered to the new heavens and the new earth (Is 65:17; 66:22; Rev 21:1). It will find its consummation when God will one day be "all in all" (1 Cor 15:28). Creation is not a rigid reality, but an event that has not been concluded. It is open for the future that God himself will be for man.

105–106; Just as creation has a beginning and a goal, so it has its *center in Jesus*
136–138 *Christ.* The Old Testament prepares for this conviction by declaring that God created everything through his word (Gen 1). In the New Testament, *the* Word is Jesus Christ (Jn 1).

> He is the image of the invisible God, the first-born of all creatures. In him everything in heaven and on earth was created, things visible and invisible, whether thrones or dominations, principalities or powers; all were created through him and for him. He is before all else that is. In him everything continues in being (Col 1:15–17).

The meaning of creation is ultimately disclosed to us by Jesus Christ. Through him, even the dark aspects and riddles of worldly reality, such as suffering and dying, are illuminated with meaning (GS 22). Conversely, the Christian may discover in all created reality vestiges and fragments that point to the reality of Christ; the believer understands Jesus Christ as the recapitulation and fullness of "all things in heaven and on earth" (Eph 1:10).

1.3 The Mystery of Creation

The fundamental Christian perspective on creation leads to *individual truths of the Christian faith in creation.*

1. *The freedom of creation*. Although many people think that the world is a product of chance, of blind fate, or of some necessary natural law, the Christian faith confesses that this world is willed, created, loved, and affirmed by God. The world springs from the free will, the goodness, and the love of God, who without any necessity and of his own free decree willed to let creatures participate in his being. "For you have created all things; by your will they came to be and were made!" (Rev 4:11). Even without the world, God would have been blissful as God; he did not need us and the world, but he willed us and the world. Everything that exists, not least ourselves, exists just because God said, I will you to be; you are because I will you, because I love you. "Because he is good, we are" (Augustine).

2. *Order in creation*. Again and again we read: "God spoke . . . , and it came to be." In the Book of Wisdom we read: ". . . you . . . have made all things by your word" (Wis 9:1; cf. Jn 1:3; Rom 4:17). In being created through the Word of God, creatures are grounded in meaning and intelligibility. Through the Word, God separates cosmos from chaos, light from darkness, the heavens from the earth. The Bible says that God has created all his works with wisdom (Ps 104:24; Pr 8:27). For the Christian, then, the world is not the expression of an irrational, chaotic power of life; it is rationally ordered. "You have disposed all things by measure and number and weight" (Wis 11:20). The world is the realization of divine ideas. How else is one to explain the wonderful order of the world, newly discovered by science, except as the work of an ordering Spirit? In his investigation and thought, man is able to search out and to approach the creative thoughts of God. To believe in God the Creator requires us to hold fast to the intelligibility and rationality of the world.

3. *The goodness of creation*. The biblical account of creation repeats that God made all things good (Gen 1:4, 10, 12, 18, 21, 31). This repeated formula tells us that everything comes from the goodness of God and so shares in the goodness of God. From this insight the early Church was able to resist gnosis, a worldly wisdom widespread at that time, which rejected the material world as evil and repudiated the Creator God of the Old Testament. In the Middle Ages, the Church had to defend the goodness of creation against the pessimistic notions of the Cathars and other dualistic sects (DS 800, 1333, 3002; NR 277, 301, 316). With this doctrine of the universal goodness of creation, the ground is cut out from under every false asceticism, from every sceptical and pessimistic flight from the world, and from contempt for the world. That is good news precisely for our modern world, which hovers "between hope and anxiety" and wonders "uneasily about the present course of events" (GS 4).

4. *The essence of creation.* In spite of occasional parallels, the way the Bible speaks of creation differs from that of the creation myths of the surrounding religions, which tell of a battle between God and the powers of chaos or of a battle of the gods among themselves. According to the Bible, God creates effortlessly, as it were, and altogether sovereignly. He also creates differently from the way men do, since men always presuppose some material that they recast or reshape. With God there is never any talk of pre-existing, given material. He is not a demiurge (an architect of the world). In order to express the uniqueness of the creative activity of God, Scripture (2 Macc 7:28; Rom 4:17) and Church doctrine (DS 800, 3025; NR 295, 322) speak of *creation from nothing.* This does not mean that nothing is the material out of which the world is made, that the world is at bottom insubstantial. Rather, it affirms the absence of every pre-existing matter. Positively, this says that God is the sole and exclusive ground of the world; the world depends fully on him and has a share in God's being in all that it is. For a world that has suffered and still suffers the anxiety of the anonymous powers and superhuman forces of fate, this is a comforting thought. It tells us that all that we have and are, indeed all that is, is a reality bestowed by God and attributable to God.

5. *The independence of creation.* Through its radical dependence on God, the world is essentially and infinitely different from and distinct from God, who is absolutely independent. Precisely in its radical dependence, the world is something independent from God. Creation from nothing lends the creature a proper dignity before God. Creation is not a degradation and humiliation but an empowerment to being from God and toward him. The Second Vatican Council speaks of an *autonomy of the world* and of its different domains, when correctly understood (GS 36, 41, 56, 76; AA 7). Culture, science, economics, politics, and the other worldly domains possess a relative independence: their own truth, goodness, order, and inherent laws. Man must *respect the dignity proper to creatures and to their rhythms*; he may not deal with them however he pleases. The Christian must *behave appropriately* in the world and in the different domains of the world. The will of God encounters the Christian concretely in and through the world's order and structures. The correctly understood independence of which the Council speaks must, of course, be distinguished from any claim to absolute autonomy for the world. This modern secular conception is incompatible with faith in the creatureliness of the world.

6. *The meaning of creation.* Since creation is wholly from God, its independence is also wholly for him, for his glory and honor. The first meaning of creation is the *glorification of God.* The Psalms often express this quite pointedly:

O Lord, our Lord,
> how glorious is your name over all the earth!
> You have exalted your majesty above the heavens (Ps 8:2).

The heavens declare the glory of God,
> and the firmament proclaims his handiwork (Ps 19:2).

In their song of praise, the three young men, whom King Nebuchadnezzar had thrown into the fiery furnace for refusing to worship his idolatrous image, summon the entire creation—heavens and earth, sun, moon, and stars, dew and rain, lightning and clouds—to praise God: "Bless the Lord, all you works of the Lord, praise and exalt him above all forever" (Dan 3:57). The creation's praise of God meets us again and again in the history of Christian piety. Perhaps best known is the "Canticle of the Sun" by St. Francis, which he composed "to the praise and honor of God" as he lay ill at San Damiano:

> Thou most high, almighty, good Lord,
> Thine are the praise and the glory,
> The honor and every blessing.
> To thee alone, most high, are they due,
> And no man is worthy even to say thy name.
> Praise be to thee, thou Lord of mine,
> With all thy creatures,
> Especially the lord brother, the sun,
> For he is the day,
> And bestoweth light upon us through himself.
> And he is beautiful and radiant in great splendor.
> Thy emblem doth he bear, thou most high.

In a similar way, Francis addresses the moon, the stars, the wind, precious and chaste water, fire, earth, flowers and herbs, but also sickness, distress, and death. He has something like a sibling's relationship to his fellow creatures, and so calls them brother and sister.

To say that the glorification of God is the first meaning of creation does not at all suggest that God is somehow egoistic or narcissistic. God's glory is the glory of his love. God's honor is at the same time the salvation of man. "The glory of God is man fully alive" (Irenaeus of Lyons). Creation also serves the *joy of creatures*, which are allowed to participate in God's glory and which find their ultimate fulfillment precisely in glorifying God. Man finds his ultimate fulfillment not in having and enjoying, but in festival and celebration, in thanks, glory, and praise. The Eucharist, the thanks-giving, in which bread and wine represent the entire creation, is therefore the center of the world's meaning, the liturgy of the world, as it were, and the anticipation of its definitive consummation. Paul expresses the right order in this way: "All these are yours, and you are Christ's, and Christ is God's" (1 Cor 3:22–23).

1.4 God Preserves and Sustains the World

79–81   We often think of creation as an event lying unimaginably far back in the past, something like the "big bang" that many natural scientists posit. After this primordial happening, reality is thought to have developed over some twelve billion years into the imposing order and fullness that encounters us today. God is also sometimes imagined as a giant clock maker who constructed the world once upon a time and now lets it run its own course according to the laws he gave it then (deism). But these pictures are not the notions of biblical faith in creation. For faith, there is not only the single act of creation, but also a permanent *preservation of the world by God*.

> They all look to you
> to give them food in due time. . . .
> If you hide your face, they are dismayed;
> if you take away their breath, they perish
> and return to the dust.
> When you send forth your spirit, they are created,
> and you renew the face of the earth (Ps 104:27, 29–30).
>
> And how could a thing remain, unless you willed it;
> or be preserved, had it not been called forth by you? (Wis 11:25).

Creation is both a primeval event and a present event. It coexists with every instant. In the preservation of the world, the act of *creation is always a new present*; it sustains, permeates, and encompasses all. Without this active preservation, everything would sink back into nothingness. We could not take a single breath without God's sustaining, willing, and affirming us. Is this not a comforting thought? Faith in the constant, efficacious presence of the Creator for his creation dispels the feelings of the emptiness, artificiality, and hollowness of the world that threaten us so often. This faith makes the world a mystery always filled with God and always close to God.

The preservation of the world and its order is also of existential importance because *the cosmos is continually threatened by chaos*. The story of the flood describes this constant danger. The end of that same story also promises the permanence of the world order: "As long as the earth lasts, seedtime and harvest, cold and heat, summer and winter, and day and night shall not cease" (Gen 8:22). *The* enemy of life is death. For that reason, *the* act of preserving the world happens when God does not allow man to be extinguished even in death, but sustains him, preserves him, and awakens him to new life. The God who "calls into being those things which had not been" is at the same time the God who "restores the dead to life" (Rom 4:17). This happened once for all in the *death and Resurrection of Jesus Christ*. Only for this and only because of this is the world preserved. Everything has its permanence in Jesus Christ (Col 1:17).

1.5 God's Hidden Providence

Faith in creation gains its ultimate depth and its existential earnestness as faith in God's providence. But great *existential difficulties* also block this faith in providence. We frequently fall into situations where we ask: Why must I suffer this? Why me of all people? Men have often spoken and still speak—as the case may be—of a blind, good, or evil *fate*. They have often been (and still are) of the opinion that this fate is written in the stars and can be ascertained by interpreting the stars (astrology). We speak of a lucky dog, a child of fortune, a lucky fellow on whose life a lucky star shines, or of an unlucky fellow who is practically pursued by misfortune. Consciously or unconsciously, various relics of superstition persist today —talismans, fear of unlucky numbers, belief in good and bad omens, among other things.

The Bible too proceeds from the fact that life and reality as a whole have an order that presides over men as a power. But the Bible sees this power not as an anonymous fate, but as *personal guidance* by God. We are told of this personal guidance in the Old Testament stories of individual figures: of Joseph in Egypt; of Moses, who as a little boy was drawn out of the waters of the Nile through God's care; or of Tobias, to whom God gave an accompanying angel during his journey. In a particularly expressive way, this personal guidance figures in the best-known psalm:

> The Lord is my shepherd; I shall not want. . . .
>   he refreshes my soul.
> He guides me in right paths
>   for his name's sake.
> Even though I walk in the dark valley
>   I fear no evil; for you are at my side
> With your rod and your staff
>   that give me courage (Ps 23:1, 3–4).

The same thing is said in another familiar psalm: "You who dwell in the shelter of the Most High . . ." (Ps 91). The Book of Wisdom also bears witness to a quite general divine providence: "He himself made the great as well as the small, and he provides for all alike" (Wis 6:7). Above all,

Jesus shows repeatedly that his living, working, and dying unfold wholly under the will of the Father. So he can exhort us also to have an almost childlike trust.

> "Do not worry about your livelihood. . . . Look at the birds in the sky. They do not sow or reap, they gather nothing into barns; yet your heavenly Father feeds them. Are you not more important than they? . . . Stop worrying, then. . . . The unbelievers are always running after these things. Your heavenly Father knows all that you need" (Mt 6:25–26, 31–32; cf. 10:26–31).

The New Testament summarizes the message of Jesus in these words: "Cast all your cares on him because he cares for you" (1 Pet 5:7).

These are not just the idyllic thoughts of pious but unworldly men. The faith in providence of both the Old and the New Testaments is rooted in the *great context of God's whole plan of salvation*. God leads mankind through many steps (the covenants with Noah, Abraham, Moses, and David) up to the New Covenant in Jesus Christ and its consummation at the end of time. Through his Spirit, he also leads the Church, in order to prepare through her the all-encompassing Kingdom of God. Providence for the individual serves this all-encompassing plan of salvation. So the key to Jesus' faith in providence lies in the exhortation: "Seek first his kingship over you, his way of holiness, and all these things will be given you besides" (Mt 6:33). This does not advocate a naïve optimism. It says, rather, to make God and the care for his Kingdom the content of your life, and the world around you will change.

Faith in providence means that the immeasurably large creation and God's all-encompassing plan of salvation are directed to the *individual person*. Indeed, the meaning of creation and of history is decided in the individual. God's providence should not be misunderstood as a plan hovering over man's head. It presupposes the concurrence of the man who entrusts himself to God's care. In the measure that a man accepts God's will and changes his life, his "fate" will also change. The man who comes into agreement with God also comes into agreement with the world. Things and events then lose their strangeness; they appear in a special way as "caused" by God. Where this happens, God has already become "all and in all" for the believer. Even if the believer cannot change external circumstances, they do change because he knows that nothing can separate him from the love of Christ (Rom 8:35) and that "the sufferings of the present" are "as nothing compared with the glory to be revealed in us" (Rom 8:18).

The intimate connection between the all-encompassing providence of God and the freedom of man is seen especially in the *prayer of supplication*.

The invitation to pray shows that man has access to God and can know himself to be accepted by him. It shows that God hears man, listens to him, and affirms him. Man is in no way degraded to a servile figure by petitionary prayer. On the contrary, supplication has been planned and included in God's providence from all eternity. God's almighty providence does not eliminate the initiative of man, but includes it and takes it into its service. When man places his situation before God in the prayer of supplication, he may be certain beforehand of a hearing. Jesus himself tells us:

> "If you are ready to believe that you will receive whatever you ask for in prayer, it shall be done for you" (Mk 11:24; cf. Mt 7:7; 21:22; Lk 11:9).

Many will ask in amazement: If God in principle answers every prayer, what about the prayers that apparently or really are not answered, about which God is silent, although we have practically stormed him? The answer is not easy. But in the light of the very clear declarations of Jesus, we must respond that God answers every prayer in a way surpassing all our hopes. If he does not answer a prayer in the way we wish, it is because this wish does not correspond to what is truly best for us. St. Augustine says: "Good is the God who often does not give us what we want so that he may give us what we should want." St. Thérèse of Lisieux says: "And if you do not answer me, I shall love you even more." Precisely when God corrects our wishes and deepens our faith, our hope, and our love, he reconciles us in prayer with our situation and bestows on us a peace that transcends all understanding (Phil 4:7).

All this shows that God's providence ultimately remains a *mystery*, the mystery of the ever-greater God and of his ever-greater love. Faith in providence does not simply dissolve the mystery of existence or simply make it transparent. It does not give us an insight into the thoughts of God, nor does it explain to us the details of God's ordinances and guidance in the world. Neither does God make our own life history transparent to us so that we can stand over everything and be spared darkness and tribulation. God is a hidden God especially in his guidance of history (Is 45:15).

> How deep are the riches and the wisdom and the knowledge of God! How inscrutable his judgments, how unsearchable his ways! For "who has known the mind of the Lord? Or who has been his counselor?" (Rom 11:33–34).

But what belief in fate treats as simply incomprehensible, faith in God sees as a mystery which is not solvable but which elicits trust. Where belief in

fate finds indifference and emptiness at the core of history, faith finds the providential love of the Father. Even if we have no insight into the "how" of divine ways and guidance, we may still recognize *signs* in which God's guidance can be experienced in faith. Faith can assure and strengthen itself in the conviction that "God makes all things work together for the good of those who love him" (Rom 8:28).

2. Heaven and Earth

Referring to Holy Scripture, the confession of faith names God the "maker of heaven and earth". "Heaven and earth" indicates what are the two extreme ends of reality in the ancient world view. "Heaven and earth" means reality as a whole. The Creed means to say that God has created absolutely everything. But it adds at once that God has created the *whole of reality in a certain order*. The Nicene Creed qualifies the graphic expression "heaven and earth" by the abstract concepts "seen and unseen". In this way it distinguishes a spiritual and a material created reality. The two together constitute the whole of creation, the entirety of reality. Between the two, there opens up the existential space of man.

2.1 Earth: The Place Where Man Lives

The earth is first of all the *material* from which God lets plants and animals emerge (Gen 1:11, 24; 2:19). Man is also taken from it; to it he shall return (Gen 2:7; 3:19). He must till it by the sweat of his brow in order to earn his bread (Gen 3:17–19). The earth is the whole of the material world, *the place and the condition of man's existence*. It is the abode of man and the arena of history. It has been created by God for man.

The Bible sees the earth's beauty and splendor, as well as its utility and solidity, as occasions of praise and thanks to God, the Creator of heaven and earth. The Old Testament does not exclude prosperity and wealth from this view. The Bible does urgently warn against the dangers of wealth so far as it can become "mammon", that is, an idol (Prov 11:28; Mt 6:19–21, 24; Mk 10:23–25). In principle, though, even wealth is a gift of God, when it is justly acquired (Prov 10:22, among others). *Contempt for the world and denigration of the material are completely foreign to the Bible.* Indeed, the Bible rehabilitates matter in the face of dualism, which views matter as a principle of evil and the earth as the prison of man.

Scripture speaks moreover of a *new earth* (Is 65:17; Rev 21:1). When the form of this world passes away (1 Cor 7:31), there will be a definitive transfiguration even of material reality (Rom 8:21). In the sacraments, material realities such as water, bread, and wine serve as signs and means of new life even now. Our possessing and using material goods, however, cannot and may not ever be an end in itself or the ultimate fulfillment of existence, but must be directed to the ultimate goal of man and the world, the Kingdom of God. St. Augustine says that we may employ earthly goods, but we may not enjoy them as ultimate values.

The Bible does not disdain nature, nor does it reject the *cultivation* of the earth and human *culture*. The earth only becomes the dwelling and living space of man through his creation of culture. The Old Testament wisdom literature describes man's creation of culture in agriculture, city-building, technology, commerce, justice, the wisdom tradition itself, education, and politics, among others. The Bible by no means views the earth as a material that serves the unlimited exploitation and the egoistic consump- 99–100 tion of man. On the contrary, ethical consequences follow from faith in God, the "maker of heaven and earth". Because God is the Creator and Lord of the earth, the earth possesses its own dignity as God's creation. It is entrusted to the responsible and careful dominion of man (Gen 1:28–30; 2:15). The Bible speaks deliberately of a commission to care for and preserve the earth. This point of view is important, especially in our present situation. New orientations and new forms of self-moderation in dealing with our environment are necessary today, especially for the sake of a future that will respect the dignity of life.

Further consequences follow for the question about the *right to and limits of property*. Because God is the Creator and Lord of the earth and because he has made it for all men, man can "own" the earth only as its custodian. His right to property is explicitly protected in the seventh commandment (Ex 20:15, 17; Dt 5:19, 21), but the prophets unambiguously subordinate this right to the obligation to care for the socially weak. The prophets Amos and Isaiah criticize with perfect clarity the oppression and exploitation of the poor, the corruptibility of judges, and the ruthlessness and partiality of the officials (Am 5:10–12; 8:4–8; Is 5:8–10; 10:1–3, among others). Even if Jesus denies that he is judge and arbiter (Lk 12:13–14), he still knows from the prophet Isaiah that he is sent to bring the good news to the poor and to proclaim the release of prisoners (Is 61:1–2; Lk 4:18). The primitive congregation of Jerusalem voluntarily held goods in common as a sign of the dawning lordship of God (Acts 2:44–45; 4:32–37). The same ideal has been a constant inspiration in the Church's history for 234–235 those Christians who have been called to renounce personal property and to practice the community of goods in a religious order. For all Christians, the lordship of God over the earth implies that the earth's goods are to be distributed justly, so that all have a share in them and so that each one may find space and the proper conditions for life (GS 69).

2.2 Heaven: The Hope of Man

344–346

Today we find it more difficult to understand the creation of heaven than the creation of earth. *What is heaven?* For us, as for the Bible, the heavens are first of all the visible firmament arching over the earth. A second meaning is found in our present usage. We say, for instance, that someone feels as if he were in heaven, that he has heaven on earth. In this second meaning, heaven is the realm of human striving, hoping, dreaming that transcends everything visible, tangible, calculable, and producible. It alone grants us breadth, height, and depth, prospect and perspective. The Creed means to speak of this when it says that God has created a world of the invisible beyond the earth. The world is more than materialism, whether theoretical or practical, believes it to be. Materialism mistakes the heights and depths, the wealth and fullness of reality.

For the Bible there is no doubt that *God alone is the heaven* of man, the fulfillment of his deepest wishes and longings. Heaven is where God is, where man encounters him and is close to him. The New Testament deliberately uses the "Kingdom of heaven" as synonymous with the "Kingdom of God". When the Creed says that God created heaven, it includes beings who stand especially close to him and continually glorify him. In the Christmas story, there are heavenly hosts who praise God, singing, "Glory to God in high heaven" (Lk 2:14). Holy Scripture and the Church's tradition of faith call these beings *angels*. They are, so to speak, the invisible attendants and guardians of man's longings and hopes.

2.3 The Angels

Today there are many *objections and difficulties* about angels. True, Scripture does express the doctrine of angels to a large extent in mythological language and in particular historical representations. Nor can we deny a historical development of the notion of angels. Christian piety not infrequently rendered angels as innocuous, cute, and tasteless. Speaking seriously about angels is difficult also because we run up against the limits of human expression. The great teachers of the Church knew this. For that reason, we must be reserved with speculations about the number, the species, the distinctions and orders ("choirs") of angels. On the other hand, we should also see that reality is deeper and more comprehensive than a narrowly understood reason suspects. Reality has a level below and a level above without which totality, fullness, and perfection would be lacking in creation. Without angels it would then be materialistically constricted and would not have that mysterious (numinous) depth and height that many poets and thinkers have described. The figurative language of myth is a means of expressing an essential dimension of reality—a dimension hardly graspable in purely conceptual terms.

Scripture witnesses to the existence of angels unambiguously and in many passages.

> By the word of the Lord the heavens were made;
> by the breath of his mouth all their host (Ps 33:6).

> In him everything in heaven and on earth was created, things visible and invisible, whether thrones or dominions, principalities or powers
> . . . (Col 1:16).

Beyond the witness of Holy Scripture, the witness of the liturgy is most important. Angels have their place at the center of the liturgy, at the Sanctus of the Eucharistic Prayer. Supported by such witnesses from Scripture, the liturgy, and the rest of tradition, the Church's doctrinal proclamation has officially declared the existence of angels several times (DS 455–457, 800, 3002; NR 288–290, 295, 316).

What are the angels? According to Holy Scripture, they are definitely creatures. We may honor, but not worship, them (DT 17:3; Rev 22:8–9). In accordance with the Bible (Heb 1:14), the confession of faith specifies them as an invisible, spiritual creation. That does not mean that they stand apart from the visible world and operate only sporadically in it. They represent individual domains of creation before God.

The most proper *task of the angels* is the glorification of God. We read many times in Holy Scripture, "Bless the Lord, all you his angels" (Ps 103:20; 148:2; Dan 3:59). In the Sanctus, the Church joins in the threefold cry of the angels before the throne of God (Is 6:3; Rev 4:8). The angels enact the most important meaning and goal of creation: the glorification of God. But angels are also included in the history of God with men. They too are created in Christ and with an orientation toward him (Col 1:16). For that reason, the great teachers of the Church hold that angels are endowed by God with supernatural grace. They are God's servants and messengers in his dealings with men (Heb 1:7). Especially in the revelation of Jesus Christ, they appear as interpretative messengers (Lk 1:11–13, 26–28; Mt 28:2–4; Acts 1:10–11). Finally, the angels are personal figures of God's protection and care for the faithful. In the well-known psalm (and hymn), "You who dwell in the shelter of the Most High", the angels ground trust and confidence in God: "For to his angels he has given command over you, that they may guard you in all your ways" (Ps 91:11). The angels are "ministering spirits, sent to serve those who are to inherit salvation" (Heb 1:14). Proceeding from such declarations, the pious belief developed that God has assigned a special *guardian angel* to each believer, indeed to each person. This conviction meets with scepticism today, especially when trivialized as a false, childish belief. Properly understood, however, it finds support in Jesus' saying about children: "Their angels in heaven constantly behold my Father's face" (Mt 18:10). This belief affirms once again that the visible world possesses an invisible dimension of depth, and that every individual, especially the small child, possesses an infinite value before God. The angels are helpers and guarantors for us that our hope and longing do not grope in the dark; rather, heaven stands open for us.

2.4 The Devils

In a quite different way, the height and depth of reality stands forth in the Bible's and the Church's conviction concerning the existence of *evil spirits*, demons, Satan, or the devil. There are not only protectors and guardians of human hope, but also begrudgers, enemies, and tempters who throw man's longing and hope into confusion, violently suppress it, or drive it to excess, to demonic proportions. There is a devil, the father of lies (Jn 8:44). He is the tempter who wants to embitter and obstruct our journey to heaven.

Difficulties and misunderstandings about devils are even greater than those about the angels. The language both of Holy Scripture and of the Church's tradition of faith is here especially conditioned by historical world views. On the other hand, 105–108   the existence of evil, of the wicked, destructive, perverse, monstrous, absurd, and diabolical, is an *experiential reality* for us. So is the impression that this evil not only comes as the expression and consequence of human freedom, but that it possesses a cosmic dimension. Biblically speaking, our horizon is heaven, toward which human freedom tends; but prior to any of our decisions, it is constricted, obscured, confused. We are barred from paradise as if by cherubim and flaming swords of fire (Gen 3:24).

The *biblical witness* presents this situation in the language of mythical images; it describes a reality that is hardly to be grasped in purely conceptual terms. The graphic expressions of the collapse of heaven, of the fall of the angels (2 Pet 2:4; Jude 6), of evil spirits in the air, in the realm between heaven and earth (Eph 2:2; 3:10; 6:12), touch man's situation very exactly. They indicate that we have to battle with more than flesh and blood (Eph 6:12). The evil "powers and dominations" (Eph 1:21; Col 2:15, among others) represent the revolt and resistance of the world against God and against his order; they also show that many domains of reality are inimical to man. They ruin God's good creation and seek to harm man in the bodily realm, even to the point of being able to possess his bodily and psychic forces and so to alienate man from himself (diabolical possession). As rulers of this world (Jn 12:31; 14:30) and as gods of this present age (2 Cor 4:4), the evil powers frustrate the hope and the longing of man, or they drive that hope and longing to excess, like the serpent in the garden of paradise, who says, "You will be like gods" (Gen 3:5). In this way, the devil is the father of lies (Jn 8:44). He reinterprets the truth about man. He darkens the distinction between yes and no, which is clear in itself, and confuses the order of the world as given by God. The devil becomes a tempter for man, but one who can gain power over him only if man consents to him.

The Bible makes clear both the power and the impotence of the evil spirits above all in *connection with the appearance of Jesus*. The Gospel of Mark in particular describes the whole life and work of Jesus as a battle with Satan (Mk 1:23–28, 32–34, 39; 3:22–30). With Jesus, though, the stronger one comes who defeats the strong one. In Jesus the lordship of God dawns, because he drives out demons by the power of God (Mt 12:28; Lk 11:18; 10:18). Because Jesus Christ has definitively defeated the powers and dominations (Eph 1:21; Col 2:15; Rev 12:7–12), fear of the demons is un-Christian. We are exhorted, instead: "Stay sober and alert! Your opponent the devil is prowling like a roaring lion looking for someone to devour. Resist him, solid in your faith . . ." (1 Pet 5:8–9). 130–131; 269–270

Church teaching follows the witness of Scripture. The evil power binding men cannot stem from a primordial evil principle independent of God; this would deeply contradict the Christian faith in God, the almighty Father. So the power can be traced back only to creatures who were created good by God, but who—as the Fourth Lateran Council (1215) says—have become evil through their own decision (DS 800; Nr 295). According to Church teaching, there is then not only an evil power but also the evil one or, rather, evil ones. In this way, Catholic teaching does justice, on the one hand, both to the human experience of the unfathomableness of the world and to the biblical witness; on the other hand, the teaching shows the limits of the importance and influence of the evil spirits. They are in the end only finite, created by God and to that extent permanently dependent on him. Their accursed dominion is broken by Jesus Christ and is more and more overcome by the work of the Holy Spirit. Hope has the last word.

With "heaven and earth", the *existential space of man* is marked off and a space is opened up in which the history of God with man can take place. All declarations about the material world and the spiritual world of angels and demons are but border and background for the central proclamation of faith. We may not make these declarations the center of proclamation or an object of faith important for its own sake. Conversely, neither may we favor a narrowly anthropological view that overlooks the cosmic dimension that these declarations enunciate. In what the Bible and the Church say about angels or demons, the point is to stress the universal-cosmological dimension of the history of God with men. The teaching gives this history its dramatic character and its universal dimension.

3. Man: Center and Crown of Creation

3.1 What Is Man?

Heaven and earth are the two dimensions of reality; they mark off the space in the center of which man stands. "Believers and unbelievers agree almost unanimously", the Second Vatican Council states, "that all things on earth should be ordained to man as to their center and summit" (GS 12).

But is not this declaration countered by the experience that man is in many respects a paltry being? We know today that our earth is not the center of the cosmos and that most natural scientists believe that man is 15–17; caught up in the evolution of life. So we must ask again: *What is man?* This 101–103 has been the primordial question of Western mankind. Even the Bible asks it (Ps 8:5; 144:3; Job 7:17).

This question finds *differing, even contrary answers* today. On the one hand, man is defined optimistically and idealistically as a free being who must decide on his own what he is to be. Man himself becomes the highest standard; he thinks he must emancipate himself from every dependency in order to actualize only himself. On the other hand, there is a materialistic

> image of man, absolutely devoid of mystery, which shows only a
> man of pure needs, a man without longing, a man thus without the
> ability to grieve or to be truly consoled or to understand consolation
> as something other than purely empty comfort (*Gem. Synode, Unsere
> Hoffnung* I, 1).

The image of man in the Marxist world view is very widespread: man is seen as the "ensemble of social relations", as the product and producer of society, worth only what he provides to society and its progress.

All these answers are partially correct, but in their one-sidedness they miss the complex reality of man, whose mystery cannot be easily captured in a single answer. More disquieting than such one-sided conceptions is the fact that today many men no longer even pose the question about the 19–21 meaning of their humanity: they flee from it and lose themselves. Perhaps this is the deepest *crisis of contemporary man*. Beyond all other organisms, man is the one able to ask about himself; in this question he encounters an insoluble mystery concerning himself. All answers to the question about the mystery of man, however rich or profound, remain fragmentary if they do not understand man in terms of his ultimate ground and goal.

3.2 Man as Creature

The Bible's fundamental answer to the question "What is man?" is that *man is a creature of God*. He owes his existence and nature to God. He is willed and held in existence by God; he exists because God has called him by name. God says, I will you to be. The basic act of man's existence must, then, be thanks and trust.

> I give you thanks that I am fearfully, wonderfully made;
>   wonderful are your works.
> My soul also you knew full well;
>   nor was my frame unknown to you.
> When I was made in secret,
>   when I was fashioned in the depths of the earth.
> Your eyes have seen my actions;
>   in your book they are all written;
>   my days were limited before one of them existed.
> How weighty are your designs, O God;
>   how vast the sum of them!
> Were I to recount them, they would outnumber the sands:
>   did I reach the end of them, I should still be with you (Ps
>   139:14–18).

Can such declarations of God's immediate creation of man still hold in view of the modern *theory of evolution*? In principle, the same answer is to be given to this question as to the question about the evolution of other organisms: God's creative power as all-encompassing cause does not exclude, but includes, the "secondary causes" empowered by him. 79–81; 110–112

Church teaching, however, distinguishes between the genesis of man and that of other organisms. It leaves the descent of the human body from prehuman organisms to scientific discussion, but holds fast to the immediate creation of the human soul by God (DS 3896; NR 332).

This means that man is more than the result of a biological evolution. He is not a chance product of development; every individual man is willed by God in a unique and quite personal way. Every man is a unique creative thought of God, an answer that has become a person in response to the personal call of God. This is the deepest reason for the dignity of man as a person with a spiritual soul. In the realization of his creative call, God also uses secondary causes. This holds both for the genesis of the first man from prehuman forms of life (hominization) and for the becoming of each individual man in the act of generation. Parents cooperate in transmitting life in the love of God, the Creator, and are, as it were, interpreters of this love (GS 50). 101–103; 331–332; 335–337

The declarations of faith concerning the special creation of man by God express man's special position among the other creatures and ground his unique dignity. In what exactly is this dignity grounded?

3.3 Man's Likeness to God

The Bible distinguishes the creation of man from the creation of other organisms. This can be seen in Genesis. The earlier, second creation narrative only briefly indicates the creation of other creatures but describes the creation of man in detail and so places him at the center of creation. Man ("adam") is taken from the earth ("adamah"), yet God breathes the breath of life immediately into his nostrils (Gen 2:7). The first and later account of creation considers man as the high point of creation. It introduces it with particular solemnity and calls what distinguishes man from the rest of reality his *likeness to God*.

> Then God said: "Let us make man in our image, after our likeness. Let them have dominion over the fish of the sea, the birds of the air, and the cattle, and over all the wild animals and all the creatures that crawl on the ground."

> God created man in his image;
>   in the divine image he created him;
>   male and female he created them (Gen 1:26–27).

What is this likeness to God? Various answers can be given. Man distinguishes himself from other organisms through his upright carriage, the sign of his nobility. Man is appointed lord over the earth and the other creatures; they are committed to him for his use and care. He is called as the "vicar of God" to represent God's lordship in the world. Man distinguishes himself through his spiritual soul; he is given reason and free will (Wis 2:23). Each of these interpretations contains something correct. The decisive thing is, of course, that the Bible sees man's special position not by comparing him with what is below, the animals, but with what is above, God himself. Of all organisms, man is the only being that corresponds to God, that can hear and answer God. Man is created as a *partner to God* and called to communion with God. Man becomes truly human by turning to God and recognizing the lordship of God. The meaning and the fulfillment of his existence is the glorification of God, in which he lends his voice to a mute creation. The Psalms express this magnificently:

> O Lord, our Lord,
>   how glorious is your name over all the earth!

What is man that you should be mindful of him,
  or the son of man that you should care for him?
You have made him little less than the angels,
  and crowned him with glory and honor.
You have given him rule over the works of your hands,
  putting all things under his feet.
O Lord, our Lord,
  how glorious is your name over all the earth! (Ps 8:2, 5–7,
    10; Sir 17:1–10).

Man's likeness to God places him in a fourfold network of relations from which a *fourfold vocation* results: to praise God, to love his neighbor, to live and care for the world, and to esteem and pay heed to himself.

1. Man stands in *relationship to God*. This relationship is not added externally and subsequently to man's being human; it constitutes him in his entire existence and essence. It means that *man is a being profoundly related to God*. He faces God and so can be addressed by and for God. He can forget his relationship to God, repress it, and pervert it, but he can never shake it off. Man's whole life, whether he knows it or not, is a question about God and a search for him. This constitutes man's greatness and dignity, but also the reason for his creaturely humility. Within this tension, he stands tempted by both arrogance and despair. Man can find his true dignity only in humility and in the magnanimity of serving God and glorifying him.

2. Man's relationship to God and his cooperation with God are reflected in man's social nature. Man is not a solitary being; "by his innermost nature man is a social being; and if he does not enter into relations with others he can neither live nor develop his gifts" (GS 12). The most important part of this is that God created man *as male and female* precisely to be social (Gen 1:27). As images of God, both sexes are, in their difference, of equal rank and equal value. Any discrimination because of sex contradicts the Christian faith. But both sexes can find their fulfillment only in turning toward each other and in being with one another. The covenant between man and woman is thus a biblical image of God's covenant with men (Hos 1–3; Is 54; Eph 5:21–33). Their mutual love is at the same time a service to life. In the union of male and female, man is allowed to participate in God's creative activity. "God blessed them, saying: 'Be fruitful and multiply; fill the earth and subdue it' " (Gen 1:28). Married people have to fulfill this commission to serve life, according to the essence of love, in personal, human, and Christian responsibility before God and one another (GS 50–51; FC).

63–64;
316–317

3. Because of his special position, man stands in a special relation to the rest of creation. Man may and should make the rest of creation serviceable

90–92 and delightful. His *dominion over the world* does not mean, however, freedom for capricious and egoistical exploitation of nature; it calls, rather, for care and responsibility for life. The Bible sees man's dominion over the world symbolized in his giving a name to birds and animals (Gen 2:19–20). Through this naming, man recognizes what things and animals are and so brings them to themselves. The rest of creation also has its intrinsic value and its inherent laws given by God; man must respect these if he does not want to destroy his world.

4. Finally, man also stands *in relationship to himself*. The Bible speaks in this connection of the *heart of man*. "Heart" does not refer to a central bodily organ; it is understood as a symbol for the personal center of man. It is the interior, the place where man can hear God, obey him, but also refuse him. We might say that the heart is the *person of man*. Personality implies that man is present to himself in all openness for God, men, and the world, so that each man possesses unique value and unique dignity in himself and bears responsibility for the deeds he commits and omits. He possesses more than exteriority; he is occupied with himself in his inner thoughts and can reflect upon himself. He can laugh at himself, become annoyed with himself, feel ashamed, and be satisfied or dissatisfied with himself. We know ourselves and other men only when we know what is going on in our and their innermost thoughts. Man, who as a person is related to himself and confronted with himself, is at the same time related to God. His personal vocation is a communion with God, which finds its fulfillment in and through Jesus Christ.

The declaration of man's likeness to God has important *practical consequences*.

The dignity of every man before God grounds the *dignity of man* before other men. It is the ultimate ground of the fundamental equality and brotherhood of all men, independent of race, nationality, sex, descent, education, or class. In the ancient world, this was a revolutionary declaration. It is so even today, when one thinks of the differences and discriminations that still exist among men. Because something of the glory of God is reflected on the countenance of every man, *the life of man* is *holy and inviolable* (Gen 9:6). The fifth commandment, "You shall not kill" (Ex 20:13; Dt 5:17), holds because God has laid his hand on every man, especially on the powerless, the small, and the poor. God alone is Lord over life and death. Many consequences follow:

> All violations of the integrity of the human person, such as mutilation, physical and mental torture, undue psychological pressures; all offenses against human dignity, such as subhuman living conditions, arbitrary imprisonment, deportation, slavery, prostitution, the selling of women and children, degrading working conditions where men

are treated as mere tools for profit rather than free and responsible persons: all these and the like are criminal: they poison civilization; and they debase the perpetrators more than the victims and militate against the honor of the Creator (GS 27).

Man may never use another man as a thing; he must esteem him as an independent being responsible for himself and worthy of respect.

The dignity of man before God also implies man's dignity before himself, the right and the duty of *self-respect* and self-love. We should love our neighbor as ourselves (Mk 12:31). We may be and should be worth something to ourselves and should pay just as much attention to our health as to our honor and our reputation. The dignity of man requires that he seek his fulfillment not first of all in what he has, but in what he is. "It is what a man is, rather than what he has, that counts" (GS 35). Precisely in the haste and hurry of everyday life, we can forget and lose ourselves and so no longer come to reflect on ourselves. This too goes against the value and dignity of man.

3.4 The Nature of Man

On the basis of the vocation and the dignity of man, our question can be posed yet again: What is man? What is the essential state of man? The Bible's answer matches our modern experience and knowledge very well. We experience man not as a composition of two parts, a material body and a spiritual soul; we understand man as a *unity and totality*. For instance, when the body is sick and ailing, the whole man suffers; conversely, bodily diseases may have psychic causes. So too when the Bible speaks of man as the likeness of God, it always means the one and the whole man. It describes him by referring to individual bodily functions or organs such as breath of life, flesh, heart, loins, and soul, which in addition to their literal meaning have a figurative meaning designating the whole man. When the New Testament says that the eternal Word became flesh (Jn 1:14), it means that Jesus Christ has become man. *Man does not have a body and a soul; he is a body, and he is a soul and a spirit.*

15–17;
96–97

335–337

The Church's teaching of faith has constantly defended the unity of man in body and soul against both a one-sidedly materialistic and a one-sidedly spiritualistic interpretation (DS 800, 3002; NR 918, 316). Referring to the teaching of St. Thomas Aquinas (thirteenth century), the Church teaches that the spiritual soul is the substantial form of the body (DS 902; NR 329). This means that body and soul are not two separate beings that are only subsequently united. The body cannot exist at all without the soul; it is the soul's form of expression and form of existence. Conversely, the human spiritual soul is essentially linked to the body, and it cannot be understood except in relation to the body. The Second Vatican Council summarizes this teaching: "Man, though made of body and soul, is a unity" (GS 14).

Salvation too is intended for the one, whole man. Jesus teaches the Kingdom of God not only as an inner, spiritual reality. Jesus' proclamation of the Kingdom brings with it his healings of the sick. "The blind recover their sight, cripples walk, lepers are cured, the deaf hear, dead men are brought to life, and the poor have the good news preached to them" (Mt 11:5). For the same reason, we should glorify God in our bodies (1 Cor 6:20; Rom 12:1). The body will indeed die; but the Christian hopes that he will be transformed into a new, glorified body (1 Cor 15:35–49; Phil 3:21).

Within this unity of body and soul we must *distinguish between body and soul.* This distinction corresponds to our everyday experience. Man can in spirit step outside his body and turn toward it for observation or reflection; he can also be absent in spirit. He can suppress the body and its needs—or he can let himself be overcome by them and thereby lose his personal freedom and dignity. Finally, the body of man can be old and weak while his spirit is still young and fresh. Man obviously has many sides that cannot be reduced to a single principle.

Man's *bodiliness* unites the elements of the material world; "Through him they are thus brought to their highest perfection and can raise their voice in praise freely given to the Creator" (GS 14). But man is not only a part of nature or an anonymous element in human society. Through his *spirituality* he transcends the totality of things and penetrates into the spiritual, the deeper structure of reality. "So when he recognizes in himself a spiritual and immortal soul, he is not being led astray by false imaginings that are due to merely physical or social causes. On the contrary, he grasps what is profoundly true in this matter" (GS 14). "Man's most secret core, and his sanctuary" is *conscience*. "There he is alone with God, whose voice echoes in his depths." "Deep within his conscience man discovers a law which he has not laid upon himself but which he must obey. Its voice, ever calling him to love and to do what is good and to avoid evil, tells him inwardly at the right moment: do this, shun that" (GS 16). "It is, however, only in freedom that man can turn toward what is good." This *freedom* is a sign of man's likeness to God. "Man's dignity therefore requires him to act out of conscious and free choice, as moved and drawn in a personal way from within, and not by blind impulses in himself or by mere external constraint" (GS 17). Today we highly treasure this freedom and passionately aspire to it, and rightly so. Man's dignity includes his free *self-determination* (autonomy); man wishes to shape and must shape his individual and social life in responsibility for himself.

This autonomy does not oppose man's creaturely dependence on God. God and man are not two competitors. The creaturely freedom of man is rather sustained and empowered by the creative freedom of God. As a bestowed freedom, it can never be absolute. We attain our freedom only when we liberate ourselves from servitude to our passions and persevere in pursuing our goal in the free choice of the good. Freedom *from* inner and outer dependence is only possible through freedom *for* the good. It finds its highest expression where individual Christians and Christian communities, such as Francis of Assisi and his friars, attempt to live by trusting entirely in God's care, without material security.

The Church's teaching on the nature of man also contains important *motives for man's moral action*: the basic axiom is the *greatest possible unity and mutual penetration of soul and body*. Bringing this about is a constant task. Man must realize his reason and will in concrete deeds and express his soul in sport, play, art, and culture. Conversely, he must integrate his bodily needs into the whole of his person and its meaning. Such a cultivation of the body is, however, to be distinguished from a cult of the body, of health, or of beauty. It is important to protect the priority of the spirit and to endeavor to obtain wisdom, which ordains all to the ultimate goal of man (GS 15). Whenever sexuality is made independent and is no longer   316–317 ordered into the whole of a personal partnership, where the satisfaction of drives and the gaining of pleasure become primary, there can no longer be talk of real love. Sexual activity is good just so far as it is an expression of love. Just as there is a bodiliness inimical to the spirit, so there is also a spirituality inimical to the body. Unfortunately, the Church too, not in its official teaching but in its pastoral, pedagogical, and ascetical praxis, has not infrequently succumbed to this hostility to the body. The bodily needs and abilities of man were often devalued and repressed instead of being cultivated. In the original Christian image of man, there is no room for such a contempt of the body. True care of the soul must include care of the body and concrete help for life. It must use not only words, abstract concepts, and moral principles, but also images, symbolism, and songs in order to address the whole man and to include him in the event of salvation.

The unity of body and soul shows itself especially in language, through which we express our thoughts, intentions, and innermost selves and so communicate them to others. *Truth* is an essential dimension of man. In falsehood, on the other hand, man's inner unity and the foundations of trust in the human community are destroyed. The eighth commandment says, "You shall not bear false witness against your neighbor" (Ex 20:16; Dt 5:20). Truth belongs to the nature and the dignity of the person, both as an individual and as a member of society.

In striving for integration, man runs up against the *limits of his freedom*. He is limited by nature, by the freedom of others, by his own life history, and by the social milieu. These are often frustrating obstacles despite our good will. We do not simply *have* our freedom; it is imprisoned in many ways and must first be set free. Freedom is ultimately a gift. Indeed, it is a gift from Jesus Christ. "If the son frees you, you will really be free" (Jn 8:36).

3.5 Called by Grace to Communion with God

We are remarkable beings. We are tied down by the conditions and limitations of this world through our body and yet are full of dreams, desires, and hopes that cannot be fulfilled by anything or anyone in the world. *Man is a being of infinite hope.* The heart of man is so great and so wide that God alone is great enough to fill it.

22–23

> As the hind longs for the running waters,
>   so my soul longs for you, O God.
> Athirst is my soul for God, the living God.
> When shall I go and behold the face of God? (Ps 42:2–3).

82;
136–138
97–102

The mystery of man is first disclosed to us fully in Jesus Christ. Only by knowing Jesus Christ can anyone know man entirely. Jesus is *the* image of God (2 Cor 4:4; Col 1:15); he is the first to disclose entirely to us our likeness to God and the first to fulfill it in us. As the Son of God, he is simultaneously the new Adam, the new man (1 Cor 15:47–49; Rom 5:14). "Christ, the new Adam in the very revelation of the mystery of the Father and of his love, fully reveals man to himself and brings to light his highest calling" (GS 22). In him we have been predestined by God "to share the image of his Son, that the Son might be the first-born of many brothers" (Rom 8:29). The song of praise that begins the Letter to the Ephesians summarizes all of this beautifully:

> Praised be the God and Father of our Lord Jesus Christ, who has bestowed on us in Christ every spiritual blessing in the heavens! God chose us in him before the world began, to be holy and blameless in his sight, to be full of love; he likewise predestined us through Christ Jesus to be his adopted sons—such was his will and pleasure— that all might praise the glorious favor he has bestowed on us in his beloved. . . . God has given us the wisdom to understand fully the mystery, the plan he was pleased to decree in Christ, to be carried out in the fullness of time: namely, to bring all things in the heavens and on earth into one under Christ's headship. In him we were chosen . . . we were predestined to praise his glory by being the first to hope in Christ (Eph 1:3–6, 10–12).

185–187;
205–208

The *newness* that Jesus Christ bestows on us is not grafted onto our human nature. As men, we are already predisposed on the basis of our likeness to God that was given in creation to *communion with the triune God*, but we are unable to reach this by our own efforts. This communion is realized in a unique way in Jesus Christ, the incarnate Son of God. Through his Spirit we are accepted as children of God (Rom 8:14–17; Gal 4:4–6). When we receive through Christ a share in the divine nature (1 Pet 1:4), God bestows on us infinitely more "than we ask or imagine" (Eph 3:20). Still, what we have already received is only an inkling and a foretaste (2 Cor 1:22; Eph 1:13–14); it will be consummated only when we see God face to face (1 Cor 13:12). For "eternal life is this: to know you, the only true God, and him whom you have sent, Jesus Christ" (Jn 17:3).

344–345

Theology later distinguished between man's *natural likeness to God–a likeness given in creation–and his supernatural likeness to God bestowed by grace*. It originally grounded this distinction in the difference between "image" and "likeness" (Gen 1:26, 28). Even if this scriptural interpretation seems no longer tenable, it nonetheless fully corresponds to the full perspective of Holy Scripture. For Scripture, creation is only the beginning and the foundation; it is not abolished in the history of salvation, but surpassed. If theology speaks in this connection of the supernatural character of the order of salvation, it is because we do indeed—consciously or unconsciously—long and hope for this salvation, this communion with God, on the basis of our creaturely relation to God, but are unable to reach it by our own power. Salvation cannot be achieved either by evolution or by revolution. The personal communion of life with God can be bestowed on us only by God out of pure grace, i.e., without any merit, freely and gratuitously, beyond our nature. And yet precisely as a gift, salvation is the all-surpassing fulfillment of man. *Nature and grace* are not related as two strata, for instance, or as two orders placed one on top of the other, which have nothing to do with each other. Both orders realize the one plan of salvation in Jesus Christ.

This distinction between natural and supernatural likeness to God differs from that found in *Protestant doctrine*. In general, Protestant theology relates the concept of likeness to God only to the communion with God through grace, but not to the vocation to partnership with God given in the nature of man. There are consequences for the understanding of sin as rupture and loss of the communion with God established through grace, as well as for the question of human cooperation in the justification and sanctification of the sinner. We have begun to overcome this difference today by understanding our natural likeness to God as a vocation coming from Jesus Christ, ordained to him and to participation through grace in his reality.

110–112;
197–198;
203–204

324–325

The intimate connection of nature and grace is expressed in the famous Scholastic principle: *the grace bestowed in Jesus Christ presupposes nature and brings it to fulfillment*. Grace is addressed to one who is free to accept or reject it. To that extent, grace presupposes a relatively stable nature, the human person and his freedom. It presupposes this person, though, as "something" open, something that points dynamically beyond itself and finds its fulfillment in God alone.

Jesus Christ discloses to us why *man is the being that infinitely surpasses himself* (Pascal), that is always newly underway, that can stop nowhere.

New horizons always open before man, who cannot find his final satisfaction in anything worldly, but who is without rest or repose. Jesus
Christ teaches us to understand man as a being of infinite hope and
longing, but also a being haunted by abysmal fear of personal failure. Man
oscillates between hope and anxiety, not just today, but always. "For you
have created us for yourself, and our heart is restless until it rests in you"
(Augustine).

4. Where Does Evil Come From? The Meaning of History

4.1 A Difficult Question with Many Answers

Everything said so far about the greatness and beauty of creation and
about the vocation of man can seem unrealistic and naively optimistic.
How is one to praise the God "who governs all so splendidly" in the face
of the hell of Auschwitz, of Hiroshima, of the Gulag Archipelago—to
name just a few of our century's sites of horror? Even the Psalms are
familiar with the experience that things go well for the wicked, but badly
for the just (Ps 73:3–12). The question "Why must the just man suffer?"
occupies the Book of Job in particular. Job is something more than the
patient sufferer who speaks the oft-quoted saying, "The Lord gave and
the Lord has taken away, blessed be the name of the Lord!" (Job 1:21). Job
contends with God. He rises up and curses the day of his birth (Job 3:2–3).
He cries, "I loathe my life" (Job 10:1). Job rejects the too-easy answers that
his friends give him in the face of unjust suffering. God appears to him as
the always greater and the wholly other whose ways are unfathomable
and whose wisdom is inscrutable (Job 40:2–4; 42:2–4).

Nonetheless, men have repeatedly tried to gain an insight into the ups
and downs of history. *Two basic models for the interpretation of history* have
been developed. The first sees history as a great cycle. At the beginning
stand the "good old days", the golden age; the silver, the bronze, and the
iron age follow. History might seem a great process of decline, but at the
extreme low point a reversal takes place. At the end, the beginning
returns; the circle is closed. The second model sees history as an ascending
line, the line of progress on the way to the better and the higher. History is
not the eternal return of the same (as in the cyclical model), but the coming
of the new and of a future that has not been here before. Beginnings of this
view are found in the Old Testament prophets' hope for the future. We
meet a secularized form of this view in the modern belief in progress and
in the Marxist utopia of a future kingdom of liberation, a classless society
free of domination.

We must ask whether these two interpretations really do justice to mankind's experience of suffering. Does man's suffering allow itself to be ordered into some general schema? Do such interpretations take seriously enough the suffering of each individual?

Given its fundamental concern, Holy Scripture does not try to offer us any immanent interpretation of history. The Bible does insist that everything comes from God and returns to him. But the course of history does not allow itself to be forced into any schema, whether of decline or of progress. History is, as Augustine showed in his *City of God*, a constant *battle between two kingdoms*: the Kingdom of God and the kingdom of evil (of Satan). They are distinguished by two different kinds of love: love of God and love of self. Usually the two are intertwined. For that reason, one must not rush to interpret individual historical events as signs of God or as monstrous prodigies of the evil one. We must admit instead that God is a hidden God who has appeared to us unambiguously only in Jesus Christ. From Jesus Christ alone do we have the standard by which to judge history and life. "It is therefore through Christ, and in Christ, that light is thrown on the riddle of suffering and death which, apart from his Gospel, overwhelms us" (GS 22). The full Christian answer to the question of the meaning of suffering will become clear to us only later, in the treatment of the cross of Jesus Christ.

4.2 The Origin: Man's Original State and Paradise

The biblical interpretation of history declares that God did not will and did not make the world as we find it concretely now. He willed and wills life, not death; he abhors injustice, violence, and deceit. He does not will man to suffer; he wills the happiness of man in communion with him. In order to express God's original will and plan, the Bible tells the *story of paradise*.

> Then the Lord God planted a garden in Eden, in the east, and he placed there the man whom he had formed.
> The Lord God then took the man and settled him in the garden of Eden, to cultivate and care for it. The Lord God gave man this order: "You are free to eat from any of the trees of the garden except the tree of knowledge of good and evil. From that tree you shall not eat; the moment you eat from it you are surely doomed to die" (Gen 2:8, 15–17).

To understand this narration correctly, we must know that Holy Scripture describes God's mysterious workings not so much in conceptual statements as in images. These images are taken from the human realm and are borrowed in part from the myths of a given time. God speaks to us in a human language that the men of a certain age, with their notions understood. Since it is expressed in figurative language, the story of paradise should not be understood as a *kind of historical report* on the beginnings of human history. Even less should we imaginatively amplify these images (though they are very reserved in comparison with those of other myths) and imagine paradise as a realm of fantasy. On the other hand, this figurative language bearing a mythological imprint cannot be dismissed as meaningless for us today or interpreted in a purely spiritual and symbolic way, as if no historical reality at all were at stake. The Bible here makes a declaration precisely on the historical origin of evil and of ills in the world. It says: God created the world good. Evil and ills in the world do not have their origin in God; they first arose in history. They are not the fault of God but of men. The paradise story is a large-scale *justification of God* (theodicy) in view of the world's concrete state.

What the paradise story expresses in images, the Church's proclamation of faith explains conceptually in the *doctrine on man's original state*. Taking up older formulations, the Council of Trent (1545–1563) states that Adam, the first man, lost "the holiness and justice in which he was instated" by transgressing God's command (DS 1511; NR 353). By "*holiness and justice*" the Council means man's original communion and friendship with God, his being on a "first-name basis" with God, as the paradise story relates. The core of both the paradise narrative and the doctrine on man's original state is thus not a paleontological (prehistorical) but a theological declaration. God not only created man good, even very good; he also let him participate beyond that in the divine life.

110–112 According both to Holy Scripture and to the Church's teaching, man's life of grace had repercussions on the whole of his life. The original "holiness and justice" radiated out to the different domains of human existence. In the technical language of theology, there were *preternatural gifts of the original state* as consequences of supernatural grace. Man was not divided in himself; body and soul were wholly integrated. Man was thus free from concupiscence (inordinate desire), that is, free from the resistance of his various instinctive forces against his basic personal orientation. Secondly, man was also free from the obfuscation and the confusion of his spiritual powers. That does not mean that he had more knowledge than we have today, but he did possess greater and deeper wisdom. He was able to understand everything as coming from God and as ordained to him. No experience of the meaninglessness and absurdity of existence gnawed at him. Thirdly, being at one with himself and with God, man was also one with the world. No suffering impinged on him from without. Work was not the burden and plague that we often feel it to be today (Gen 3:17–18).

330–331 Man was finally and above all free from death as an anonymous power presiding over him, against which his natural will to life must rise up and which he now experiences as something dark and foreign, as rupture and breach. According to the Apostle Paul, death came into the world through sin (Rom 5:12). Death is the drastic sign that by sin man is alienated from God, the source of life. What was life without death? Holy Scripture and the Church's teaching of faith tell us nothing; speculations are useless. Life in paradise was a promise that revealed God's original plan and will for man. But man refused this promise even at the beginning and so frustrated God's plan from the first.

Why does the Bible tell us all this? It is not to satisfy our historical curiosity. Its declarations about paradise and man's original state are not important for their own sake. They merely represent the background against which we can begin to understand the present situation of mankind as a state of alienation that God did not will and did not create. Where, then, does evil come from?

4.3 Adam's Sin and the Original Sin of Mankind

"Through one man sin entered the world and with sin death" (Rom 5:12). That is Paul's lapidary statement. It summarizes what is vividly recounted in the first pages of the Bible as the *narration of the fall of man*.

Man lets himself be seduced by the serpent. Breaking God's commandment, he grasps at the tree of life and so falls prey to death. This first sin is not a trivial matter of man's having grasped at a forbidden fruit and having illicitly eaten it. Nor is there any suggestion of sexual misconduct. Something more is at stake. What is broken is not the sixth but the first commandment. God alone is the Lord of man and the source of his life. Man transgressed his creaturely limits; he mistrusted God and willed to grasp at life himself. He wanted to take matters into his own hands and to direct them. In doing so, he chose death. Sin consists in disobedience (Rom 5:19). The consequences of alienation from God are great. Man is alienated from his fellow man. Male and female, originally meant for mutual help and support in love, become the temptation and ruin of each other. Man also is alienated from himself; he grows ashamed because he stands naked. Man is alienated from life; the birth of new life takes place in pain. Finally, man is alienated from his environment; by the sweat of his brow he must earn his bread (Gen 3:1–24).

The Bible does not tell only this one story of the fall. The one story triggers the avalanche of a further history of sin, in which the *social dimension* of sin stands forth. In the story of the murder of Abel by Cain, man transgresses against his fellow man. He begrudges the other the love and benevolence of God; he becomes fatally jealous (Gen 4). A vicious circle of guilt and revenge among men is set in motion (Gen 4:23–24). In a strongly mythical narration about the marriage of men with the sons of heaven and the subsequent birth of the "heroes of old", man in general is seen to have lost the measure of the human. He transgresses in regard to the superhuman, the heroic, the herculean. The consequence is the descent of the flood's chaos (Gen 6). In the story of the tower of Babel, finally, man transgresses against the cultural realm as well. The result is a babel, a confusion in which no one understands anyone anymore. Peoples drift apart and often fall into opposition; each must live in isolation and dispersion (Gen 11).

157–158 In the New Testament, Paul takes up this narrative. He describes the first Adam in relation to the second, *the new Adam, Jesus Christ*.

> Through one man sin entered the world and with sin death, death thus coming to all men inasmuch as all sinned. . . . From Adam to Moses death reigned, even over those who had not sinned as did Adam, that type of the man to come. . . . For if by the offense of the one man all died, much more did the grace of God and the gracious gift of the one man, Jesus Christ, abound for all. . . . If death began its reign through one man because of his offense, much more shall those who receive the overflowing grace and gift of justice live and reign through the one man, Jesus Christ (Rom 5:12, 14, 15, 17).

This text goes beyond the declarations of the Old Testament. Through Jesus Christ the universality and radicality of sin is disclosed to us; he first shows us the true situation of salvation and perdition. The universality of sin's power, which reigns as the power of death over mankind, is now explicitly established. Still, the knowledge of sin's universality is only *the negative formulation of the universality of salvation* in Jesus Christ. Because we know that in Jesus Christ salvation is given for all, we can recognize that outside of Jesus Christ there is perdition. The declaration on sin has no independent importance. It illustrates the universality and the superabundance of the salvation brought by Jesus Christ. The hopeless situation of mankind is embraced by the greater hope and the certainty that Jesus Christ bestows the fullness of salvation on us. Indeed, salvation in Jesus Christ surpasses the original calling and grace. For that reason, the Easter Vigil liturgy speaks of a *felix culpa*, a happy fault.

The *dogmatic teaching on the sin of Adam and original sin* was clarified in the fifth century. This happened in the dispute of St. Augustine with Pelagianism. Pelagianism affirmed that sin is only an individual deed committed as a free decision and so spreads only through bad example and its imitation. In principle, the Pelagians held that man is free to decide for sin or for God. This put the necessity of grace in question. *St. Augustine*, the "teacher of grace", rose up against this teaching. Different synods took up his reasoning, with the Synod of Orange (529) summarizing the teaching (DS 371–372; NR 350–351).

Further clarification was provided in the dispute with the Reformers and their understanding of sin. According to the *Reformers*, turning away from God leads to the radical perversion of man. The essence of original sin is evil desire and inclination, that is, disinclination toward God, lack of true fear of God, and lack of true faith (CA 2). Man thus loses the original likeness to God (Apol. 2). In justification and baptism, man is indeed reborn, but evil desire and inclination continue to exist. The justified are "sinners and just at the same time". *(margin: 104–105; 197–198; 203–204)*

In opposition to this, the *Council of Trent* (1545–1563) taught that Adam lost "the holiness and justice in which he was instated" on account of the sin by which he transgressed the commandment of God. He fell out of communion with God and fell prey to the power of the devil. He was not totally perverted but was changed "for the worse in body and soul". This one sin of Adam was transmitted to the whole human race "through propagation, not through imitation", so that it "dwells in all and is proper to each". Through the merits of Jesus Christ, original sin is truly washed away in the sacrament of baptism. Baptism is a real regeneration through which we put aside the old man and put on the new one created according to God (Eph 4:22; Col 3:9–10). The concupiscence remaining after baptism is not sin itself but rather its result. It stems from sin and inclines one to sin again. It was certainly not the intention of Trent to include the Virgin Mary, Mother of God, in this general situation of perdition caused by original sin (DS 1511–1516; NR 353–358). *(margin: 149–150)*

The *evil concupiscence* (inordinate desire) of which Tradition speaks should not be restricted to sexual desire. There is also spiritual concupiscence or arrogance. Concupiscence is the disintegration of man, the disparate striving of his various instinctive powers, the recalcitrance of both body and spirit against the basic orientation of the person; it is the inclination to evil. *(margin: 108)*

Old and New Testament teaching on the universality of sin was developed in the Church's tradition in the doctrine on the original state and on original sin. This doctrine encounters many misunderstandings and causes serious *difficulties* for many Christians today. A first difficulty arises because many scientists today suppose that at the beginning of mankind's history there was not a single human couple (monogenism), but that human life developed rather by a process of *evolution*, perhaps in several places (polygenism or even polyphyletism). The Church's Magisterium held, to the contrary, that it is not evident how the latter *(margin: 79–81; 96–98)* opinion is compatible with the doctrine about the sin of Adam and original sin (DS 3897; NR 363). The doctrine of one original human couple at the beginning was meant to express the unity and the equality of all men. Today it is often remarked that "Adam" in biblical language is not only the name of an individual man, but also a collective designation for "man" and "mankind". The Second Vatican Council has also spoken with great reserve about this question. It speaks of men's having fallen "in Adam" (LG 2) but also formulates it more generally by speaking of "man" and his sin (GS 13). The meaning of the Church's teaching can be preserved if it is firmly asserted that mankind, which forms a unity, rejected God's offer of salvation in the beginning and that the loss resulting from that rejection is a universal reality from which no one can free himself by his own strength. If this is firmly asserted, then the question of monogenism or polygenism is a purely scientific one, not a question of faith.

A second objection is more difficult, but also leads us farther. The answer to it opens a way *to understand the doctrine of original sin*. The words "inherited sin" appear to many to be a self-contradiction. An inheritance is something taken over by birth without personal merit; sin, on the other hand, is a personal deed for which one is responsible. That seems to lead to a dilemma: either the sinful state is taken over through an inheritance and so is not sin, or it is indeed sin, but then cannot be called an "inheritance". These difficulties are resolved when we give up the individualistic image of man that stands behind them and recall the *solidarity of all men*. No one ever starts out wholly from scratch; no one begins, as it were, from zero. Each man bears most deeply the imprint of his life history, the history of his family, of his people, of his culture, even of all mankind. Moreover, he finds himself in a situation determined by guilt. We are born into a society in which egoism, prejudices, injustice, and dishonesty reign. That does not mold us only in the sense of an external bad example; it determines our reality. No one lives for himself; all that we are, we are together with others. So the general sinfulness dwells within all; it is proper to each. Our sin has an effect on others. There is a network of common implication in guilt, a general solidarity in sin from which no one can loose himself. This holds even for *small children*. They are personally innocent; they have their life, though, only in the form of participation in the life of adults, especially of their parents. For that reason, they are implicated in the history of the adults even more than the adults themselves.

The general situation of perdition molds and determines each man most deeply in what he is and what he does. The state of original sin is actualized in the individual (personal sin). Man makes the received, general perdition his own; he sins into it. This intertwining and *interpenetration of personal sin and original sin* can never be wholly elucidated. Since sin destroys the inner

(margin note: 209–210)

logic of the world and of man, it always has something contradictory about it. Just as God and man and their relationship are mysteries, the disruption of this relationship is also a mystery.

What follows for the *understanding of original sin*? According to Catholic teaching, original sin is the general perdition of man and of mankind. Man's descent through the succession of generations can no longer mediate his true future, communion with God. Man lacks his true fulfillment in holiness and justice, as well as participation in the life of God. Alienation from God alienates man from the world, from his fellow man, and from himself, and thus deprives him of the gifts of the original state. The Apostle Paul has movingly described the inner conflict produced by sin:

> I cannot even understand my own actions. I do not do what I want to do but what I hate. . . . This indicates that it is not I who do it but sin which resides in me. . . . The desire to do right is there but not the power. What happens is that I do, not the good I will to do, but the evil I do not intend. . . . My inner self agrees with the law of God, but I see in my body's members another law at war with the law of my mind; this makes me a prisoner of the law of sin in my members. What a wretched man I am! (Rom 7:15, 17–19, 22–24).

Following this presentation of Catholic doctrine on the sin of Adam and original sin, we may well ask whether the doctrinal differences that once divided the churches on this question continue to exist, or whether they have been resolved ecumenically since then. We can treat this question in detail only later, when we talk about the central controversy between the Reformers and the Catholic 194–204 Church, the doctrine of justification. But this much is already clear: the differing understanding of the sin of Adam and of original sin, as well as the question of whether the natural likeness to God survives after sin or not, has consequences for man's cooperation in justification and sanctification.

This is, however, not only a doctrinal problem; it leads to *differing attitudes* 197 toward reality. Pelagianism engenders a kind of optimism, as occurred above all in connection with the Enlightenment's belief in progress. The unfathomableness of evil and the necessity of redemption are easily underestimated by this view. The Protestant doctrine of man's radical depravity through sin and of his loss of the natural likeness to God often leads, on the other hand, to a more pessimistic judgment on human nature and culture. The Catholic doctrine, according to which human nature was indeed wounded but not totally destroyed through the loss of the communion with God in grace, takes a realistic middle road to a certain extent. It agrees with the Reformation doctrine that man can do absolutely nothing for his salvation without saving grace. Nonetheless, it places a greater trust in the natural and cultural possibilities of man. These differing attitudes have had and still have a lasting effect; they determine the atmosphere in the separated churches and the relations between them.

The doctrine of the universality of sin has great *practical importance*. It means that every man is a sinner. "If we say, 'We are free of the guilt of sin', we deceive ourselves; the truth is not to be found in us" (1 Jn 1:8). This doctrine *destroys the illusion* we create for ourselves and no longer allows us to avoid our guilt, to minimize it, or to keep looking for scapegoats elsewhere: in others, in circumstances, inheritance and predisposition, structures and relations. The doctrine of original sin also tells us, though, that we must be careful about the *concrete imputation of personal guilt*; we may not judge hastily and condemn. In the end, only God sees into the heart of man. He does not will to condemn, but to forgive. The confession of sin becomes possible only with the knowledge of forgiveness. We may not *detach* the doctrine of the universality of sin *from the context* in which it stands with Paul, which is the universality of salvation in Jesus Christ. If it is isolated from that, a false fear of sin, a pessimistic view of the world and of life, even a dualistic devaluation and contempt of the human body and of the cultural achievements of man, can take place. The Christian is realistic enough to see the abyss of sin, but he sees it in the light of the greater hope that is bestowed on us in Jesus Christ. The most important function of the doctrine of original sin is to refer us to Jesus Christ as our sole salvation.

4.4 Mankind's Hope of Salvation

The Bible gives sin neither the first nor the last word. Man can indeed resist God's plan through disobedience and deeds of violence, but God's will to save is stronger than all power of sin. It is effective from the very beginning. So the biblical story of the fall ends not with a word of punishment or imprecation, but with a promise of salvation, the *proto-evangelium* (proto-Gospel).

For a long time, this proto-evangelium was seen in what God says to the serpent:

> "I will put enmity between you and the woman,
>   and between your offspring and hers;
> He will strike at your head,
>   while you strike at his heel" (Gen 3:15).

This saying was originally an imprecation and not a blessing. It describes the battle between the species, between man and serpent. It shows that human life will not let itself be definitively subdued. Thus the Church Fathers interpreted the imprecation as a word of promise and understood it as referring to Jesus Christ. He is seen as the "offspring" who will crush the head of the serpent and deliver mankind from the curse of sin. This interpretation has had a lasting influence on the fine arts as well as on the texts of hymns:

> Jacob's star has climbed the sky,
> Has quieted the wistful sigh,
> Has crushed the head of serpents sly,
> And smashed the gates of hell.
>
> (from the hymn "*Quem pastores laudavere*")

Scripture's original promise does not depend, of course, on this single passage and its interpretation. Every biblical story of a fall ends with a promise of salvation. They all show that *God wills not the death of the sinner, but his life*. Even the story of the fall in paradise shows that God lets his grace prevail. Though man was threatened with death for his fall of disobedience (Gen 3:3), he is allowed through God's long-suffering to continue to live. So Adam is a type of the new Adam who is to come (Rom 5:14). That life continues and can be passed on is expressed in the honorific name of the woman. She is Eve, the mother of all the living (Gen 3:20). God continues to care for the life and survival of men; this is also seen in his giving them leather garments and protecting them from the adversities of nature (Gen 3:21). From the very beginning God seeks, if not to reconcile, then at least to make bearable the disrupted relation between man and world. After Cain's murder of his brother Abel, God explicitly declares himself the protector of life; this protection holds even for Cain, the wicked murderer (Gen 4:15). Finally, after the chaos of the flood, God founds an order of life that is new in several respects: the permanence, order, and rhythm of nature are guaranteed (Gen 8:21). Nature is to serve man as a means of life. The life of man, who is the likeness of God, is holy and inviolable; the human legal community is meant to protect it (Gen 9:1–7). In the orders of nature and of culture, then, something of God's salvific will for all men becomes clear.

    140

In the New Testament as well, *creation as a whole and all mankind await the coming Redeemer*. The New Testament knows that man can recognize God in the order of nature, especially in the voice of his conscience. It says that *the whole created order was created in Jesus Christ and ordained to him* (Col 1:16). The Word that became man in Jesus Christ was always the life and light of men, illuminating every man (Jn 1:4, 9). God wills the salvation of all men in the one and only mediator, Jesus Christ (1 Tim 2:4–5). The world is filled with good hope, like a woman expecting a child. Even fallen creation, made subject to futility, lifts up its hopeful head as it awaits, with the groans and pangs of birth, its liberation from servitude and exile (Rom 8:18–22).

    25–27
    82;
    136–138

    217–220

A well-known Advent song also shows the universality of this hope in reference to the prophet Isaiah, who includes not only all peoples, but also heaven and earth in this hope:

> Let justice descend, O heavens, like dew from above,
> like gentle rain let the skies drop it down.

> Let the earth open and salvation bud forth;
> let justice also spring up!
> I, the Lord, have created this (Is 45:8).

The Church Fathers found everywhere vestiges and fragments of the Logos, which has appeared in its fullness in Jesus Christ. They speak of God's great pedagogy of salvation running through the whole history of mankind and of a *preparation for the gospel even among the pagans*. The Second Vatican Council took up these considerations to say explicitly, despite many narrower formulas of the past, that the *salvific will of God is universal* and does not exclude even atheists:

> Those who, through no fault of their own, do not know the Gospel of Christ or his Church, but who nevertheless seek God with a sincere heart, and, moved by grace, try in their actions to do his will as they know it through the dictates of their conscience—those too may achieve eternal salvation. Nor shall divine providence deny the assistance necessary for salvation to those who, without any fault of theirs, have not yet arrived at an explicit knowledge of God, and who, not without grace, strive to lead a good life. Whatever good or truth is found amongst them is considered by the Church to be a preparation for the Gospel and given by him who enlightens all men that they may at length have life (LG 16).

From the declarations of Holy Scripture and the Church's tradition of faith, we can draw the following conclusions:

1. Sin has tainted the world and man, tearing them within. It has upset them, but not destroyed them absolutely. Man lacks that communion with God to which he most deeply tends, but he remains, *even in the state of sin, the likeness of God*. Even in his deepest degradation, he preserves his dignity as a man. Every purely pessimistic or even dualistic world view must be ruled out by these considerations.

2. In the natural order, *God's salvific will in Jesus Christ has effect from the very beginning*. God's willing is always effective; it accomplishes what it wills. For that reason, the universal salvific will of God takes its effect in a universal yearning for salvation and in a universal hope for salvation. These can be consciously expressed, as in the religions of mankind, or they can manifest themselves unconsciously, as in cultural and artistic configurations and social utopias, but especially in the seeking and searching for truth and in the striving for the good, and even in man's will to survive.

3. The fallen world is like a broken mirror (J. H. Cardinal Newman). It still reflects something of God's glory, but it also distorts the image of God to such an extent that it can assume demonic traits and instill anxiety

97–101;
111;
197–198

and horror in men instead of hope and trust. *The religions and human culture remain ambivalent.* So man, consciously or unconsciously, continues to search for an unambiguous and definitive sign of salvation, one capable of purifying the many other signs and of bringing them to fulfillment. The Christian is able to say, "What you are worshipping in ignorance I intend to make known to you" (Acts 17:23). In *Jesus Christ*, all these promises have been fulfilled; in him, the fullness of time has come (Gal 4:4).

PART TWO

JESUS CHRIST

I

JESUS CHRIST: OUR LORD AND GOD

1. The Confession and Its Claim

The confession "We believe in one Lord, Jesus Christ" is the *center of the Christian confession of faith*, even considered externally. It is the center that radiates out in all directions and gives all other declarations their proper place.

We can see this already in the *name "Jesus Christ"*. "Jesus" (in Hebrew, *jeshua, jehoshua*) was a very popular name with the Israelites; it meant "Yahweh is salvation". The Greek word "Christ" (the anointed one) translates the Hebrew term for Messiah (*mashiach*). Originally, the name Jesus Christ was itself a confession: Jesus is the Christ, the Messiah sent by God and anointed with the Holy Spirit. He is the fulfillment of the Old Testament hope; in him God has carried out his promise to send a savior for the world. "For there is no other name in the whole world given to men by which we are to be saved" (Acts 4:12).   173–174

With this message about Jesus Christ, a great *claim* is made. Paul knew well that the proclamation of Jesus Christ appears to many as foolishness and as a scandal (1 Cor 1:18–20). In a quite different way, the question must arise for us today: Is the claim at all tenable? Without a doubt, our perspective has expanded enormously since the time of the Bible. We are today better informed about the history of mankind before the coming of Jesus Christ. We know about the many religions and the high cultures of pre-Christian antiquity. We are familiar with cultures of vast regions of Asia, Africa, America, and Oceania that came into contact with Christianity only very late and are but slightly Christianized even today. In view of these incontestable facts, how can we say that salvation is in Jesus Christ alone? Is not such an absolute claim either presumption   217–219
or naïveté? Others ask us, in light of the modern evolutionary world view, how we can declare Jesus Christ the head and center of the cosmos.

These are very serious questions. But they cannot be solved by relativizing the claim that the confession of Christ makes on us. This much is already clear: absolutely everything in Christian faith stands or falls with the answer to this question: Who is Jesus Christ? The Christian believes in Jesus Christ, lives from him and for him. In imitation of Jesus and in friendship with him in thought, desire, and action, the Christian wholly accepts the God of Jesus Christ in the service of men. The Christian believes that in Jesus Christ the fullness of time has appeared; he considers the whole of reality as coming from him and as ordained to him. So Christianity is not primarily a sum of doctrines and commandments, of institutions and structures, though all these things are important in their places. Primarily, however, Christianity is Jesus Christ and communion with him. So the question returns more urgently: Who is Jesus Christ? What can we know of him? What does his unique and universal claim mean for our understanding of the world and its history?

2. The Earthly Jesus

2.1 What Can We Know of Jesus?

By far the most important source for the life, work, and way of Jesus is the New Testament. The four Gospels tell us of him in detail. The first three Gospels, those of Mark, Matthew, and Luke, are called the synoptic Gospels and belong together. The Gospel of John has a character of its own. We also know of other individual sayings of the Lord, which the New Testament has not passed on but which are preserved by early Church Fathers. The extra-biblical reports about Jesus (those of Flavius Josephus, Tacitus, Pliny the Younger, Suetonius, the Talmud) are late, meagre, and unhelpful. Still, no serious researcher disputes any longer that Jesus really lived in Palestine and that he died on a cross in Jerusalem around the year 30 A.D. under the Roman governor Pontius Pilate.

43–44   A difficult problem was raised by *modern historical* research into Jesus. To it, the biblical and ecclesiastical confession of Jesus, the Christ, our Lord, seemed to be a later retouching of the original, "historical" Jesus of Nazareth. This research thus set about freeing the image of Jesus from the "fetters of dogma" in order to re-emphasize the "simple Jesus of history". But what usually resulted from this was new images of Jesus after the mind of their creators. A given image of Jesus corresponds only too easily to the taste of a given time: Jesus as political Messiah, as moral teacher, as apostle of interiority, as friend of the poor, as hippie, as superstar. The rise of the later confession of Christ was explained either as an intentional deception by his disciples (Reimarus), as unintentionally poetizing saga and legend (Strauss), or, according to the schema of the history of religions, as derived from Old Testament and Jewish piety, from the contemporary Hellenistic environment, or from the prevailing social milieu. Between the "earthly Jesus" and the "Christ of faith" there arose a gulf that no longer seemed to be bridgeable.

At the beginning of our century, it was increasingly clear that an adequate reconstruction of the life of Jesus and an exact picture of his personality were impossible. The newly published or republished novelistic presentations of the life of Jesus, as well as the corresponding film adaptations, are historically worthless. *The Gospels are not historical reports in the modern sense of the word; they are witnesses to the faith of the first communities and of the evangelists.* They see the earthly work of Jesus in the light of deeper insights gained on Good Friday, Easter, and Pentecost. The so-called form-critical method has shown that the Gospels have their original setting in the early communities, in proclamation, catechesis, liturgy, apologetics, and church order. The so-called redaction-critical method has shown further that the four evangelists were not merely scribes of the communities, but that they edited according to their own literary and theological conceptions the oral and written traditions received by them. Historical representation and the witness of faith are most intimately linked in the Gospels. If one detaches Jesus from the primitive Church's perspective of faith, confession, and life, then everything dissolves into statements that are no more than highly probable. *We do not "have" Jesus at all except in the confession of the Church.*

38–41; 42–43; 211–212

Out of the wreckage of liberal research into the life of Jesus, Bultmann's school arose to make a new beginning. It was theologically uninterested in the life and personality of Jesus and wanted to found the faith exclusively on the proclamation (kerygma) of the Risen Christ believed to be present. For it, everything depended on the new self-understanding of man awakened by the *Christ-kerygma*. But this approach failed to recognize that *the Gospels bear witness to their kerygma by telling the story of Jesus and stories about Jesus.* If faith in Christ is detached from the story of Jesus, faith becomes a general world view or a myth that no longer confesses the concrete Jesus Christ as Lord. Even the primitive Church had to counter this tendency to devalue what was human in Jesus Christ: "Every spirit that acknowledges Jesus Christ come in the flesh belongs to God, while every spirit that fails to acknowledge him does not belong to God" (1 Jn 4:2–3). The task of the Holy Spirit is precisely to remind us of Jesus, his word, and his work (Jn 14:26; 16:13).

132–133

Such insights have led since the 1950s to further reconsideration and to a *new question about the historical Jesus*. It is more and more frequently admitted that *there is no basis for resignation and scepticism* with respect to the stability of historical knowledge. Suitable criteria can be developed for ascertaining the "very words, deeds, and intentions" of Jesus. Even if we cannot write a "life of Jesus" in the sense of a biography, or draw a personality sketch; even if there will always be differing historical opinions about details, the Jesus of history encounters us so freshly and unmistakably that today there is a broad consensus among scholars on the basic features of his proclamation and on his work. It has again become clear that the Gospels pass on the message and the work of Jesus dependably and faithfully. There is still no other way to a real understanding of Jesus than the way

172–173

the primitive Church itself traveled: *we look back from Easter at the historical Jesus, and we present his earthly appearance and ministry by looking forward to Easter, in the light of the Resurrection and exaltation.*

The Second Vatican Council has used and confirmed the most important results from the development of research about Jesus. It affirms three levels in the Gospels (DV 19):

1. *The earthly Jesus*: "Holy Mother Church has firmly and with absolute constancy maintained and continues to maintain that the four Gospels just named, whose historicity she unhesitatingly affirms, faithfully hand on what Jesus, the Son of God, while he lived among men, really did and taught for their eternal salvation, until the day when he was taken up" (cf. Acts 1:1–2).

2. *The Apostles and the apostolic Church*: "For, after the ascension of the Lord, the apostles handed on to their hearers what he had said and done, but with that fuller understanding which they, instructed by the glorious events of Christ and enlightened by the Spirit of truth, now enjoyed."

3. *The Evangelists*: "The sacred authors, in writing the four Gospels, selected certain of the many elements which had been handed on, either orally or already in written form; others they synthesized or explained with an eye to the situation of the churches, the while sustaining the form of preaching, but always in such a fashion that they have told us the honest truth about Jesus."

2.2 The Message of Jesus

56–58;
192–193;
348–352

At the center of Jesus' ministry there stands his *message about the coming of the Kingdom of God*. The evangelist Mark summarizes this good news in this way: "After John's arrest, Jesus appeared in Galilee proclaiming the good news of God: 'This is the time of fulfillment. The reign of God is at hand! Reform your lives and believe in the gospel!' " (Mk 1:14–15). With this message, Jesus proclaims the *fulfillment of the Old Testament's hope*. The very cry "The Lord is king" (Ps 93:1; 96:10; 97:1; 99:1; Is 52:7) announces the eschatological Kingdom of God through which the fullness of life is to be bestowed on Israel and on the peoples of the world. According to the messianic texts of the Old Testament, this divinely granted salvation is mediated through an eschatological, ideal king appointed by God. In the religious and political predicament of an epoch's end, the hope for the coming of the royal lordship of God becomes the central content of people's expectation; they long for the realization of the ideal of a just ruler, which was never fulfilled on earth (Dan 2:44; 7:27). In the mind of the peoples of the ancient Orient justice is not primarily impartial adjudication, but help and protection for the helpless, the weak, and the poor. So Jesus' message of the coming of the Kingdom of God must be understood in the context of *mankind's question and mankind's longing for peace, freedom, justice, and life.*

The decisive element in Jesus' message of the coming of God's lordship is that the fulfillment of this hope of mankind is not the deed and achievement of man, but *solely God's deed and God's gift*. The coming of the lordship of God means the coming of God himself. For Jesus, the Kingdom of God is not something of this world (political, social, cultural), not a future utopia, and not a program of reform. It contains a promise that can be fulfilled neither by technology, nor by the economy, nor by science. Behind this message there lies an understanding of existence that knows both that man is bound to this world and that the meaning of his existence is not exhausted in the world. Man finds his ultimate fulfillment only in communion with God, the original ground and goal of his life. Man cannot himself fulfill this hope. For that reason, we as men cannot "build" the Kingdom of God. Much less can we bring it about by force through moral, social, scientific, cultural, or political effort. We can only pray for its coming: "Thy kingdom come" (Mt 6:10). For Jesus, a hopeful prospect for the future is inseparably linked with the appeal to God. Hence this exhortation: "First the Kingdom of God!" (Mt 6:33). It is necessary to give God what is God's (Mk 12:17). In the final reign of God, "God will be all in all" (1 Cor 15:28).

116–117

The God whose sovereign coming Jesus proclaims is at the same time his Father and the Father of us all. Here too Jesus stands squarely in the Old Testament tradition (Hos 11:9; 14:5). But Jesus dares to address God in a way that the Old Testament would find unusually intimate; he calls him *Abba, Father*. He proclaims the God who is goodness, grace, and mercy. In God's name and place, he grants forgiveness to sinners (Mk 2:5; Lk 7:48). The New Testament summarizes the message of Jesus by saying only, "God is love" (1 Jn 4:8, 16b).

57–59;
66–67

For man, the message of the coming of the Kingdom of God is good news, a *message of salvation*. In his "inaugural sermon" in his home town, Nazareth, Jesus recalls the Old Testament expectation:

> "The spirit of the Lord is upon me;
>   therefore he has anointed me.
> He has sent me to bring glad tidings to the poor,
>   to proclaim liberty to captives,
> Recovery of sight to the blind
>   and release to prisoners,
> To announce a year of favor from the Lord" (Lk 4:18–19).

With the coming of the Kingdom of God, the lordship of the evil powers and dominations inimical to God, who once enslaved man, is now vanquished. The *kingdom of life, freedom, peace, and love* is now to dawn. As distinct from John the Baptist, Jesus sees the coming of God's lordship not primarily as judgment, but as mercy, joy, and grace. He compares the Kingdom of God to a wedding (Mt 22:1–14) or to a large and rich harvest (Mk 4:26–29; Mt 9:37–38). These are only images, but Scripture tells us that we cannot speak of the Kingdom of God except in images and parables.

328–329;
348–350

> We cannot simply "translate" them, we can really only protect them, remain true to them, and resist their dissolution in the language of our concepts and arguments, empty of mystery, which indeed responds to our needs and our plans but not to our longing or our hopes (*Gem. Synode, Unsere Hoffnung* I, 6).

This message may seem foreign to the oppressive reality of this world. Jesus promises the complete actuality of the Kingdom of God as occurring only in the future, but it is *already* beginning *now* in a hidden, unassuming, inconspicuous way. But it will gain ground in the world through the power of God. So Jesus describes the coming of the Kingdom of God in the parables of the sower, of the growth of the seed, of the mustard seed, and of the leaven, to name a few (Mk 4; Mt 13). The Kingdom of God is a reality even now wherever God's forgiving and reconciling love is found. For that reason, the evangelist Luke combines three parables about the loss of something in the middle of his Gospel: the lost sheep, the lost drachma, and the lost son (Lk 15). In the last parable, man's great fragility is described. He falls prey to the temptation of passing goods and thereby misses his true calling. He loses himself and remains lost when left to himself. But in this hour of the gospel, Jesus proclaims that God has mercy on the sinner and, full of love, draws him to himself. At the same time, Jesus defends this gospel against the hard-heartedness of men who see God's mercy but do not want to understand it. "But we had to celebrate and rejoice! This brother of yours was dead, and has come back to life. He was lost, and is found" (Lk 15:32). The gospel challenges everyone to reflect before God on himself and his relationship to other men. It is meant to give him courage and hope. Because God accepts every man, man may also accept himself and all others. Wherever such love is found, the lordship of God is already dawning in a hidden way.

349–351

The hope for the coming of the Kingdom of God is being fulfilled here today. Jesus expresses this especially when he ties *his message to his person*. With his coming, the Kingdom of God begins to spread. "Blest are the eyes that see what you see. I tell you, many prophets and kings wished to see what you see but did not see it, and to hear what you hear but did not hear it" (Lk 10:23–24). Jesus' consciousness of acting with God's authority shines through many of his words and is expressed in his deeds. To those who doubt his message, he says, "You have a greater than Solomon here. . . . You have a greater than Jonah here" (Lk 11:31–32). In his exorcisms, through which the power of the evil one is broken, the coming of God's lordship manifests itself (Lk 11:20). In his teaching also, which differs from that of the scribes, the people recognize a divine authority (Mk 1:22, 27).

95;
130–131;
269–270

Jesus' claim to authority also expresses itself in the mysterious use of the title the *Son of Man*. We encounter it often, and it impressed itself deeply upon the primitive Church. This title contained the hidden claim of Jesus to be savior and judge. The Son of Man has authority to forgive sins on earth (Mk 2:10); he is "lord even of the Sabbath" (Mk 2:27). Whoever confesses Jesus, "the Son of Man will acknowledge him before the angels of God"; whoever denies him before men "will be disowned in the presence of the angels of God" (Lk 12:8–9). This mysterious title "Son of Man" stems from Jewish expectations. Originally it referred to the majesty of the coming savior and judge, but Jesus applies it to his own abasement (Lk 7:34; 9:58), even to his suffering and death (Mk 8:31; 9:31; 10:33), and to his surrender to death "for the many" (Mk 10:45). But the Son of Man will also come one day "in the clouds with great power and glory" (Mk 13:26; 14:62; Dan 7:13); he will judge all the peoples (Mt 25:32). In Jesus' use of the title the Son of Man, the primitive Church recognized his hidden authority on earth, his way through the cross to the Resurrection as determined by God, and his future appearance in divine glory. This is also the way of the Kingdom of God: it grows from its hidden presence in the earthly work of Jesus, through the time in which men are tested, to its completion at the end of the world.

Where God's lordship, mercy, and love become manifest, man is called to do *God's will* entirely and in everything (Mt 7:21). Jesus announces the will of the Father "with authority". In spite of all the radicality of his message, this authority is characterized by a peculiar freedom in interpreting the law. Jesus traced individual regulations again and again back to God's original will. Man should not hide behind the correct fulfillment of the law; he should direct his gaze to the man who needs his help. After the beatitudes about the poor and the oppressed (Mt 5:3–12; Lk 6:20–26), there come warnings to the rich (Mt 6:24; Mk 10:23, 25; Lk 16:19–31) and accusations against the powerful who abuse their power (Mk 10:42). Jesus confronts the influential and ruling classes with this statement: "Tax collectors and prostitutes are entering the Kingdom of God before you" (Mt 21:31).

The *beatitudes* of the Sermon on the Mount are fundamental. Luke reports four beatitudes: "Blest are you poor", "Blest are you who hunger", "Blest are you who are weeping", and "Blest shall you be when men hate you . . . because of the Son of Man" (Lk 6:20–22). The reversal of every earthly standard of value is meant, especially with Luke, in an entirely realistic way. But there is no earthly upheaval, no social or political program. The beatitudes of the Sermon on the Mount can be understood only in the whole context of Jesus' proclamation of the approaching Kingdom of God. The Gospel of Matthew "spiritualized" and expanded the beatitudes in the spirit of Jesus' message. It speaks of those who are "poor before God", and it calls those blessed "who hunger and thirst for justice". It adds the beatitudes for the non-violent, the merciful, the pure of heart, and the peacemakers (Mt 5:5–10). Those who have nothing to expect from the world expect all from God; they accept the message of God's lordship and mercifulness in order to love and live from it. This poverty, already described in the Old Testament, and this service in the cause of peace in the spirit of the gospel, which are required here of the disciples of Jesus, are not some new law that can immediately be applied to the whole of society. The beatitudes of the Sermon on the Mount appeal rather to the heart of man to let itself be grasped by God's mercy and love. They set standards indirectly for behavior in this world. Their concrete application in the realm of society and of politics is not possible, of course, without human skill.

Jesus summarizes his moral requirement in the *double commandment of love of God and love of neighbor*. He thus ties together two individual commandments of the Old Testament (Dt 6:5; Lev 19:18, 34).

> " 'Therefore you shall love the Lord your God
>   with all your heart,
>   with all your soul,
>   with all your mind,
>   and with all your strength.'
>
> This is the second,
>
> 'You shall love your neighbor as yourself' " (Mk 12:30–31).

These and other teachings, which directly urge a change of human conduct and indirectly one of social relations, have greatest weight in the *requirement to love one's enemies* (Lk 6:27–36). They have their deepest foundation in the words "Be compassionate as your Father is compassionate" (Luke 6:36). The dawn of God's lordship and love explains Jesus' radical requirements, since the Kingdom of God obligates one to the Father's love for one's fellow men. With this moral message, Jesus gave no immediate instructions for action but set standards that gave obvious pointers for the encounter with men and the co-existence of peoples. "For the promises of the Kingdom of God are not indifferent to the horror and the terror of earthly injustice and subjugation, which destroy the countenance of man." The hope for the Kingdom of God does not make us indifferent to questions of peace, of justice, and of freedom in the world; it makes us more sensitive to all of these.

Jesus does not require anything that he himself has not first lived. He travels the way first. His own behavior is characterized by love, mercy, faithfulness, peacefulness, and willingness to forgive. He "has not come to be served but to serve" (Mk 10:45). Thus, the message of Jesus *calls us to imitation*.

> "Follow me" (Mk 1:17).

> "If a man wishes to come after me, he must deny his very self, take up his cross, and follow in my steps. Whoever would preserve his life will lose it, but whoever loses his life for my sake and the gospel's will preserve it" (Mk 8:34–35).

This call, with all that it comprises and means, with all that it requires and promises, is most characteristic of what has been handed down to us by the earthly Jesus. This call went forth at first to those who were also to be his companions and messengers during his earthly work. The primitive Church after Easter passed on this call to all those who believe in Jesus Christ. All are to become disciples of Jesus and to follow him according to their talents and calling, according to their abilities and possibilities, but each one with the same resolution and radicality. When the words of Jesus are applied to the life of later believers and congregations by the primitive Church, this is not a falsification of Jesus' intention. It is a living reception of his unfading voice.

2.3 The Life and the Deeds of Jesus

Jesus worked not only through words, but also through his life, which provoked sensation, amazement, and contradiction. Among the most original parts of the Jesus-tradition are stories of his fellowship at table 153–154 with tax collectors, of his forgiving words for prostitutes and other public sinners (Mk 2:13–17; Mt 11:19), of his violation of Sabbath and purification regulations (Mk 2:23–3:6; 7:1–23), and of the cleansing of the temple (Mk 11:15–19). As with the appointing of the Twelve (Mk 6:7–13), we 238–239; have here a question of *symbolic actions* that render Jesus' message and 311–312 intentions clear, even as they disclose his personal manner. This way of acquainting men with the meaning and requirements of the lordship of God through gestures and signs, which are then interpreted through words, reminds us of the Old Testament prophets and their symbolic

100–102;
282–283 actions. We are to understand the celebration of the Last Supper in the same way, the supper that Jesus held with his disciples before his death to announce the "New Covenant" of God (Mk 14:17–25). *The whole life and work of Jesus makes manifest the hidden reality of God, his powerful, saving presence, and his call to men.* For that reason, Jesus can say in the Fourth Gospel, "Whoever has seen me has seen the Father" (Jn 14:9).

The *extraordinary deeds* of Jesus that we call *miracles* are particularly important here. In them, something of the promise of the prophets is fulfilled: "The blind recover their sight, cripples walk, lepers are cured, the deaf hear, dead men are raised to life, and the poor have the good news preached to them" (Lk 7:22; Is 35:5–6).

79–81 These miracle accounts in the Gospels cause many problems for us today. Our ordinary concept of miracle, which is influenced by *modern science* and which questions the possibility of a breach of the laws of nature, is foreign to the Bible. For the Bible, it is a question of faith in God, the Creator of the world and Lord of history, who is "wonder-ful" in all his works, but who can also reveal his power in extraordinary deeds. The Bible gives no thought to "how" such things happen, especially not to their relation to the natural causes and forces that God can use. So the presentation of miracles seems to us unreflective and naïve. In addition, there 43–45;
122 are *historical problems*. The biblical miracle accounts are constructed according to determinate narrative patterns common at that time. Several superimposed layers make understanding miracles more difficult for us: we encounter a thinking that has become foreign to us, that has a different relation to nature and a different conception of "historical" reports; we meet a different mode of presentation that prefers the stereotypical over the concrete elements of events.

In spite of these difficulties, even strict *historical criticism* cannot doubt that extraordinary, inexplicable events, especially healings, occurred through Jesus. The healing reports frequently contain exact information about the persons involved, with names and circumstances. The throng of people, the spreading reputation of Jesus, the helplessness of his opponents who could not deny his deeds, the tradition of miracle accounts beginning shortly after Easter, at a time when the witnesses to the appearance of Jesus still lived—all of this cannot be understood in any other way. *Modern natural science* deliberately limits itself in its consideration of reality to immanent factors; it deliberately abstracts from the question of God. That is thoroughly justified in terms of the methodological presuppositions of the natural sciences. But the consideration of the world from the point of view of the laws of nature is but one of the ways to understand reality. Faith cannot accept any absolute version of this mode of consideration. Faith in the living God, the Creator of heaven and earth, would lose its content if it no longer reckoned with the possibility and reality of God's working in an extraordinary way in time and history. Faith without that possibility would be a contradiction in terms.

The wondrous deeds of Jesus were not spectacular events; Jesus always refused "signs from heaven" (Mk 8:11–13; Lk 11:29; Jn 6:30). The miracles were intended to bring one to reflection and so to lead one to faith. On the other hand, only believing eyes and ears were able to grasp what was happening in the work of Jesus (Mt 11:4–6; Lk 10:23–24). His miracles remain deeds with a symbolic value, intended to make clear God's saving will and to be *portents of the dawning lordship of God*. "But if it is by the finger of God that I cast out devils, then the reign of God is upon you" (Lk 11:20; Mt 12:28). The raisings from the dead are intended to show most intensely the life-awakening power of God, which the men of that time already saw at work in the healings of the sick. The stilling of the storm on the Lake of Gennesaret (Mk 4:35–41) is a rescue miracle that illustrates the power of God's assistance present in Jesus. The great feeding of the multitude, which draws together various motifs, is at heart a miracle of generosity that presents us with God's rich goodness, the distribution of his gifts—given during Israel's wandering in the desert, now again through his Messiah—and the fellowship of Jesus with the disciples and the people (Mk 6:34–44; 8:1–10). It should become clear in the miracles that God is the victor over sickness and suffering, over death and evil. In all this, the *authority of Jesus* and his glory, which is still hidden in his earthly life, should also rise resplendent. The miracles show that in Jesus "the kindness and the love of God" has appeared (Tit 3:4).

95;
126–127;
269–270

307–309

3. Jesus Christ: The Son of God Become Man

3.1 Jesus Christ: Our Brother

The forceful, engaging, and in many respects strikingly new proclamation of Jesus, his sudden and remarkable appearance in history, above all his wondrous deeds—these led then and still today lead to the question: Who is Jesus? Many answers have been given: perhaps he is the resurrected John the Baptist, the returned Elijah, or one of the prophets (Mk 6:14–15; 8:28). Since then, the list of proposed answers has grown much longer. Of course, what matters is not what other people say about Jesus; Jesus asks his disciples and each one of us: "And you . . . who do you say that I am?" (Mk 8:29).

Surely, we must first say that *Jesus is a man*, truly human like us all. The Gospels describe him in his whole humanity: he is born from a human mother, grows and matures, learns a trade, asks questions, and feels compassion. He takes delight in other people, especially in children. He also becomes angry at men's hardheartedness, and he fears and suffers pain and finally dies on a cross. Jesus is a man with body and soul. He lived fully and suffered fully the heights and depths of being human. *He is our brother* (Jn 20:17; Rom 8:29; Heb 2:11). The Letter to the Hebrews summarizes the witness of the Gospels in this way: "For we do not have a high priest who is unable to sympathize with our weakness, but one who was tempted in every way that we are, yet never sinned" (Heb 4:15). So Jesus was a man like us in everything, with the single exception of sin. As distinguished from all other men, he did not stand under the law of sin. He was, rather, wholly open to the will of the Father and to the service of men. He says of himself that he "has not come to be served but to serve" (Mk 10:45). *He is the man for others* who in obedience to the Father gives his life at the end "for the many", i.e., for all (Mk 10:45). Jesus himself expresses this law of substitution, which determines his whole life and even more his death, at the Last Supper: My body for you—my blood for you (1 Cor 11:24–25; Lk 22:19–20). In this being-for-you, for-us, and for-all, Jesus is the appearance in human form of the kindness and the love of God (Tit 3:4).

154–157;
157–158
281–284

The *true humanity of Jesus* is just as important to the faith of the New Testament and of the Church as is the true divinity of Christ. In New Testament times, faith in Jesus as a kind of divine being would not necessarily have been anything at all special or extraordinary. But faith in the Son of God who died like a criminal on the cross was "a stumbling block to Jews and an absurdity to Gentiles" (1 Cor 1:23). For the First and Second Letters of John, the confession of "Jesus Christ as coming in the flesh" is the decisive test. Whoever does not confess this is the anti-Christ (2 Jn 7; 1 Jn 4:3). False doctrines soon appeared that affirmed that Jesus had only an apparent body and that he only apparently suffered. The martyr-bishop Ignatius of Antioch wrote against this view around the year 110 in his letter to the congregation of Smyrna. If Jesus only apparently lived and suffered, he argued, then we too are only apparently redeemed. Such a view, he showed, dissolves everything in Christianity into a pseudo-reality.

To say that Jesus, the Son of God, is at the same time truly and wholly a man is not only a factual truth, but also a *saving truth*. Only if God has bodily assumed our flesh and blood has he also redeemed us in our humanity. God has gathered together our whole being-human in Jesus Christ (Irenaeus of Lyons). There is no longer any human dimension after Jesus that would in principle be without God or distant from God. In Jesus Christ, God has accepted and sanctified everything human. Salvation and redemption are never only an interior salvation of the soul; they touch the whole man. The *humanity of salvation* also means that salvation is bestowed on us in Jesus Christ in a human way. The humanity of Jesus is not God's disguise or an inert instrument; even less is Jesus a kind of marionette controlled by God. Jesus accomplishes our salvation through his human obedience and service. Through his obedience he atones for the disobedience of Adam. Only if Jesus Christ is both true God and true man can he redeem us (Anselm of Canterbury).

3.2 Jesus Christ: Our Lord

In Jesus' humanity something more-than-human also becomes clear. As we have shown in detail, this is expressed above all in Jesus' unique, essential, intimate relationship with God, his Father. For that reason, Jesus claims with unprecedented authority to speak the word of God and to act in place of God. In the call to discipleship, he demands unconditional allegiance from his disciples. Through the Resurrection and the exaltation of Jesus, God confirms this claim and enthrones Jesus as Lord (*kyrios*).

174–179

The confession of Jesus Christ as Lord belongs to the *oldest core of the biblical tradition and of the formation of the Christian confession*. As the Christ hymn in the Letter to the Philippians shows, Paul already found this confession in the Christian communities when he converted to Christ. There we read, "Jesus Christ is Lord" (Phil 2:11; cf. 1 Cor 12:3). In the Letter to the Romans, Paul cites a similar confession known to the early Christian congregations: "For if you confess with your lips that Jesus is Lord, and believe in your heart that God raised him from the dead, you will be saved" (Rom 10:9). This confession seems to be a liturgical formula. In the oldest Palestinian congregational liturgy, Christians gathered for the eucharistic celebration cry out, "Maranatha" (1 Cor 16:22; cf. Rev 22:20; Did 10:6). This cry can be translated as "Our Lord has come" or "Our Lord, come!" This was probably its original meaning. Even today, the confession of "our Lord Jesus Christ" plays a central role in the liturgy. We need think only of the cry "*Kyrie eleison*", "Lord, have mercy." All liturgical prayers close with the formula "through Christ, our Lord". The New Testament calls the Eucharist as a whole the "Lord's Supper" (1 Cor 11:20); the day on which we gather for it, the "Lord's day" (Rev 1:10).

281–283;
284–285;
343

With the confession "I believe in one Lord, Jesus Christ" we stand at the beginning of our Christian faith and at its innermost center. So the question becomes more urgent: *What does this confession mean?* How are we to understand it today?

In non-theological English, the word "Lord" survives only as a title for the nobility. It is a faint echo of the time when the lords were the freemen, the nobles, the superiors, the authorities, who distinguished themselves from the slaves and serfs as well as from the common man and the ordinary people. We find such domination distasteful, given our modern democratic sensibilities. Even if there still are various inequalities in social life, everyone is equal in principle before the law. Christianity too speaks of the brotherhood of all men. These few observations show that the confession of Jesus Christ as Lord represents anything but vacuous, flowery language. This is a claim that demands a response. The confession of Jesus Christ as Lord calls into question the *standard and orientation of our lives*.

In the Old Testament, "Lord" is a title of dignity that belongs to God alone. In the New Testament, "Lord" translates the Old Testament name of God, *Yahweh*. When the early Church claims this title for Jesus Christ, it means to say that the lordship of God is dawning in Jesus. In him God

65–70   himself appears on the scene; indeed, Jesus is himself of *divine nature*. To confess that Jesus Christ is Lord means that he is the fulfillment of the Old Testament hope. In him the ground and goal of all reality has become tangible in space and time. Time, which is without rest and repose, which

104–105;   passes away again and again, has reached its fullness. That *toward which*
136–138   *man tends, and with him the whole world, has appeared*: God himself and communion with him. Whoever wishes to know who God is and what man is must look to Jesus Christ and take his bearings from him. He must confess him as his Lord. He must follow after him in order to attain life and salvation.

In antiquity, "Lord" was also the title and mark of honor accorded the Roman emperor as ruler of the world. The title asserted that the emperor was divine, that he ruled over men and peoples in order to guarantee life, order, and peace. When early Christianity claimed this title for Jesus Christ, it said that it is not the emperor but Jesus Christ who guarantees life, order, and peace. Jesus is the true ruler of the world. Because of this belief, the first Christians came into conflict with the Roman state and its cult of the emperor. The persecutions of Christians during the first centuries, with their many martyrs, made clear the seriousness of the confession of Jesus Christ as Lord. Today this confession has a crucial and liberating meaning in regard to all who pose as saviors and benefactors of mankind, and who claim the requisite power and prestige. The confession

159–160;   of the one Lord *grounds Christian freedom* from the many false lords. It is not
201–202;   only a claim, then, but a consolation, a message of salvation.
209–210

3.3 Jesus Christ: The Son of God in the Flesh

The confession of Jesus Christ, our Lord, leads to the most important
65–70;   confessional formula: Jesus Christ is the Son of God. We have already
173–174   spoken of this in some detail. We must now speak about how Jesus, the

eternal Son of God, became man in time. This confession can be found in the oldest texts of the New Testament, such as in the Christ hymn of the Letter to the Philippians:

> Though he was in the form of God,
>   he did not deem equality with God
>   something to be grasped at.
> Rather he emptied himself
>   and took the form of a slave,
>   being born in the likeness of men.
> He was known to be of human estate,
>   and it was thus that he humbled himself,
>   obediently accepting even death,
>   death on a cross (Phil 2:6–8).

The Gospel of John says the same in its prologue:

> The Word became flesh
>   and made his dwelling among us,
>   and we have seen his glory:
> The glory of an only Son coming from the Father,
>   filled with enduring love (Jn 1:14).

The Church's confession of faith summarizes the witness of Holy Scripture in these words: "For us men and for our salvation he came down from heaven . . . and became man." The declarations of Holy Scripture and of the Church's confession of faith were elaborated by the Church's doctrinal tradition into the teaching of *Jesus Christ as true God and true man*. This fundamental truth of our salvation was formulated summarily by the fourth general council, the *Council of Chalcedon* (451). The Council of Ephesus had earlier taught the unity of divinity and humanity in Jesus Christ against the false doctrine of the Nestorians. The new clarification had become necessary because the monk Eutyches and his adherents understood the unity one-sidedly and falsely; they thus denied the permanent distinction of the two natures. They claimed that the humanity of Jesus was absorbed into his divinity like a drop of honey in the sea. They therefore spoke of only one nature in Jesus Christ. Pope Leo the Great especially objected to this view. When his letter to the Patriarch Flavian of Constantinople was read out at the Council of Chalcedon, the Council Fathers cried: "That is the faith of the fathers, that is the faith of the apostles! . . . Peter has spoken through Leo." The Council itself formulated the faith in Jesus Christ in this way:

143

> One and the same is perfect in divinity and perfect in humanity, true God and true man . . . consubstantial with us according to his humanity. . . . We confess one and the same Christ . . . in two

natures without confusion or alteration, without division or separation
(DS 301–302; NR 178).

The fifth general council, the Second Council of Constantinople (553),
finally arrived at the formula of *one divine person in two natures* (DS 424–425;
NR 183–184). The Third Council of Constantinople (680–681) made clear
that this unity of God and man in Jesus Christ takes nothing away from
Jesus' being human. It does not impair it, diminish it, or curtail it. Taking
up human willing into the will of God does not eliminate human freedom,
but unbinds it and completes it (DS 556; NR 220). St. Maximus the
Confessor, the most important theologian of the seventh century, whose
tongue and hand were amputated for his courageous confession of the true
faith, best grasped the deep meaning of this doctrine. He taught that the
greater the unity of God and man, the more the distinction of both is
protected.

These are not purely theoretical formulas; they have a deep meaning for
our salvation. They hold fast to the saying that God's Son became man
"for us men and for our salvation". They declare that unity with God,
including the highest possible and fully unique unity in Jesus Christ, takes
nothing away from man. It cannot oppress or do violence to anything
human; rather, it sets it free, "without confusion or alteration". At the
same time, salvation means the most intimate communion of God and
157–158 man—a mutual penetration, a *"wonderful exchange"*. God becomes man
that we may partake of the divine nature. "Therefore, the Redeemer
became the Son of Man so that we might become sons of God" (Leo the
Great). For that reason, we pray in the Eucharist, at the preparation of the
gifts, "By the mystery of this water and wine may we come to share in the
divinity of Christ, who humbled himself to share in our humanity." A
new beginning for all men is made in Jesus Christ. What happened in his
Incarnation in a unique way is to become the lot of all men. We are to
attain the fulfillment of our being human through communion with God.

The fundamental dogma of the Council of Chalcedon was further developed in the
period following. From the truth of the true human nature of Jesus Christ it was
deduced that Jesus Christ possesses as true man a *true human spiritual soul* and a *true
human will*, which is wholly subordinated to the divinity in free obedience. This
was solemnly declared by the sixth general council at Constantinople (680–681)
against the false doctrine of one will in Jesus Christ (monotheletism; DS 556; NR
220). The human freedom of Jesus there proclaimed is the foundation and
presupposition of his obedience, through which he has redeemed us. This dogma
shows once again the humanity of God's salvation through Jesus Christ.

Just as truly human freedom of will belongs to Jesus Christ, so does truly human
knowledge. Holy Scripture tells us that his wisdom increased (Lk 2:52) and that he

learned obedience through suffering (Heb 5:8). So Jesus possessed a *human experiential knowledge* and a *human self-awareness*. According to the witness of Holy Scripture, of course, Jesus knew himself to be wholly one with God, his Father. This unique connection of knowledge and certainty is what is meant by the doctrine of *Jesus' immediate vision of God* already during his earthly life (DS 3812; NR 245). This doctrine must be understood in such a way that it does not suppress, cover over, or make unreal Jesus' normal experiential knowledge or indeed his experience of suffering, his struggle with the will of the Father (Mk 14:33–36), and his cry "My God, my God, why have you forsaken me?" (Mk 15:34). On the contrary, Jesus' fundamental and steadfast certainty of God has proved itself again and again precisely in such human experiences. Only in this way is Jesus the one who "inspires and perfects our faith" (Heb 12:2). Only in this way can the fullness of time dawn in the midst of history.

3.4 Jesus Christ: The Fullness of Time

82;
104–105
134–135

The confession and even the name of Jesus Christ claim that in Jesus Christ the messianic time, the fulfillment of history promised by God, has dawned. The Apostle Paul elaborates on this confession: "But when the designated time had come, God sent forth his Son born of a woman, born under the law, to deliver from the law those who were subjected to it, so that we might receive our status as adopted sons" (Gal 4:4–5). In Jesus Christ, then, that for which mankind has always longed, that for which every individual man consciously or unconsciously hopes, has become reality in a unique way surpassing all expectation. The heart of man is so wide that only God is great enough to fill it. This has happened once for all through the Incarnation of the Son of God in Jesus Christ. In Jesus Christ the whole fullness of God has appeared (Col 1:19) in order to fulfill and to unite everything (Eph 1:10).

The New Testament uses various images and ideas to proclaim that Jesus Christ is the fullness of time. In him the *life* and the *light*, which always shone in the world, have become fully radiant (Jn 1:4, 9). In Jesus, the manifold *wisdom* and the eternal *mystery* of God have appeared (Eph 3:9–10), so that in him "every treasure of wisdom and knowledge is hidden" (Col 2:3). In him, God has brought everything together in the fullness of time and united everything in heaven and on earth (Eph 1:10). Indeed, the New Testament goes even a step further to say that *everything has been created in Jesus and ordained to him* (1 Cor 8:6; Heb 1:2; Jn 1:3). He is the first and the last (Rev 1:17; 22:13).

> He is the image of the invisible God, the first-born of all creatures. In
> him everything in heaven and on earth was created, things visible and

invisible, whether thrones or dominations, principalities or powers;
all were created through him, and for him. He is before all else that is.
In him everything continues in being (Col 1:15–17).

The early Church Fathers often discovered in all reality—in nature as in
culture, in religions as in philosophies—vestiges, seeds, and fragments of
the divine *Logos* (reason, spirit, wisdom). This *Logos* has come in its entire
fullness in Jesus Christ. Jesus Christ is thus the *head and recapitulation of all
reality* (Irenaeus of Lyons). The Second Vatican Council says that Jesus
Christ is "the key, the center, and the purpose of the whole of man's
history" (GS 10). Elsewhere the Council says: "The Lord is the goal of
human history, the focal point of the desires of history and civilization,
the center of mankind, the joy of all hearts, and the fulfillment of all
aspirations" (GS 45). In him, there stands illumined the "mystery of man"
(GS 22).

These are not abstract speculations or empty phrases. Such declarations
have *concrete consequences*. Paul expresses them thus: "All these are yours,
and you are Christ's, and Christ is God's" (1 Cor 3:22–23). Because
everything has its permanence in Jesus Christ, all reality belongs to the
Christian. Nothing is "taboo" for him; he may make use of everything
and take delight in everything. Because he has only one Lord, he is free in
relation to all others (1 Cor 8:6). He must use this Christian freedom, of
course, as does Jesus Christ, who lives wholly from God, his Father, and
for him, who wills nothing for himself but all for others. Jesus Christ
becomes for Christians the key to understanding the world and to living
in it. In Jesus Christ, the Christian may be and should be wholly open to
the world, but not in order to conform himself to the world (Rom 12:2).
The Christian wants, rather, to ordain all to Jesus Christ and to fill all with
the Spirit of Jesus. No violence is done to anyone or anything. On the
contrary, in Jesus Christ the deepest meaning of all reality is made clear.
Without Jesus Christ, no one can fully understand either man or the
world. Human work also receives its ultimate meaning through the
relation of all reality to Jesus Christ. Our work participates in the work of
the Creator but also has importance for the Kingdom of God (GS 39).

In order to realize the universal salvation of the world and to bring
everything to fulfillment in Jesus Christ, God needs men who will place
themselves wholly in the service of this task. We see the relation of this
human mediation to the Incarnation of God especially in Mary, the
Mother of the Lord.

II

BORN OF THE VIRGIN MARY

1. Mary Belongs in the Gospel

The gospel bears witness for us to Mary as the mother of Jesus. She was chosen by God as the mother of his Son. For that reason, the Church confesses her as Mother of God and as our mother. Today many Christians have great *difficulties* with the confession that Jesus was "born of the Virgin Mary". The difficulties are not only related to the obscurely intelligible or even unintelligible fact of virgin birth. They concern more fundamentally the fact that Mary appears in the Creed at all. Evangelical Christians worry that Marian devotion could obscure faith in Jesus Christ, the mediator between God and man. It is indisputable that there have been and still are excesses of Marian piety. But there are also opposite scruples and qualifications that would overlook Mary's place in the Creed of the Church, where she belongs precisely because she belongs in the gospel, as Holy Scripture shows. We must proceed from this biblical image of Mary. Genuine Marian piety must always be inspired by Scripture and be critically measured by it.

Holy Scripture mentions Mary in the first instance because she is the human mother of Jesus. In Hebrew she is named *Miriam*. She is one of the common people, one who hopes with her people for the advent of the redeemer from the house of David. In the hour of fulfillment, she speaks the "Yes" of faith and voluntarily places herself in the service of salvation and of her people's hope (Lk 1:38). But the New Testament witness to Mary does not limit itself to the childhood stories in Matthew and Luke. Mary meets us again during the earthly life of Jesus (Mk 3:20–21; Lk 11:27–28; Jn 2:1–12). Here she is the seeker and questioner who is not spared grave disappointments. She too stands on the way of the cross. But Mary persists with her original "Yes" of faith to the very end, and so stands at the foot of the cross with the disciple whom Jesus loved (Jn 19:25–27). For this reason, she is honored as the Mother of Sorrows. Finally, we encounter Mary once again in the midst of the earliest community at Jerusalem, with whom she prays for the coming of the Holy Spirit (Acts 1:14).

We can understand the place of Mary in the New Testament only if we

139

115;
151–152

see that Mary belongs to the long *history of great women in the Old Testament*. At the very beginning stands Eve. Created according to God's image and likeness, she is of equal rank with the man and is commissioned with him to represent God's lordship in creation. But instead of being Adam's helper, she becomes a co-temptress for him. Even so, she is promised that she will be the mother of all the living (Gen 3:20). That promise continues. Because of it, a son, Isaac, is bestowed on Sarah even in her advanced age (Gen 18:10–14). Something similar happens at the births of Samson (Jg 13) and of Samuel by Hannah (1 Sam 1). In all these stories, God bestows new life against every human expectation and hope in order to fulfill his promise. God chooses the weak and the powerless in order to put the strong to shame (1 Cor 1:27). In difficult moments for the people of Israel, he calls women to be their rescuers: Deborah, Judith, and Esther.

Mary has a unique place in the history of this promise. She stands at the moment of its final fulfillment. Her place is in the fullness of time when God sends his Son, "born of a woman" (Gal 4:4). Mary responds to her task with the "Yes" of faith (Lk 1:38). Thus she is the true daughter of Abraham: "Blest is she who believed" (Lk 1:45). She is addressed at the annunciation of the birth of Jesus by the same words that the Old Testament uses to address Israel, the daughter of Zion: "Hail!" (1:28). "Shout for joy, O daughter Zion! sing joyfully, O Israel! Be glad and exult with all your heart, O daughter Jerusalem!" (Zeph 3:14; Jl 2:23; Zech 9:9). Mary is thus the daughter of Zion, the *representative of Israel in the hour of the fulfillment of its hope*.

Mary herself summarizes the *New Testament fulfillment* of the Old Testament promise in her song of praise, which we call the Magnificat after its first word in Latin (Lk 1:46–55). It is full of allusions to texts of the Old Testament and especially to Hannah's song of thanks after the birth of Samuel (1 Sam 2:1–10). By this song, Mary proves to be the prophetess who stands beside, indeed above, the great women and men in the history of her people. With them, Mary knows that honor and glory, praise and thanks, are due to God alone. For that reason, she proclaims the reevaluation of all earthly values. "He has deposed the mighty from their thrones and raised the lowly to high places. The hungry he has given every good thing, while the rich he has sent empty away" (Lk 1:52–53). With this song of praise, which throughout shows the imprint of the spirit of the Old Testament, Mary anticipates at the same time the gospel of the New Testament. We hear in it the beatitudes of the Sermon on the Mount for the poor, the weak, the mourning, and the persecuted. *With her whole existence she bears witness to the gospel of Jesus Christ*: the first will be last and the last will be first (Mk 10:31). That is why the Magnificat has become a part, even the high point, of the solemn daily divine office of the Church at vespers. Mary becomes the representative of the song of praise that the Church owes to God because of his great deeds in history.

Mary is *the great archetype and pattern of the Christian faith*. She is the archetype of Advent hope, of total surrender in faith, and of service in the spirit of love. She is the pattern of man listening to God's word and praying to God. She preserves and ponders in her heart what she has seen and heard from God (Lk 2:19, 51). In her faith, Mary remains the questioner and the seeker. She is the afflicted one, the Mother of Sorrows, who unites herself at the foot of the cross with the sacrifice of her Son. Not least is she the poor, humble handmaid of the Lord.

Both Catholic and Evangelical Christians can say all this of Mary. The German Evangelical Adult Catechism writes under the heading "Mary Belongs in the Gospel" the following: "Mary is not only 'Catholic'; she is also 'Evangelical'. Protestants can tend to forget that. But Mary clearly is the mother of Jesus and closer to him than his closest disciples. With what humanity the New Testament depicts this closeness, without concealing Mary's distance from Jesus! An example of this distance can be seen in Luke, who tells so much of Mary. A woman from the crowd says to Jesus: 'Blest is the womb that bore you and the breasts that nursed you!' Jesus replies: 'Blest are they who hear the word of God and keep it' (11:27–28). But does that not apply precisely to Mary? She is depicted as the exemplary hearer of God's word, as the handmaid of the Lord who says 'Yes' to the will of God, as the blessed one who is nothing of herself but gains everything through God's goodness. Mary is the pattern for men who let themselves be opened and gifted by God, of the community of believers, of the Church" (pp. 392–393).

The Catholic Church sees in these common declarations about Mary a solid biblical foundation for her Marian devotion and for her dogmatic declarations about Mary. We are not concerned here with the wild proliferations and isolated further developments of what might seem a modest biblical point of departure. If one considers the New Testament declarations within the whole of the history of salvation, it becomes clear why the Tradition of the Church has designated *Mary as a type of, that is, a pattern for, the Church* (LG 53, 63).

Through her faith and her relation to Jesus Christ, Mary is a vivid image of the person redeemed by him. She embodies in a unique way what the Church and Christ mean. But Mary is not only a radiant archetype of the Church; she is also the Church's pattern. She precedes the Church and first makes the Church possible. Through her "Yes", which as representative she speaks for all, she becomes God's entrance into the world. So the Church Fathers call Mary the *new Eve*, who "through her obedience became the cause of salvation for herself and the whole human race." "Thus was the knot of Eve's disobedience untied through the obedience of Mary" (Irenaeus of Lyons).

These declarations do not deny at all that Jesus Christ alone is the salvation of all men. Mary is only the humble handmaid. She is redeemed by Jesus Christ as we all are. But God wills to include the free "Yes" of his creature in the act of redemption. Mary's *fiat*, her "Yes", her saying, "I am the servant of the Lord. Let it be done to me according to your word" (Lk 1:38), expresses the fundamental fact that God wills to form a covenant with men, to enter into dialogue with them, and to bestow his communion and friendship on them. *Mary's acceptance of the salvation rendered possible by God's grace is an essential element in the event of salvation.* Mary and her "Yes" belong essentially to the completion of salvation history. Without Mary, the full content of the meaning of faith in Christ cannot be safeguarded. Were Mary to be stricken from the gospel, the human element would become a mere disguise for God's speaking and acting in history. In Mary, on the other hand, the creature's dignity before God is assured.

The Second Vatican Council, then, says rightly that, "having entered deeply into the history of salvation, Mary, in a way, unites in her person and re-echoes the most important doctrines of the faith" (LG 65). In Mary we see who Jesus Christ is and what he means to us as salvation and hope. That is Mary's greatness and her humility.

2. Mary, the Mother of the Lord

2.1 Mary, the Mother of God

We learn from the New Testament in many places that Mary is the *mother of Jesus* (Mt 1:18; 2:11, 13, 20; 12:46; 13:55; Jn 2:1; Acts 1:14). The Christmas story tells very vividly how Mary carried Jesus nine months just like every other mother and bore him when her time had come (Lk 2:5–7).

More is intended here than physical motherhood and a purely private relationship between Jesus and Mary. She is not the mother of the Lord only bodily; her faith is an essential part of her motherhood. Before she conceived Jesus bodily, she had received and conceived him in faith. Of Mary we say not only, "Blest is the womb that bore you and the breasts that nursed you", but even more, "Blest are they who hear the word of

God and keep it" (Lk 11:27–28; 8:21). Elizabeth already praises Mary's belief: "Blest is she who believed" (Lk 1:45). Through her "Yes", Mary the mother of Jesus becomes at the same time a figure of salvation history. So it is that Luke gives her the title *Mother of the Lord* (Lk 1:43).

Luke's story of the annunciation tells us even more exactly what Mary's being a mother means: she is not only mother of Jesus and mother of the Lord, but also mother of the Son of God. "The Holy Spirit will come upon you and the power of the Most High will overshadow you; hence, the holy offspring to be born will be called Son of God" (Lk 1:35; Gal 4:4). This declaration recalls the Old Testament narrative according to which the glory of God went in front of Israel in the form of a column of cloud (Ex 13:21), or even took up its dwelling in the midst of Israel in the sacred tent of meeting (Ex 40:34). The cloud symbolizes God's powerful presence in the midst of his people. If, according to the New Testament, Mary is overshadowed by the Spirit of God, then she is the new dwelling of God, the new tent of the covenant, in which God's Word has made its dwelling among us (Jn 1:14).

On the basis of such biblical declarations, the Church taught at the third general council, the *Council of Ephesus* (431), that *Mary is the Mother of God*. 135–136 This confession is held by all Christians. Even the Reformers of the sixteenth century hold fast to it. Of course, we ought not to misunderstand the expression "Mother of God". Mary did not give birth to God as God. To say that would be to depart from the gospel for a pure mythology that speaks of a feminine principle in the divinity or even of a quaternity instead of a trinity. Mary, as she is described by the Bible and believed by the Church, is and remains a creature! She did not give birth to God as God, but to Jesus Christ according to his humanity that is essentially united with his divinity. The confession of Mary's motherhood of God is ultimately a confession that Jesus Christ is true God and true man in one 135–137 person. When the Church honors Mary as the Mother of God, she wishes to glorify Jesus Christ, who is the mediator in his person between God and man.

2.2 Mary, Our Mother

We find the title "Mother of God" for the first time in a prayer already recorded around the year 300. We still say this prayer today in a somewhat expanded form:

> Remember, O most gracious Virgin Mary, that never was it known
> that anyone who fled to your protection, implored your help, or

sought your intercession, was left unaided. Inspired with this confidence we fly unto you, O Virgin of virgins, our Mother; to you we come, before you we stand, sinful and sorrowful. O Mother of the Word Incarnate, despise not our petitions, but in your mercy hear and answer them. Amen.

This prayer beautifully expresses how Mary the Mother of God is also our mother. As our mother, she has no other task than to lead us to Jesus Christ, her Son. As mother of Jesus Christ, Mary is the gate of salvation for all who belong to Jesus Christ. She is the mother of the members of the body of Christ whose head is Jesus Christ (LG 53). Thus Mary cares in her motherly love for the brothers and sisters of her Son who are still on their pilgrimage and hence exposed to dangers and afflictions. She is "invoked in the Church under the titles of Advocate, Helper, Benefactress, and Mediatrix" (LG 62).

We cannot imagine the Church's treasury of prayer without the *intercession*, the help, and the assistance of Mary. The closing of the "Hail Mary", the best-known of all prayers to Mary, makes this particularly clear. "Holy Mary, Mother of God, pray for us sinners now and at the hour of our death." What is self-evident in the Catholic tradition of prayer and song is contradicted by Reformed Christianity. Evangelical Christians can thoroughly honor Mary (and the saints in general) as models in faith; they refuse, though, to invoke Mary for her intercession and help (CA 21). According to the Catholic understanding, such an invocation is to be fundamentally *distinguished from adoration*, which is due to God alone and never to a creature, and so not to Mary either (LG 66). Nor does the invocation of Mary deny or obscure the truth of Jesus Christ as the sole mediator of salvation (1 Tim 2:5–6). St. Ambrose said that the intercession of Mary neither detracts from nor adds to the dignity and efficaciousness of the one mediator. Mary's intercession depends wholly on the act of redemption in Jesus Christ and draws from it all its force (LG 61–62). Her intercession ultimately results from the fact that all members of the body of Christ are in solidarity with one another. "If one member suffers, all the members suffer with it; if one member is honored, all the members share its joy" (1 Cor 12:26). According to the Catholic understanding, trust in the intercessory mediation of Mary expresses in a particular way the mystery of God's availing himself of some individuals in order to bestow salvation on others. Thus the human race as a whole is honored in Mary.

In order to express devotion to and trust in Mary, Catholic piety has used many titles for her. In addition to those already named, Mother, Advocate, Helper, and Mediatrix, there are many others, often effusive and hence easily misunderstood by non-Catholic Christians. Understood in context, these titles can have a thoroughly correct sense. This holds especially for the title "*Mediatrix of all*

Margin notes:
226–227
234–235; 253–254
253–255

Graces". This designation in no way excludes or even obscures the fact that Jesus Christ is the sole mediator. It means to express only that Mary, with her "Yes", has accepted on behalf of all the coming of this mediator of all graces, so that Jesus' mediation of salvation is permanently accompanied by her intercession. In order to say that Mary surpasses the other saints in fullness of grace, she is invoked and honored as the *Queen of Heaven*. The most popular form of this title occurs in the *Salve Regina*: "Hail, Holy Queen, Mother of Mercy" (eleventh century), or in the *Regina caeli*: "Queen of Heaven, rejoice!" (twelfth century). Finally, in order to express the unique position of Mary as pattern for the Church, we call her not only mother of Christians but *Mother of the Church*.

With these and many other forms of Marian devotion, we must attend to the exhortation that Pope Paul VI directed to the Church in his apostolic letter on Marian devotion (1974). The Pope asked for a *renewal of Marian devotion* that, bearing a biblical orientation and a trinitarian and christological imprint, would be considerate of those of a different faith, maintain the integrity of Catholic Tradition, and correspond to the forms of expression of the given time and culture. With the Second Vatican Council (LG 67), he explicitly warns against *false forms of Marian piety*. These transgress the limits of true doctrine, are credulously and curiously interested in the latest miracle reports, and exhaust themselves in external practices or indulge in superficial sentimentality. *The ultimate goal of all Marian devotion must be the glorification of God and the Christianization of life.* In this respect, Catholic Marian piety has borne rich fruit.

3. The Virgin Mary

3.1 Difficult Historical Facts

"Born of the Virgin Mary"—this sentence from the Creed has a *biblical foundation*. The two childhood stories in Matthew (1:18–25) and Luke (1:26–38) support it. According to the Lucan annunciation story, Mary asks the angel who announces the Incarnation of Emmanuel in her womb, "How will this be since I do not know man?" (Lk 1:34). What is meant is, "since I am a virgin and unmarried". The angel's answer explains the conception of Jesus Christ through Mary as the creative, wondrous deed of the Spirit of God: "For nothing is impossible with God" (Lk 1:37). Matthew's narrative is even clearer. In a dream an angel explains to Joseph, Mary's fiancé, how Mary will become a mother: "It is by the Holy Spirit that she has conceived this child" (Mt 1:20). Matthew recognizes in this the fulfillment of the Old Testament promise, which he cites according to the Greek translation: "The virgin shall be with child, and bear a son" (Is 7:14).

However unambiguously the confessional declaration of the virgin birth of Jesus may be substantiated in these two texts, it causes many *difficulties* today when we interpret the biblical texts with the help of the modern historical-critical method. There are at least three historical difficulties.

1. The texts in Matthew and Luke are not historical reports in our present sense of what is historical. Of course, they cannot be dismissed as unhistorical sagas or legends either. We must understand them as pious, edifying narratives (*Haggadah*) that retell Old Testament tradition in the light of the New Testament fulfillment. Event and theological interpretation, report and confession, are indissolubly woven together. Such narratives contain a historical core. Nevertheless, we ought not primarily to analyze them for historical facts, but listen to them for their declaration of faith. So the question is often posed: Is the motif of the virgin birth merely a means for expressing a declaration of faith, or does it itself belong to the declaration of faith?

2. Other strata and texts of the New Testament, especially the Pauline letters, do not, as distinguished from Matthew and Luke, mention the motif of the virgin birth. In the Gospels Jesus is occasionally even designated explicitly as the son of Joseph (Mt 13:55; Lk 4:22; Jn 1:45; 6:42). Elsewhere we read simply of the parents of Jesus (Lk 2:27, 41, 43, 48). So the virgin birth seems to be a particular and relatively late tradition. Then the question is posed: If all the traditions of the New Testament are not familiar with the virgin birth of Jesus, cannot faith in Christ today also manage without it?

3. The motif of the virgin birth in Matthew and Luke stands in a larger tradition. The Old Testament records a series of miraculous birth stories for great savior figures: from Jacob, Isaac, and Samuel all the way up to John the Baptist. This tradition is supposed to be taken up and at the same time surpassed by the motif of the virgin birth. Jesus is thereby supposed to be proclaimed as the surpassing fulfillment of the Old Testament. Many researchers even derive this motif from Hellenistic or Egyptian parallels. So the question arises: Is the motif of the virgin birth a more or less common literary symbol of the time that must be understood only as a form of expression for a theological teaching?

The *answers* to these questions we can only sketch here. It has already become clear that one cannot conclude from the literary form of the Haggadah to the fictional character of the story. The two New Testament texts remain open to a factual understanding, and there can be no doubt that they themselves meant their declarations literally. The argument that these texts in their present form belong only to a later level of Tradition has nothing to do with its objectivity. For the truth of a text does not depend on whether it is later or earlier. Moreover, as is clear from their strongly Semitic language, both texts contain much earlier traditions that go back to the Palestinian communities. Their credibility is further strengthened by the fact that Matthew and Luke bear witness to this earlier tradition independently of one another. Even the fact that Jesus is designated in many places of the New Testament as the son of Joseph is not a compelling objection. According to Jewish law, both one's own and one's adopted sons bore the name of the father.

There remains the argument from the history of religions. Derivations from the

Hellenistic or Egyptian realm do not withstand careful examination. There are related motifs but no real parallels; moreover, analogies are not genealogies. It is otherwise with the correspondences in the Old Testament. They are of fundamental importance for the two New Testament texts, always keeping in mind that the New Testament not only repeats the Old Testament but also surpasses it. This statement is important for the question whether Isaiah 7:14 in the original Hebrew text speaks of a virgin, as it does in the Greek translation and the interpretation of the Church Fathers, or of a young woman, i.e., a girl of marriageable age, as most exegetes today think. In either case, Isaiah bears witness to the miracle of a new beginning wrought by God, in which faith must place its trust. The New Testament sees this miracle in the virgin birth of Jesus.

Church dogma speaks not only of the virgin birth of Jesus. The fifth general 95–96 council at Constantinople (553) already expanded the confession to include the *dogma of the perpetual virginity of Mary*. This dogma declares that Mary remained a virgin not only *before* the birth of Jesus but also *during* and *after* it (DS 422, 427, 437; NR 181, 185, 192). Even Luther held fast to this doctrine (Smalcaldian Articles), though most Protestant interpreters of Scripture today do not. They refer to the statements of Scripture that speak of the brothers and sisters of Jesus (Mk 6:3; Mt 27:56; 1 Cor 9:5), as well as of James, the brother of the Lord (Gal 1:19). Catholic scholars reply that there are good grounds according to ancient linguistic usage for understanding by this phrase the close relatives of Jesus—male and female cousins, for instance.

It does not follow, of course, that the confessional declaration of the virgin birth of Jesus can be historically proved. On the other hand, the historical objections against it are not compelling either. We conclude that the New Testament texts, when considered purely historically, allow the interpretation of the Church Fathers, which has been recorded in the Creed. Ultimately, there remains *a mystery* about these texts *that is inaccessible to purely historical consideration*. It is disclosed to us for the first time when we read the texts in the light of the Church's Tradition as expressed in the Church's confession of faith. It is the Church's confession of faith that gives us clarity and certainty on these matters.

3.2 A Deep Theological Meaning

The New Testament bears witness to the virgin birth of Jesus as a miracle worked by God. The true question is thus whether one believes that God is really the almighty Father. If something like a virgin birth were excluded in principle, would we even ask about God and faith? The world would then be understood as a system hopelessly closed in on itself. The real objection raised today by many against the virgin birth is not historical, but scientific or philosophical. It springs from the world view accepted by many today. In this perspective, the virgin birth appears to be, if not impossible, at least extremely improbable. But this objection is found not only today but at the time of the Gospels too. Still, is the humanly improbable impossible for God? Or is it not true, rather, that nothing is impossible for him (Lk 1:37)?

129–131   This does not mean that the faith must accept all possible miracles and credulously believe every alleged miracle. God's wondrous deeds stand in the service of his coming lordship. The virgin birth is the absolutely unforeseeable miracle that has dawned with the coming of Jesus Christ. The virgin birth of Jesus is a *bodily sign of God's new beginning*. It is a sign of our powerlessness and inability to procure our own salvation. When men no longer knew any way out, God made a new beginning in a miraculous way through the power of his Spirit to create anew. Virginity is linked elsewhere in the New Testament to the coming of the Kingdom of God for just this reason (Mt 19:12; 1 Cor 7:7, 32–34).

Mary's virginity is also closely connected to her motherhood of God. If God has deliberately not used the normal means of human generation in the Incarnation of his Son, this is because the virgin birth corresponds symbolically to the Incarnation. For the virgin birth expresses with unsurpassable clarity that Jesus as Son of God depends on his Father in heaven alone; whatever he is comes from the Father and is ordained to the Father. The virgin birth is a *sign of the genuine divine sonship of Jesus*.

Faith's confession of the perpetual virginity of Mary, of her virginity not only before but also during and after the birth of Jesus, has a deep symbolic meaning. Unfortunately, the dogma of the *virginity during birth*, in connection with certain apocryphal writings, has often given rise to inappropriate considerations about the nature of Jesus' birth. By this arises a misunderstanding of the deep meaning of this declaration for salvation history. According to Genesis 3:16, the painful bearing of children is a sign of deep disturbance connected with life itself and is a consequence of original sin. Now that new life appears and redemption from original sin begins, life no longer comes into the world under the sign of death and its harbinger, pain. Creation, once torn, now becomes whole and intact again. It was not the physiological event of birth that was different; rather, the virgin birth was a sign of man's being saved and healed through a personal cooperation. So the tradition records Mary's joy at the birth of her Son. The ancient Marian song *Ave maris stella* (ninth century) calls her the "*felix caeli porta*", the "happy gate of heaven".

140–147   The *virginity of Mary after the birth* of Jesus means that Mary brought no more children into the world. Faith here confesses a final radiation of her "Yes" and of her unconditional availability to God and his will. Mary was wholly absorbed by her task within salvation history. The perpetual virginity of Mary is a sign of her holiness, of her being singled out for the service of God and his people. This truth of faith was historically of great importance for the ideal of the freely chosen unwedded state. The ideal does not devaluate marriage, but rather elevates it to an independent ministry in the Church and in society. The high esteem for virginity and the esteem for marriage as a sacrament, i.e., as a sign of salvation, are necessarily connected in the Catholic understanding.

4. Mary, the Blessed and Glorified One

Only with the theme of the blessing and glorification of Mary do we come to the *Catholic Marian dogmas in the strict sense*. These are the dogma of Mary as immaculately conceived (declared in 1854) and the dogma of Mary as assumed into heavenly glory (declared in 1950). In substance, these truths are also familiar to the Orthodox church, but there they belong more in the realm of liturgy and piety than of dogma. The Reformed churches, in contrast, can respect the piety out of which these dogmas have grown, but they can hardly join us in accepting their presuppositions. Both dogmas are only indirectly and implicitly contained in Scripture. They result from a faithful synthesis of the biblical witness of   42–45
Mary and her position in the history of salvation, but not from individual texts in the Bible. This interpretation is guaranteed for us by the Church's witness and practice of faith. The task of the Catholic Church's proclamation, doctrine, and instruction must be to teach us to understand these dogmas not as an isolated element or an external addition to the common faith, but as an objective expression of our common faith in Christ.

4.1 Mary as a Sign of Blessing

"Blessed" is a title granted to Mary already in the New Testament (Lk 1:28). She is "full of grace" because she found favor with God, in his unfathomable election, and because she wholly accepted God's call in faith. So Mary is first of all a pattern for each one of the elect, of the believers, and of those blessed. She tells us that God is found at every   188–191
man's beginning, that he has written every man in the palm of his hand from all eternity and has called him by name. God encompasses the life of each of us with unfathomable redemptive love. By calling us into existence, he calls us at the same time to communion with him.

Mary is, then, a sign that God and his grace precede our very being and   196–198
even more our every act. God anticipates us, so that we are nothing of ourselves, but everything from God and in him.

But Mary is more than a pattern for the election and blessing of every Christian. She is the blessed one in a unique sense that results from her

141–143   unique position in the history of salvation. In her, in the fullness of time, the election of Israel is concentrated. The promise given to Israel becomes reality when her "Yes" accepts on behalf of all mankind the "Yes" of God (Thomas Aquinas). "Let it be done to me according to your word" (Lk 1:38). This is not her own supreme moral and religious achievement; it is possible only as a response in faith sustained and made possible by the grace of God. Mary, who by her "Yes" made possible the coming of the fullness of grace, must herself be "full of grace".

Against this background, the *dogma* that Pope Pius IX proclaimed in 1854 becomes intelligible.

> The blessed Virgin Mary was preserved pure from every stain of original sin in the first instant of her conception through a singular gift of grace and privilege of almighty God with a view to the merits of Christ, the redeemer of the human race (DS 2803; NR 479).

This dogma of the "immaculate conception" of Mary provokes the apparently ineradicable misunderstanding that generation and conception are normally something tainted or tainting. Quite apart from the fact that such a misunderstanding contradicts the Church's doctrine of the goodness of creation, this doctrine implies nothing about the religious or moral state of Mary's parents at her conception; it speaks only about the immaculately conceived one herself. We are to believe that she was *free*

108–114   *from original sin from the first moment of her existence*. She was not conceived, like others, at a distance from God, but was wholly encompassed from the very beginning by God's love and grace. For that reason, she remained in her later life *wholly without personal sin*. She is, as the Orthodox church says, the "all-holy one"—holy from the very beginning and in all dimensions.

A long and difficult path led to this dogma. Great saints and theologians stood for and against it. Even a saint and fervent devoté of Mary such as Bernard of Clairvaux in the twelfth century opposed the introduction of the feast of the immaculate conception (December 8th). The basic question was how this truth of faith could be reconciled with the fact that Mary, like all of us, was redeemed through Jesus Christ in whom alone is salvation. The answer that the theologians of the Franciscan order, especially John Duns Scotus, finally gave and which later entered into the formulation of the dogma is this: The act of redemption takes effect with Mary in advance and has with her the form of preservation from sin. We can find such an anticipated effect already under the Old Covenant, but only as the shadow of which Mary is the reality. To the whole "Yes" of faith there comes in the fullness of time the fullness of the act of redemption. Mary is indeed a member of the human race in need of salvation. *She is the perfect, exemplary, pure case of redemption.* In her and in her alone, the Church is without stain or wrinkle (Eph 5:27), where it is otherwise only an eschatological hope. Mary, the all-holy, is a sign of the grace of election, call, and sanctification for us sinners. We may therefore pray, "Holy Mary, Mother of God, pray for us sinners . . ."

4.2 Mary as a Sign of Hope

The most recent Marian dogma concerns the *bodily assumption of Mary into heavenly glory.* There is no direct biblical witness for this dogma either. In the Tradition, this article of faith is attested to only from the sixth century on. It figures first in legendary reports which, although they possess no historical value, nonetheless express a conviction of faith. As the feast of "Mary's Going Home", known since the fifth century, and later called the "Assumption of Mary" (August 15), shows, the Church has affirmed this conviction of faith for many centuries. So the dogma does not express some new content, but a centuries-old tradition. It has its roots indirectly and implicitly in the total context of Holy Scripture. In the Gospel of Luke, we read of Mary, "Blest is she who believed"(Lk 1:45). Because she was the one wholly blessed and wholly believing, the promises of faith hold for her in a special way—and so with the resurrection to eternal life promised to the whole man, body and soul.

In this sense Pope Pius XII proclaimed the *dogma* in the year 1950: "It is a truth of faith revealed by God that the immaculate, ever virgin Mary, the Mother of God, was assumed body and soul into heavenly glory after the completion of her earthly life" (DS 3903; NR 487).

In this truth of faith, we do not find a historical tradition concerning the time, place, and circumstances of Mary's death (Jerusalem or Ephesus?). About such historical details we know nothing dependable. The truth is solely a tradition of faith. As distinguished from the Resurrection and exaltation (ascension) of Jesus Christ, attested by the appearances of the Risen One, there are no witnesses for the assumption of Mary into heavenly glory. It is an event wrought by God, but we cannot date it historically. Unlike the Resurrection and exaltation of Jesus Christ, which is the ground of our hope in our own resurrection, Mary's assumption is only its fruit and so a confirmation of our own hope. 169–171; 174–176 170–173; 333–334; 336–338

Two considerations can help us understand this article of faith. In the first place, there is the particularly *close connection of Mary with Jesus Christ, her Son,* and with his way. Communion with Christ is a communion with his cross and Resurrection. All Christians are called in principle to that. Because of her unique connection with Jesus Christ, we see anticipated in

334–339
115; 140 Mary that to which we are only called, the resurrection of the body. A second consideration sees Mary as the new Eve, *the new mother of life*. She bore the author of life and contributed through her "Yes" in a special way to the victory of life over death. Of her it is true even now that "death is swallowed up in victory" (1 Cor 15:54). Thus Mary shines through her glorification as a "sign of certain hope and comfort to the pilgrim People of God" (LG 68).

What does this dogma mean for us? At a time when some idolize the flesh and others hate it because they feel hopelessly locked into structures and systems, it would be of little use were the Church to proclaim only programs, principles, and challenges. In Mary, she gives us *the shining pattern for a genuinely Christian hope*. It is a hope for the entire man. Even the flesh will be saved. But it is a hope that moves, not downwards through sensualization from below, but upwards through transfiguration and glorification from above. This hope is valid because Jesus Christ was awakened from the dead. He is its beginning and permanent ground. In Mary it becomes clear that this hope is fruitful for us all and that it includes the completion of the whole man. Thus is Mary the pattern for the hope of all Christians.

III

CRUCIFIED FOR US

1. Jesus' Way to the Cross

1.1 How Did Jesus' Death on the Cross Come About?

Since the days of the New Testament, the cross has been considered as *the* sign of salvation. At baptism, we are signed with the sign of the cross; with the sign of the cross we receive the blessing of God time and again; with it we sign ourselves. The cross is *the* Christian symbol that we display publicly and privately. In the cross, the self-humbling of God, which began in the Incarnation of Jesus Christ and in his birth through Mary, reaches its goal. So the cross is for Paul the *summary of the whole Christian message of salvation*. Paul wishes to know "nothing but Jesus Christ and him crucified" (1 Cor 2:2).

We should not, of course, in all these expressions, forget the *scandal of the cross*. The cross as the sign of salvation is at the same time a sign of contradiction that raises many questions. We face these questions when the cross affects us personally: in grave illness, incurable suffering, great disappointments, failures, and blows of fate; in misfortunes, catastrophes, and in the encounter with death. Why did God choose precisely this way of redemption and expose the most innocent of all men, his own Son, to cruel death on the cross? Is God so vindictive and cruel that he needs a "scapegoat"? The cross thus confronts us anew with a question about God. But that is not all. For many, there is also a difficult question about how this one act of suffering and dying of Jesus can redeem us in our suffering and dying, in our guilt. What does it really mean to say that we are redeemed?   183–184

Let us begin by asking how, *seen historically*, it could come to pass that a man who proclaimed nothing but the love of God and summoned men to love one another, who healed the sick, bore up the poor and despairing, but condemned rebellion and violence as well—how such a man could be executed. Historically, reasons enough can be found in the struggle for power of social groups and political currents to make the elimination of an irritating, popular leader and an annoying admonisher easily comprehensible. Even John the Baptist had shared this fate of not a few

129–130

men of God and prophets in Israel. Jesus came into conflict with the influential ruling classes of his people by turning to the oppressed classes, by criticizing the Pharisaical practice of the law and the Sadducean administration of the temple, and by his open message and his provocative acts. Even the mass of people who thronged to him as a physician and wonderworker, who eagerly listened to his sermons, did not advance to a clear and resolute faith.

The course and the background of the *trial of Jesus* before the Council are not easy to discern historically. A man from the circle of Jesus' closer disciples, Judas Iscariot, obviously betrayed him to the high priests for money. The politically influential circles of the Sadducean priestly nobility probably then arranged Jesus' extradition to the court of the Roman procurator, Pontius Pilate, who was violently hated by the Jews on account of his rigorous and provocative administration. The outcome of the trial is unambiguous, given the title put on the cross, "King of the Jews" (Mk 15:26), which is attested to by all four Gospels. Whereas Jesus was condemned before the Council on religious grounds, Pontius Pilate had him executed on the cross as a political rebel. This interplay shows that we must be reserved in any judgment about the "guilt" of the Jews. In no case is the whole Jewish people to be made responsible for the rejection of Jesus, and not even the Jewish authorities of that time bear sole responsibility. Jewish and Roman authorities together brought about the downfall of Jesus.

In view of the growing hostility of powerful groups, *Jesus himself* must have reckoned with his violent death, especially with the vivid reminder of the fate of John the Baptist. According to the Gospels, Jesus foresaw his death and interpreted it in three passion prophecies as a salvific death willed by God (Mk 8:31; 9:31; 10:33–34). The interpretation of the early Church's Tradition, however, has already entered into these passion prophecies. But in other sayings and discourses of Jesus (Mk 10:38–39; 12:1–8; Lk 12:50; 13:32–33), there are various allusions that suggest a

282–284

presentiment of death. Within the context of the Last Supper, a saying has been handed on that shows Jesus' certainty about his own death as well as his unbroken conviction of the coming of the Kingdom of God: "I solemnly assure you, I will never again drink of the fruit of the vine until the day when I drink it new in the Kingdom of God" (Mk 14:25; Lk 22:16, 18). This saying shows that Jesus accepted his death, in spite of all human failure, not as an anonymous fate but as the will of his Father: "*Abba* (Father). . . . May your will be done, not mine" (Mk 14:36). Even if, indeed precisely if, the hidden thoughts of God were not yet clearly unveiled to Jesus at his entrance into suffering and death—that too belongs to his self-abasement—he nevertheless still affirmed in this darkness the will of the Father. "Son though he was, he learned obedience from what he suffered; and when perfected, he became the source of eternal salvation for all who obey him" (Heb 5:8–9).

Jesus experienced every kind of humiliation in his Passion: groundless arrest, betrayal by someone in his own circle, the flight of his closest friends, inhuman interrogation and cruel tortures, false accusations, perjuries, the political shifting of blame onto the shoulders of an innocent and defenseless man, derision, condemnation as a lawbreaker and criminal, condemnation to death, physical collapse under the cross, defamation, sensation-mongering, and the experience of abandonment by God. *"Ecce homo!"* "Look at the man" (Jn 19:5). See what men are capable of and what men can and must suffer!

1.2 Did Jesus Understand His Death as a Salvific Death?

The question whether Jesus himself attributed a salvific meaning to his death is important particularly for describing Jesus' understanding of his person and mission. This question is difficult to answer historically. Interpretations by the early community have entered into every tradition. There are good grounds, however, even historically, for believing that Jesus carried through to the end in obedience to his Father and for his service to men. Of particular importance are the Last Supper and words   282–284 that interpret it. The interpretative words have not been handed down to us uniformly; but they cannot be explained away as background projections based on the eucharistic celebration of the primitive community. In all forms of the tradition, there is mention of the "Covenant" (Mk 14:24; Mt 26:28) or of the "New Covenant" (Lk 22:20; 1 Cor 11:25) that Jesus has founded through his blood. In all the texts, there are also the important and suggestive words about the self-surrender "for you" or "for the many", which means in Scripture "for all". "Many" means the totality for which the one surrenders oneself (Is 53:11). The words of the Last Supper are accompanied by special gestures of sharing, bestowing, and self-surrender. All this supports the conviction that Jesus understood his death as a saving death and that he looked beyond his death to the community of disciples and instituted a memorial of his death for this community which would at the same time contain the promise of the future Kingdom of God.

It turns out that the message of the coming of God's saving lordship is intrinsically connected with the faith in the salvific meaning of Jesus' death on the cross. Jesus' proclamation of the nearness, indeed of the symbolic dawning, of God's lordship demands that the divine offer of salvation be accepted. With the rejection of his message and the repudiation of his person, there arose a new situation. Jesus accepts it in obedience as the "hour" determined by the Father (Mk 14:35, 41; Jn 12:23, 27–28; 13:1; 17:1). The hardheartedness of men cannot overthrow God's plan of salvation. So God opens up a last way of rescue for mankind with the self-surrender of his Son.

There is a problem only if one interprets this utmost proof of the love of God as the execution of his punitive justice and thus understands Jesus only as the "scapegoat" for mankind. Then there arises an unbearable tension between the God whom Jesus proclaimed and the one who willed his death for the salvation of mankind. But this interpretation misses the deep meaning that lies in the dying of the one for the many: it is the utmost proof of the love of God. "Yes, God so loved the world that he gave his only Son, that whoever believes in him may not die but may have eternal life" (Jn 3:16; Rom 8:32).

2. The Salvific Meaning of the Death of Jesus on the Cross

2.1 God's Salvific Will

The shameful death of Jesus on the cross was for the Jews a judgment by God, even a curse (Gal 3:13), for the Romans a disgrace and, as not a few witnesses prove, a ground for contempt and scorn. Paul writes: "Yes, Jews demand 'signs' and Greeks look for 'wisdom', but we preach Christ crucified—a stumbling block to Jews and an absurdity to Gentiles" (1 Cor 1:22–23). It was therefore a difficult task for the primitive Christian proclamation to come to terms with this scandal of the cross. But the early Church remembered Jesus' own words at the Last Supper. In the light of Jesus' Resurrection by God, she saw clearly that this very offensive death was indeed brought about on the superficial level of history by the unbelief and enmity of men, but that *God's will, God's plan of salvation, even God's love*, ultimately stood behind it. The Church recognized in Jesus' way through suffering and death a divine *"must"* (Mk 8:31; Lk 24:7, 26, 44), one already prefigured in the Old Testament. For that reason, one of the oldest of New Testament traditions, which Paul already found in the communities when he converted, says that Jesus Christ died for us *according to the Scriptures* (1 Cor 15:3).

Different attempts to interpret the deeper divine meaning of Jesus' death followed. According to one early interpretation, Jesus shares the *lot of the prophets* who had been rejected and killed by Israel (Lk 13:34; Mt 23:29–31, 35). Hence violent death awaited him in Jerusalem, the city of God, "since no prophet can be allowed to die anywhere except in Jerusalem" (Lk 13:33). The ancient passion account taken over by Mark describes Jesus as the *innocently suffering just one* persecuted by men. It finds Jesus' fate foreshadowed in Psalm 22. The fourth song of the *suffering servant of God* in the Book of Isaiah (Is 52:13–53:12), which was interpreted by the New Testament as a prophecy about Jesus Christ, became of particular importance. Thus Paul recognizes in the death of Jesus the unfathomable *love of God*, who did not spare even his own Son but gave him up for us (Rom 8:32, 39; Jn 3:16), in order to reconcile the world in him with himself (2 Cor 5:18–19). The cross is the absolute sign of the self-emptying love of God.

2.2 Jesus' Vicarious Expiatory Death

Jesus' own self-surrender to the will of the Father "for us" is the response of Jesus to God's surrender of his Son. To see the death of Jesus as the vicarious surrender of life leads us into the *very center of the New Testament witness*.

At first, of course, this thought is not easy for us to think through. It may be helpful to remember that the *notion of substitution* corresponds to a basic human given: the solidarity of all men. The Bible appropriates this notion in a new way as a *fundamental law of the whole history of salvation*. Adam acted as the representative of all mankind and brought about a solidarity of all in sin. Abraham was called a blessing for all generations (Gen 12:3), Israel a light for the peoples (Is 42:6). Holy Scripture concretizes this idea through the thought of vicarious suffering, which is found already in the fourth song of the servant of God:

109–113

> Yet it was our infirmities that he bore,
>   our sufferings that he endured. . . .
> But he was pierced for our offenses,
>   crushed for our sins,
> Upon him was the chastisement that makes us whole,
>   by his stripes we were healed. . . .
> And he shall take away the sins of the many,
>   and win pardon for their offenses (Is 53:4–5, 12).

The notion of substitution, which is so central to the Bible, is especially suited to clarify for faith how the death of Jesus can have a salvific meaning for us. The consequence of the solidarity of men in sin was solidarity in death. There we see, above all, the lost and hopeless situation of men. By becoming one with us in death, Jesus Christ, the fullness of life, makes his death the *foundation for a new solidarity*. His death now becomes a source of new life for all who stand under the fate of death.

As the accounts of the Last Supper show, the interpretation of the death of Jesus as vicarious suffering and dying dates back in its core to Jesus himself. This very old saying shows as much: "The Son of Man has not come to be served but to serve—to give his life in ransom for the many" (Mk 10:45). The interpretation of the death of Jesus as vicarious suffering entered into the oldest tradition of the community (1 Cor 15:3) and was taken up and deepened in the New Testament in many places (Jn 10:15; 1 Jn 4:10; 1 Pet 2:21–25; 1 Tim 2:6, among others). Paul took up the notion of substitution in a special way and even spoke of an exchange of places between us and Jesus Christ. He goes so far as to say that Jesus Christ was cursed for us (Gal 3:13); indeed, that he, the sinless one, was made to be sin for us, so that we might become in him the justice of God (2 Cor 5:21). "For your sake he made himself poor though he was rich, so that you might become rich by his poverty" (2 Cor 8:9). This thought of a *"wondrous exchange"* was taken up with variations by the Church Fathers.
135–136 Irenaeus of Lyons says of Jesus Christ (around the year 200), "Because of his infinite love, he became what we are to make us perfectly what he is." According to Irenaeus, Jesus Christ as the new Adam recapitulated the whole human race in himself and reunited it with God.

The understanding of the cross as *expiation* and *satisfaction*, which are today so difficult for us to understand, must be understood in this context. Behind the notion of the death or, rather, of the blood of Jesus as an expiatory mediation for our sins (Rom 3:25; 1 Jn 2:2; 4:10), there stands again the notion of a great solidarity of the people or, rather, of all mankind in good as well as evil. Because the sin of a given individual affects all and "poisons" the social order, every fault needs an expiatory reparation. Since sin is directed against God, however, man himself cannot achieve this reparation. Only God himself, as Anselm of Canterbury (eleventh century) makes so clear, can achieve this. It is God who establishes reconciliation and thus marks a new beginning (2 Cor 5:18). The expiation motif leads back to the thought of substitution and to the motif of the compassionate love of God. In terms of the history of piety, the principle of substitution and expiation has been an important factor especially in the theology of martyrdom and in devotion to the Sacred Heart of Jesus.

It is similarly difficult for us today to understand the biblical idea of the *sacrificial*
288–292 *death* of Jesus. The account of the institution of the Lord's Supper in Matthew and Mark invokes it already when it speaks of the "blood of the Covenant" (Mk 14:24; Mt 26:28). For Paul, Jesus is the paschal lamb that has been sacrificed (1 Cor 5:7). For John, he is the Lamb of God "who takes away the sin of the world" (Jn 1:29). If

we wish to understand the deeper meaning of the notion of sacrifice, we have to be clear that what matters with a sacrifice is not primarily the external offerings. The offerings presented are only meaningful as signs of a personal attitude of sacrifice; this inner attitude must, of course, be manifested and embodied. With Jesus, personal self-surrender becomes one with the offering; his sacrifice is a self-sacrifice; he is the sacrificial priest and the offering all in one. His sacrifice was the perfect sacrifice, the fulfillment of all other sacrifices, which are but shadowy types of this one sacrifice presented once for all (Heb 9:11–28). For that reason, the Letter to the Hebrews can say that this sacrifice is not an external material offering, but the self-surrender of Jesus in obedience to his Father (Heb 10:5–10). Through this vicarious and complete self-surrender, alienated mankind becomes wholly one with God again. Through his unique sacrifice, Jesus is *the one mediator* between God and men (1 Tim 2:5).

One and the same theme runs through all these declarations. They announce in ever-new ways the anticipatory and redeeming love of God, which Jesus Christ has obtained vicariously for us once for all through his obedience and through his self-surrender. He does so in order to establish peace between God and men as well as among men. So the Letter to the Ephesians says, "It is he who is our peace" (Eph 2:14). In him, the alienations that sin has caused between God and man, among men, and in man himself, are healed and reconciled. The cross is finally a sign of victory over all powers and dominations hostile to God and man, a sign of hope.

2.3 A Sign of Hope

The message of the cross *cannot be separated from the Resurrection and exaltation of the Lord.* The Gospel of John shows this most clearly: Jesus' exaltation on the cross is conjoined with his exaltation and glorification at the right hand of the Father. Crucifixion, exaltation, and glorification are for John an indivisible, integral event (Jn 3:14; 12:34). In the moment of death, Jesus speaks the victorious "Now it is finished" (Jn 19:30). John sees the cross as a judgment on both the world and the power in the world opposed to God (Jn 12:31). The cross exposes sin, injustice, and deceit as it reveals the greater love, justice, and truth of God. It is God's strength and wisdom. Through the cross, God has disarmed "the principalities and powers. He made a public show of them and, leading them off captive, triumphed in the person of Christ" (Col 2:15).

The victorious character of the cross also makes possible the understanding of Jesus' death on the cross as a ransom (Mk 10:45; 1 Tim 2:6). The Apostle Paul says that we have been bought at a dear price (1 Cor

6:20; 1 Pet 1:18–19). He thus describes the death of Jesus as a liberation from the slavery of sin (Rom 7; Jn 8:34–36), from the devil (Jn 8:44; 1 Jn 3:8), from the powers of the world (Gal 4:3; Col 2:20), from the law (Rom 7:1; Gal 3:13; 4:5), and above all from death (Rom 8:2). The freedom *from* the powers that grip man, holding him back from his true fulfillment, is at the same time the gift of a new freedom *for* God and neighbor. While this *Christian freedom* has consequences for political and psychological liberation, it is by no means exhausted in them. As Pope Paul VI made clear in his apostolic letter on evangelization in today's world, Christian freedom meant an integral liberation that embraces man in all his dimensions (EN 30–44). For precisely that reason, Christian freedom is not a purely this-worldly program of liberation. It is a liberation by and for God, since its goal is freedom in God and in communion with him.

209–210

The *liturgy of Good Friday* expresses this victorious, liberating character of the passion of Jesus Christ. The cross is carried in solemn procession into the church; it is then elevated before the congregation and venerated.

> This is the wood of the cross
> on which hung the Savior of the world.
> Come, let us worship.

A sign of victory, the cross is also a sign of hope. The hymn to the cross, *Vexilla regis prodeunt* (sixth century), expresses the certainty of this hope.

> The kingly banners now appear,
> The cross ascends from nighttime drear,
> On which true life for us did die,
> To win through death new life on high.
>
> O Cross, through which our hopes prevail,
> Your conquest over death we hail!
> Increase the grace of God within,
> And wash away our deeds of sin.

The victory of the cross, the victory of love over hate and violence, of truth over deceit, of life over death, is of course still hidden. Hate, deceit, and violence still reign in the world. New life is bestowed on us only in the form of the cross. The history of hope in which Jesus proves himself as the living Son of God is not a history of unbroken success, not a history of victors according to our standards. Only on the way of the cross is the victory of the cross promised to us. God's self-humbling into the misery of human suffering and death has united us with him again in this, our concrete situation. The cross is a sign of hope for definitive liberation and for the definitive victory of God. So we pray again and again at the stations of the cross: "We worship you, O Christ, and we praise you, for by your holy cross you have redeemed the world."

3. Christian Life and the Cross of Christ

The cross of Jesus has an immediate, existential meaning for Christian life. The imitation of Jesus is only possible as an *imitation of the cross*. "If a man wishes to come after me, he must deny his very self, take up his cross, and follow in my steps" (Mk 8:34). Through baptism, every Christian is 273–275 included in the passion of Christ so that he may one day receive a share in Christ's life also (Rom 6:3–8). In the celebration of the Eucharist, the cross 288–294 is made present once again (1 Cor 11:26). Moreover, the whole life of the Christian stands under the sign of the cross.

> Continually we carry about in our bodies the dying of Jesus, so that in our bodies the life of Jesus may also be revealed. While we live we are constantly being delivered to death for Jesus' sake, so that the life of Jesus may be revealed in our mortal flesh (2 Cor 4:10–11).

The imitation of the cross can take many forms: persecution, being slandered, poverty, obedience, selfless service, inner and outer discipline, discouragement and sorrow, loneliness, sickness and suffering, and death in its various forms.

Through the cross, even the darkest question in human life is answered —the question about the *meaning of suffering* and of the power of death. "It 330–331 is therefore through Christ, and in Christ, that light is thrown on the riddle of suffering and death which, apart from his Gospel, overwhelms us" (GS 22). This is not an answer that rationally illuminates all darkness. It is not a higher harmony or a global solution. Nor should the cross be misused as a means of empty consolation. God's suffering with and for us on the cross obligates the Christian to help bear the burdens of others and to exert himself wherever suffering can be eliminated or ameliorated. But even when we have done everything in our power, there remains much suffering that we cannot change with the best of wills. The cross can bear man up in this night of suffering and death. With his gaze on the crucified Jesus, a man may be full of "hope against all hope" (Rom 4:18). For nothing can "separate us from the love of God that comes to us in Christ Jesus, our Lord" (Rom 8:39).

Still, with his knowledge about the victory of the cross, the Christian may not become triumphalistic and forget *the permanent scandal of the cross*. The "sacred head surrounded by crown of piercing thorn" suggests itself more, especially to our epoch, than does the cross as a sign of victory. The Crucified One bears witness to God's love especially for the downtrodden, the offended, the oppressed, the hungry, the exiled, and the tortured, for all who are full of anxiety and would despair of the meaning of their lives. The Sermon on the Mount's blessings for the poor, the mourning, the powerless, and those hungering for justice (Mt 5:3–6; Lk 6:20–22) are definitely confirmed on the cross of Jesus Christ. In the hungry, the foreign, the homeless, the naked, the sick, and the imprisoned, the Crucified One abides (Mt 25:35–36, 40). This conviction should make us Christians sensitive to our society's growing insensitivity to suffering, which it attempts to repress or mark as taboo. The cross should enable us to suffer and to have compassion. So the cross is not only a short formula and summary of the whole gospel, but also a sign of the genuineness of a Christian life.

4. Descended into Hell

The article of faith concerning the descent of Jesus Christ into the realm of death is one of those truths that have been largely forgotten. It is unintelligible and foreign to most Christians, who find the present version particularly unpalatable: "descended into hell". This declaration reminds us of a three-story world view that we find antiquated. Perhaps we even see in it mythical motifs of the descent of the gods into the underworld. What are we to do today with such declarations?

We come closer to the meaning intended in the Creed when we see that the immediate background of this declaration is the Old Testament *notion* of the realm of the dead (sheol). According to this notion, the dead live a shadowy existence. Their true plight is that they are closed off from God, that they live *far away from God and are abandoned by him* (Ps 6:6; 88:11–13; 115:17). When it is said of Jesus that he descended into the realm of death, this does not mean only that he entered into our common fate of death. It means that he also entered into the whole abandonment and loneliness of death, that he took upon himself the experience of meaninglessness, of the night, and—in this sense—of the hell of being human. The article of faith about the descent into the realm of death does not recall an outdated world view. It uses the language of that world view to describe a permanent, profound dimension in man, one that does not lie only in the beyond but already begins in the midst of this life.

331–332

The *Church's Tradition* has found a basis for the article of faith about Jesus' descent into the realm of death in a passage in the First Letter of Peter: "It was in the spirit also that he went to preach to the spirits in prison" (3:19; 4:6). The interpretation of this difficult text is, of course, disputed. The original thought was doubtless not of a descent into hell, but of an ascent into heaven. Some then thought that the evil spirits   94–95 inhabited the air between heaven and earth. These spirits wish to obstruct man's way to heaven and to make this life a hell for him. In this figurative sense, the interpretation of the Church's Tradition is thoroughly correct. Through his ascension into heaven, Jesus has *conquered hell* and bestowed on us anew the way to heaven, which is hope. Other interpreters wanted to read the First Letter of Peter as depicting a descent into the realm of the dead and a victory over the evil powers and dominations. They spoke of Jesus' preaching in the netherworld, of his breaking open of the gates of hell, of a battle in hell for the liberation and redemption of the deceased, and of Christ's triumphal victory march through Hades. All of this goes beyond the content of this declaration of the faith. Even so, these images have a deeper meaning. The extreme passion, the extreme night of obedience, the ultimate solidarity of Jesus with the dead in their abandonment and loneliness, his entering into the entire hell of being human—all these are the *victory of God over death and over the powers of darkness and death*.

The article of faith about Jesus' descent into the realm of death is, then, a *message of salvation*. For the Orthodox Church, the descent into the realm of death is interpreted in the light of Easter, the central event of salvation. This article asserts that in Jesus' death God's omnipotence takes on the most extreme powerlessness in order to fill the emptiness of death with his life and so to burst open the bonds of death. The affirmation of Jesus' descent into the realm of death expresses once again the fact that the death of Jesus has brought about the death of death and has established the paschal victory of life. Jesus' solidarity with the general human fate of death expresses further the *universality of salvation*. In Jesus' death, the   188–189; long-deceased generations are also redeemed. His salvific death gives   218–220 meaning to all the suffering and sacrifices of history. Through him, redemption is given precisely to the small and the powerless, to the long-forgotten, to the many nameless persons whose suffering no further social progress can reconcile. The mystery of Good Friday already foretells the paschal victory of life over death and the exaltation of the Crucified One as Lord of the world.

IV

ROSE AGAIN, ASCENDED INTO HEAVEN

1. "Blest Are They Who Have Not Seen and Have Believed"

With Jesus' violent and shameful death on the cross, everything seemed to end. In the account of the disciples on the road to Emmaus (Lk 24:13–35), for instance, the Gospels mirror the disappointment and resignation of the disciples, who thought that all their hopes had now to be buried. For Jesus had tied his "cause", the coming of the lordship of God, so closely to his person that this "cause" simply could not continue after his death. No one could continue to maintain and uphold the ideas and ideals of Jesus as the ideas and ideals of Socrates have been continued after his death. That was impossible for a Jew, who would have had to understand the cross as God's judgment. Nevertheless, the gospel of Jesus Christ spread through the known world shortly after Good Friday with a dynamic force that we can still barely imagine. How did this sudden change come about? How can one explain this forceful *beginning of Christianity*, which continues to have force today? 126–127

According to the unanimous witness of the New Testament, this new beginning has its ground in the Resurrection of Jesus. Without the Resurrection of Jesus, the Apostle Paul tells us, the proclamation would be empty and faith meaningless; our vain hope would then make us more pitiable than all other men (1 Cor 15:14, 19). *The Resurrection of Jesus is the foundation and, together with the message of the cross, the center of the Christian faith.*

Of course, many people have *problems* with the Resurrection of Jesus. Its message conflicts with the harsh experience of reality, above all the reality of death. Nothing seems to be so definitive as death. So questions were posed about the Resurrection from the very beginning. The Gospels tell us of the incipient doubts, of the unbelief and obstinacy of Jesus' disciples. The episode of "doubting Thomas" is described in an especially impressive way (Jn 20:24–29). These accounts show us that questioning and critical investigation also have their rightful place in the face of the Easter message. Jesus himself says to Thomas: "Blest are they who have not seen and have believed" (Jn 20:29).

Even in New Testament times there were attempts to explain away the message of the Resurrection and the empty grave as a deception by the disciples (Mt 28:13). Since the Enlightenment, we have heard, beyond hypotheses about deception and theft, new hypotheses about confusion and apparent death. Some wished to derive the Easter faith from ancient religious ideas and expectations (the evolution theory) or to explain the appearances of the Risen One as purely subjective visions (hallucinations). Yet all these rational "explanations", when faced with the un-ambiguous and unanimous witness of the New Testament, create more problems than they solve. These "explanations" are concerned from the start only about causes immanent to the world. They thus miss the perspective of Jesus and of Holy Scripture. Today these hypotheses have been practically given up by serious theology.

Today, though, new questions are being posed. Some ask how the message of the Resurrection is to be understood. Is it an "objective" happening in space and time on the basis of which the one who had previously died on the cross now lives? But how does he live? Certainly the Risen One does not merely return to his old life; rather, he lives a new life in the power of God. But how are we to think of this new life? Is the Resurrection only a symbol or a cipher intended to express the definitive and abiding meaning of the earthly Jesus and his "cause"? Is it only a symbol of the indestructability of life and of love? But would not the biblical message of the Resurrection be utterly emptied by such interpretations? What then does this article of faith, Jesus' Resurrection, mean?

Both the central, fundamental character of the message of the Resurrection and the question it raises are reasons for us to listen attentively to the witness of Holy Scripture about Jesus' Resurrection and the appearances of the Risen One to his disciples. Here we can find the answer to our question.

2. The Biblical Witnesses of the Resurrection

2.1 The Early Confessions of the Resurrection

The New Testament's declarations of the Resurrection distinguish themselves by a remarkable reserve. Unlike many later apocryphal writings and many artistic representations, the New Testament presents *no description of the event of Resurrection itself*. Neither does it report anywhere that someone observed the Resurrection. A veil of impenetrable mystery hangs before the event of the Resurrection.

In the New Testament, we find first of all some very old, well-established formulas of confession that bear witness to the faith in the Resurrection (Rom 1:3–4; 10:9; Phil 2:6–11; 1 Tim 3:16). Perhaps we hear an ancient liturgical acclamation already in Luke: "The Lord has been raised! It is true! He has appeared to Simon" (24:34). A very early witness of the Resurrection is the pre-Pauline formula of faith that Paul recalls for the Corinthians:

> I handed on to you first of all what I myself received, that Christ died for our sins in accordance with the Scriptures; that he was buried and, in accordance with the Scriptures, rose on the third day; that he was seen by Cephas, then by the Twelve (1 Cor 15:3–5).

According to this ancient, rhythmically constructed confession, the Resurrection is a *unique act of God* toward Jesus Christ who died on the cross. So the New Testament often employs, alongside the word "resurrection" familiar to us, the concept of "reawakening". Holy Scripture uses the passive formulation "has been awakened" as a paraphrase for God's action, which remains mysterious to men and which cannot be adequately captured by any image or concept.

In this unique and mysterious act of God toward the Crucified One, *faith and history* are most intimately linked. The earthly and crucified Jesus stands in the midst of history; the testimony of the Apostles to the appearances of the Risen One is also a historical event. The Resurrection of Jesus as an act of God's power, on the other hand, while historically fixed by his death, surpasses the human-historical horizon of experience. By God's deed, Jesus of Nazareth, once crucified, has been taken up in his bodiliness into the glory of God, so that he now lives with God. So the Resurrection is not a "historical event" in the usual understanding, i.e., an event that can be generally verified, compared with other events, incorporated into the course of history, and given conceptual clarity. Of course, Christian faith cannot relinquish the fact that Jesus' Resurrection happened in time and history. But this event is distinguished from the miracles that Jesus worked during his earthly life. The Risen One does not return to this world and to this life (like the young man of Naim or the daughter of Jairus); he enters, rather, into the trans-temporal world of God that is not perceivable by the senses. The Resurrection is an event that occurred in the realm of history, was enacted in the historical person of Jesus of Nazareth, completed his own history, and introduced the completion of all history. It is in principle accessible only to faith because it is possible only through God.

This peculiar interlacing of faith and history shows itself especially in the confession that Jesus rose *on the third day*. For the Old Testament, the third day is the day of a change for the better, of salvation (Hos 6:2; Jon 2:1). According to Jewish tradition, God will never leave the just in distress longer than three days. This hope for salvation has been fulfilled by Jesus Christ in a quite extraordinary manner. In him, salvation does not come within history; the seriousness of the end and of failure in death is allowed to stand. At the same time, God's power and faithfulness prove themselves precisely in ultimate hopelessness and effect an absolute transformation. Death has been conquered by death, and so something surpassing all history has happened in history.

Where does faith find this certainty? As the Creed says, faith's certainty in the Resurrection is justified because the Risen One *appeared* to witnesses chosen by God. To translate more exactly, he "made himself visible to them" or "revealed himself to them" (1 Cor 9:1; Gal 1:16). The New Testament does not give us any detailed description of the concrete events of the appearances. The "how" of the appearances is pushed into the background by what is essential: a *personal encounter* and a *revelational event*, in which the Lord, awakened by God to new life and enthroned in divine glory and lordship, revealed himself to his disciples. The many rationalistic attempts to interpret and explain away these Easter appearances as purely natural founder because of the clear witness of the New Testament. The experiences of the disciples, which they had struggled to express, become intelligible only if the disciples experienced a revelation from the risen Lord, in which they recognized Jesus as they had known him in his earthly life, but now in a new mode of being. Even Paul understands his encounter with Christ outside Damascus as a revelation graciously bestowed upon him and overwhelming him—a revelation of the risen, living Lord who dwells with God (Gal 1:15–16; 1 Cor 9:1; 15:8–10; Phil 3:12). He proclaims just what those men do to whom the first appearances were given (1 Cor 15:11).

The appearances of the Risen One express two things: the Risen One appears in the world and so makes a concrete claim on his disciples. But he is no longer of this world. He appears in God's glory and bears witness that God stands on his side, that he himself has been enthroned in God's glory. By showing himself as the victor over death, the Crucified One proves that he is the *kyrios*, the Lord, by whose glorification the message of the coming of the lordship of God has been definitively confirmed.

2.2 The Easter Narratives of the Gospels

Beyond the succinct Easter confessions, the New Testament includes more detailed Easter narratives: the conclusion of the four Gospels. Mark relates only the discovery of the empty tomb by the women hurrying to it and the angel's proclamation (Mk 16:1–8), but fuller accounts are found in the other Gospels. These differ more than slightly as regards places and names of persons, not to mention individual narrative features. These differences must be judged according to each narrative's literary genre and objective. The narratives bear witness to the common Easter faith of the communities; they defend it against doubters and opponents, unfolding it for the life of the communities in the Lord's presence. The appearances of the Risen One at the meal fellowships (Lk 24:30, 41–42; Jn 21:5, 12–13) show especially well the connection with the earliest Christian celebrations of the Eucharist. So the variety and multiplicity of the narratives do not call the common message of the Resurrection of the Crucified One into question. On the contrary, they confirm and corroborate it. In this chorus of witnesses, the early Church experiences the certainty of the Lord's Resurrection and of his abiding presence.

A separate tradition concerns the women's visit on the first day of the week and their discovery of the *empty tomb* (Mk 16:1–8). Despite many critical questions, there is no reason to doubt the historical fact of the empty tomb. Indeed, there is no attempt in first-century Judaism to dispute this fact. Of course, an empty tomb and a missing corpse are not, seen historically, a proof for the Resurrection. Other possibilities suggest themselves to critical reason (for example, theft, deception, removal, confusion). For the primitive Church, then, the empty grave was not the ground of the Easter faith, but only a demonstrative and confirmatory sign of the Easter message. Only in connection with the Resurrection of the Risen One does the empty tomb become a revealing witness that the Crucified One has risen and entered even in his bodiliness into the glory of God. From this there grew early on the veneration of the holy tomb that, located as it is on a credible site, constantly reminds one of the Resurrection of Jesus Christ.

The striking narratives of eating with the Risen One and the accounts of the empty tomb are intended as expressions of the *bodiliness of Jesus' Resurrection*. Of course, the narratives also make clear that this is a special kind of body. Wholly spiritualized and transfigured through the glory of God, it is nonetheless quite real. We can understand why the Easter narratives are necessarily indefinite on many points. They are declarations at the limit, trying to grasp something no longer expressible in words. So they are pervaded by a characteristic tension. The risen Lord is close to his disciples, and yet he withdraws from them again and again. This singular mixture of strangeness and familiarity shows that in the Easter event the absolutely hidden and mysterious glory of God, in which the Resurrection takes place, erupts into the historical world of space and time as a promise and as a hope of future transfiguration.

337–339

2.3 Witnesses to the Resurrection

The appearances of the Risen One are not purely private experiences for the Apostles; they are always connected with the *commission to give authoritative missionary witness*. The appearances do not allow a distanced and neutral, a purely "objective" and general, consideration. They require one to believe and to be a witness. Most splendid in this respect is Matthew's account of the appearance of the Risen One on a Galilean mountain:

> "Full authority has been given to me
> both in heaven and on earth;
> go, therefore, and make disciples of all the nations.
> Baptize them in the name
> 'of the Father,
> and of the Son,
> and of the Holy Spirit.'
> Teach them to carry out everything I have commanded you.
> And know that I am with you always, until the end of the world!"
> (Mt 28:18–20).

237–239   Through these appearances of the Risen One and through the mission given during them, the *Apostles* are appointed as the *foundation of the faith of the Church* and as the leading authorities for the Church in all times. It is thus important that Cephas or Simon Peter is named first each time (1 Cor 15:5; Lk 24:34; Jn 20:3–8; 21:15–19); he is the original witness of the faith in the Resurrection.

212–214   The appearances of the Risen One have a *foundational meaning for the Church*. They show that the Church is always and essentially apostolic. There is no other access to the center of the Christian proclamation, to the message of the death and Resurrection of Jesus, than by the witness of those to whom the Risen One disclosed himself in his new being. Their witness gains persuasive force when we see that all of the first witnesses were ready to die for their message and so to seal the witness of their faith with their own blood. This witness calls everyone to a daring faith that, with the Apostles, risks life in the hope of the new life that has dawned in the Resurrection of Jesus Christ. The words of the Risen One apply precisely to the Easter faith: "Blest are they who have not seen and have believed" (Jn 20:29).

3. The Meaning of the Resurrection

3.1 The Fulfillment of Hope

The most ancient attestation of the Resurrection already indicates its deeper meaning. It says that, "in accordance with the Scriptures, [he] rose on the third day" (1 Cor 15:4). The Resurrection of Jesus is seen as the fulfillment of the promises of the Old Testament, the fulfillment of the hope of Israel. From the beginning, God was for Israel the living God, the Lord over life and death (Num 27:16) and the "fountain of life" (Ps 36:10). With him, there is hope that he will never finally abandon life to death.

> Because you will not abandon my soul to the nether world,
> nor will you suffer your faithful one to undergo corruption.
> You will show me the path to life,
> fullness of joys in your presence,
> the delights at your right hand forever (Ps 16:10–11).

> Yet with you I shall always be;
> you have hold of my right hand;
> With your counsel you guide me,
> and in the end you will receive me in glory (Ps 73:23–24).

This hope begins in the Old Testament as undetermined and open. Only in the later texts, from a time of oppression, of bloody persecution and of martyrdom, does the hope grow stronger and become an expectation of the resurrection of the dead at the end of time (Dan 12:1–2; 2 Macc 7:9, 11, 14, 22–23, 29). So when the New Testament makes what is for Jews the unprecedented declaration that God has raised Jesus from the dead, it declares that *the eschaton (the final age) has dawned*. In Jesus Christ, God has made this hope a reality. He has thus confirmed Jesus' message about the coming of divine lordship. Jesus' death was not a meaningless end, but a definitive beginning. In him the new creation has already begun.

331–334;
336–338

In the *Easter Vigil liturgy*, we hear in detail the message of the Resurrection of Jesus as the fulfillment of hope, not only for Israel, but for all creation. In the first reading, the liturgy reminds us of the first creation. Just as God then called what did not exist into existence (Rom 4:17), so he now calls the dead to life in the new creation. In Jesus' Resurrection, God stands by his creation; he affirms life in the face of death. The second reading announces the Resurrection as the fulfillment of the salvation history that began with Abraham. In the third reading, the Resurrection appears as the fulfillment of the deliverance of Israel from out of Egypt. The passage through the Red Sea is the prefigurement of Jesus' passage through death into life. So the Easter proclamation (the *Exsultet*) sings: "This is the night when first you saved our fathers: you freed the people of Israel from their slavery and led them dryshod through the sea." The other readings interpret Easter as the fulfillment of the prophetic promise to renew the chosen people Israel by giving them a new heart and a new spirit.

From the Resurrection our gaze turns not only backward, but even more forward. Jesus Christ is the first of those fallen asleep who are awakened to new life (Acts 26:23; 1 Cor 15:20; Col 1:18). In him, the future is newly and definitively disclosed; hope is finally restored to all. Jesus' Resurrection is the surety that at the end life will be victorious over death, truth over deceit, justice over injustice, and love over hate. The Resurrection of Jesus Christ grounds the *hope for our own resurrection* to eternal life (Rom 6:5; 1 Cor 15:12–22; Phil 3:11; 2 Tim 2:11). This is a hope not only for man's soul and spirit, but for the re-formation and transfiguration of our bodies and even of the entire cosmos. Everything is included in this hope—except evil. Man's desires and his actions, if they are motivated by love, are permanently secured in the reality of the new creation, even if they fail in history (GS 39).

327–328;
333–334;
336–342

3.2 Jesus' Resurrection as a Revelation of God

Whenever the New Testament speaks of the Resurrection of Jesus, it characterizes it as the act of an all-powerful God. Through the Resurrection, God fully reveals himself as the Lord over life and death. He holds everything in his hand, to him everything belongs—and so we can rely on him unconditionally in living and dying. Even the Old Testament says:

48–49

> The Lord puts to death and gives life;
> he casts down to the nether world;
> he raises up again (1 Sam 2:6).

So Paul defines God in reference to Judaism as the "*God who restores the dead to life*" (Rom 4:17; 2 Cor 1:9). The description "who raised Jesus, our Lord, from the dead" (Rom 4:24; 8:11; 2 Cor 4:14; Gal 1:1, among others) practically becomes the New Testament's definition of the essence of God. Jesus' Resurrection makes uniquely clear who God is: he is the one whose power embraces life and death, being and non-being; he is the living God, who is life and bestows life, who is creative love and faithfulness; he is the one on whom we can rely unconditionally, even when all human possibilities are shattered.

Faith in the Resurrection of Jesus is not something added to faith; it is the *epitome of faith in God*, who is the all-encompassing power of life. In

36

deciding for or against the Easter faith, we ultimately decide whether we think that men can live by their own possibilities and those of the world alone, or whether we dare to accept God wholly in our living and dying, to live wholly from God and ordered to him. In the Easter faith, there is a fundamental decision about the orientation and the meaning of all existence—a decision about whether we will to take God's being God seriously. Paul impressively describes a life permeated by strong faith in the Resurrection:

> We are afflicted in every way possible, but we are not crushed; full of doubts, we never despair. We are persecuted but never abandoned; we are struck down but never destroyed. Continually we carry about in our bodies the dying of Jesus, so that in our bodies the life of Jesus may also be revealed. While we live we are constantly being delivered to death for Jesus' sake, so that the life of Jesus may be revealed in our mortal flesh (2 Cor 4:8–11).

In his apostolic labors, Paul illuminates (is an epiphany of) the reality of the death and Resurrection of Jesus Christ. Like the Apostle, every Christian should express the death and Resurrection of Jesus Christ in his living, working, and dying. He should strive for what lies in heaven, where Christ sits at God's right hand. He should direct his mind to the heavenly and not to the earthly (Col 3:1–2). This does not mean, as Paul himself shows best, that the Christian disdains earthly goods or diminishes his exertions for God's cause in this world. The earthly ought to be oriented toward the definitive future and toward drawing strength for life and work in the world from hope for the heavenly.

3.3 The Resurrection as Revelation and Glorification of Jesus Christ

The Gospels let us see in many passages that Jesus was misunderstood during his earthly life, not only by the people but also by his disciples. Despite the extraordinary and sensational events of his ministry, in which the uniqueness of his person and of his mission stood forth, his mystery was still hidden from them. The Easter revelation first led them to the clear knowledge and full certainty that he is the promised Messiah, the Son of God—the Savior not only of Israel, but also of the pagans. The Gospels are written in the light of this Easter faith and interpret Jesus' words and deeds through faith.   123–124

Through the Resurrection, God confirmed the message and the claim of Jesus. God's power in raising Jesus removed what would have been an otherwise insuperable scandal for the Jews: How could the one crucified

121   on the cross be the promised Messiah, the Christ of God? He who was rejected by the leaders of his people and executed by the Romans is proved by the Resurrection to be the innocent and just one (Acts 3:14–15), the Son of David installed in his messianic position of power. "[He] who was descended from David according to the flesh . . . was made Son of God in power according to the spirit of holiness, by his resurrection from the dead . . ." (Rom 1:3–4). By his Resurrection, Jesus became the glorious Messiah, though differently from what the Jews had expected. The cross was not deprived of its offensiveness, but it was included in God's plan of salvation (Mk 8:31; 1 Cor 2:7–9).

65–70;   With the Resurrection, Jesus' relationship to God also comes fully to light. If in his earthly life Jesus already hints at something of his unique, immediate relationship to God, the Father, the *mystery of the divine Sonship* becomes fully evident to the disciples in the Risen One, Christ clothed with divine power and dwelling with God. Paul counts it as irrefutably certain that God "chose to reveal his Son" to him before Damascus (Gal 1:16). The previously unbelieving, doubting Thomas falls to his knees as he encounters the Risen One and exclaims, "My Lord and my God!" (Jn 20:28).

134–137

The titles of majesty and dignity with which the early Church expressed its faith in the person of Jesus Christ—Messiah, Lord, Son of God, Servant of God, among them—draw their strength and take their meaning from faith in the Resurrection. This faith is the creative source of a developing Christology. The Christology means to say not only who the earthly Jesus was in the past, but who he is in the present, as the exalted Lord.

4. He Ascended into Heaven

4.1 Exaltation and Ascension into Heaven

The New Testament expresses Jesus' confirmation and his enthronement in a position of divine power primarily by the concept of "*exaltation*". In doing so, it interprets Psalm 110 messianically, as the early Church did: "Sit at my right hand till I make your enemies your footstool" (Ps 110:1). Already in Peter's "Pentecost sermon" (Acts 2:34), we find the message that Jesus Christ has been exalted to God's right hand. But it pervades the whole New Testament (Acts 5:31; 7:56; Rom 8:34; Eph 1:20, among others). The declaration that Jesus has received the place of honor next to God is, of course, meant figuratively: Jesus has received a share in the glory, lordship, power, and divinity of God. He is now "the Lord" or, 133–135 rather, "our Lord" (1 Cor 1:9; 6:17, among others). Exaltation means Jesus' enthronement in a position of power equal to God. We hear this in the ancient hymn to Christ from the Letter to the Philippians:

> Because of this, God highly exalted him
>   and bestowed on him the name above every other name,
>
> So that at Jesus' name every knee must bend
>   in the heavens, on the earth, and under the earth,
>   and every tongue proclaim to the glory of God the Father:
> JESUS CHRIST IS LORD! (Phil 2:9–11).

This hymn teaches that the exalted Jesus is the *cosmocrator*, ruler over the world, over the living and the dead (compare Rom 14:9). To him as the *pantocrator* everything is subjected—heaven and earth, even the powers and dominations opposed to God. Even if his lordship remains hidden under the struggles and afflictions of the present time, even if it is still covered over by the world's evil, it cannot be defeated. "Christ must reign until God has put all enemies under his feet" (1 Cor 15:25). So the Book of Revelation calls him the "King of kings and Lord of lords" (Rev 19:16).

Luke presents essentially the same truth with the *ascension of Jesus into heaven* (Lk 24:50–51; Acts 1:9–10). We should not understand this as some sort of space flight. The cloud that hides Jesus from the gaze of the disciples is an Old Testament symbol of the powerful appearance and presence of God. By it we understand that Jesus has entered into God's world and God's glory, which surpass space and time. Luke tells us that the ascension into heaven happens in the context of a final appearance of the Risen One who has already entered into the heavenly world (Lk 24:26). The ascension into heaven is not an event separate from Jesus' exaltation; rather, it emphasizes a particular aspect of it. It is the final appearance of the Risen One. With it, the disciples become clearly conscious that while Jesus has left those who immediately experienced his presence (Lk 24:51), he will one day come again (Acts 1:11). The ascension also makes clear, of course, that Jesus, by having entered into the glory of God, is close to his disciples in a new way, in the way of God. Jesus is now always with us, is present from God and as God.

According to Luke, *forty days* separate the Resurrection from the ascension of Jesus Christ into heaven. By the number forty, Holy Scripture designates a particularly holy time: the people Israel wandered for forty years through the desert; Moses dwelt on Mount Sinai for forty days "before God"; Elijah was underway to Mount Horeb for forty days; and Jesus was tested in the wilderness for forty days. The forty days after

Easter are the time when the Exalted One still appeared bodily to his disciples. With the ascension into heaven, a new time has begun—the *time of the Church*. In it the one who has returned home to God is close to those who are his in a new way. He sends them the Holy Spirit from the Father (Acts 2:4–5) and endows them with the strength to continue his work on earth (Acts 1:8). With the succession in salvation history of the Resurrection, ascension into heaven, and outpouring of the Spirit, Luke tries to express the continuity between the time of Jesus and the time of the Church. In the forty days, the two times overlap, so to speak. The time of the Church is thus linked to the time that Jesus dwelt visibly on earth. The ascension of Jesus Christ into heaven is less an ending than a new beginning. It inaugurates the time in which Jesus Christ, the exalted Lord, continues his work in the Church and in history through the Spirit.

4.2 The Lordship of Jesus Christ

The lordship of Jesus Christ, who is exalted at the right hand of the Father, is described in Holy Scripture and in the Church's tradition of faith in many ways. In more recent times, the doctrine of the *threefold office* of Jesus Christ—prophetic, priestly, and kingly—has been affirmed.

226–227

1. *The prophetic office of Jesus Christ.* In the New Testament, Jesus is frequently described as the prophet promised in the Old Testament (Acts 3:22; Jn 1:45; 6:14; Dt 18:15). Likewise, he is often called the teacher (Mk 10:17, among others). The Fourth Gospel calls him the light of the world (Jn 1:8; 8:12; 12:46) and the truth (14:6). Jesus has come into the world for the purpose of bearing witness to the truth (18:37). He is the definitive truth about God, man, and the world. Among the many elusive hopes and illusions in the world, he is the light that lets us see men and things without distortion. Jesus discloses to us, in the darkness and blindness that are consequences of sin and signs of our being lost, the

104–105;
136–138

meaning of our existence, the meaning of suffering and death. As *the* prophet, Jesus Christ is the key to the understanding of man; without Jesus Christ, man cannot fully comprehend himself and his world. In Jesus Christ, God reveals "man to himself" (GS 22). That is why Jesus Christ is celebrated in the liturgy of Christmas and Epiphany as the light of the rising sun, the winter solstice of the world. The Easter Vigil liturgy hails Jesus Christ in the symbol of the Easter candle with the threefold cry: "*Lumen Christi*"—"Christ, our light".

254–255

The prophetic office of Jesus Christ is exercised in the *proclamation of the Church*. In the word of proclamation, the exalted Lord is abidingly present among us. For this reason, the book of the Gospels is solemnly carried in and venerated at festive liturgies. The presence of Jesus Christ in the word is not, of course, limited to the liturgical proclamation or to the official proclamation of the Church. Jesus Christ is present wherever his gospel is attested to in word or deed, wherever his truth brings itself to bear in the daily life of family and society (LG 35).

2. *The priestly office of Jesus Christ.* The New Testament already inter- 154–157;
prets Jesus' self-surrender to the will of the Father and his vicarious 157–158
ministry for us as a priestly ministry. The Letter to the Hebrews in
particular describes the cross as a sacrifice presented once for all by which
the exalted Christ is "a priest forever" (Heb 7:17, 21, 23–24). He lives 158–159;
forever to make intercession for his own (Heb 7:25). Through his sacrifice, 288–292
Jesus has once for all reconciled man to God, and man to man, bestowing
new life on us. Life, which was alienated from itself and damaged in 205–208
manifold ways, becomes whole again. The fulfillment of life bestowed by
Jesus Christ does not consist, of course, in egoistic self-realization, but
in self-emptying love. We see this meaning of life already in nature.
Everything that lives lives only in transition to something else; living
things must leave themselves in order to preserve themselves. "Unless the
grain of wheat falls to the earth and dies, it remains just a grain of wheat.
But if it dies, it produces much fruit" (Jn 12:24). This is fully true of new
life in Jesus Christ: "Whoever would preserve his life will lose it, but
whoever loses his life . . . will preserve it" (Mk 8:35).

As high priest, Jesus Christ is especially present in the *celebration of the* 284–286
Eucharist. Even in the Gospels' Easter stories, the Risen One appears in the
context of meal celebrations (Lk 24:30–31, 36–42; Jn 21:9–14). Indeed, the
whole liturgy is an act of the priestly office of Jesus Christ (SC 7). In every 262–265
sacrament, Jesus Christ is the true minister. Jesus' priesthood realizes itself
not only in the ordained priesthood but also in the common priesthood of
all Christians. The ministry of the laity presents "spiritual sacrifices" to
God (1 Pet 2:5; Rom 12:1; LG 34) through prayer, apostolic efforts,
married and family life, daily work, intellectual and physical recreation
when done in the Spirit, and the burdens of life patiently borne.

3. *The kingly office of Jesus Christ.* In the ancient world, the king was
considered a representative of God, even the son of God. He represented
the cosmic and political order within which alone a fulfilled human life
was possible. The king, the kingdom, the city, and the state have been
from ancient times not only political concepts, but religious symbols of
hope. The Old and New Testament message about the kingly lordship of 124–126
God carries this hope forward. Since the lordship of God dawns in Jesus
Christ, in his cross and in his exaltation, the New Testament can also call 159–161;
him king. But just as he is the Messiah of the cross, he is also the King on 174–176
the cross (Mk 15:2, 18, 26; Jn 19:14–15, 19–22). We see this most clearly

when Jesus—mocked, beaten, humiliated, and stained with blood by the clamorous crowds, bearing a crown of thorns on his head—is asked by Pilate: "Are you the King of the Jews?" Jesus answers affirmatively, but adds immediately: "My kingdom does not belong to this world." His kingdom consists in his bearing witness to the truth and gathering men in the truth (Jn 18:33–37). Only in this sense is he the "King of kings and Lord of lords" (1 Tim 6:15; Rev 19:6).

208–210;
216–218;
343;
350–352
The kingship of Jesus Christ implies no theocratic kingdom, whether in the Church, in the state, or in society. The kingly lordship of Jesus Christ is *not a utopia or an ideology for this world*. Neither is it, of course, a purely inner, purely spiritual notion, a salvation understood purely privately. Jesus Christ wills to penetrate everything with his Spirit, with his truth, and with his life, the private as well as the public, the family as much as the world of work and leisure. As the Second Vatican Council teaches, the lordship of Christ is realized wherever men realize the kingly freedom of
134–135;
159–160;
201–202;
209–210
the sons and daughters of God, wherever they conquer the reign of sin in themselves through self-denial and through a holy life, wherever they no longer allow their bodies to be ruled by sin but offer their members "to God as weapons for justice" (Rom 6:13). The Kingdom of Christ is a kingdom of holiness and of grace, a kingdom of justice, of love, and of peace (Preface for the feast of Christ the King). When Christians promote progress in the world "through human labor, technical skill and civil culture", thus serving "the utility of all men according to the plan of the creator and light of his word", Christ will "increasingly illuminate the whole of human society with his saving light" (LG 36).

216–218
There is no external separation of the Kingdom of God or the Kingdom of Christ and the kingdom of the world. They are mixed together in the Church as well as in society and the state. St. Augustine has shown in his famous book *The City of God* that the two kingdoms are distinguished rather by *two manners of love*, love of self and love of God, life according to the flesh and life according to the spirit. So wherever there is selfless love,
212–214;
216;
223–224
whether within the Church or outside it, the Kingdom of Christ is already dawning there. The Church is to be a sacrament, a sign and an instrument, of the unity of men with God and with one another (LG 1). The task of Christians and of all men of good will is to work toward a universal civilization characterized by love (Paul VI).

5. He Will Come Again in Glory

With the Resurrection and exaltation of Jesus Christ, a new world and a new mankind begin once for all. But the Kingdom of Christ still struggles with the powers of evil. For that reason, the Church's confession of Christ concludes with a *prospect of hope* for the definitive completion of the lordship of Jesus Christ: "He will come again in glory to judge the living and the dead."

This confession of the Second Coming of Jesus Christ and of the eschatological judgment provokes many questions for us today. How can we imagine it within our evolutionary world view? Can we still imagine anything at all by it? We cannot take up this question here but must come back to it below when we consider in detail the question of eschatological hope. Here we ask only what the hope formulated in the confession of faith means today and what strength it has for transforming our lives in the present world.

339–343

This way of posing the question agrees with the *intention of the New Testament*. Holy Scripture is not particularly interested in speculations about the when, where, and how of the Second Coming of Jesus Christ. Indeed, it rejects such speculations. For "as to the exact day or hour, no one knows it, neither the angels in heaven nor even the Son, but only the Father" (Mk 13:32). So we are not seeking information about a near or distant future; we are confronting a *decision here today* in light of this future. "Be constantly on the watch! Stay awake! You do not know when the appointed time will come" (Mk 13:33). The decision of the coming judgment is already being made now: "If anyone in this faithless and corrupt age is ashamed of me and my doctrine, the Son of Man will be ashamed of him when he comes with the holy angels in his Father's glory" (Mk 8:38; Jn 5:24). Both the earthly life and ministry of Jesus and his ascension into heaven and exaltation occur within this *horizon of the future*. The epoch of the Church, which begins with Jesus' ascension into heaven, ends with the Second Coming of Jesus Christ in glory (Acts 1:11). That is why the Apostles have the commission to proclaim and to bear witness before all people: "He is the one set apart by God as judge of the living and the dead" (Acts 10:42). This and many other declarations of the New Testament (Acts 17:31; Rom 14:9; 2 Tim 4:1; 1 Pet 4:5) are summarized in the Nicene Creed: "He will come again in glory to judge the living and the dead." This affirmation declares that the lordship of Christ, the *victory of life and of love*, which has begun in a hidden way with the Resurrection and exaltation, is definitive and will become finally manifest. At that time our hope for eternal life and for resurrection from the dead will be fulfilled.

The Second Coming of Jesus Christ and the subjection of all powers

348–352   and dominations opposed to God are directed to *God's being all in all* (1 Cor 15:28). When in the fourth century Marcellus of Ancyra falsely concluded from this declaration that Jesus Christ would divest himself of his human nature at the end of time and enter again into God, the First Council of Constantinople (381) rejected this, adding a phrase to the Creed: "and his kingdom will have no end". Jesus Christ is the definitive "Yes" and "Amen" of God to all that God has promised (2 Cor 1:20), the "Yes" and "Amen" to man and the world. The humanity of Jesus Christ has a definitive importance in God and for God. For that reason, the lordship of Jesus Christ will be an eternal lordship (Lk 1:33).

339; 343;   Even this article of faith has an eminently *practical meaning*. On the one
350–352   hand, confession of the eschatological judgment of God through Jesus Christ contradicts our dreams of progress and harmony, with which we like to connect our notion of salvation. The teaching about judgment says that not everything will come out even in the end. At the end of history, there will be a definitive separation of good from evil, the victory of the good and the condemnation of evil. That is what makes for the seriousness of our decisions today. On the other hand, the teaching about judgment contains a promise: the specifically Christian understanding of the equality of all men as in practice responsible for their lives before God. This gives an inalienable hope to all who suffer injustice, even as it urges us onward in the historical struggle for universal justice.

Our hopeful gaze into the future sharpens even more our vision of the present and our historical responsibility here and now. The future, which has definitively begun with Jesus Christ, is realized through the work of the Holy Spirit, who makes present the work of Jesus Christ in us, in the Church, and in the world. This is the theme of the third part of the confession of faith.

PART THREE

THE WORK OF
THE HOLY SPIRIT

I

NEW LIFE IN THE HOLY SPIRIT

1. The Reality of the Holy Spirit

1.1 Are We Redeemed?

The good news of the redemption of the world through Jesus Christ appears to be refuted almost automatically by the unredeemed state of the world. How can this message stand in the face of injustice that cries out to heaven, of deceit, violence, hunger, and torture? How can it stand in the face of loneliness, meaninglessness, faithlessness, of sickness, guilt, and death? How can it stand in the face of our continuing sinfulness? Is not our world grace-less in the truest sense? Did Jesus die in vain?

These questions are as old as Christianity itself. From the very beginning, the Christian message of the world's salvation had to confront two other answers. There was and still is the *answer of Judaism*. It shares with Christianity the Messianic promise of salvation. But whereas Judaism still hopes for the Messiah and the Messianic times, Christianity announces that in Jesus, who is the Christ, the Messiah has already appeared and that the salvation of the world has already dawned. In this, Christianity also opposes one of the most influential doctrines in the ancient world, the *answer of gnosis*, which has reappeared today in new forms. In gnosis, there is no redemption *of* the world, but rather redemption *from* the world. The gnostic seeks to "escape" from the evil system of this world. He flees either into pure interiority, into undamaged nature, or, through mystical ecstasy, into a wholly other world. In opposition to this, Christianity proclaims that God has so loved this world that he surrendered his only Son and sent him into the world so that it might be saved through him (Jn 3:16–17).

The Christian message is a message of a *salvation that does not come from this world, but that is nonetheless the salvation of the world* (Jn 17:11, 14, 16, 18). On the one hand, Christianity speaks of a salvation that does not come *from* this world. It bears witness to salvation that comes from God. Only God can make a wholly new beginning; he alone can be man's ultimate fulfillment. On the other hand, Christianity bears witness to the fact that this salvation in Jesus Christ is present once for all *in* the world and *for* the

world. But how can this message be credibly asserted in the face of the
world's distress? Where, how do we encounter the reality of salvation?

1.2 The Holy Spirit as the Reality of the New Covenant

The Church's confession of faith answers the question about the reality of
redemption by saying: "We believe in the Holy Spirit, the Lord, the giver
of life." What does this mean?

69–72   As we have already seen, Scripture understands the Holy Spirit as the
creative power in all life. He animates all, binds all together, and guides all
toward eschatological salvation. He is active particularly in *Jesus Christ*, in
159–161;   his conception, baptism, public work, death, and Resurrection. In the
170–173;   death, Resurrection, and glorification of Jesus, the Spirit has ushered in
348–352   the *beginning of the new creation*. It will one day be completed in the
transfiguration of all reality. Jesus is the Christ, the one anointed with the
Holy Spirit. According to the Gospel of Luke, Jesus applies to himself the
prophet's promise: "The spirit of the Lord is upon me; therefore he has
anointed me" (Lk 4:18; Acts 10:38; Jn 1:32). Our redemption and our
salvation consist in our participation in the fullness of the Spirit found in
Jesus Christ. We are Christians, i.e., anointed ones, by sharing in Jesus
Christ's anointing with the Spirit.

This participation in Jesus Christ is bestowed on us by the Holy Spirit
himself. The Spirit has been sent to make Jesus Christ—his person, his
word, and his work—ever present in history. All of reality is filled by the
Holy Spirit, the Spirit of Jesus. So Paul says: "The Lord is the Spirit, and
where the Spirit of the Lord is, there is freedom" (2 Cor 3:17). He means
that *the Spirit is the active presence and the present activity of the exalted Lord in
the Church and in the world*. But the Spirit is more than the gift of new life in
Jesus Christ; he is also the giver of this gift, a distinct divine person.
Wherever he works, the eschatological kingdom of freedom dawns. The
gift of the Holy Spirit received in faith is the reality of the New Covenant
(Thomas Aquinas).

Luke has expressed this in his account of the *outpouring of the Holy Spirit on Pentecost*
(Acts 2:1–13). For the Jews, Pentecost began as a harvest feast; by the first and
second centuries A.D. it had become a day commemorating the making of the
covenant on Sinai. Luke knows this; he intends by his account to represent the
dawning of the eschatological time of salvation, the fulfillment of the prophetic
promise (Joel 3:1–3), of the proclamation of the Lord (Acts 1:8). In doing so, Luke
takes up biblical images that were already employed for theophanies in the Old
Testament, especially at Sinai. The raging storm shows the strength of the Holy

Spirit, who is the breath and storm of new life. The tongues of fire, which alight individually on each of those gathered, show that the disciples are enabled and encouraged to bear witness. Speaking and understanding foreign languages, together with the list of foreign peoples, signifies that the worldwide mission entrusted to the disciples puts an end to the Babylonian confusion of languages. Disrupted mankind is now united again. Because of the apostolic mission, the peoples are to be gathered into the one people of God. Pentecost fulfills the prophetic promise that the Spirit of God will be poured out at the end of time on all flesh, on great and small, young and old, Jew and Gentile (Joel 3:1–2; Acts 2:17–18; 10:44–48).

The New Testament describes the individual aspects of the Holy Spirit's reality and activity in many ways. According to the *Acts of the Apostles*, the Spirit is active especially in the Church's mission. It is he who leads the Church in mission and who discloses again and again new missionary fields and tasks. He accompanies her mission with visible deeds and with extraordinary charisms, such as glossolalia (speaking in tongues) and prophecy. While emphasizing the freedom of the Spirit, Luke is also concerned to demonstrate the continuity in the Spirit's activity. We see it especially in the brotherly fellowship of the Gentile Christian congregations with the primitive Jerusalem congregation.

Paul too is familiar with extraordinary gifts of the Spirit. In him, however, the 228–230 emphasis falls not on conspicuous phenomena but on everyday Christian life. The Spirit is not so much the strength of the extraordinary as the strength to do the ordinary in an extraordinary way. The Spirit shows himself particularly in the confession of Jesus Christ (1 Cor 12:3) and in the building up of Christian communities (1 Cor 12–14). Paul also understands the Spirit as the driving force in the life of each believer. The believer should let himself be led not by the flesh but by the Spirit (Gal 5:16–17; Rom 8:12–13). He should bring forth fruits of the Spirit: "love, joy, peace, patient endurance, kindness, generosity, faith, mildness, and chastity" (Gal 5:22–23). The Spirit effects a double openness in man: the openness for God, which expresses itself above all in prayer (Gal 4:6; Rom 8:15–16, 26–27), and the openness to one's neighbor. The selfless service of love is the true Christian freedom (Gal 5:13). In this we see already the liberation of creation from its transitoriness and servitude—a liberation for which creation waits and hopes. The Spirit is the first fruit, giving Christian hope a sure ground (Rom 8:18–27).

The manifold witness of Holy Scripture to the reality and activity of the Holy Spirit can be summarized in three points:

1. The Holy Spirit, the gift and love of God in person, discloses the reality of creation to us. *Grace in a broader sense* is already active in creation. 114–117 So the believer takes nothing simply for granted; for him everything is a gift and a present from God. Even in the plainest and most everyday things, incidents, and encounters, he can experience traces of God's love and of his Spirit, being filled with joy and thanks. Since the Spirit directs all of reality to its definitive completion, his reality and activity show

themselves especially where new life is awakened, where reality pushes beyond itself. This is especially clear in men's historical seeking and striving for life, justice, freedom, and peace. We may recognize traces of God in a particular way where men break out of the prison of their egoism, where they find their way to one another in love and pardon, where they forgive one another, do good, and offer help, without expecting or asking recompense. Man finds himself and his fulfillment not in egoistic self-seeking, but in giving, bestowing, and sharing. Wherever there is love, something of the world's final completion and transfiguration is anticipated even now.

2. Man first finds his deepest fulfillment, of course, where he is unconditionally and definitively accepted and affirmed as a person. Only God can bestow such absolute love. He does bestow it by bestowing himself on man, taking him up into communion and friendship with himself and letting him participate by the Holy Spirit in the divine life. In this way, men become a new creation (2 Cor 5:17; Gal 6:15). When this happens, we speak of *grace in the true sense of the word*. Grace is friendship and communion with God. Grace is God's love poured out into our hearts through the Holy Spirit (Rom 5:5; DS 1530, 1561; NR 801, 829). Holy Scripture even speaks of the indwelling of the Holy Spirit (1 Cor 3:16; 6:19; 2 Cor 6:16); this means his living presence in the faithful. Through the indwelling of the Holy Spirit, the Father and the Son are also present in us (Jn 14:23). By grace we are received into the life and love of the triune God in order to share it.

This friendship with God takes effect in different ways. It shows itself in man himself. The Holy Spirit heals and sanctifies him. He sanctifies him by joining him to God, making him whole and entire. The Spirit brings about order, discipline, and moderation in man. The fruits of the Spirit show themselves next in our behavior toward others—in friendliness, helpfulness, reconciliation, selflessness, but also in a commitment to that justice without which love would be hollow and empty. The Spirit also brings about friendship and communion with Jesus Christ. Paul uses "in the Spirit" and "in Jesus Christ" as interchangeable expressions. This communion with Jesus Christ shows itself concretely in reading and meditating on Holy Scripture, in efforts to imitate Jesus according to the Sermon on the Mount, in communion with Christ in the sacraments, and not least in service to needy brothers and sisters, in whom we encounter Jesus Christ himself (Mt 25:34–45). Finally, the Spirit brings about joy in God, in the liturgy, and in prayer. Particularly in prayer, the Holy Spirit gives us the experience of being God's children. Only in the Holy Spirit are we able to cry "Abba, Father". "The Spirit himself gives witness with our spirit that we are children of God" (Rom 8:15–16). Because

205–207

76–78

communion with God is the deepest fulfillment of man, whoever opens himself to the working of the Spirit will be filled with deep inner peace, with consolation and joy. This is the experience of all great Christians, especially the saints.

3. All these effects of the Holy Spirit are only a foretaste of future glory (2 Cor 1:22; Eph 1:14). They are only a *beginning and anticipation of the definitive completion*. The Spirit is the power of hope and the strength of a life lived out of hope. Suffering from the still-unfinished world, suffering under the power of evil in its many forms, experiences of injustice, rejection, persecution, even martyrdom (which is still a concrete reality for Christians in many parts of the world)—these too belong to the experience of the Holy Spirit. In such situations, which arise in one way or another for every Christian, the Spirit gives us the strength. He is himself the strength to endure and to resist; he lends us courage and magnanimity so that in spite of all opposition we may stand up for Christ and his kingdom. The Spirit is strength in suffering and dying. That is why many medieval hospitals were called Holy Spirit hospitals. A hymn summarizes all this by referring to the Spirit as the Consoler: "You who are called the Consoler". We hear of the manifold saving work of the Holy Spirit in many songs. The prayer of St. Augustine is especially striking:

348–352

> Breathe in me,
> Thou Holy Spirit,
> That I may think what is holy.
> Move me,
> Thou Holy Spirit,
> That I may do what is holy.
> Attract me,
> Thou Holy Spirit,
> That I may love what is holy.
> Strengthen me,
> Thou Holy Spirit,
> That I may guard what is holy.
> Guard me,
> Thou Holy Spirit,
> That I may never lose what is holy.

We can sum up all this by saying that the Holy Spirit discloses to us our origin in God and his grace, even while he gives us hope for God and his kingdom. He works as well in our present lives by healing and sanctifying, reconciling and comforting. This brings us to consider the procession of all reality from God and its return to him.

2. God Eternally Predestines to Salvation

The most fundamental statement about our blessedness is this: God has chosen, called, and accepted us from all eternity. God has always already gone ahead of us with his helping grace. Before we ever asked about God and his grace, before we set out for him and sought to prove ourselves worthy of him through a good life, before we even existed at all, God had already chosen us out of pure love and had predestined us to communion with him. As the beginning of the Letter to the Ephesians says, God has bestowed on us "every spiritual blessing" from all eternity.

> God chose us in [Jesus Christ] before the world began, to be holy and blameless in his sight, to be full of love; he likewise predestined us through Christ Jesus to be his adopted sons—such was his will and pleasure—that all might praise the glorious favor he has bestowed on us in his beloved (Eph 1:4–6).

This *doctrine of predestination* seems to many people to be a very dark topic. They see in it a presumptuous attempt to penetrate into the hidden mystery of God's will. In reality, the doctrine is an essential part of the gospel, an important part of the encouraging, consoling *good news*. The point of this doctrine is not to pry impertinently into the mystery of God's will, but to assert with certainty that "God makes all things work together for the good of those who love God and are called according to his decree" (Rom 8:28), so that nothing in this world can separate us from the love of God that is in Christ Jesus, our Lord (Rom 8:39). This message can be a firm foothold amid the world's adversities. It proclaims that God is eternally in Jesus Christ "Emmanuel", God with us and for us.

In principle, this good news holds for all men. *God's salvific will is universal.* God "wants all men to be saved and to come to know the truth" (1 Tim 2:4). He does not will the death of the sinner, but wants him to change his ways and remain alive (Ex 33:11; 2 Pet 3:9). The universality of the divine salvific will has been re-expressed emphatically by the Second Vatican Council:

114–116;
217–220

> Those who, through no fault of their own, do not know the Gospel of Christ or his Church, but who nevertheless seek God with a sincere heart, and, moved by grace, try in their actions to do his will as they know it through the dictates of their conscience—those too may achieve eternal salvation. Nor shall divine providence deny the assistance necessary for salvation to those who, without any fault of theirs, have not yet arrived at an explicit knowledge of God, and who, not without grace, strive to lead a good life. Whatever good or

truth is found amongst them is considered by the Church to be a preparation for the Gospel and given by him who enlightens all men that they may at length have life (LG 16).

The election and calling of man, of every man, implies, of course, that God accepts man as man and takes him seriously. For that very reason, God wills man's free response and consent. Indeed, God in his love makes the realization of his salvific will depend on our freedom. That means that through our own fault we can also miss salvation. *Predestination in the stricter sense* holds only for those who also attain eternal salvation with God's grace.

Unfortunately, this good news was in the past often mixed with an anxiety-producing message of terror. In thinking to follow St. Augustine, the great teacher of grace, many deduced from particular declarations in Holy Scripture about individual obduracy (e.g., Ex 7:3; 9:12; Is 6:10; Mk 4:12; Rom 9:18), and from Paul's declarations in Romans 9–11, a doctrine of double predestination: some are chosen from all eternity for salvation, others are not. At times, a few people even presumed to know that only the smaller number of men was predestined to salvation, whereas the majority belonged to the mass of the damned. The Church, however, rejected these extreme doctrines of predestination (that of the monk Gottschalk in the ninth century, for instance, or that of Calvin in the sixteenth century). The Church has held fast to the contrary doctrine: "Almighty God wills that all men without exception come to salvation, even if not all are saved in fact. That some are saved is the gift of the Savior; that others are lost is the fault of those who are lost" (DS 623, 1567; NR 835). Jesus Christ did not die only for the elect, nor only for the faithful, but for all men (DS 2005, 2304; NR 875). That is what is meant when we say that all possess sufficient grace, but that grace does not become efficacious grace in all.

But these definitions, though correct in themselves, do not solve the *problem*. How is the absolute primacy of God secured if the efficacy of God's saving work depends on human consent? Must the failure to attain salvation not ultimately fall back on God, who indeed bestows sufficient grace on all men, but not efficacious grace? How are we to reconcile the two declarations, that God wills the salvation of all men, but that there are men who through their own fault do not attain salvation? How are *God's predestination and human freedom* to be related?

The *dispute over grace* in the sixteenth and seventeenth centuries between Dominican and Jesuit theologians revolved around this difficult problem. The pope finally left the problem open and forbad mutual accusations of heresy. That was a wise decision. As it was then posed, the question was insoluble. The relation between God's freedom and the freedom of man remains an insoluble mystery for us. The relation between the freedom of God and of man cannot be described in such a way that one takes away from God what one gives to man—or vice versa. The freedom of God's love is so infinitely great that he not only permits finite human freedom but renders it possible, sustains it, encourages it, liberates it, and fulfills it. This relationship between God and man is disclosed to us once for all in Jesus Christ. For that reason, the problem of predestination can be illuminated only by Jesus Christ. This point was lost in the traditional discussion of predestination, and was the reason why the dispute got stuck in many useless questions.

In its original sense, the doctrine of divine predestination says three things:

1. The point of departure of the doctrine of God's predestination is not an abstract decree of God's will, not a general principle, but concrete *election in Jesus Christ* (Eph 1:4–6, 11–12; 3:2–13). In Jesus Christ, God speaks a pure "Yes", and not "Yes" and "No" at the same time. So election and rejection are not co-equal or parallel. There is only election to salvation. That is why we speak not abstractly and indeterminately of predestination, but concretely and determinately of the predestination to salvation. This predestination happens in Jesus Christ. God's election determines us "to share the image of his Son" (Rom 8:29). God made him to be sin for us (2 Cor 5:21); all men, even sinners, are called to salvation in Christ.

2. God's salvific will in Jesus Christ directs itself not to the isolated individual, but to the *people of God* as a whole. The individual is addressed as a part of the great community of the people of God, as a member of which he is saved (Dt 7:7–8; 14:2, among others). For that reason, election is spoken of not in the singular but in the plural (Eph 1:4–6; 1 Pet 1:1–2; 2:5–10). The election of one man is in the end also the salvation of the other (Rom 11:31–32). Thus election of the individual is always *election to representative service for others*. Election is not a privilege of those who have a "monopoly" on salvation; it is a singling out for service in the salvation of all. To the question whether only few will be saved, Jesus answers with the appeal, "Try to come in through the narrow door" (Lk 13:24). This appeal becomes the Risen One's missionary commission, a call to proclaim the gospel to all creatures (Mk 16:15). There are no predestined or privileged families, peoples, or races, no members of a master race superior to second-class men. To prevent such a falsely interpreted doctrine of election, Holy Scripture tells us that God chooses precisely the weak to shame the strong (1 Cor 1:26–28).

3. For the *individual*, God's predestination is the quintessence of the gospel. What matters is not ultimately the willing and striving of man, but only the mercy of God (Rom 9:16; Eph 2:8). The certainty of election is our greatest support and the strongest consolation. But it also cancels every natural security and relates us wholly and entirely to God's grace. Precisely because God effects both the willing and the achieving, we must work out our salvation in fear and trembling (Phil 2:12–13). For where

136–138

212–215;
224–226

217–222

man does not conform to grace, it becomes a judgment on him. The
saying "The invited are many, the elect are few" (Mt 22:14) shows that
election is not a sure possession; it is both a gift and a task. It does not
exclude man's responsibility but, quite the contrary, sets it free and lays
the most extreme claims on it. It confronts man with the possibility of
forfeiting his life by his own fault and falling prey to eternal ruin. So the
certainty of election gives no assurance, but is ultimately a *certainty of hope*.   199–201;
It relies on God's faithfulness alone, hoping that he who has begun the   345–347
good work will also complete it (Phil 1:6). Just as election proceeds from
God, so it flows back in the end in praise of God:

> How deep are the riches and the wisdom and the knowledge of God!
> How inscrutable his judgments, how unsearchable his ways! For
> "who has known the mind of the Lord? Or who has been his
> counselor? Who has given him anything so as to deserve return?" For
> from him and through him and for him all things are. To him be glory
> forever. Amen (Rom 11:33–36).

3. The Historical Realization of Grace:
The Justification of the Sinner

3.1 Justice and Justification according to
The Witness of Holy Scripture

The Old and New Testaments answer the question about the meaning of
grace and of salvation with a wide range of images and concepts. Holy
Scripture speaks of life, light, peace, freedom, justice, reconciliation,
sanctification, redemption, and rebirth, to name a few. From these rich
and varied images and concepts, the concepts of justice and justification
became especially important through the influence of St. Augustine and
even more through the Reformation. The original sense and fundamental
meaning of these concepts is no longer immediately intelligible to us. We
must exert ourselves to discover their original sense. So we must begin by
entering into the biblical and ecclesiastical Tradition in this chapter. We
will then be able, in the next chapter, to talk about their meaning for
today.

The theme of justice and justification already plays a major role in the
Old Testament. Of particular importance is the characterization of Abraham
on the occasion of the making of the covenant: "Abraham put his faith in

the Lord, who credited it to him as an act of righteousness" (Gen 15:6). These words show that justice in this context means faithfulness to the covenant and behavior according to it. The covenant is the great proof of God's grace for Israel; he bestows life and land on the people as well as on the individual. The just man is the one who stands by this covenant and its order. He is just before God, just in relationship to others, and just before himself. But the prophets already accused Israel of seeking to ground its existence not on God and his will, but on its own insight and strength. The unbelief of Israel broke communion with God. Judgment threatens Israel. But even in the Old Testament, the message of judgment is not the last word (Hos 14:5). There is the stronger promise that God will restore Israel at the end of time through his creative action, making a new covenant with it (Jer 31:31–33). Indeed, certain (apocalyptic) sectors of Judaism at the time of Jesus expected the manifestation of God's justice, his faithfulness to the covenant at the end of time.

123–131   It is characteristic of *Jesus' message and appearance* that he criticized the self-righteousness of the pious of his time and turned to sinners. He has "come to call sinners, not the self-righteous" (Mk 2:17; Lk 19:10). In the parable of the prodigal son, the wayward brother is reinstated in his filial rights and justified (Lk 15:11–32). "To those who believed in their own self-righteousness while holding everyone else in contempt" (Lk 18:9) Jesus tells the parable of the self-righteous Pharisee and the tax collector. Of the tax collector who confesses, "O God, be merciful to me, a sinner", Jesus says, "This man went home from the temple justified but the other did not" (Lk 18:13–14). This message leads Jesus to take sinners into communion with himself and to eat with them (Mk 2:15–16; Mt 11:19; Lk 15:2; 19:7). Jesus understood these meals as anticipated celebrations of the eschatological marriage feast in the Kingdom of God. Thus the new justice proclaimed by Jesus means new communion with God and new community among men. Because God accepts every man, even the sinner and the godless, men can and must also accept one another. Because God justifies us, we no longer need to justify ourselves, no longer need to "achieve" our lives.

The Apostle *Paul* understood the message of Jesus in a particularly deep way; he asserted it against the Judaism of his time in a *message about the justification of the sinner*. Paul long and zealously sought justice by observing the precepts of the law. He was "above reproach when it came to justice based on the law" (Phil 3:6; Gal 1:14). Then Jesus Christ appeared to him on the road to Damascus (Acts 9:1–9; Gal 1:15–16), and Paul considered everything up to that point as loss, for the sake of Christ (Phil 3:7–8). He now announced the central content of the gospel of Jesus Christ:

But now the justice of God has been manifested apart from the law, even though both law and prophets bear witness to it—that justice of God which works through faith in Jesus Christ for all who believe (Rom 3:21–22; 1:17).

For we hold that a man is justified by faith apart from observance of the law (Rom 3:28).

We can understand these declarations only if we recognize that for Paul *the great turning point has come with the cross and Resurrection of Jesus*. Though all men are sinners and have broken the covenant with God, God has held fast to the end in Jesus Christ with his faithfulness to the covenant; in his justice, God has reconciled the world to himself out of pure love (2 Cor 5:18). For that reason, God's justice is not bound to the conditions of the law and its fulfillment, but only to faith in Jesus Christ. Jesus has been made justice for us (1 Cor 1:30); in him God's justice is bestowed on us. So God's justice is not one that distributes according to merit, rewarding the good and punishing the evil. It is God's own justice, his faithfulness to the covenant and love. It proves itself as a *justice that bestows and creates anew*, making the sinner just without merit, out of pure grace. This concerns not only the individual. The covenant with Abraham already invokes a universal promise (Gen 15:5–7): Abraham's offspring are to "inherit the world" (Rom 4:13). In the faith that depends on God, hoping against hope, the original creation is restored (Rom 4:17–18). In upholding covenant justice, *God's new justice in the world* is upheld: the coming of the lordship of God, the lordship of love. 159–161; 170–173

What Paul proclaimed, in the disputes with contemporary Jews, as the justification of the sinner by God, he elsewhere calls salvation, redemption, reconciliation. We find different notions and concepts in other writings of the New Testament. The Letter of James found it necessary to take a position against misunderstandings of the Pauline doctrine of justification; it emphasizes that faith without works is useless (Jas 2:20). This does not contradict Paul on this point, for Paul too teaches that Christians must be rich in the "harvest of justice" (Phil 1:11) and in the "fruit of the Spirit" (Gal 5:22). Faith must be active in love (Gal 5:6). The New Testament proclaims the one message of God's salvation in Jesus Christ in differing images and concepts according to the changing formulations of the question and situations.

These differing images and concepts have a deep material *connection*: the common point of departure is *Jesus' message of the coming of the lordship of God*. This is at the same time the salvation of man. God's faithfulness to the covenant, his *justice* in spite of all the unfaithfulness and sin of man, is now manifest. God's unconditional *love* is now brought to bear, because 205–206 through Jesus Christ God accepts every man who accepts this message in faith without any exception and without any conditions. This unconditional acceptance is the end of our enmity with God; it is the *forgiveness of sins, liberation* from the power of sin. This is also liberation from the power of death, from the power of the pressure to perform according to the law, from meaninglessness, hopelessness, and radical disorientation. Positively, acceptance by God means new *communion and friendship with him, reconciliation*, and *peace*. Because this *New Covenant* becomes real in the blood of Jesus (Mt 26:28; Mk 14:24), there dawns a *new creation* in which a new home is given to wandering man. His life has meaning again; he is in the *light*. He is reborn to a *new life*. Wherever God's loving lordship becomes concrete reality, men are reconciled with one another and called to the *service* of justice, of love, and of friendship. This is what we mean when we speak of justification by grace.

3.2 The Catholic/Protestant Controversy

In the Reformation of the sixteenth century, the issue of the justification and sanctification of man became the fateful question around which the unity of Western Christianity was broken. For the Reformation, the doctrine of justification was "the article with which the Church stands and falls".

How did this momentous splitting of the Church come about? Which questions of faith were (and are) under discussion?

Considered historically, *various economic, social, political, and religious factors* converged in this controversy. Through the rise of the national states, the unity of Western Christendom was already weakened. The beginning of the sixteenth century was also a time of spiritual upheaval. One need only think of the Renaissance, of humanism, and of the revolutionary new discoveries of Copernicus and Columbus, or of the invention of the printing press. In the Church there were influential reform movements, religious renewals, and new forms of piety (the *devotio moderna*, for instance). On the whole, though, *the Church at the end of the Middle Ages had fallen into a grave inner crisis*. Popes and bishops were variously entangled in worldly quarrels and interests; their personal lives often failed to accord with their religious offices. In many places pastoral care was lacking in vigor. Popular piety was externalized to a great extent, becoming at times even superstitious. There was a great deal of confusion in theology. Such deplorable states of affairs made a reform of head and members urgently necessary. Yet these external factors were rather the *climate* in which the Reformation was able to gain such rapid ground in so many places. Its real *causes* lay deeper. St. Clemens Maria Hofbauer (d. 1820) once remarked that the Reformation happened "because the

Germans have and had the need to be pious". This *genuinely religious impulse of the Reformation* cannot be ignored, and it should prevent us from "explaining" the splitting of faith through a one-sided imputation of personal guilt.

The point of departure of the Reformation was *Martin Luther's* (1483–1546) question: "How do I find a gracious God?" This was for Luther a question of life and death that stirred him most deeply and cast him into despair. In this question, he saw at issue man's standing justly before God. He did not find the answer in the absolution of the sacrament of penance, but in a new understanding of Holy Scripture. Through reading the Letter to the Romans, he discovered anew what God's justice means (Rom 1:17): not the justice that judges man according to his works and punishes him for his sins, but the justice that God gives man from pure grace on account of Christ. The Augsburg Confession formulates the *doctrine of justification* in this way: "Men cannot be justified before God through their own strengths, merits, or works, but they are justified without any effort on their part on account of Christ through faith . . ." (CA 4). For Luther and the Lutherans this doctrine of justification was not just one article of faith among others; it was *the center and the criterion of Christian faith*. This article describes what Jesus Christ means "for me". Because this article proclaims Jesus Christ as the only mediator of salvation, one cannot "yield or surrender anything of it, even if heaven and earth were to fall" (Smalcaldian Articles).

204

Luther's understanding of the justice of God corresponded thoroughly to the Catholic Tradition. By one-sidedly making this doctrine into the criterion of the whole faith, however, and given the prevailing circumstances, Luther very quickly fell into *conflict with the existing Church order*. In his Ninety-Five Theses on Indulgences published in 1517, Luther objected to the indulgence practice of the Dominican Tetzel because he saw in it a false conception of the forgiveness of sins. In the disputes that followed, Luther appealed to "Scripture alone", which he interpreted in the sense of the article on justification. The Church's authority to expound Scripture in a binding way was called into question. Luther declared that the pope, who refused to permit the preaching of the gospel interpreted in Luther's sense, was the Antichrist. Criticism of the Church was thus not the point of departure that led to the Reformation position. On the contrary, Luther's understanding of scriptural authority and the doctrine of justification gained from it were the point of departure and the criterion for his criticism of the existing Church, its sacraments and offices. The entire Church was now to be judged by the criterion of the gospel of justification by faith alone. This understanding thus came to break with the essential, traditional forms of life in the Church. The *differing understandings of the Church, its sacraments and offices*, came ever more clearly into the foreground and showed themselves as the true reason for the break from the unity of the Church.

304–307

204;
215–216;
238–239;
247–248;
263–264;
287–288;
290–291;
312–313;
324–325

The Reformers Huldrich *Zwingli* (1484–1531) in Zurich and especially John *Calvin* (1509–1564) in Geneva were, with Luther, important figures. In spite of many fundamental agreements with Luther, Calvin placed other emphases on the doctrine of justification. As distinct from Luther, Calvin did not regard this doctrine as the core of all doctrines; in his major work, *Institutes of the Christian Religion*, he placed it within the doctrine on the Holy Spirit. Calvin's leading doctrine was the honor of God and obedience to God's ordinances in all domains of life. In this, he stood close to the Catholic Tradition. On the other hand, he sharply opposed the Catholic understanding of faith in the doctrine of divine predestination, but also in sacramental doctrine, particularly as regards the Eucharist.

An initial *reaction by the Catholic Church* came with the condemnation of various Lutheran theses in a bull threatening excommunication, "Exsurge Domine" (1520). The general council, demanded and planned for so long yet repeatedly postponed, finally convened, but unfortunately only after much maneuvering and much too late. The *Council of Trent* (1545–1563) did not condemn the Reformers themselves nor their doctrines as a whole; it did anathematize, though, many of their theses. Moreover, it introduced one of the greatest reforms in Church history. In the Decree on Justification (1547) (DS 1520–83; NR 790–851), the Council offered its own global presentation of the Catholic doctrine of justification from out of the Tradition. As distinguished from Luther, the Council did not make the doctrine of justification into the criterion and perspective for the whole, but developed it rather in the context of the whole of the traditional faith and life of the Church.

43–44;
46–48;
204

Here the *decisive point of controversy* became clear. The Reformers were convinced that they had rediscovered with their doctrine of justification by faith alone the original meaning and center of Holy Scripture and so brought it to bear on later distortions of the gospel. Yet even for the Catholic theologians who opposed them, Holy Scripture possessed unconditional authority. The problem was not Holy Scripture as such but the *correct interpretation of Holy Scripture*. The Reformers' formulation of the question was not identical to that of the Apostle Paul in the Letter to the Romans. Paul proclaimed in his dispute with the Jews that salvation is bestowed without any preconditions through Jesus Christ alone. In the controversy of the sixteenth century, on the other hand, the discussion involved Christians on both sides, all of whom recognized Jesus Christ as the sole mediator of salvation. The question was now *What does Jesus Christ mean "for us" and how is the salvation of Jesus Christ mediated to us?* This became the question whether through certain Church ordinances, declared as necessary for salvation, new conditions for salvation were not established. At issue was a new expression of the central content of Holy Scripture that would be relevant for this changed formulation of the question. Scriptural doctrine did not simply stand against Church doctrine. The issues were rather the correct interpretation of Holy Scripture and the way to make Scripture relevant. In this connection, the Council of Trent affirmed *scriptural interpretation by the We of the Church* against the scriptural interpretation of the Reformers, which bore the imprint of their personal experience of the faith.

3.3 The Catholic Doctrine of Justification and Sanctification

Most Christians today find the doctrine of justification difficult to understand. Here we must examine the old formulas and present their material content anew. We are dealing here with the *foundations of Christian existence*.

The message of grace is in a certain sense the heart of the whole of Christianity.

1. The first and fundamental declaration of the Catholic doctrine of justification in reference to the witness of Holy Scripture concerns *the absolute impossibility* of man's self-redemption and *the absolute necessity of redemption through Jesus Christ*. Jesus Christ alone is the salvation of man; he is "the sun of justice" (DS 1520; NR 790). According to the Gospel of John, Jesus says, "No one can enter into God's Kingdom without being begotten of water and Spirit" (Jn 3:5) and "Apart from me you can do nothing" (Jn 15:5). St. Augustine underscores the fact that this latter text does not say, "You can do little without me"; it says, "You can do nothing". "Be it then much or little, it can not happen without the One without whom nothing can happen". So the Council of Trent teaches:

> Whoever affirms that man can be justified before God through his works which are accomplished by the strength of human nature or in the teaching of the law without the divine grace that exists through Jesus Christ is to be excommunicated (DS 1551; NR 819).

This teaching firmly declares that the supernatural grace of God is absolutely necessary for man's every salvific action. That is true even for the first desire for salvation and for the beginning of faith and salvation. Grace always precedes man's knowing and willing and always accompanies them: "It is God who, in his good will toward you, begets in you any measure of desire or achievement" (Phil 2:13). Christian existence is wholly and entirely an existence owed to another. Here the Church agrees fully with the Reformers. Together we pray the well-known hymn to the Holy Spirit, "*Veni Sancte Spiritus*" (from around 1200):

> Where thou art not, man hath naught,
> Nothing good in deed or thought,
> Nothing free from taint of ill (cited in CA 20).

The thesis of the absolute necessity of grace for man's salvific action contains in principle *no moral or cultural pessimism*.

According to Catholic doctrine, man in the state of sin (and therefore without grace) is not barred from knowing any moral truth or accomplishing any morally good deed. His cognitive power and his moral freedom are indeed deeply wounded through sin, but they are not destroyed. Hence the possibility of considerable moral and cultural achievement is not to be disputed. The doctrine excludes only a natural optimism in relation to salvation. The moral freedom remaining to the sinner is related only to the domain of the humanly good, not to salvation. In spite of all differing emphases and many extreme formulations of the Reformers, a fundamental agreement with the Church is possible in this question (CA 18).

205

113–114;
116–117

104–105;
110–111;
203–204

The controversy especially concerns whether grace enables man to consent to his justification and *to cooperate* with it. The Reformers speak explicitly of unfree will; for them, man's full passivity in the process of justification is fundamental. In opposition to this, the Council of Trent speaks repeatedly of a human cooperation (DS 1554; NR 822). It does not mean by that, of course, an autonomous freedom in relation to God, but only a bestowed freedom. This way of speaking is scripturally legitimate. The Apostle Paul designates himself explicitly as God's *co*worker (1 Cor 3:9; 2 Cor 6:1); he speaks of grace working with him (1 Cor 15:10). God protects the dignity of the creature, which even the sinner cannot lose. He does not treat us as inert blocks; he respects us as men! God's activity in all is not only his activity alone. "He who created you without you does not justify you without you. Thus did he create you without your knowledge, but only with the consent of your will does he justify you" (Augustine). This question of creaturely cooperation in the process of the mediation of salvation still represents a *fundamental problem* in relation to the Reformation. Of course, even according to Catholic doctrine the meaning and goal of justification is not the glory of man, but the glorification of God and of his grace in Jesus Christ (DS 1528, 1583; NR 798, 851). But the glory of God is a man fully alive (Irenaeus of Lyons). For that reason, glorifying God means taking man's dignity seriously. Within this total perspective, Catholics and Protestants can find a way to each other in order to prepare a solution for the differences which still exist.

205–208

2. The essence of justification is described in the New Testament as rebirth, new creation, renewal, and sanctification; as removal from the state of death into that of life (1 Jn 3:14), as passage from the state of darkness into that of light (Col 1:13; Eph 5:8). Accordingly, the Council of Trent defines justification as "the transference from the state in which man is born as a son of the first Adam to the state of grace and acceptance as a child of God through the second Adam, Jesus Christ, our Savior" (DS 1524; NR 794). Justification by God thus effects a *real and essential transformation of man*. It does not only declare him just, but it makes him to *be* just; it changes him and creates him anew. This comprises two things: the forgiveness of sins and "the sanctification and renewal of the inner man" (DS 1528; NR 798). *Justification is also sanctification*, by which we have communion with God in the Holy Spirit through Jesus Christ.

According to Luther, the justified believers are *"just men and sinners at the same time"*. Luther means to express the paradoxical character of Christian existence, in which even the justified man still stands under sin. The greatest saints always held themselves to be the greatest sinners. The Council of Trent sought to do justice to this fact in another way by speaking of an abiding inclination to sin (concupiscence). If one proceeds from such declarations, an understanding on this point seems possible today to many theologians. That the remaining differences over points of departure and ways of thinking or speaking, especially on the place of the doctrine of justification within the whole, still have their consequences is shown by the later development of the Reformation, which resulted above all in the *Book of Concord* (1580). This is counted among the Lutheran confessional writings. The *Book of Concord* distinguishes strictly between *justification* and *sanctification*, whereas the Council of Trent (1545–1563) sees them as a unity. These differing declarations have further consequences for the relation of faith and works, to which we now turn.

3. *Man's justification is possible only in faith.* This is the unambiguous teaching of Holy Scripture. In the conclusion to the Gospel of Mark we read explicitly, "The man who believes in it and accepts baptism will be saved; the man who refuses to believe in it will be condemned" (Mk 16:16). The Apostle Paul, as we have seen, emphasized with particular clarity the meaning of faith (Rom 1:17; 3:22, 28). "Without faith, it is impossible to please him. Anyone who comes to God must believe that he exists, and that he rewards those who seek him" (Heb 11:6). So it is that the Council of Trent can declare, "Faith is the beginning of salvation for man, the foundation and root of all justification; without it no one can please God (Heb 11:6)" (DS 1532; NR 803). As J. A. Möhler wrote, "Faith is thus the *beginning* of salvation, not however a beginning that could ever be left behind again during this lifetime, perhaps after significant progress had been made; at the same time, it is the permanent *foundation* on which the whole edifice of salvation is erected, but not an underlying mass without organic connection to the rest of the edifice, for it is the *root* of justification". All this is possible because faith, in its deepest essence, means incorporation into Jesus' innermost attitude. Christian existence is existence in faith and from faith.

36–39;
206–208

Luther's famous formula *"by faith alone"* is based on his seeing faith not only as the beginning, but as the quintessence, of salvation. Nevertheless, because he feared justification by works, Luther refused to admit that a faith determined and moved by love is necessary for justification. Catholic doctrine, of course, does not understand love as a self-righteous work of man, but as a gift of grace. In this sense, it says that only a faith alive in graciously bestowed love can justify. Having "mere" faith without love, merely considering something true, does not justify us (DS 1559; NR 827). But if one understands faith in the full and comprehensive biblical sense, then faith includes conversion, hope, and love—and the Lutheran formula can have a *good Catholic sense*. According to Catholic doctrine, faith encompasses both trusting in God on the basis of his mercifulness proved in Jesus Christ and confessing the salvific work of God through Jesus Christ in the Holy Spirit (DS 1562; NR 830). Yet this faith is never alone. It includes other acts—

turning away from sin and turning toward God, fear of God, hope in God, and love of God (DS 1559; NR 827). These are not external additions and supplements to faith, but unfoldings of the inner essence of faith itself.

4. The question whether *the grace of justification could be experienced* was of particular importance and is so all the more today. To be sure, there can be no objective assurance about grace. God, the origin and content of grace, is an impenetrable mystery to man. God's grace and mercy are indeed beyond all doubt for the one who believes; but we have this certainty only in an act of faith. If we look to ourselves, because of our weakness we can never know with assurance whether we find ourselves in a state of grace or not (DS 1534; NR 804). We may perhaps not be conscious of any sin, but we are not therefore justified (1 Cor 4:4). So we must seek salvation "in fear and trembling" (Phil 2:12). Even so, given God's mercy, we may *hope* to attain salvation.

190–191; This *certainty of hope can be experienced by way of signs*. Paul himself
345–347 exhorts us: "Test yourselves to see whether you are living in faith; examine yourselves. Perhaps you yourselves do not realize that Jesus Christ is in you" (2 Cor 13:5). Among such signs of hopeful certainty, Thomas Aquinas names joy in God and the things of faith, distance from the seductive power of the world, and the judgment of conscience that one is not guilty of serious sins. St. Ignatius Loyola refers in his "Rules for the Discernment of Spirits" particularly to the experience of spiritual consolation: inner courage and inner strength, inner peace, a love that places God before all else, inner joyfulness, and an inner attraction to spiritual things.

For *Luther* the *question of the certainty of salvation* was the point of departure for his development. The experience of the certainty of salvation was inseparably linked for him with justifying faith. *Calvin* even spoke of a certainty of predestination. The *Council of Trent* (1545–1563) saw in this an "empty and impious fiducial faith", which in the assurance of the forgiveness of sins even boasts of its sins (DS 1533; NR 804). In substance, the Reformation doctrine and the Catholic Tradition of faith's certainty in hope are much closer to each other, however, than the sharp formulations of both sides suggest. The *real problem* lies deeper, of course. In Luther's doctrine about the individual's certainty of faith, we see a concern that was to become fundamental for the whole modern era—the concern to find certainty. By refusing the doctrine of the individual's certainty of faith (DS 1563–64; NR 831–32), the Council of Trent points to a Catholic solution of the certainty problem. Certainty is possible only within the community of the Church, in mutual recognition of grace and in the hope that grace inspires, as well as in being borne up in common by the We of faith and hope.

5. Since justification is an inner renewal of man, it must lead to a new life. "Mere" faith does not suffice; the faith that grounds one's whole life

on God and his grace is wholly absorbed with God and his will. So this new life proves itself by *keeping the commandments*. Christian existence is existence in obedience to the will of God.

In the Old Testament, the Ten Commandments, the charter of the covenant (Ex 20; Dt 5), belong to a covenant granted by God from grace. When Jesus was asked about the way to life, he answered, "If you wish to enter into life, keep the commandments" (Mt 19:17). For him, it is not enough to say, "Lord! Lord!" in order to enter into the Kingdom of heaven. It is essential to do the will of the Father (Mt 7:21). In the parable of the merciless official, Jesus shows that God's forgiveness of guilt demands forgiveness among men as its consequence (Mt 18:23–25). Whoever loves Jesus will also keep his commandments (Jn 14:15). The Apostle Paul deduced from the Christian's liberation from the power of sin that the believer should no longer be a slave to sin, but should live as a new man and offer his body "to God as a weapon for justice" (Rom 6:13).

It is with strong biblical foundation, then, that the Council of Trent teaches the necessity and the possibility of fulfilling the commandments (DS 1536–39; NR 806–8). The Council even stresses that Jesus Christ is not only the Redeemer, but also the Lawgiver (DS 1571; NR 839). Paul too speaks of the "law of Christ" (Gal 6:2). With Paul, the Council here resists a false understanding of Christian freedom that would use freedom from the law as a pretext for self-seeking, instead of understanding freedom as selflessness in love (Gal 5:13).

This brings us to the *Reformation doctrine of the "freedom of a Christian"*. Luther employed this paradoxical formulation: "A Christian is a free lord over all things and subject to no one. A Christian is a ministering servant of all things and subject to everyone." The Augsburg Confession (1530) speaks of "new obedience" and says "faith must bring forth good fruits" (CA 6) and "Our people are accused unjustly of forbidding good works" (CA 20). Furthermore, the Reformers know a *double* (in some cases even threefold) *use of law*: the civil or political use, for the regulation of human co-existence, and the theological use as expression of the will of God. In this latter sense, the law overtaxes man; it convicts him of his sin and refers him to the gospel. This frees him from the law and lets him fulfill the will of God from within.

The Council of Trent did not explicitly treat the doctrine of Christian freedom. But this doctrine too has a long *Catholic Tradition*. According to the Catholic understanding, the law of Christ is not a new legal code so much as a law of the Spirit (Rom 8:2). To that extent, it is a law of freedom (Jas 1:25) that moves us from within to fulfill the will of God. "The law was given so that grace would be sought; grace was given so that the law would be fulfilled" (Augustine). Thomas Aquinas calls the law of the New Covenant a law of freedom because it is not given from without, but consists in the grace of the Holy Spirit received in faith. The

difference from the Reformation position is not so much a matter of dogma as of
the concrete living of Christian life, of the concrete relation to the world, and
perhaps especially of differing forms of speech and thought. The Catholic teaching
presents clearly the correspondence between the inner law of the Spirit and the
outer commandment. For that reason, the obligation to obey the commandments
of God and (in another way) to obey the ordinances of the Church is more
concrete. This concreteness can entail the danger of legalism, just as the Reformation position can turn into lawlessness. The two positions can be a mutual
corrective for each other.

6. The sore point of the doctrine of justification is the question of the
344–346   *merit in good works.* Does not an affirmation of merit return to holiness of
works and self-righteousness? To this question we must answer first that
Jesus himself speaks in many places of a reward in heaven (Mt 5:12; 19:29)
and of a judgment according to human works (Mt 25:34–35, among
others). The same holds in the writings of Paul (Rom 2:6; 1 Cor 3:8; 15:58,
among others). This is not a matter of justification by works. Rather,
Christians are like branches on the vine. Only in Jesus Christ can they bear
fruit; without him, they can accomplish nothing (Jn 15:5). *Our merits are
ultimately his grace.*
The Council of Trent stands firmly on this scriptural declaration when
it teaches us

> to hold out the prospect of eternal life simultaneously as grace that is
> promised to the sons of God through Jesus Christ and as reward that
> is paid exactly according to God's promise for their good works and
> merits (DS 1545; NR 815).

> This power [of grace] always precedes their works, accompanies
> them, and follows upon them, and without it they can in no way be
> pleasing or acceptable before God (DS 1546; NR 816).

> Thus, far be it from a Christian to trust in himself or to seek his glory
> in himself and not in the Lord (1 Cor 1:31) whose goodness toward all
> men is so great that he lets his own gifts to them become their merits
> (DS 1548; NR 817).

This explanation shows that grace, which is active in and through our
cooperation, is not a rigid and static reality, but something highly dynamic,
even dramatic. Justification is indeed bestowed once for all, and yet it sets
in motion a *lifelong process* of sanctification: with the help of grace, we
must prepare ourselves for sanctifying grace (DS 1525–27; NR 795–97).
Through the works accomplished by the power of grace, sanctifying
grace is able to grow (DS 1635; NR 805). Grace, though, can also be lost
through sin (DS 1544; NR 814), just as it can be bestowed again after one

has repented (DS 1542–43; NR 812–13). The whole life of the Christian is a struggle with sin and a constant penance; it always needs renewal and deepening. Even after we have done everything, we remain useless servants (Lk 17:10).

297–301

The *Reformation's polemic against justification by works* was necessarily linked with the formulas "by grace alone" and "by faith alone". But even the Reformers speak of works as fruits of faith and as its certifying signs. Works are necessary for salvation, but they do not effect salvation; they have no value of merit before God (CA 6, 20). In relation to the meritoriousness of the fruits of justification, clearly differing declarations are made by the two teachings (DS 1581–82; NR 849–50).

Still, today we see a much closer agreement on what is meant than may appear at first sight. This *objective convergence* is clearly expressed in St. Thérèse of Lisieux's prayer of consecration "to the merciful love of the good Lord": "I wish to accumulate no merits for heaven, I wish to work only for the sake of your love, in the sole intention of pleasing you. . . . At the evening of life I shall appear before you with empty hands, for I do not ask you, Lord, to count my works. All our works of justice are stained in your eyes. I thus wish to clothe myself with your own justice and by your love to receive eternal possession of you." Many of the opening prayers in the Mass describe our situation similarly. Obviously, Catholic and Protestant Christians stand close to one another, despite differing dogmatic formulations, when they speak not *about* God and *about* the faith, but stand *before* God in faith and speak *to* God in prayer. Are we today, then, not in agreement on matters of justification, matters over which our fathers in the sixteenth century separated from one another?

3.4 Agreement on the Doctrine of Justification?

When we look back today after four hundred and fifty years at the sixteenth-century disputes over the doctrine of justification, we must say that the questions at issue in them are *permanent questions* for Christians. It would not be good if these questions no longer meant anything to us. Of course, we clearly feel today the *distance of time*. Both the Reformers and the Fathers of Trent were men of their times, and they spoke the language of their times. The Catholic side was indebted to the styles of thinking and speaking inherited from medieval scholasticism; Luther showed in many matters the imprint of the late medieval problematic (nominalism). The two sides often spoke past each other. To this misunderstanding were added the mutual distortions of polemics. But what both sides often said in exaggerated polemics at a time when unity was fragmenting we see more calmly and objectively today when the denominations are moving toward one another again. We can understand that many controversies arose through semantic and even real misunderstandings and were only apparent oppositions. When we look instead to what was meant by the contradictory formulations, and especially to the personal acts of faith, we see in many questions an *amazing nearness and a deep commonality*. We can be thankful for that. It is the Spirit of God himself who is leading us together (UR 1, 4).

43–44;
46–48;
113–114;
196–203;
263–265;
286–287;
290–291

The ecumenical discussion of the last decades has led to great progress in the doctrine of justification. Many Catholic and Protestant theologians are today of the opinion that the doctrine of justification need no longer separate the two churches, but that an *agreement in this question is possible*. Two aspects of the doctrine must be conceived together: the grace of God, and the cooperation of man rendered possible by it in faith and action. The Catholic and the Protestant doctrines about this relation do not exclude each other in principle; they do not indeed coincide, but they are open to each other.

194–196

The chief difference that still exists despite this rapprochement concerns the *position of the doctrine of justification in the whole of the Church's faith and life*. There are still essential differences in the understanding of the Church,

215–216;
238–239;
247–248;
263–265;
286–287;
287–289;
290–291;
312–313;
324–325

its sacraments and offices. If one looks at the entire context of the doctrine of justification, it becomes clear that the disputes 400 years ago did not rest only on misunderstandings or different conceptual systems, forms of thought, and emphases. In reality both parties did not mean the same thing. There are indeed *objective differences* between the doctrine of the Reformers and of the Catholic Church.

104–105;
110–112;
197–198;
324–325

On these individual questions, we see *a difference in the general understanding of the common Christian inheritance*. While the Reformers stress the rupture of sin and its abiding power in the life of the justified, Catholic doctrine sees rather the unity of creation and redemption, which was disturbed by sin but not destroyed. For that reason, Catholic teaching can present more clearly the healing and sanctifying meaning of grace and the meaning of man's cooperation in the work of salvation. Thus Catholic teaching describes man's standing *before* God and his relationship *to* God not only in personal categories, but also in categories of being (ontological categories) *about* the reality of sin and about the new reality of grace.

232–233

Any overcoming of the differences which still exist will require a patient *dialogue* in which old prejudices and misunderstandings are removed and both sides strive to obtain a deeper mutual understanding. Only in this way can they grow together in common obedience to the word and work of Jesus Christ. This will also require expressing anew the message of the justification and sanctification of man in the language of our times, while remaining fully faithful to Holy Scripture and to the Tradition of faith. We must now turn to this task.

4. Grace as Beginning and Dawning of the New Creation

4.1 The New Man

The biblical message about God's justice and his faithfulness and love answers a *permanent human question and need*. This question is today as current as ever. Indeed, we now experience with particular urgency that we cannot liberate ourselves from our grace-less situation by our own strength. Whatever we undertake falls under the law of the encompassing setting of futility, which no one can escape by his own strength. Every attempt at self-liberation creates new conflicts and alienations. So without redemption we move in a vicious circle. But man cannot give up hoping for final justice, truth, and love. This hope seeks a qualitatively new beginning, one that cannot be generated from our history of failure. Salvation is possible only from God. 196–197

Jesus proclaims this new beginning in the message of the *coming of the lordship of God*. This message is for him the essence of salvation and of grace; it must therefore also be the point of departure and the foundation of our speaking about grace and salvation. The coming of God's lordship is synonymous with the manifestation of his faithfulness, justice, graciousness, mercy, and love. It bestows a new future on man and with it a new home, a new realm for human living. The lordship of God brings justice as the right order between God and man. Scripture describes this justice as life, light, salvation, and peace. The grace of God's lordship bestows communion and friendship with him and gives a share in his life. The God-man *Jesus Christ* is the New Covenant of God in person, since in his person divinity and humanity are indissolubly and most intimately linked. In his death and in his Resurrection, new life has definitively appeared and hope has been definitively fulfilled. For that reason, Jesus is the prototypical realization of grace. Every blessing for man consists in being taken into the reality of Jesus Christ. Through grace we become adoptive sons and daughters according to the image of the one and only Son. Our being children of God is realized in the *Holy Spirit*. Only in the Spirit can we address God as "Abba, Father" and be brothers and sisters to one another. Grace ultimately consists in the fact that the love of God has been poured out into our hearts through the Holy Spirit (Rom 5:5), that the Holy Spirit dwells in us (Rom 8:9, 11) and that we are temples of the Holy Spirit (1 Cor 3:16–17; 6:19; Eph 2:22). In the Holy Spirit, through Jesus Christ, we have a share in the life and the love of the triune God. The promise of the Old Testament is thus fulfilled: 123–130; 191–193

I will make with them a covenant of peace; it shall be an everlasting covenant with them, and I will multiply them, and put my sanctuary among them forever. My dwelling shall be with them; I will be their God, and they shall be my people (Ezek 37:26–27).

104–105;
185–187

All of this means that grace is not a tangible quantity. *Grace is God himself in his self-communication to us through Jesus Christ in the Holy Spirit.* Fundamentally, grace means that we are unconditionally accepted, affirmed, and loved by God through Jesus Christ in the Holy Spirit and that we are wholly one with him in this love. Grace is personal communion and friendship with God, personal participation in the life of God. Unconditional acceptance in the encounter with the infinite love of God is the ultimate and highest fulfillment of man; it is man's salvation.

The living and creative presence of God and intimate communion with him presuppose man's preparation for God, borne by God's grace. The result is the inner transformation of man. The love of God is indeed

197–199

creative; it reshapes man and sanctifies him. So grace bestows a *new being* on man; it is the gift of rebirth to new life, the reality of the new creation. St. Augustine says, "Because you have loved me, you make me lovable." In this sense, personal communion with God brings about the divinization of man, which is his true humanization. In divinization, man finds his highest fulfillment.

We can accordingly distinguish between uncreated grace, God himself in his loving self-communication to man, and *created grace*, which both prepares man for and is, as it were, the radiation of God's love in man. In created grace, one can again distinguish between the abiding state of the person, *sanctifying grace*, and the character of individual acts of knowing and willing, *actual or helping grace* (the grace that illumines and strengthens). Many may find these distinctions meaningless at first. Basically, though, they mean that the *one* grace of God is a dynamic reality; it is a transformation of man that encompasses his whole life. Actual grace serves either as the preparation for sanctifying grace or as the effect and intensification of sanctifying grace in the action of man. Grace takes possession of a man progressively. For that reason, we cannot think that grace is our possession. St. Bonaventure, who after Thomas Aquinas is the most important Church Doctor of the Middle Ages, uses this formulation: "To possess God means to be possessed by God." Grace does not belong to us; rather, by grace we belong to God. Grace is the way we have already been taken into God's lordship and because of this, into God's service.

A life rooted in grace means a life rooted in *faith, hope, and love*. We call these three the *theological virtues* because they are bestowed on us by God (*theos*) and because they have God as their goal.

In *faith*, man bases his whole existence on God. God is the support and substance of his life. This attitude of trusting faith is possible only as a response to the historical revelation of God's faithfulness and dependability. Faith is always at the same time a personal trust in God and an affirmation of the truths that are believed. The two aspects together constitute a living faith that is moved by love, as distinguished from a dead faith that merely considers something to be true. Living faith is a light for man; it bestows orientation, perspective, direction, and meaning upon him. With the "eyes of faith" he sees more and more deeply than he is able to see with his natural eyes and with the natural light of reason. Faith as personal surrender to the mystery of God is essentially shrouded in darkness because our eyes, as long as we do not yet live in the vision of God, cannot grasp the dazzling light of God and are, as it were, blinded by him. We can indeed be challenged in our faith by questions and doubts. Still the certainty of faith is beyond every doubt. It is based not on human insight but on the truth of God himself "evident" to us in faith. This divine truth also definitively discloses to us the truth about ourselves and about the world. Faith is an inestimable gift of grace for man.

In *hope*, man guides himself by God's faithfulness grasped in faith and aims wholly at the coming Kingdom of God that has already dawned in Jesus Christ. The Christian subordinates earthly goods to the Kingdom, places them last for its sake, and endures sufferings and persecutions of every kind with courage and patience. Christian hope resists both despair, which anticipates failure, and presumption, which places false trust in one's own capabilities and achievements and in earthly assurances that anticipate success. Hope preserves one especially from spiritual slothfulness, from clinging to this-worldly things, from any repugnance toward going beyond the earth and its fulfillments, and from listlessness and lukewarmness in living out one's faith. Hope frees us from the dullness and weariness of everyday life. In the face of all purely this-worldly attitudes, hope directs itself to the ever-greater, all-encompassing, and all-surpassing, highest good, to God himself as the fulfillment of man and to a world that will be fully revealed only in the future.

Love is that friendship and communion with God that enables man to love God "with all his heart and all his soul" (Mk 12:30 par.), in order to become wholly one with him even now. Love of God is a full, unlimited, unreserved "Yes" to God and to his commandments (Jn 14:15–17; 15:9–10; 1 Jn 1:3–6). It is a "Yes" that only a friend can speak, because he knows the beloved entirely and understands him (Jn 15:15). This love of God is the standard and fullness of Christian life; whoever lacks it is spiritually empty (1 Cor 13). So far as man forgets himself in his love for God and goes beyond himself in loving surrender to God, he also finds in God his own true fulfillment. For that reason, man may also love created goods in God and with God and take delight in them. Virtue is ordered love (Augustine). Since God loves every man absolutely, true love of God is always linked with love of neighbor (Mk 12:30–31 par.; Jn 13:34; 1 Jn 2:8–10; 1 Cor 13). Indeed, love of neighbor is the criterion for the genuineness of love of God (1 Jn 4:20–21). The love of God that is linked with love of neighbor bestows joy, peace, and compassion. It brings about zeal and enthusiasm for God and his Kingdom. The new man who lives by faith, hope, and love already has begun that full communion with God in the new, future world.

The grace of the Holy Spirit and its realization in faith, hope, and love are a first share in the future glory of God's lordship (2 Cor 1:22; Eph 1:14). We are redeemed in hope (Rom 8:24), and we are reborn to a living hope (1 Pet 1:3). Grace is the strength and power of future glory present even now. So theology understands *grace as the beginning and foretaste of eternal life*, as the anticipation of the vision of God "face to face" (1 Cor 13:12). Cardinal Newman expressed this in a well-known verse: "In grace, glory is away from home; in glory, grace is at home." Just as all grace comes from God, so it leads back to him and to his Kingdom.

344–345

4.2 The Renewed World

The dawning of the Kingdom of God does not happen only in the interiority of the heart. Beginning in the Old Testament, God's salvific action occurs in concrete historical events. God's election of Israel is experienced in deliverance from Egyptian slavery, in being led through the Sea of Reeds and through the wilderness, in the entrance into the promised land, and in the founding of the Davidic kingship. Jesus' proclamation of the coming lordship of God is accompanied by wondrous deeds of power—healing the sick, feeding the hungry, and bearing up and encouraging the hopeless. *Inner grace is normally linked with outer grace.*

The connection of these two is seen in every Christian life. We normally experience God and his salvation first of all through our parents, in our family, in encounters with others, in love and forgiveness, in words that touch the heart, in times of great joy or of great suffering, but also in books, in art, and in nature. These experiences illuminate what grace is: forgiveness and bestowal of a new beginning, liberation from guilt, anxiety, and meaninglessness. To say the same thing positively, grace is love, trust, truth, community and friendship, comfort and hope. Christian faith always sees more at work in human experiences than the merely human. Human experience is a sign and a symbol of the working of God's

Spirit; he works to bring about God's Kingdom in the midst of a grace-less world.

Grace not only encounters us *from without*; it also works *outward* again. So far as God takes possession of man by his Spirit, new life can and must have an effect in deeds of truth and justice, in works of peace and reconciliation. A life nourished by grace must produce *signs of the beginning redemption of the world*. New life from God must become concretely visible in our lives by way of signs; the love of God must be embodied and concretized in the love of neighbor.

177–179;
216–218;
343;
350–352

> If anyone says, "My love is fixed on God",
> yet hates his brother,
> he is a liar.
> One who has not love for the brother he has seen
> cannot love the God he has not seen.
> The commandment we have from him is this:
> whoever loves God must also love his brother (1 Jn 4:20–21).

The Tradition has summarized what this means concretely in *the seven corporal and the seven spiritual works of mercy*:

> To feed the hungry, to give drink to the thirsty, to clothe the naked, to harbor the homeless, to visit the sick, to ransom the captive, to bury the dead.
> To instruct the ignorant, to counsel the doubtful, to admonish sinners, to bear wrongs patiently, to forgive offences willingly, to comfort the afflicted, to pray for the living and the dead.

Today, some attempt to describe the incipient redemption of the world as *liberation*. We see this not only in theology but also in magisterial declarations, especially in the apostolic letter of Pope Paul VI on evangelization in today's world (1975). In these texts we must understand the word "liberation" in a deep and comprehensive sense; it cannot be restricted to political or psychological liberation. The freedom into which Jesus Christ has freed us (Gal 5:1) is *freedom graciously bestowed by God*. It expresses itself chiefly in thanks, in glory and praise of God and his salvific deeds, and in the prayerful "Abba". Freedom before God liberates us at the same time for freedom and service in the world.

134;
159–160;
201–202

Concretely, liberation by Jesus Christ means liberation from sin, the law, and death. *Freedom from sin* means that the grip of evil, which makes us unfree, is broken. Sin often embodies itself in oppressive structures, in alienating human, economic, and political situations, which for their part then are the occasion for selfish behavior, envy and conflict, discord and violence. Christian freedom must prove itself by changing such unjust situations as much as possible and by bringing about freedom, justice, and

111–113

200–202
truth. *Liberation from the law* in grace means liberation from all mere legalism which, in merely external observance of the law, seeks fulfillment through works, labor, achievement, success, esteem and power. This false fulfillment produces exhaustion, pressure, and stress. So freedom from the law means, for instance, having places and times for leisure, 108–109; enjoyment and celebration, sociability and relaxation. *Liberation from death* 329–337; can and must lead to removing anxieties insofar as possible, to awakening 339 courage and hope, and to serving life against a widespread mentality inimical to life—making room for it, cherishing and protecting it. This means feeding the hungry, caring for the handicapped and elderly, and protecting the life of the unborn.

It is clear that while Christian liberation cannot be limited to political liberation, neither can it be a purely interior attitude or a purely private 18–19 practice. It has a *political dimension* and necessarily includes commitment to justice, peace, freedom, and truth. The Christian must advocate an order of private and public life in which grace—understood in a more universal sense—is not an empty word.

All this should not be understood in a visionary sense. We cannot build the Kingdom of God; only God can do that. Of course, God wills to act among us and through us. The message of the Kingdom of God does not call for a natural utopia, but for an eschatological hope—and still this hope should and will already become concrete in this world as signs. In the Holy Spirit and his freedom there are *signs of the coming Kingdom of God*; God's lordship is manifest in this world in a fragmentary way and in shadowy sketches. Of course, change of external circumstances is of little use if the hearts of men are not also changed—just as the hearts of men can hardly change as long as the circumstances, understood humanly, suppress all hope and generate self-centered and violent attitudes and actions. There is no room for dichotomies. In the Christian understanding of salvation, we deal with the whole man and the whole world. This integral liberation happens concretely because man is called out of the power of sin and into a new context for life, into the community of believers and of the redeemed. He becomes a member of the Church. The Church is *the* great sign of God's salvation in the world.

II

THE CHURCH AS SACRAMENT OF THE SPIRIT

1. Difficulties with the Church

To the question about the place of the Holy Spirit, the Church's creed answers with this declaration: "We believe in one holy, catholic, and apostolic Church." The Church confesses that in it and through it the Spirit of Jesus Christ continues to work in history. She believes that she is the place, even the sacrament—the sign and instrument—of the working of the Holy Spirit.

Hardly any other declaration of faith excites so much misunderstanding, contradiction, even hostility as this one. Many practicing Catholic Christians have difficulties with the Church. Not a few of them say: "Jesus, yes—the Church, no!" The *principal objection against the Church* is that she has betrayed in her history the original message of Jesus. For Jesus—so runs the objection—was poor and stood up for the poor. The Church, on the other hand, is rich, makes pacts with the rich and powerful, and has failed when confronted with social questions. Jesus preached love to the point of loving one's enemies; the Church, on the other hand, is intolerant and persecutes her opponents with brutal cruelty, as is most evident in the Inquisition. Jesus called men to discipleship, to the practical works of love; the Church, on the other hand, demands obedience to infallible dogmas. Jesus behaved in an unbiased, open, and understanding way toward women; the Church, on the other hand, has devalued women and disparaged sexuality. She begrudges man his happiness and offers him the empty consolation of the beyond. For others, the Church is intellectually, culturally, and scientifically behind the times and radically antiquated.

What should a Catholic Christian say to this "list of sins"? He does not need to gloss over or cover up anything. The Church above all, which proclaims the forgiveness of sins, can confess her own guilt while trusting in God's forgiveness, as Pope Hadrian VI did at the Imperial Diet in Nuremberg (1522–1523) or Pope Paul VI during the Second Vatican Council (1962–1965). The Christian does not need to deny the *dark sides of the Church's history*. He may, though, in all modesty also recall the *bright sides*: the Church of the martyrs who resisted the powerful; the Church of the saints who lived the gospel in a heroic way; contemporary witnesses like St. Maximilian Kolbe, Mother Teresa, and many others; works of charity exercised at all times and today above all in the service to the Third World's poor; the contribution of the Church to peace both in the Middle Ages and in the present; the contribution of Christianity to the recognition of the unique dignity of the person, of the dignity of women, and of freedom of conscience. Imagine for a moment the history of our Western culture without the Church and ask what would be left of it. Imagine that the social and charitable institutions of the Church in our present society did not exist and ask how things would look then. And most important of all: the Church has kept the memory of Jesus Christ alive to our present day. Without her there would be no gospel and no Holy Scripture. Without her we would know nothing of Jesus Christ and of the hope he has brought us.

39

Neither one-sided polemics nor one-sided apologetics does justice to the Church. Moreover, bright and dark aspects of the historical Church cannot be balanced against one another. Any final judgment on the Church can only be made by the Christian in faith. That is why we recite "We *believe* in the Church". The Church is included within our faith in God's salvation through Jesus Christ in the Holy Spirit. She is ultimately *a reality of faith*. The believer confesses that God's Spirit is at work in the externally visible and at times quite miserable form of the Church, with all her historical contingency and sinful fragmentation. The believer disputes nothing and excludes nothing of what is visible in the Church, which always needs purification and renewal. He sees in the visible reality of the Church, however, a deeper and more comprehensive reality at work. What Paul says of himself applies even more to the Church; she bears the riches of Jesus Christ in earthen vessels, showing that the abundance of strength comes from God and not from us (2 Cor 4:7).

223–224

234–236

2. The Church in God's History with Men

2.1 The Church in Salvation History

The origin of the Church reaches back to the beginnings of mankind's history. God calls and sanctifies us not as isolated individuals but as beings that tend toward community and can find fulfillment only in community (LG 9; GS 32). No one can believe by himself and be a Christian by himself; no one can preach the gospel to himself. Everyone depends on others who bear witness to the gospel for him and who sustain and support him in his faith. Each is taken into the great chain of believers and into the community of believers, which encompasses all times and places. From the beginning, God did not call men as individuals, as dispersed believing souls; rather, he gathered a people in whom and through whom each individual is sustained and in whom each sustains the others.

The gathering of the people of God is *prefigured from the beginning of the world*. It begins at the moment when sin destroys communion with God and of men with one another. The gathering of the people of God is, so to speak, God's reaction to the chaos caused by sin. The Church Fathers believe that it begins already with Abel the just and happens in a hidden way among all peoples (LG 2, 13, 16). "At all times and in every race, anyone who fears God and does what is right has been acceptable to him (cf. Acts 10:35)" (LG 9).

The *preparation* and the public history of the gathering of the people of God begins with the *calling of Abraham*, to whom God promised that he would become the ancestor of a great people (Gen 12:2; 15:5–6). The true preparation begins with the *election of Israel* to be God's special possession (Ex 19:5–6; Dt 7:6). Through its election, Israel is a sign for the eschatological gathering of all peoples (Is 2:1–5; Mic 4:1–4). Yet the prophets soon accuse Israel of breaking the covenant and becoming a prostitute (Hos 1; Is 1:2–4; Jer 2, among others). They announce a New Covenant through which God will choose a new people for himself (Jer 31:31–34).

Jesus refers to this promise. His whole proclamation and his public life refer to the Kingdom of God. Through this message, he introduces the eschatological gathering of Israel. This gathering lays the *foundation* for the Church. We see this most clearly in his calling the Twelve out from the wider circle of his disciples into closer communion with him and giving them a special share in his mission of proclamation (Mk 3:13–19; 6:6b–13). The number twelve is not accidental; the Twelve represent the twelve tribes of Israel (Mt 19:28; Lk 22:30). The Twelve are therefore also the foundation stones of the New Jerusalem (Rev 21:12–14). Moreover, in the meals he takes with those who are his own, Jesus anticipates the eschatological feast in heaven. This is clearest at the Last Supper on the evening before his death (Mk 14:22–25, par.). The eucharistic celebration of the early Church community continues these common meals with Jesus and realizes them in a new way for the changed situation after his death and Resurrection. The Church, her proclamation, her celebration of the Eucharist, and the authority of the apostolic office are all established by the earthly Jesus. 123–131 243–244; 311–312

The Church has her true foundation in the *cross and Resurrection of Jesus Christ*. The foundational meaning of the cross for the Church is expressed especially when the eucharistic texts speak of the Blood of the Covenant (Mk 14:24) or the New Covenant (Lk 22:20; 1 Cor 11:25). The death of Jesus is the ground of the New Covenant and of God's people in that covenant. The Gospel of John says that Jesus draws all to himself as the 169–171

One elevated on the cross and to the right hand of the Father (Jn 12:32). The Church Fathers interpret the blood and water that stream from the opened side of the crucified Jesus (Jn 19:34) as symbolizing the two fundamental sacraments of the Church, baptism and the Eucharist. We say with the Fathers that the Church sprang from the wound in the side of Jesus (SC 5). The cross cannot be separated from the Resurrection and its foundational meaning for the Church. By the event of Easter, the dispersed flock of disciples was gathered again; at the same time the Easter witnesses received the mission to make all peoples disciples of Jesus and to baptize them (Mt 28:19–20). Finally, the founding of the Church is completed at Pentecost through the outpouring of the Holy Spirit. The Church is made 184–185 known publicly as the new people of God taken from out of the many peoples of the earth (Acts 2; LG 2, 5). The Holy Spirit is the vital principle of the Church.

It follows that the Church was not founded or instituted by a particular word or by a particular act of Jesus. The Church is rooted in the whole of the history of God with man; she grows out of the dynamics of the whole 225–226 of salvation history. So we can speak of a *gradual founding of the Church*: she was foreshadowed from the beginning of the world, prepared through the history of the people of the Old Covenant, established through the work of the earthly Jesus, realized through his cross and Resurrection, and finally revealed by the outpouring of the Holy Spirit (cf. LG 5).

The Church, grounded in the whole of what has *already happened* in God's history with men, is *still* underway toward her *eschatological completion*. She is a pilgrim Church that bears in the sacraments and institutions of the present age the form of the new world. The Church takes her "place among the creatures which groan and travail yet and await the revelation of the sons of God (cf. Rom 8:19–22)" (LG 48). In the Church, the forces of the coming Kingdom of God are already active; in the celebration of the liturgy especially, the eschatological glorification of God is already anticipated (LG 50–51; SC 8). But the Church is not yet the Kingdom of God. She shares rather in Jesus' taking on the form of a slave. She is the 234–236 Church of the poor and the suffering; she is the Church of sinners. She is always in need of purification and must perpetually travel the way of penance and of renewal. She is, finally, the persecuted Church, which must travel its way through trials and tribulations (LG 8). The Church is only a "seed and beginning" of the Kingdom of God on earth (LG 5). She is a Messianic people and "a most sure seed of unity, hope, and salvation for the whole human race" (LG 9). What does this mean for the mission of the Church in history and society?

2.2 The Church in History and in Modern Society

Something of the Church's essence is already clear at her origin: the gathering of the Church is meant for her mission in the world. *Gathering and mission* belong inseparably together.

The concrete realization of the Church's mission has taken differing forms in the course of history. The *early Church* understood herself as a new people promised to God in the midst of a world of many peoples. She was the little flock in the great Roman empire. She was willing to give the emperor what belonged to the emperor (Mt 22:21), loyally recognized the state order, and included the emperor and the empire in her intercessions. She also knew, of course, that she was not of this world (Jn 17:16) and that she had to obey God more than men (Acts 5:29). This attitude led to the *persecutions of Christians* during the first centuries and to serious conflicts between State and Church. Yet the blood of Christians proved to be the seed of new Christians (Tertullian). The growing importance of Christianity led to the recognition of Christianity as a legal religion by the Emperor Constantine in the Edict of Milan (313); his successor, Theodosius, made it the official state religion in 360. This *Constantinian turn* marks one of the most important changes in the Church's history. The Church became a political and social power and succumbed too often to the temptations of power and wealth.

In the *Middle Ages*, the Church and the Empire formed the one Christendom, in which spiritual and secular elements were indissolubly linked. The bishops were at the same time imperial princes; the emperor and queen claimed spiritual authority. Whereas a state ecclesiasticism (Caesaro-papism) prevailed in the *East*, first in Byzantium and then in Moscow, a battle for the freedom of the Church from the State occurred early on in the *Western Church*. In the West, the Church constituted herself under the guidance of the pope as more and more independent, a hier-archically ordered entity. In this powerful "papal Church", the call for ecclesiastical freedom became quickly enough a call for freedom from the external hierarchical power of the Church—a call for a purely spiritual understanding of the Church. In the late Middle Ages, the demand for a reform of the Church in head and members grew stronger. Since this reform did not come soon enough, one of the worst catastrophes of Christendom came about, the splitting of the Church in the wake of the Reformation.

Luther distinguished between secular government and the Church. He particularly criticized the connection between ecclesiastical offices and functions of secular sovereignty. The Church is for him the community of true believers. It exists wherever the gospel is preached purely and the sacraments are administered according to the gospel (CA 7). Luther saw the Church as not ruled through external force like a secular government, but as having no force except the word of God alone (CA 28). The external proclamation and dispensation of the sacraments, together with an office instituted by God, do indeed belong to the Church (CA 5). But Christ's lordship over the Church is hidden under the visible form of the Church. The true Church, according to Luther, is hidden. The consequence of this

195–196;
204;
232–233;
247–248;
324–325

distinction between the visible and the hidden Church was, of course, that Luther had to entrust the external protection and the external order of the Church to the princes; he thus brought the Church into a new dependency on secular power that has lasted into our own century.

According to Catholic conviction, the visible side of the Church as well as her sacramental and hierarchical constitution belong to the true Church. Thus, the *Roman Catholic Church* of the modern era has understood herself as an independent, visible, hierarchically constituted entity in relation to the State. After the Enlightenment, the French Revolution, and secularization, the Church was often forced into the role of a fortress in a state of siege. This was the historical context of the First Vatican Council (1869–1870) and of its definition of the

249–251   primacy of jurisdiction and of the infallibility of the pope.

The *Second Vatican Council* (1962–1965) marks another fundamental turning point. For the first time in her history, the Church sees herself confronted with a global situation. Her form, which has been "Western" to a large extent, must now become the form of a worldwide Church. So the Council deliberately abandoned the so-called Constantinian form of the Church, which had in any case become antiquated historically.

177–179;   The *point of departure and the foundation* for a correct understanding of the
208–210;   Church's relation to the modern world is the message entrusted to the
350–352   Church of the coming of the Kingdom of God. The goal of the Church is eschatological salvation, which can be fully realized only in a future world (GS 40). The Church is indeed constituted as a visible structure (LG 8; GS 40), but she is distinct from the political community in her task and competence and is tied to no political system. By presenting her proper
83–85   and independent mission, the Church recognizes at the same time the *legitimacy of specialized secular domains*, especially of the State (GS 36, 56, 76; AA 7). She defends religious freedom as an expression of the dignity of the person (DH).

This *distinction between the domains of competence for the Church and the world* (society, culture, politics, among others) does not imply a *separation*.
136–138   Jesus Christ is the key and center, the goal of all of mankind's history. He is the point toward which all the efforts of history and of culture converge, the center of mankind, the alpha and the omega (GS 10, 45). This message is the source of mission, light, and strength for the upbuilding of the human community (GS 42; AA 5). So the Church claims the right "to pass moral judgments even in matters relating to politics, whenever the fundamental rights of man or the salvation of souls requires it" (GS 76; DH 14). "One of the gravest errors of our time is the dichotomy between the faith which many profess and the practice of their daily lives. . . . Let there, then, be no such pernicious opposition between professional and social activity on the one hand and religious life on the other. The

Christian who shirks his temporal duties shirks his duties toward his neighbor, neglects God himself, and endangers his eternal salvation" (GS 43).

In the realm of the world the Church should not work by worldly means; it should, rather, *penetrate the temporal order from within with the spirit of the gospel*. "It is to be a leaven and, as it were, the soul of human society in its renewal by Christ" (GS 40). The Council cites the Letter to Diognetus (from the second or third century): "What the soul is in the body, let Christians be in the world" (LG 38). This is where we find the mission and the responsibility of the laity in particular. Yet we must distinguish in each case between what can be said and done in the name of the Church in a way binding on all and what individual Christians as members of human society advocate according to their Christian consciences (LG 36; GS 76). As regards the latter, Christians may come to differing judgments on the basis of and within the boundaries of their common faith (GS 43).

What does this entail for the *Church's service to the world*? Because the Church insists that man finds his fulfillment in God alone (GS 21, 41), she is "the sign and the safeguard of the transcendental dimension of the human person" (GS 76). The Church advocates the dignity of the human person and the priority of that dignity over institutions and material goods. The Christian message of hope for the new earth and the new heavens is at the same time an encouragement to commitment in the world, because everything that is done in love and out of love will enter purified and transfigured into the final state of reality (GS 39). Since the Church is by her mission and nature tied to no particular form of human culture and to no particular political and economic or social system, she is able by her universality to be a bond of peace and of reconciliation between men, between races and classes, peoples and cultures (GS 42). The Church watches over and safeguards man's dignity and man's unity. She must remain the conscience of society whenever there is a question about fundamental human values or human co-existence. The Church must always point to the transitoriness of the world and so resist making earthly things absolute, making them idols—whether they be money, power, or pleasure. The Church thus serves the greater freedom and hope of man.

348–352

In this dialogue between the Church and the world, *the Church receives considerable help from today's world*. The Church must declare the message of Christ in the symbols and languages of different peoples and clarify this message with the wisdom of the philosophers (GS 44). The Church takes on and furthers the aptitudes, abilities and customs of a people insofar as they are good; she also purifies, strengthens, and enhances them (LG 13).

49–50;
225–226
Contemporary questions, secular sciences, literature, and art can contribute much to an understanding of the faith, making it more exact, more profound, and more adequate to the times (GS 62). We see again how the Church is the people of God on the way. She not only lives and works in history, she herself has a history. The Church grows to the full stature of Christ (Eph 4:13).

2.3 The Church's Mission of Salvation

188–189;
223–224
In carrying out her mission of salvation, the Church has experienced many decisive changes brought about by the concrete circumstances of time and place. But whatever those changes, she remains *the one all-encompassing sacrament of salvation* at all times and for all times (LG 48). All men are called to her; she is necessary for all. There is only one mediator of salvation, Jesus Christ (Acts 4:12; 1 Tim 2:5). Only the man who believes in him and is baptized in his name can attain salvation (Mk 16:16; Jn 3:5). This implies the *necessity of the Church for salvation*, since faith and baptism are the door through which we enter into the Church. "Hence they could not be saved who, knowing that the Catholic Church was founded as necessary by God through Christ, would refuse to enter her, or to remain in her" (LG 14; cf. AG 7).

The positive declaration that salvation is possible only in and through Jesus Christ, but that one encounters Christ in the Church, is often formulated negatively: "*There is no salvation outside the Church.*" This statement can be misleading and today seems utterly unintelligible to many people. They ask whether we are really to believe that all men of good will who have never heard of Christ and the Church, but who live good, just, and pious lives, are going to hell. Does this hold even for the non-Catholic Christians? How would such a doctrine be compatible with God's justice and love for all men? How would it foster Christian solidarity with all men?

The statement, "There is no salvation outside the Church", was originally directed as an admonition to Christians who were in the Church but on the verge of leaving her. In this context, the sentence intended to say that those who leave the Church also lose salvation. Only *later* did this statement receive a more general sense; it was then related to all who did not in fact belong to the Roman Catholic Church. Many formulations of it are very narrow. That holds especially for the bull *Unam sanctam* of Pope Boniface VIII (1302) (DS 875; NR 430) and the Decree of the Council of Florence for the Jacobites (1442) (DS 1351; NR 381). These sharp formulations must be seen against the background of the prevailing world view. They proceed from the belief that the gospel is attested to in all the world, and so they presuppose that it can only be a man's own fault if he is not in the bosom of the one Roman Catholic Church. When at the beginning of the *modern era* new continents and cultures fully untouched by Christianity were discovered, the Church stated (as early as 1713) that there is grace outside the visible Roman Catholic Church (DS 2429). Pope Pius IX taught explicitly that God does not refuse his grace to those who live according to their conscience, but who through no fault of their own do not know the Church of Christ yet do the will of God as they are able to recognize it in their situation (DS 2866). Pius XII reaffirmed this explicitly (DS 3869). The *Second Vatican Council* has confirmed this doctrine, developed it, and substantially deepened it. It recalled the declaration of Holy Scripture that God wills the salvation of all men (1 Tim 2:4), but also that man must make the salvific will of God his own (LG 16).

The statement "There is no salvation outside the Church" means that *the Church is the one, all-encompassing sacrament of salvation*. Whoever rejects it by his own fault cannot be saved. Neither can someone be saved, of course, who belongs to the Church only externally, according to the body but not according to the heart. Someone who does not know the Church through no fault of his own can be saved if he does the will of God according to the best of his knowledge and conscience, according to the way he recognizes it concretely in his situation.

Since the Church is the one all-encompassing sacrament of salvation, but many men in fact do not belong to the Church through no fault of their own, there are *different ways and degrees of belonging to the Church*. *Full incorporation* into the community of the Church belongs to those who in the possession of the Spirit of Christ are connected with it "by the bonds constituted by the profession of faith, the sacraments, ecclesiastical government, and communion". Baptismal candidates (catechumens) who, "moved by the Holy Spirit, desire with an explicit intention to be incorporated into the Church, are by that very intention joined to her" (LG 14).

232–234;
275–277

> The Church knows that she is joined in many ways to the baptized who are honored by the name of Christian, but who do not however profess the Catholic faith in its entirety or have not preserved unity or communion under the successor of Peter (LG 15).

They are linked to the Church through Scripture, the confession of faith of the ancient Church, and in some cases, the episcopal office and the Eucharist. To these are added communion in prayer and in other spiritual goods, as well as in the gifts and graces of the Holy Spirit (LG 15). Those who have not yet received the gospel are *related* to the Church in different ways. This holds chiefly of the people of the Old Covenant, but also of Moslems who confess the faith of Abraham, and finally even of those who

seek the unknown God in shadows and images—even of those who have
not yet come to an explicit recognition of God, yet strive to lead a just life
with the help of grace (LG 16). Belonging to the one Church of Jesus
Christ is realized in many different degrees.

The comprehensive possibility of the salvation of all men does not
release the Church from her *missionary commission*. Through sin, the
knowledge of God that we can derive from creation has been obscured.
Men have often confused the truth of God with lies and served creation
more than the Creator (Rom 1:21–25). The message of Jesus Christ lets the
light of creation shine brightly again; only in him is the deepest mystery of
man disclosed (GS 22).

Today the missions are met with many *questions and critical objections*. The Church's
development work and the efforts of the missionary churches to eliminate circumstances unworthy of man are generally esteemed. But one hears objections that the
missions repress native religions, destroy the natural cultures and social structures,
and alienate men from their ancestral forms of life. The missions are said to create
an alienated Church that is an instrument for extending Western culture. They
allegedly communicate our crises and problems to other cultures. It is surely true
that missionaries were all too often children of their times and so not infrequently
brought Christianity to other peoples in Western forms. But often enough they
also helped to make Western colonialism and imperialism more bearable. Of
particular importance were the exertions of St. Peter Claver (d. 1654) against the
slave traffic and on behalf of the blacks, the pastoral activity of St. Turibius of
Mogrovejo (d. 1606), the patron of Lima and of Peru, as well as the battle of St.
Bartolomé de las Casas (d. 1566) for the human rights of the Indians.

Since then, the *situation of the missions has changed in a far-reaching way*. On the one
hand, there is now a universal missionary situation. On the other hand, native
local churches have arisen on all continents, taking independent responsibility for
the propagation and the deepening of Christianity in their own regions. The older
churches of Europe and North America must support such churches with both
personnel and finances. But the older churches also experience that they are not
222 only giving, but also richly receiving. The missions today engender a *worldwide
exchange among the different local churches*. These new forms of the missions correspond
to the fact that we now depend in all spheres on reciprocal worldwide exchanges.
But economic and technological exchange alone does not create a family of
mankind, and developmental aid, however urgently needed, does not solve
questions of meaning. In order for men of all peoples and races to become friends,
there must be a unity of hearts in the confession of the one God.

The true *basis of the missions* is the commission received by the Church
from the Lord himself: "Go, therefore, and make disciples of all the
nations" (Mt 28:19; Mk 16:15). The missions are not something added to
the Church; even less are they reserved to a few missionary priests,

brothers, and sisters. All Christians are called to give witness. The Church is essentially missionary (AG 2). The mission, the sending out, begins in God himself. The Father sends the Son, the Son sends the Holy Spirit, and in the strength of the Holy Spirit the disciples know themselves to be sent to share the love and light that they have experienced. Mission is so fundamental that we can say that the Church originates in a mission and realizes herself in her mission.

The *goal of the missions* is not the spreading of Western culture or the propagation of the Church in our form, but "the evangelization and the implanting of the Church among peoples or groups where she has not yet taken root" (AG 6). "Implanting" means that the Church should everywhere be rooted in the culture and customs of life of the people (AG 15). So far as the wealth of Jesus Christ is bestowed on all people and, conversely, so far as the riches of the peoples and their cultures become native to the Church, both the Church and the world strive toward their eschatological fullness. This is what the Second Vatican Council taught: "Missionary activity is nothing else, and nothing less, than the manifestation of God's plan, its epiphany and realization in the world and in history; that by which God, through mission, clearly brings to its conclusion the history of salvation" (AG 8).

2.4 The Church as Particular Church and as Worldwide Church

The Church lives in space and time. She embodies differently the mission given to her once for all by Jesus Christ in the individual epochs of her history. She also exists in a specific place according to specific forms of life—in traditions, in social, cultural, and political circumstances and mentalities. The Church is at the same time the worldwide universal Church and the church of a particular place.

When the New Testament speaks of the Church it sometimes means the universal Church; in other places, it means the specific local church in such places as Jerusalem, Corinth, and Rome. St. Paul speaks, for instance, of the "church of God which is in Corinth" (1 Cor 1:2; 2 Cor 1:1). He means that the local church of Corinth is not only a section, an administrative district, as it were, of the universal Church; it is, rather, the Church of God represented and realized in Corinth. The essence of the whole Church is realized by the local church in its historical situation. But precisely because the *local church is the representation and the realization of the one Church of God*, it cannot exist in isolation. It must stand in communion with all other local churches. Paul himself struggled, at the risk of his life, to obtain this unity and community.

In the earliest period, the Church as a communion had her center in the primitive community of Jerusalem. Later, this primacy passed to the church of Rome, which Ignatius of Antioch (around 110) already designated as first in love. The unity of the Church showed itself during the first centuries especially in the communion (*communio*) of the different local churches. It was realized in a shared faith, in reciprocal admission to the Eucharist, in intercession, in hospitality, and in correspondence among bishops. The synods too proved themselves quite early as important instruments and forms of expression for the communion of churches. In the second millennium, after the rupture of communion with the churches of the East, a more monolithic understanding of unity developed in the West; the local churches figured more or less as parts of the Roman Church. The Second Vatican Council (1962–1965) took up and renewed the ancient Church's idea of the community of local churches. It taught clearly that *the one and only Catholic Church exists in and from the local churches* (LG 23). The Council described the local churches as particular churches "in which the one, holy, catholic, and apostolic Church of Christ is truly present and active" (CD 11).

293–295

249–250

> This Church of Christ is really present in all legitimately organized local groups of the faithful, which, insofar as they are united to their pastors, are also quite appropriately called churches in the New Testament. For these are in fact, in their own localities, the new people called by God. . . . In them the faithful are gathered together through the preaching of the gospel of Christ, and the mystery of the Lord's Supper is celebrated. . . . In these communities, though they may often be small and poor, or existing in the diaspora, Christ is present through whose power and influence the one, holy, catholic and apostolic Church is constituted (LG 26).

230–233;
250–252
235–238

Accordingly, the Council has given more room in the liturgy as well as in the entire life and discipline of the Church for *legitimate diversity within unity*. It has thus emphasized the catholicity of the Church once again (SC 13, 37; LG 13, 24; AG 19).

275–276

When speaking of a particular or local church, the Second Vatican Council usually means the church under the leadership of a bishop—a diocese, a bishopric (CD 11). For the individual Christian, however, the *parish* under the leadership of a priest is normally the immediate place where he experiences the working of Christ in the Holy Spirit. The individual Christian in an increasingly secularized society must find a home in a parish so that he can live his faith. The Second Vatican Council speaks also of the local congregation as deserving "to be called by the name which is given to the unique people of God in its entirety, that is to say, the Church of God" (LG 28; SC 42). Yet just as the bishopric can exist only within the communion of the whole Church, so the local parish congregation depends on communion with the bishop and the diocese. Through baptism, we are members of the one Catholic Church in all times and all places.

In the broadest sense, the Church of Christ exists wherever two or three are together in the name of Jesus (Mt 18:20). The most important units of the Church are *Christian marriages and families*, which the Second Vatican Council explicitly designates as *a kind of domestic church* (LG 11). But various other groups—associations, domestic communities, neighborhoods or spiritual communities in a locality, as well as Church associations and groups—also serve the upbuilding and growth of the parish community and of the universal Church. They help the individual to sink roots and to find a home in the Church. 293–294

If the Church is such a many-sided and manifold thing in time and space, it becomes even more important to ask: What is the Church? What is her enduring essence?

3. The Essence of the Church

3.1 The Church Is a Mystery

It is clear that the Church is a genuinely human entity but that she is at the same time more than something visible or perceptible. Ultimately, the Church can be adequately understood only within the *perspective of faith*. 212–213 The reality of the Church is grounded in the saving decree of God, the Father, and in the saving work that he effects through Jesus Christ in the Holy Spirit. The Church is a *single, complex reality*. On the one hand, she is 215–216; the visible, earthly Church, which needs regulations and structures for the 232–233 fulfillment of her mission. She is constituted and ordered in this world as a society realized in the Catholic Church which is led by Peter's successor and by the bishops in communion with him. On the other hand, the Church is a spiritual reality, filled with the Spirit of Christ, which can be fully grasped only in faith (LG 8). In her, God's mystery of salvation, which has come into the world once for all with Jesus Christ, is abidingly and concretely present in history (Eph 3:3–12; Col 1:26–27).

In order to express both of these aspects, the Second Vatican Council teaches that the Church is in Jesus Christ *the sacrament, i.e., the sign and* 188–189;
217–222; *instrument, of the universal salvation of mankind* (LG 1, 9; GS 42, 45; AG 1, 266–267; among others). A visible element does belong essentially to the Church, 295–296 but it is only a sign and instrument of the spiritual dimension of the Church. This implies two things. First, the Church is a means for the re-presentation and transmission of salvation. But she cannot be defined in terms of her function alone. So, second, as re-presenting sign she is also the fruit of the work of salvation. The Church is the mystery of salvation become public in the world.

The Church's mysterious reality cannot be reduced in its essence to any single concept. The Church can be described only with the help of a *multitude of mutually complementary images and concepts*, each of which captures only a single side of her essence. The New Testament calls her the Church of God, the people of God, land to be cultivated, the field of God, the flock, edifice, temple, and house of God, the family of God, the Church of Jesus Christ, the body of Christ, the bride of Christ, the temple of the Holy Spirit. The Church Fathers added other images. They described the Church especially as the community of believers and as the communion of saints (of those sanctified through the sacraments)—a declaration that appears in the Creed. The Greek and Latin words for Church are important here. They are *ekklesia* or *ecclesia* respectively; they define the Church as assembly and as congregation. The English word "church" comes from the Greek *kyriakē* and means "house of the Lord". It affirms that the Church belongs to the Lord Jesus Christ.

These various images and concepts point in different ways to God, the Father, in whose eternal decree and election the Church is grounded; to Jesus Christ, God's Son, through whose salvific work she enters into history; and to the Holy Spirit, in whose strength she is held together, is constantly rejuvenated, and always works. "Hence the universal Church is seen to be", as the Second Vatican Council says, "a people brought into unity from the unity of the Father, the Son, and the Holy Spirit" (LG 4). In order to unfold this *trinitarian mystery of the Church*, we will discuss three biblical images for the Church: the people of God, the body of Christ, and the temple of the Holy Spirit.

3.2 The Church Is the People of God

"The people of God" is a central concept in Vatican II's declarations on the Church. Since Vatican II, this phrase has contributed much to the renewal of the Church's self-awareness and life. It has helped to overcome an individualistic manner of living the faith and to strengthen the conscious-ness that every member of the Church shares in responsibility for her. When Holy Scripture describes the Church as the people of God, it means that salvation is not intended for the isolated individual by himself alone, but for a community into which the individual is taken up to obtain a personal share in salvation. This community is not formed by the belated coalition of religiously like-minded. Like a people or a family, the Church is given from the start to the individual; the individual is taken up into the Church, grows into her, is sustained by her, and takes on responsibility for her. This holds in principle for all Christians, for the hierarchy as well as for the laity. The people of God does not mean just the people or—as is often misleadingly said today—the foundation as distinguished from the hierarchy. It means all Christians in their totality as well as in the multiplicity of their gifts, ministries, and offices. *All are the Church, the people of God!* 239–243

But the Church is not a people in the ordinary sense of the word. It is not a community linked by common descent, history, and culture. Nor does it proceed from a people as a natural and historical entity, even less as the result of the forces of a particular group or class. The Church is the *people of God*—the people that God has singled out and called from among the peoples, his own special possession, with which he has formed a covenant. She is one universal people residing in and drawn from all peoples, races, and classes. The Church is at the same time a holy people. A person is not born into the Church but is incorporated into it through faith and through baptism, the sacrament of faith and of rebirth to new life (Jn 3:5). So the assembly of the people of God is not a civil-political 274–277 assembly, brought together to confer and decide on common matters. It is an assembly brought together to hear what God has decided, said, and done, in order to thank him for his salvific decrees and deeds. The Church is the community of believers which assembles as a community of worship, thanksgiving and praise, with God himself effectively present in her midst, and which is sent into the world to bear witness to the gospel through word and deed.

God's fundamental promise to *his people of the Old Covenant* is "I will be your God, and you will be my people" (Lev 26:11–12; Ezek 37:27; 2 Cor 6:16; Heb 8:10; Rev 21:3). This promise connects the Church with Israel, the people of God of the Old Covenant. The Apostle Paul presents this connection in detail (Rom 9–11). The Second Vatican Council reaffirmed this common history after a long history of alienation, estrangement, and 56–57 guilt (NA 4). Without this connection with the Old Covenant, in which the Church is prepared and prefigured (LG 9), the Church could not be understood. Of course, we must also see the breach between Israel and the Church, *God's people of the New Covenant*. The new people of God, the new and true Israel, also includes the Gentiles, who were not originally the people of God (1 Pet 2:10). In the *Church of Jews and Gentiles* (Eph 2:11–22), the promise to Abraham that all peoples would attain blessing in him has been fulfilled (Gen 12:3; 18:18; 22:18; Gal 3:8).

The New Covenant people of God comprises men of all peoples and races. "There does not exist among you Jew or Greek, slave or freeman, male or female. All are one in Christ Jesus" (Gal 3:28; 1 Cor 12:13; Col 3:11). Because the Church is not linked to a particular form of culture or to a particular political, economic, or social system, because she encompasses all peoples, cultures, races, and classes, she can be a sign and instrument of unity and peace for mankind (GS 42). The Church is the *Messianic people of God*, the sign of hope for the peoples (LG 9).

217–218;
219–222

As a sign and instrument of man's unity, the Church points beyond herself. She is an *itinerant people of God*, the people of God underway. She lives in history and has her own legitimate history. She is still on the way and not yet at the goal. As the people of God, she is not rigid and static, but dynamic, an active sign of hope. The Church lives in this world in diaspora, away from home, and has no lasting home here (Jas 1:1; 1 Pet 1:1; 2:11; Heb 3:7–4:11; 11:8–16, 32–34). So she may never settle down permanently; she must always be setting out toward him who suffered outside the gate (Heb 13:12). In the end, when God is all in all, there will be no more need of the Church as the means of salvation. Though she bears witness to much that is definitive and permanent, the Church lives as the people of God with the proclamation that she is not herself the definitive goal.

49–50;
214–215

3.3 The Church Is the Body of Christ

The comparison between the human organism and the human community was well known in antiquity. Just as in the body one member cannot exist without the others, so also in the State. Paul takes up this comparison and applies it to the Church: the Church is one body in many differing members. They all need one another; they must all cooperate harmoniously and function together (Rom 12:4–9). If one member suffers, all members suffer with it; if one member is glad, all are glad with it (1 Cor 12:26). In a particular way, the poor, weak, and persecuted members need the solidarity of all in the Church (LG 8). Yet Paul also corrects this well-known image. He compares not only the body and the Church, but also the body and Christ (1 Cor 12:12). In this second comparison, he teaches that the Church does not arise only from the cooperation of its members. *The Church arises wholly from Jesus Christ.* Only through him and in him are we members of his body.

THE CHURCH AS SACRAMENT OF THE SPIRIT

For that reason, the Letters to the Ephesians and to the Colossians can

For that reason, the Letters to the Ephesians and to the Colossians can say that *Jesus Christ is the head of the body which is the Church* (Eph 1:22–23; 4:15–16; Col 1:18; 2:19). The Church is not only compared with a body; she is *identified* with Jesus Christ in his body. St. Augustine spoke of the whole Christ, head and members. This does not mean that Jesus Christ and the Church are the same. They do indeed belong inseparably together, but the Church is not simply Christ living on, however much Jesus Christ continues to live and work in her. In spite of the unity of Jesus Christ and the Church, Jesus Christ remains the head and Lord of the Church; he is placed above the Church, while she is subordinated to him in obedience. The Church lives from Jesus Christ and for him. Led by him and filled with him, the Church nevertheless also stands before Jesus Christ. The New Testament expresses this relation and this loving engagement above all in the image of the Church as the *bride of Jesus Christ* (Eph 5:25; Rev 19:7; 21:2, 9; 22:17; Hos 2:21–22).

The Church's participation in Jesus Christ is threefold: as participation in the   176–179
prophetic office, in the high-priestly office, and in the kingly pastoral office. The building up and the growth of Christ's body is fostered by proclamation of the word of God, by celebration of the sacraments (especially baptism and the Eucharist), and by pastoral ministry.

The Church is the body of Christ, the community of those who hear the
word of God and bear witness to it before the world. She is the community   254–258
of believers. Through faith we are linked fundamentally to Christ. The
word of God is embodied in the *sacraments*. Through baptism we become   266–269;
the one body in the one Spirit (1 Cor 12:13). In the Eucharist we all take   274–277
part in the one bread, the one eucharistic body of Christ, and thus become   293–296
one body (1 Cor 10:16–17). Thus, "in the sacrament of the eucharistic bread, the unity of believers, who form one body in Christ, is both expressed and brought about" (LG 3). The Eucharist is the "source and summit" of the whole Christian, ecclesial life (LG 11). It is, according to the words of St. Augustine, "the sign of unity and the bond of love" (DS 802, 1635; NR 375, 567; SC 47). We cannot, of course, share the eucharistic bread without also sharing our daily bread with one another. The celebration of the sacraments must become effective *in deeds and in the community of love*. We encounter Jesus Christ in the poor, the weak, the outcast, the persecuted, the suffering, and the dying (Mt 25:31–46). As the body of Christ,

> the Church is compared, not without significance, to the mystery of
> the incarnate Word. As the assumed nature, inseparably linked to
> him, serves the divine Word as a living organ of salvation, so, in a   132–133
> somewhat similar way, does the social structure of the Church serve

the Spirit of Christ who vivifies it, in the building up of the body (LG 8).

In this broad sense, the Church is the place filled with Jesus Christ and his Spirit, through which he will fill all (Eph 1:23).

3.4 The Church Is the Temple of God in the Holy Spirit

The ancient world understood a temple as the place of God's effective presence in the world. Israel was unique in not possessing a permanent temple for a long time; God was present in the midst of his people on its way through the wilderness. The New Testament also characterizes the Church or the concrete community as a temple, as the place of the presence of God and of Jesus Christ. "Where two or three are gathered in my name, there am I in their midst" (Mt 18:20). The Church does not mean primarily a building of dead stones, but a *spiritual building of living stones*, the cornerstone of which is Jesus Christ (1 Pet 2:4–5).

183–187   The presence of God and of Jesus Christ comes about in the Holy Spirit. Through the Holy Spirit we become the New Covenant people of God (Jer 31:31–33; Ezek 11:19–20; 36:26–27). Through the one Spirit we also become one body in Christ (1 Cor 12:13–14). Paul says:

> Are you not aware that you are the temple of God, and that the Spirit of God dwells in you? If anyone destroys God's temple, God will destroy him. For the temple of God is holy, and you are that temple (1 Cor 3:16–17; compare 2 Cor 6:16; Eph 2:21).

If the Church's external structure is the temple and dwelling of the Holy Spirit, the Holy Spirit can be likened to the soul in the body; he is *the vital principle of the Church* (Augustine; LG 7). The Church must live from the Holy Spirit and be constantly renewed in him. He constantly rejuvenates her and confers new fruitfulness and vital strength upon her. He maintains

219–222   her in the truth (Jn 14:26; 16:13–14; DV 7–9); he leads her to the missions (cf. AG 4); he sanctifies her and all her members (LG 39–40).

The Holy Spirit is particularly the principle of Church unity in the
184–185;   multiplicity of *spiritual gifts* (1 Cor 12:4–31a; Eph 4:3, among others; LG
189–191   12; UR 2). The fullness and wealth of spiritual gifts belong essentially to the Church. The Church lives from the fullness of the Spirit, who blows where he will (Jn 3:8). The Church and her renewal cannot be simply "done"; they cannot be programmed and organized. The decisive element in the Church is not at our disposal. So the Church must pray to the Holy Spirit again and again that he may continually bring her life, renewal, fruitfulness.

There are many *false notions* about the essence and operation of the spiritual gifts (charisms). Many people think that these gifts are primarily extraordinary ones like ecstasies, visions, miracles, prophecies, and speaking in tongues, to name a few. But Paul also lists among the charisms the speech that mediates wisdom or knowledge (1 Cor 12:8), the activity of apostles, prophets, and teachers, and other administrative and helping tasks (1 Cor 12:28). In another place, Paul also names the unmarried state as a charism. "Still, each one has his own gift from God, one this and another that" (1 Cor 7:7). Both the ordinary and the extraordinary spiritual gifts must be of benefit to the upbuilding of the community (1 Cor 12:7; 14:5, 12, 26); they must also conform to the "analogy of faith", to the common faith of the Church (Rom 12:6).

Other people think that the extraordinary gifts were intended only for the Church's first generations. They forget that the saints of every generation received extraordinary gifts by which they were to bear witness symbolically and representatively for others to the power and vitality of the Spirit in the Church. Through the charismatic renewal movement in our own day, we now see much of this in a new way. Finally, we should not overestimate the charisms, whose spark Paul wished to preserve ("Do not stifle the Spirit!", 1 Th 5:19). To the Corinthians, on whom rich spiritual gifts were bestowed, Paul shows a "higher way" that stands above all charisms: the way of love, which he praises so eloquently (1 Cor 13). Love is the highest fruit of the Holy Spirit (Gal 5:22).

Charism and office are not antitheses; they can and must complement each other and be linked with each other. Ecclesiastical officeholders may not claim a charismatic competence for themselves alone. On the other hand, spontaneously appearing charisms should not be played off against clear-cut offices that were instituted as permanent. 243–247; 314–315

The early Church counted the fundamental, indispensable ministries of apostles, prophets, and teachers among the charisms (1 Cor 12:28) and regarded "apostles, prophets, evangelists, pastors and teachers" as gifts of the glorified Lord to his Church (Eph 4:11). According to the Pastoral Letters, a gift of God's grace is conferred on candidates for office by the laying on of hands (2 Tim 1:6; 1 Tim 4:14). An office is, of course, not the only form of charism. And it depends on cooperation with all other charisms, just as these other charisms must be related to the office and stand in communion with it. It is the business of an ecclesiastical office not to quench the Spirit, but to test everything and to retain what is good (1 Th 5:19–21). The charismatic essence of the Church would be misunderstood if it were described only in enthusiastic terms and played off against Church order. Precisely in those chapters in which Paul speaks of charisms in most detail, he strives to present the notions of unity and order (1 Cor 12; 14). "God is a God, not of confusion, but of peace" (1 Cor 14:33).

The established official structures of the Church and groups that perceive a new awakening of the Spirit need each other. The Church always needs the forces of renewal so that she does not ossify; for their critical correction, these forces need the Church's Tradition, which sustains faith throughout the ages until the spark is enkindled anew. The Spirit of God works in both, and God's Spirit does not contradict itself. There do arise fruitful tensions and clarifying conflicts. Still, we are told to "make every effort to preserve the unity which has the Spirit as its origin and peace as its binding force" (Eph 4:3).

Given the fullness, the wealth, and the diversity of spiritual gifts in the Church, the question arises: Where and how can one recognize in the midst of conflicts where the true Church is, where the people of God, the body of Christ, and the temple of the Holy Spirit are truly realized? What are the marks of the true Church?

4. The Marks of the Church

To the question about the marks of the Church, the Creed answers: "I believe in one, holy, catholic, and apostolic Church." This names the four essential properties that characterize the Church and make her recognizable as the true Church. To be sure, one cannot, by means of them, simply demonstrate the true Church to non-Catholic Christians. The confession of the true Church presupposes an encounter and a conversion. But the four marks of the Church do yield, when taken together, a sum that has persuasive force by its coherence and intelligibility.

4.1 The Unity of the Church

The unity and uniqueness of the Church of Jesus Christ is deeply grounded *in the mystery of the Church*. From the confession of the one God, the one mediator Jesus Christ, and the one all-pervading Spirit, there follows with an inner necessity the one Church. This has a double sense: there is according to the will of Jesus Christ one single Church (uniqueness), and this Church is one in herself (unity). We hear this in the last testament of Jesus:

> ". . . that all may be one
> as you, Father, are in me, and I in you;
> I pray that they may be [one] in us,
> that the world may believe that you sent me.
> I have given them the glory you gave me
> that they may be one, as we are one—
> I living in them, you living in me—
> that their unity may be complete.

So shall the world know that you sent me,
and that you loved them as you loved me" (Jn 17:21–23).

In the Letter to the Ephesians, we find the same basis for unity and also the exhortation to consider the gift of unity as a task:

Live a life worthy of the calling you have received, with perfect humility, meekness, and patience, bearing with one another lovingly. Make every effort to preserve the unity which has the Spirit as its origin and peace as its binding force. There is but one body and one Spirit, just as there is but one hope given all of you by your call. There is one Lord, one faith, one baptism; one God and Father of all, who is over all, and works through all, and is in all (Eph 4:2–6).

These two texts say that the unity of the Church is not a mere postulate, not a goal of Church organization, not something that must first be created artificially. It is already a reality in Christ as a fruit of the Holy Spirit. The gift of unity is, of course, also a task. Every division in the faith ultimately contradicts the will of God and the reality of Jesus Christ; division is a scandal and a sin. It darkens the image of the Church and denies to the world the service of unity, of peace, and of reconciliation with which the Church is commissioned. We cannot resign ourselves to the disintegration of Christianity into different denominations.

What is the unity of the Church? When the Acts of the Apostles 221–222 describes the early congregation of Jerusalem, it emphasizes the fact that all the faithful held fast to the teaching of the Apostles and to the fellowship, as well as to the breaking of the bread and the prayers (Acts 2:42). There was a unity in faith, in love, and in worship under the leadership of the Apostles. The Second Vatican Council speaks of the *threefold bond of unity*: the bond of the confession of faith, of the sacraments, of Church leadership and community (LG 14).

This threefold unity is not a uniformity. Within the encompassing unity, a multiplicity of ways of proclamation, of liturgical and devotional forms, of theologies, of Church laws, and of forms of social involvement and social services are possible and even desirable. Otherwise, the Church could not unite men from all different peoples, races, cultures, languages, and forms of thought and life. Only a *diversity in unity* enables her to become all things to all men (1 Cor 9:19–23). The communion (*communio*) of faith, of the sacraments, of the ministries and offices, which is founded on the common participation in the one Spirit of Jesus Christ, is realized in varied exchange and mutual recognition, in solidarity with one another and in relation to the more comprehensive whole. We should distinguish this diversity in unity from a limitless plurality, from a *noncommittal pluralism* in which there is not a multiform expression of one and the same thing, but rather irreconcilable opposites. In this case, fruitful and even vitally necessary tensions become rigid and imcompatible opposites. If such incompatible elements were to stand and exist next to one another in the Church, her unity would be dissolved. The Church would then lose her definite shape and could no longer be a sign for the world.

Heresies and schisms are forms of pluralism that abolish unity. While schism abolishes the unity of the lived community, especially of the liturgical community, heresy damages the unity of the one faith, which then necessarily leads to the rupture of the liturgical community. Of course, not every erroneous opinion is a heresy. Error becomes a heresy by being stubbornly maintained and becoming fixed. Heresy presupposes personal guilt. So we cannot immediately speak of heresy in the case of those Christians separated from the Catholic Church. In individual matters, heresy can come about both through an excess and through a defect, through reductions as well as through exaggerations and additions, through the one-sided presentation and the absolutizing of partial truths as well as through the denial of a binding truth of faith.

295–296

Secular factors (national, political, cultural, social, and racial divisions) ordinarily play a role in heresy, as do personal dispositions (dogmatism, rivalry, will to self-assertion, and arrogance, among others). But this is only part of it. The great divisions in faith also resulted from a sense of responsibility for the unadulterated message of salvation; people thought they had to separate for the sake of the truth of the gospel. This kind of division cannot be overcome by penance and confession of guilt alone; a common effort to achieve the correct understanding of the gospel must also take place. The unity of the Church must be a *unity in the truth*; love without truth would be untrue and untruthful.

222;
249–250
194–197

There have been divisions in the Church from the very beginning. Two divisions in particular have led to a breach that persists today: *the separation between the Eastern and Western Church* in the year 1054, which sealed a long-lasting mutual alienation; and *the Western division of the Church* in the sixteenth century in the wake of the Reformation, which in turn brought forth numerous divisions.

After a long epoch of polemics, controversy, and denominational isolation, a counter-tendency has arisen in the *ecumenical movement* of this century. By the "ecumenical movement" we understand Spirit-inspired repentance for the division of the Church, reflection on what is common to all Christians, and efforts to overcome the remaining differences and to restore the visible unity of the Church (UR 1, 4).

Outstanding events in the ecumenical movement are the constitution of the "Ecumenical Council of Churches" in 1948 and the Second Vatican Council (1962–1965), during which the Catholic Church committed herself officially to ecumenical concerns. The Decree on Ecumenism is normative and fundamental for this commitment.

The foundation in faith of ecumenism is not a relativism that would deny that the Church of Jesus Christ is realized in the Catholic Church (LG 8). Neither is ecumenical unity an invisible something "behind" the divided churches; nor is it a unity like that of different branches on one trunk. While the Catholic Church remains convinced that she is the true Church of Jesus Christ and that she possesses the fullness of the means of salvation, she does not deny that "many elements of sanctification and of truth are found outside her visible confines. Since these are gifts belonging to the Church of Christ, they are forces impelling toward Catholic unity" (LG 8). Among these common elements are Holy Scripture as the foundation and norm of life and action; the confessions of faith of the ancient Church; baptism as incorporation into the body of Christ; the life of grace; faith, hope, and love; and other gifts of the Holy Spirit (LG 15; UR 3). With the orthodox Churches of the East we also share the Eucharist as the sacrament of unity and the episcopal office as a ministry of unity. The Second Vatican Council teaches that the separated Churches and communities, in spite of the imperfections inherent in them according to our faith, are used by the Spirit of Christ as means of salvation (UR 3). 215–216; 276–277 295–296

It follows that the *motive* of the ecumenical movement cannot be the indifference frequently to be found in the present world, which considers traditional doctrinal differences as unintelligible and antiquated. The motive can only be obedience to the will of Jesus Christ and to the urging of the Holy Spirit. The *way* of the ecumenical movement does not lead through pragmatic compromises or false peace-making that obscures or waters down the truth of the gospel and the purity of the Church's teaching. Ecumenism presupposes each believer's own renewal through prayer, conversion, and sanctification.

Of central importance for the unity of Christians is private and public prayer. Ecumenism leads through dialogue and cooperation to the removal of prejudices and misunderstandings, to knowing and understanding one another better, to efforts at a common understanding of the Christian truth and of the persistent and divisive differences. The *goal* of the ecumenical movement is the unity of the Church. This does not mean a uniform, homogenized Church, but rather a unity that permits manifold expressions and so renders the resumption of the Church community possible. Efforts toward the unity of the Church also serve the unity, reconciliation, and the peace of the world.

4.2 The Holiness of the Church

The Church's holiness seems to stand in considerable tension with our concrete experience of Church life. No one can dispute that there is sin in the Church. But faith recognizes a deeper dimension as well. Faith sees that *holiness belongs to the Church's deepest essence*. God, who is the primordial ground of the Church, is the absolutely Holy One (Is 6:3); he chooses and creates a holy people for himself (Ex 19:6; 1 Pet 2:9). Jesus Christ, "the holy One of God" (Mk 1:24, among others), surrendered himself for the

Church in order "to make her holy" (Eph 5:26). Finally, as the temple of the Holy Spirit the Church is herself holy (1 Cor 3:17). So Scripture calls the first Christians simply "the saints" (Acts 9:13, 32, 41; Rom 8:27; 1 Cor 6:1, among others). Yet from the beginning there were weaknesses, disputes, even scandals in the primitive community at Jerusalem—and even more so in the community in Corinth. What, then, does the holiness of the Church mean?

When Holy Scripture speaks of "holiness", it does not primarily mean ethical perfection, but rather *being singled out from the domain of the worldly and belonging to God.* Christians and the Church do indeed live in the world, but they are not of the world (Jn 17:11, 14–15). The Church is holy because she comes from God and is ordained to him. She is holy because the holy God, the One who is different from the whole world, keeps faith with her unconditionally and does not abandon her to the powers of death or the transitoriness of the world (Mt 16:18). The Church is holy because Jesus Christ is indissolubly linked to her (Mt 28:20), because the powerful presence of the Holy Spirit is permanently promised to her (Jn 14:26; 16:7–9). She is holy because the goods of salvation have been permanently given to her and entrusted to her for transmission—these are the truth of faith, the sacraments of new life, ministries and offices.

From this "objective" holiness, ethical realization or *"subjective"* holiness must follow. "You shall make and keep yourselves holy, because I am holy" (Lev 11:44 [cf. 45]; 1 Pet 1:16; 1 Jn 3:3). The Letters of the Apostle Paul repeatedly exhort Christians to let a new manner of life and new actions follow from the new being of grace (Rom 6:6–14; 8:2–17, among others) and to make their whole life a divine service (Rom 12:1). All Christians are called to this holiness, whether they are laymen or clerics, whether they live in the world or in a religious community, whether they are married or unmarried (LG 39–42). "It is God's will that you grow in holiness" (1 Th 4:3).

This holiness is not a product or an achievement; it is the fruit of the Holy Spirit and his gifts. Holiness does not require extraordinary or even conspicuous deeds, but rather extraordinary faithfulness, love, and patience in everyday life, in the glorification of God and in the service of one's neighbor—especially in bearing sufferings, persecutions, and adversities of every kind. "By this holiness a more human manner of life is fostered also in earthly society" (LG 40). Although the goal of holiness is the same for all Christians, there are nonetheless different ways and forms for reaching this holiness. In all Christian states of life, one thing is decisive: the radical fulfillment of the great commandment to love God above all and to love one's neighbor as oneself (Mk 12:30–31; Jn 13:34; 15:12; 1 Cor 13).

One form for reaching holiness is *life according to the three evangelical counsels* (namely, an unmarried state freely chosen for the sake of the Kingdom of heaven, poverty, and obedience). This is a special form of Christian life that tries to answer the call to holiness. It is based on the word and example of Jesus, who lived a virginal, poor, and obedient life himself; it has always been highly esteemed by the Church. The *religious state* is based on a communal life that is meant to be lived permanently under vows in accordance with the evangelical counsels. The religious life is rooted in baptism but springs from a special call and a special grace that frees one for and obligates one to a special service for God and men. The religious orders are an important, even indispensable, sign of the holiness of the Church (LG 43–47; PC 5). The Church is indebted to them for many spiritual impulses, many apostolic and charitable efforts, but also many cultural and scientific contributions. The orders can be important signs today of fulfilled human and Christian freedom in the face of an often one-sided activism and the danger of being absorbed in the material. Each of the different and quite numerous orders bears its own stamp according to a particular calling and history. They may be, for instance, either more contemplatively or more apostolically oriented. In recent times, *secular institutes*, in which men and women, laity and clergy, live according to the evangelical counsels in the midst of the world and as a leaven for the world, have been added to the earlier forms of community (PC 11). 320

At all times, there have been those in the Church who have lived this holiness in a convincing, even heroic way recognized by the Church. We call them *saints* (in the narrower sense of the word). They are the outstanding representatives of the Church, for one can best see by their lives what the Church is. They are the credible proof of her holiness. They are at the same time a standard and a model of Christian life. Because they are linked with us in the one body of Christ, in the communion of saints, we may invoke their intercession. 143–144;
253–254

The holy Church always includes sinners and can to that extent also be called a *Church of sinners*. We must pray every day, "Forgive us the wrong we have done" (Mt 6:12). The Church has often objected to rigoristic currents that, contrary to the gospel exhortation, try to separate the weeds from the wheat in the present (Mt 13:24–30) in order to set up a Church of the pure. The Church has held on the contrary that baptized sinners belong to the Church and that the Church will be "without stain or wrinkle" (Eph 5:27) only at the end of time. In this world, the Church and all her members are daily in need of penance. The Second Vatican Council says, "Christ, 'holy, innocent, and undefiled' (Heb 7:26) knew nothing of sin (2 Cor 5:21), but came only to expiate the sins of the people (Heb 2:17). The Church, however, clasping sinners to her bosom, at once holy and always in need of purification, follows constantly the path of penance and renewal" (LG 8). 211–212

The tension between the Church's holiness and the sinfulness of her members can at times assume alarming proportions and—as in the late Middle Ages, for instance—gravely distort the face of the Church herself. On the other hand, the history of the Church bears the imprint of *reform and renewal movements*, among which stand prominently the different movements of monks and friars. The boundary between legitimate and illegitimate reform is blurred when unchangeable essential structures of the Church are subjected to change. They must be considered instead as holy, as inviolable for the Church. They must be renewed, but they cannot be changed or abolished. The soul of real renewal in the Church is personal conversion by renewal of life in the spirit of the gospel. Through such private and public penance, as well as through renewal in faith, the Church demonstrates her holiness. This is the only way that she can be a credible sign of the presence in the world of the holy and sanctifying God.

4.3 The Catholicity of the Church

The word "Catholic" does not occur in the New Testament. Ignatius of Antioch (around 110) uses it for the first time in regard to the Church (Letter to the Smyrnians, 8, 2). It originally meant "what corresponds to the whole". Applied to the Church, it means that the whole, worldwide, universal Church will announce the whole, true, and genuine faith. The true Church is catholic in distinction from communities that select only a part of the truth or wish to be a church for only a particular people, a particular culture, a particular level, and so on.

The substance of this doctrine of the Church's catholicity is very well grounded biblically. According to Holy Scripture, God himself is the all-encompassing reality who lets the fullness of his divinity dwell in Jesus Christ, in order to reconcile all to himself (Col 1:19–20) and to bring all into unity (Eph 1:9–10). Through the Holy Spirit, the Church is the fullness of Jesus Christ; through her, Jesus fills the universe (Eph 1:23). The fullness of the message of salvation and the reality of salvation reveal their whole wealth only by embracing the whole range of peoples and their cultures (Eph 3:8–12; Col 1:24–28). "The Church is catholic" means that she proclaims *the whole faith and the whole of salvation for the whole man and the whole of mankind*. Every truth of salvation and every means of salvation has its home in her.

Concretely, the catholicity of the Church is realized in *three ways*.

1. The Church is catholic because she is sent into the whole world in order to announce the gospel to all creatures (Mk 16:15; Mt 28:19–20). She is sent to *all peoples and cultures, all races and classes*. She must, on the one hand, communicate her wealth to all and, on the other hand, be herself enriched by the riches of all (LG 13).

2. The Church is catholic because she is both the *Church of a locality*, the Church in a quite particular historical place, and the *worldwide, universal Church* at the same time.

3. Every local Church and the Church as a whole need in their midst a *fullness of gifts, ministries, and states of life*—of groups that realize Christian

life in differing ways, in the married state or in the religious state, as a layman or as a cleric.

Catholicity, then, does not mean a monotonous uniformity. It is a multicolored wealth and, correctly understood, even a wealth of tensions. The Catholic Church is open; she is not a closed system within which everything can be deduced from a single principle. In order to be considered Catholic, of course, every part and every element, every group and every movement, must stand within a dialectical tension with other parts and must remain in communion with them.

Catholicity is both *a gift and a task*. The Church is the Messianic people of God which, though she does not embrace all men in fact and sometimes appears even as a tiny flock, is nonetheless a seed of unity, of hope, and of salvation for the whole human race (LG 9). The already-existing catholicity needs to be realized all the more fully through the missionary implanting   220–222 of the Church in all peoples and cultures. This can be seen in a second perspective. The catholicity of the Church is obscured by the existence of   231–233 other churches and church communities that also raise the claim to catholicity. The Church does not lose her catholicity in such divisions, but they do make it difficult for the Church "to express in actual life her full catholicity in all its aspects" (UR 4). Fully realized catholicity is possible only by means of ecumenism. When correctly understood and correctly realized, ecumenism does not reduce what is Catholic, but realizes it fully.

4.4 The Apostolicity of the Church

The Gospels report unanimously that Jesus Christ gave the Apostles the mission he had received from the Father. He commissioned them to proclaim the gospel in his stead to all peoples until the consummation of the world, relying on the strength of the Holy Spirit.

> "Full authority has been given to me
> both in heaven and on earth;
> go, therefore, and make disciples of all the nations.
> Baptize them in the name
> 'of the Father,
> and of the Son,
> and of the Holy Spirit'.
> Teach them to carry out everything I have commanded you.
> And know that I am with you always until the end of the world!"
> (Mt 28:18–20; Mk 16:15–20; Lk 24:47–48; Acts 1:8).

> "As the Father has sent me so I send you" (Jn 20:21).

"He who hears you, hears me. He who rejects you, rejects me. And
he who rejects me, rejects him who sent me" (Lk 10:16).

The Church, grounded in Jesus Christ, rests permanently on the *foundation
of the Apostles*, the foundation laid by Jesus Christ, and is linked forever to
their witness (Mt 16:18; Eph 2:20; Rev 21:14; LG 19). She can be the true
Church of Jesus Christ only if she is an apostolic Church and preserves her
identity with that apostolic beginning down through the ages. How is
that possible? The Apostles, whose witness remains in force "until the
consummation of the world", went to their death for their witness and
sealed it with their blood. But where can we encounter the word of the
Apostles today? How can they be present until the end of time? With this
question, we touch on a *sore point in the ecumenical discussion* about the true
Church.

195–196;
204;
215–216;
247–248;
263–265

211–213;
243–244;
311–312

169–171

In order to make some progress, we must begin by asking *what and who is an
apostle*? We are accustomed to speak of the Twelve Apostles. Jesus called the
Twelve to his special following and a special ministry (Mk 3:13–19; 6:6b–13).
After Easter, the *first witnesses of the Resurrection of the Lord* were called "apostles".
They were sent out by the Risen One into the whole world to announce the good
news (1 Cor 9:1–2; 15:7–8). Besides the Twelve, Paul in particular belonged to the
Apostles (Gal 1:1; 2 Cor 1:1, among others), but so also did James, the brother of
the Lord (Gal 1:19). The New Testament also has an even *broader concept of
apostle*—men and women who stand in the missionary service as delegates of the
churches. We still speak of Boniface, for instance, as the Apostle to the Germans or
of Cyril and Methodius as the Apostles to the Slavs. But this is a derivative and
improper use of the word "apostle". In its proper sense, the apostolate is unique,
because it is tied to the immediate and worldwide mission of the Risen One. The
Apostles are foundations for the Church once for all. So we return to the question:
How can the Apostles and their word be present until the consummation of the
world?

The *New Testament* contains clear references to the way in which the
apostolic mission is to be continued in the post-apostolic period. It records
that even in their lifetimes the Apostles not only employed helpers but
also commissioned men to complete and strengthen their work after their
deaths, so that the mission entrusted to them might persist until the end of
time. This emerges clearly from the farewell address that Paul gave in
Miletus, according to the Acts of the Apostles, before the presbyters of the
congregation of Ephesus:

"Keep watch over yourselves, and over the whole flock the Holy
Spirit has given you to guard. Shepherd the church of God, which he
has acquired at the price of his own blood. I know that when I am

gone, savage wolves will come among you who will not spare the flock. From your own number, men will present themselves distorting the truth and leading astray any who follow them. Be on guard, therefore. Do not forget that for three years, night and day, I never ceased warning you individually even to the point of tears. I commend you now to the Lord, and to that gracious word of his which can enlarge you, and give you a share among all who are consecrated to him" (Acts 20:28–32).

The Pastoral Letters (the First and Second Letters to Timothy, the Letter to Titus) describe this transmission of the apostolic mission. These letters were probably written by a disciple of Paul. They attest that Paul had commissioned Timothy and Titus to preserve faithfully the good entrusted to them, the pure and sound teaching (1 Tim 4:16; 6:20; 2 Tim 1:14; 4:3, among others). These two were themselves to lay hands upon other men, and to place them in the apostolic ministry (1 Tim 4:14; 2 Tim 1:6; 2:2; Tit 1:5). The transition from the apostolic to the post-apostolic period already emerges in the New Testament. It is easy to understand that this happens first in the later writings of the New Testament, because the question of how things were to continue after the death of the Apostles was first explicitly posed immediately before or after their death.

From the beginning, the *Tradition of the Church* followed these indications in the New Testament. With Clement of Rome (around 95) and Ignatius of Antioch (around 110), we find the notion of an apostolic succession already alive. Hegesippus (around 180) draws up a list of bishops. Irenaeus of Lyons (around 180) and Tertullian (around 200) provide a detailed theology of apostolic succession. The Second Vatican Council summarizes the teaching of Scripture and Tradition when it teaches "that the bishops have by divine institution taken the place of the apostles as pastors of the Church" (LG 20). In them, the mission conferred on the Apostles, indeed Jesus Christ himself, is abidingly present in the Church (LG 21).

We should not misunderstand the doctrine of apostolic succession. It does not mean that the bishops are new Apostles. The office of the Apostles is unique, but some particular apostolic functions must, according to the words of Jesus Christ, be continued beyond the time of the Apostles. So we must *distinguish between the unique office of the Apostles and the permanent apostolic office*. The bishops are successors of the Apostles only in the second sense. This succession should not be misunderstood in a purely external way, as if it were merely a chain of the imposition of hands or an uninterrupted occupation of the episcopal sees. It needs to be seen *in the total context*.

1. Apostolic succession stands in the context of the transmission of the apostolic faith and is linked to it. Succession is a form of Tradition, and Tradition is the

content of succession. A bishop who falls away from the apostolic faith loses *eo ipso* the right to exercise his office.

2. A bishop's apostolic succession is connected with the succession of the entire college of bishops. The Twelve together were representatives of Israel. So too the college of bishops continues the college of Apostles. As a member of the entire episcopate, the individual bishop stands in the apostolic succession. That is why, according to the Tradition of the ancient Church, a bishop is consecrated by at least three other bishops.

3. The Church as a whole is apostolic. Apostolic succession serves the Church. This is seen best in the practice of consecrating a bishop for ministry to a particular local Church.

The Church is apostolic so far as the faith of the Apostles is alive and fruitful in her because the apostolic mission, which is to last until the end of time, is being continued. *Form and content in the apostolic mission cannot be separated.* The apostolicity of the Church cannot be preserved through faithfulness to the apostolic Scriptures alone. There is need of a living and authoritative apostolic attestation to the apostolic faith that has entered into Scripture. Only where both are given does the true Church of Jesus Christ exist. Thus we conclude with some remarks about Church ministries and offices.

5. Ministries and Offices in the Church

5.1 The Common Priesthood of All the Baptized

We have already said that all baptized Christians *are* the Church. Everything said so far does not hold only of the pope and the bishops, of a "clerical caste" or an ecclesiastical "bureaucracy" (which is often designated by the quite inappropriate term "official Church"). The truth that all baptized Christians are the Church was, of course, largely forgotten for a long time. Even today many pastors lament the difficulty of winning over laymen as coworkers just as many laymen who would like to collaborate complain that they are given too little opportunity for responsible collaboration. We need reflection on the common priesthood of all the baptized and on the common responsibility of all in the Church and for the Church.

The *Magna Carta* of the common priesthood of all baptized Christians is found in the First Letter of Peter:

You too are living stones, built as an edifice of spirit, into a holy priesthood, offering spiritual sacrifices acceptable to God through Jesus Christ. . . . You, however, are "a chosen race, a royal priesthood, a holy nation, a people he claims for his own to proclaim his glorious works." Once you were no people, but now you are God's people; once there was no mercy for you, but now you have found mercy (1 Pet 2:5, 9–10; cf. Rev 1:6; 5:10; 20:6).

The Second Vatican Council has reiterated this truth of the common priesthood of all the baptized. It teaches that *all Christians participate in the prophetic, priestly, and kingly office of Jesus Christ*, so that all are commissioned and enabled to contribute to the Church's growth and sanctification (LG 30–38; AA 1–8). The Council deliberately noted that this truth is particularly important in our time (LG 30). It is an essential foundation of the present pastoral renewal. 273–274; 280 175–179

Who and what is a layman? In our everyday language we mean by "layman" a nonspecialist, someone who understands little or nothing of a thing, a dilettante, or at best an amateur who possesses some knowledge or capability but does not have a thorough knowledge. The Church's meaning is quite different! In the Church, the word "layman" is a title of dignity. The layman is someone incorporated into Jesus Christ and the Church through baptism. The laity is not distinguished from the clergy by being lesser Christians or second-class Christians, but only by not having an official mission in the Church. The layman is distinguished from the religious by living and working in the world. The *"secular character"* is proper to the laity in a special way. So Vatican II teaches:

By reason of their special vocation it belongs to the laity to seek the Kingdom of God by engaging in temporal affairs and directing them according to God's will. They live in the world, that is, they are engaged in each and every work and business of the earth and in the ordinary circumstances of social and family life which, as it were, constitute their very existence. There they are called by God that, being led by the spirit to the gospel, they may contribute to the sanctification of the world, as from within like leaven, by fulfilling their own particular duties. Thus, especially by the witness of their life, resplendent in faith, hope and charity, they must manifest Christ to others. It pertains to them in a special way so to illuminate and order all temporal things with which they are so closely associated that these may be effected and grow according to Christ and may be to the glory of the Creator and Redeemer (LG 31; cf. GS 43).

The laity's secular responsibility expresses an essential dimension of the Church. The Church is essentially a church in the world and for the world. The Church's ministry may not be seen only or even only

316–317 primarily in the parish. That would be a serious contraction. Marriage and family in particular are an important domain of the apostolate of the laity. They are the origin and foundation of human society (AA 11)—a church in miniature, a kind of domestic church (LG 11). But apostolate must also include the domain of education, the social milieu, the place of work, science, art, literature, economics, and politics. In these domains, which are especially important today, the mission of the Church is exercised primarily by the laity. Since the gifts of grace (charisms) are adapted to the specific needs of the Church (LG 12), the Church today needs above all charismatic laymen in the domains of science, art, technology, politics, education, and mass communication, among others, so that the Christian faith may be lived as a visible and effective example in the midst of the world. In this way, the concrete meaning of salvation for the genuine form of the human community will be made evident.

The special secular responsibility of the laity does not exclude the laity's call to *cooperation and co-responsibility in the Church*. On the contrary, the apostolate of the laity is related to both the Church and the world (AA 9). The laity are to make the world's problems, hopes, and expectations, but also its anxieties and worries, present in the Church and at the same time to search for answers in the spirit of the gospel. They are thus to seek a faith that is responsible for itself and to co-determine from that faith the life of the parish and of the Church. Parishes must increasingly shape their lives by joint and uniquely individual responsibility, always in communion with the whole Church. Today we need precisely a laity come of age in faith and in love. Here it is particularly important that *women* occupy a place of equal rank in all realms of the apostolate of the laity (AA 9).

228–230 The co-responsibility of the laity in the parish and in the Church can occur *in very different ways*. Each one has his own charism. Some exert themselves in the preparation and the celebration of the liturgy, especially as lectors, acolytes, cantors, and commentators. Others labor in catechetical or in charitable and social services, in the care of individual groups, municipal districts, families, and individuals. Still others undertake the execution of particular projects. In addition, there is responsible collaboration in various groups, circles, associations, and unions. Intercessory prayer and vicarious suffering are especially important; both make an irreplaceable contribution to the reality of the Church and her unity with the suffering Christ. Individual laymen can also be called to immediate *collaboration with the apostolate of the ecclesiastical hierarchy* and be appointed through special commission to particular Church ministries, whether on a voluntary basis or as a primary occupation, whether as a profession or as an avocation (LG 33). In particularly difficult situations for the Church, "the laity take over as far as possible the work of priests" (AA 17). In the Church in America, laymen serve especially as members of the parish council.

The Church clearly recognizes the *correspondence of rights and duties*. The new canon law makes this plain (CIC, can. 208–231). The basic right of all Christians is to receive "in abundance the help of the spiritual goods of the Church, especially that of the word of God and the sacraments from the pastors". Christians also have the right to express their needs and wishes; according to their knowledge, competence, and position, they are sometimes obliged "to manifest their opinion on those things which pertain to the good of the Church". The faithful should readily follow what their pastors say and do in the exercise of their mission. Conversely, the pastors should recognize and foster the dignity and responsibility of the laity and seek their prudent counsel. Above all, pastors should conscientiously recognize the just freedom to which all are entitled in the earthly, civil domain. "Many benefits for the Church are to be expected from this familiar relationship between the laity and the pastors" (LG 37).

The collaboration and co-responsibility of the laity makes use also of certain *institutions and councils*. Vatican II wished these to be established at all levels of the Church's life (CD 27; AA 26). These councils are to perceive impending problems and to pay attention, so to speak, to the signs of the Holy Spirit. They are to gather and transmit information, inspire and coordinate various services, advise and plan common work, care for its execution, and share their experiences after its completion. If all this is not to become empty action but true spirituality, they will often need to assemble for common prayer and liturgy. In the Church, the officeholders are not to plan, control, organize, decide, and do everything. But that brings us to the decisive question: How is the common priesthood of all baptized Christians related to the offices in the Church?

5.2 Offices in the Church   311–315

The difficulties that many people have with offices in the Church arise in part because "office" sounds so impersonal. It makes us think of an anonymous governmental authority. We think of someone "in office" as an impersonal functionary. It is true, of course, that ecclesiastical office has sometimes assumed imperious, governmental, and bureaucratic traits. Bishops were given the status of government officials by the emperor Constantine; in the Middle Ages they were even imperial princes. At the same time, there have always been selfless and zealous pastors, both among priests and among the bishops and popes. They understood their offices as the New Testament did—not as dominion, but as the selfless service of a messenger, as a personal ministry of witness.

We learn more about the essence and structure of ecclesiastical offices when we ask about their *institution by Jesus Christ* and their interpretation in the New Testament, as well as in the Church's Tradition. According to the witness of the New Testament, Jesus did indeed preach to the whole   212–213
people, but he called the Twelve into his more intimate following and let   311–312

169–171 them participate in a special way in his mission (Mk 3:13–19; 6:6b–13). The Risen One appeared not to all but only to "such witnesses as had been chosen beforehand by God" (Acts 10:41); he sent them out into the world (Mt 28:18–20). According to the will of Jesus Christ, and beyond the common calling and the common ministry, there is a special apostolic calling and a special apostolic ministry in the Church.

There were particular ministerial offices in the Church *from the very beginning*. Understandably, the authority of the Apostles stood in the foreground in the primitive Church and in the early communities. Questions about post-apostolic offices were first posed explicitly immediately before or after the death of the Apostles. Still Paul already mentions superiors and laborers (1 Th 5:12), bishops and deacons (Phil 1:1). In the Acts of the Apostles, we hear of presbyters. At the beginning, then, there was a range of office structures and titles. But the office of proclamation and leadership, the carrying on of the Apostles' activity, took on an essential meaning quite early. Evangelists, pastors, and teachers (Eph 4:11), resting on the foundation of the Apostles and prophets (Eph 2:20), see to the upbuilding of the body of Christ, of the Church. They guarantee continuity with the apostolic origin and foster the unity of all believers (Eph 4:13). In Acts 20:17–38, and especially the Pastoral Letters, the office structures begin to be standardized. This development first coalesced just after the New Testament period. Ignatius of Antioch (around 110) bears witness already to a three-tiered structure: a bishop as leader of the local Church, the presbyters who assist him, and the deacons who look after certain liturgical functions and the charitable ministries.

Vatican II summarizes the interpretation of Jesus' institution of offices through Holy Scripture and Tradition: "Thus the divinely instituted ecclesiastical ministry is exercised in different degrees by those who even from ancient times have been called bishops, priests, and deacons" (LG 28). The fullness of office belongs to the *bishops*, who "have by divine institu-
312–314 tion taken the place of the apostles as pastors of the Church" (LG 20). *Priests* share in their office (LG 28), in proclamation, in administering the sacraments (especially the celebration of the Eucharist), and in pastoral ministry (PO 4–6). *Deacons* exercise their office of service in preaching, in the liturgy, and in charitable activity (LG 29).

All ecclesiastical offices must be understood as *ministry*, imitating and following the commission of Jesus Christ. Jesus' exhortation is clear and unambiguous on this point:

> "You know how among the Gentiles those who seem to exercise authority lord it over them; their great ones make their importance felt. It cannot be like that with you. Anyone among you who aspires

to greatness must serve the rest; you must serve the needs of all. The Son of Man has not come to be served but to serve—to give his life in ransom for the many" (Mk 10:42–45).

Vatican II has put new emphasis on the *ministerial character of the ecclesiastical office*:

> In order to shepherd the people of God and to increase its numbers without cease, Christ the Lord set up in his Church a variety of offices which aim at the good of the whole body. The holders of office, who are invested with a sacred power, are, in fact, dedicated to promoting the interests of their brethren, so that all who belong to the people of God, and are consequently endowed with true Christian dignity, may, through their free and well-ordered efforts toward a common goal, attain to salvation (LG 18).

The ministry of an ecclesiastical office presupposes both a *mission and an authority*. Just as Jesus Christ received his mission from the Father, so he gave it to his disciples (Jn 20:21; 17:18). No one, no individual and no community, can proclaim the gospel to himself; even less can anyone give grace to himself. The gospel must be preached; grace must be given and bestowed. This requires authorized messengers whose message is founded in the word of Christ (Rom 10:14–17). The authority of the ecclesiastical office is grounded not on commissioning by the Church or the community, but in a mission from Jesus Christ. *The ecclesiastical office performs its ministry in the name, indeed in the person, of Jesus Christ.* Jesus himself says, "He who hears you, hears me" (Lk 10:16). Paul implores in place of Christ (2 Cor 5:20). Church office shares in the threefold office of Jesus Christ; it is Christ himself who speaks and acts through his messengers (LG 21, 28; PO 1–2).   176–179

This essential characterization of ecclesiastical offices implies *the relation between the office and the Church and the community*. More exactly, it implies a particular relation between the common priesthood of all believers and the special ministerial priesthood. Vatican II teaches:

> Though they differ essentially and not only in degree, the common priesthood of the faithful and the ministerial or hierarchical priesthood are nonetheless ordered one to another; each in its own proper way shares in the one priesthood of Christ (LG 10).

This does not mean that the officeholder is better or more perfect than the "ordinary" layman. On the contrary, as Christians they are on the same level. There are many laymen who put Church officeholders to shame by their saintly lives. The difference between the common priesthood of the faithful and the ministerial priesthood does not lie on the level of personal holiness, but on the level of ministry or of mission. On this level, the two are distinguished not by degree but by their nature. The mission expressed in the office cannot be derived from that of the community; it comes from Jesus Christ.

In summary, the ecclesiastical office stands *apart from the community* at the same time as it stands *within the community*. This tension cannot be dissolved or resolved in either direction. Like all other Christians, the officeholder needs forgiveness daily. He is sustained by the faith of the Church and of the community and must work together with all the other 228–230 charisms and ministries in the Church. His mission, though, also sets him apart in the Church and in the community. The officeholders are "set apart in some way in the midst of the people of God, but this is not in order that they should be separated from that people or from any man". Their ministry does indeed demand that they do not conform themselves to this world (Rom 12:2); it requires at the same time, though, "that they should live among men in this world" (PO 3).

The ministerial character of the ecclesiastical office also requires that the office never be conferred on the individual alone, but on the individual only in communion with other officeholders, as a participation in the one 250–251; common office. There is *collegiality of office*. Every individual bishop has 314–316 his office within the college of bishops, in communion with and under the Roman pontiff, the successor of Peter (LG 22–23; CD 4). Every priest has his office within the presbyterate of a diocese, under the leadership of the bishop (LG 28; PO 7–8). No individual priest and no individual bishop can fulfill his office in isolation as an individual, but only in brotherly connection and collaboration with others who exercise the same ministry. This common responsibility is expressed institutionally in the priests' senate of a diocese, in the bishops' conferences, and in the bishops' synod.

In spite of the fundamental firmness of the Church's doctrine, there are several weighty problems in the present Church regarding ecclesiastical office. We can only sketch them here, without attempting to treat them completely. Vatican II 312–314 has renewed the *diaconate as an independent stage of orders and one intended to be permanent* (LG 29). In the post-conciliar renewal movement, the so-called minor orders were replaced in 1972 by the commissioning of lectors and acolytes. In addition, a *range of new ministries* has arisen in the Church. These ministries have substantially enriched the life of the Church and of the communities; everyday life in the Church cannot be imagined without their service. But the real shape of the diaconate as well as of the new ministries is not yet well established on all points. The assignment of the new ministries to ecclesiastical office still lacks clarity in many respects.

Another much-discussed question is that of the *ordaining of women to the priestly office*. In their human and Christian dignity, women are of equal rank with men. For that reason, women should occupy a place of equal rank in all domains of the apostolate of the laity (AA 9). With the new ministries, women are today making an irreplaceable contribution. The Roman Congregation for the Doctrine of the Faith, however, reaffirmed in 1976 that the ordination of women to the priestly office does not seem possible to the Catholic Church because of the example of Jesus and the Church's entire Tradition. This is not an ultimately binding dogmatic decision. The arguments from Scripture and Tradition, of course, have considerable weight and must have unambiguous precedence in the Church over arguments that demand social equality of rights for men and women. The question about the *ordination of women to the sacramental diaconate* is different from the question about the priesthood. More discussion is needed, however, as is a consensus in the entire Church.

After the Council, there was a lengthy discussion about the *"democratization" of the Church*. What we have said already excludes the introduction into the Church of popular sovereignty or the principle of majority rule. In the Church, majority opinion does not decide; what decides is the gospel of Jesus Christ entrusted to particular commissioned witnesses in a special way. This does not exclude a certain democratic style and many democratic modes of procedure. They can contribute to enlivening the community, can render possible more collaboration, can improve the flow of information, and can allow decisions made after thorough consultation to be accepted and realized more readily. The councils and committees that have a common responsibility are serving this function. 195–196; 204; 215–216; 238–239; 263–265

The question of Church office also concerns one of the most important *doctrinal differences between the Roman Catholic Church and the churches and church communities that spring from the Reformation of the sixteenth century*. This question is most important, because mutual recognition is presupposed for eucharistic community (UR 22). The issues here are the divine institution of office, the sacramentality of ordination or holy orders, apostolic succession, the episcopal structure of office, and not least the Petrine office. On all these questions, ecumenical dialogue has already yielded remarkably, if not completely, common positions (see "The Spiritual Office in the Church" and the Lima document "Baptism, Eucharist, and Office"). There are even continuing discussions of the Petrine office in the Church, although discussion remains especially difficult now as ever. A common process of learning and reflection is still necessary among the separated churches. It is important to remember that the *fundamental question about the visibility of the Church and about its sacramental meaning* becomes more critical in thinking about Church offices. This is not an isolated problem. Nevertheless, it is not a hopeless one either. Even if Catholic doctrine teaches that the basic structures of the ecclesiastical office are already given and assigned to the Church by divine institution, history shows that what is permanent in the offices is still very closely connected with what is historically conditioned. We may hope that future changes and renewals will be made possible by reflection on the offices' origin and history, 215–216; 223–224; 232–234 as well as by addressing pastoral requirements. Of course, institution by Jesus Christ must remain normative.

5.3 The Petrine Office as a Ministry of Unity

The primacy and infallibility of the Petrine office are generally considered as characteristic of the Catholic understanding of the Church. While other churches and church communities see primacy and infallibility as a hindrance to ecumenical agreement, the Catholic Church sees them as a particularly important ministry of unity in the Church. No other church has yet presented a comparably convincing *model of visible unity*. Of course, that is no reason for triumphalism. Peter, whom the Lord's promise made the bedrock of the Church, was also the inconstant disciple who denied the Lord. This duality too has determined the history of the papacy. In order to distinguish in the papacy between the permanently valid and the historically changeable, we speak today of the "Petrine office". By this phrase we recall the biblical ground of the papacy's primacy and infallibility.

We encounter the prominent position of Peter in many important *New Testament* texts and traditions that derive from different places and belong to practically all the epochs in which the canonical writings arose. The first three Gospels report unanimously that Peter was the first one called and the first one sent by *Jesus* (Mk 1:16–20 par.); it is he who leads the catalogues of disciples (Mk 3:16 par.). Peter was obviously *a representative and speaker for the other disciples* even during Jesus' lifetime. His calling required a change of name. He, who was originally named Simon, received from Jesus the name *"Cephas"*, in Greek *"Petros"*, "the rock". In antiquity, a name was not simply an empty tag; it was thought to express the essence and essential function of men and things. In being renamed, Peter received from the Lord the task of being the first, the rock-solid ground for the disciples and for the Church. He was to strengthen his brothers (Lk 22:32).

169–171   This commission was confirmed by the Risen One. In the Easter accounts, we meet Peter each time as the *first witness of the Resurrection* (1 Cor 15:5; Lk 24:34; it is also indicated in Mk 16:7). Thus Peter has the prime authority according to the first twelve chapters of the Acts of the Apostles, as well as at the apostolic council in Jerusalem (Acts 15:1–35). When Peter weakened in Antioch, Paul resisted him to his face (Gal 2:14). Nevertheless, Paul recognized the authority of Cephas (Gal 1:18; 2:7–9) and strove to obtain unity even at the risk of his life, because he knew that otherwise his efforts would have been in vain (Gal 2:2). The thrice confirmed granting of the pastoral office on Peter by the Risen One (Jn 21:15–17), as well as the two Letters that entered the New Testament under Peter's name, show especially that the authority of Peter still had force after his death. These texts cannot be interpreted as showing that Peter won esteem only as the main witness of the earthly work of Jesus and as the first witness of the Resurrection.

The most important Petrine passage in the New Testament is *Jesus' saying near Caesarea Philippi*. It is handed down by Matthew as the answer to Peter's Messianic confession:

> "I for my part declare to you, you are 'Rock', and on this rock I will build my Church, and the jaws of death shall not prevail against it. I will entrust to you the keys of the kingdom of heaven. Whatever you declare bound on earth shall be bound in heaven; whatever you declare loosed on earth shall be loosed in heaven" (Mt 16:18–19).

This text raises many questions for interpretation. Even if many interpreters of Scripture do not attribute this exact wording to the earthly Jesus himself, the commission and the authority of Peter, as we have seen, are anchored in the work and teaching of Jesus. This text declares three things of Peter: (1) Peter himself—and not just the faith affirmed by Peter—is the foundation of the Church. The witness of Peter cannot be detached from Peter the witness. (2) The power of the keys means authority for the administration of God's house, which is the Church. (3) The authority to "bind and loose" means the authority of binding doctrinal decision, together with disciplinary power for protecting the Church's unity.

Obviously, these texts do not speak explicitly of a *succession in Peter's official functions*, of a Petrine office in the Church. This is the decisive point of controversy in the discussion with the non-Roman Catholic churches and church communities. Yet if we proceed from the fact that the Gospel of Matthew, the Gospel of John, and the two Letters of Peter were written after Peter's martyrdom in Rome in the year 64, it is clearly indicated that the Petrine function was of not only historical importance. It had current importance after the death of the historical Peter. Moreover, Matthew 16:18 speaks of the future ("on this Rock I *will build* my Church") and has in view the eschatological conflict between the powers of death and the new power of life come into the world through Jesus Christ. So the question of the perpetuation of the Petrine office in the Church is analogous to the question of the perpetuation of the apostolic office generally. Both will have importance for the Church until the end of time. Thus the New Testament already indicates the perpetuation of Peter's function as the bedrock of the Church and as permanent guarantor of the faith (Lk 22:32).

Since the Apostle Peter probably suffered martyrdom in Rome in the year 64, special authority accrued to the *Roman church* very early on. St. Ignatius of Antioch

221–222
(around 110) already calls the Roman church "chief in love". It was a model and criterion of faith for the other churches. Whether Rome was invoked as a court of appeal or took the initiative itself, Rome knew itself to be responsible for the whole Church in a special way. We find the *special authority of the pontiff of Rome* from the fourth century on. The doctrine of primacy is fully explicit with Pope Leo the Great (fifth century). Both the form and the content of the ancient Church's doctrine of primacy had their focal points, of course, in the *Latin Church* of the West before the schism of the East. For the *Eastern Orthodox churches*, the claim to primacy by the pontiff of Rome is today the main reason for perpetuating the schism of 1054. The extension of the primacy in the West did not come in the first instance, of course, from Roman lust for power, but from a responsibility for the freedom and the unity of the Church. This priority was more often imposed on Rome from without than demanded by Rome itself. This practice found magisterial expression first of all through the Councils of Lyons (1274) (DS 861; NR 929) and Florence (1439) (DS 1307; NR 434). The Reformation polemics against the pope as the anti-Christ, as well as the straits into which the Church came through the French Revolution and secularization, contributed to an even stronger emphasis on the papal primacy. But the true ground of this doctrine, according to the Catholic conception, is founded in the witness of revelation itself.

49;
215–216
The definition of the pope's primacy of jurisdiction and of the infallibility of his magisterium took place at the First Vatican Council (1869–1870). In relation to the *primacy of jurisdiction*, this Council taught:

> If anyone says that the Roman pontiff has only the office of inspection or direction but not the full and supreme power of jurisdiction over the universal Church, not only in things which pertain to faith and morals, but also in those which pertain to the discipline and government of the Church spread over the whole world; or, that he possesses only the more important parts, but not the whole plenitude of this supreme power; or that this power of his is not ordinary and immediate, or over the churches altogether and individually, and over the pastors and the faithful altogether and individually: let him be anathema (DS 3064; NR 448).

258–262
Since the leadership of the Church is exercised especially in the proclamation of the word, the primacy of jurisdiction is closely connected with the *doctrine of the infallibility* of the papal office. The corresponding conciliar definition says,

> When the Roman pontiff speaks *ex cathedra*, that is, when carrying out the duty of the pastor and teacher of all Christians in accord with his supreme apostolic authority he explains a doctrine of faith or morals to be held by the universal Church, he operates through the divine assistance promised him in St. Peter with that infallibility with which the divine Redeemer wished that his Church be instructed in defining

doctrine on faith and morals; and so such definitions of the Roman
pontiff from himself, but not from the consensus of the Church, are
unalterable (DS 3074; NR 454).

The Second Vatican Council confirmed both dogmas (LG 18, 23, 25). But
it also placed both of them in a larger context, recalling the responsibility
and infallibility of the entire Church (LG 12) and especially that of *the
whole college of bishops* (LG 22–23, 25). It is not only the pope who has "full,   246–247;
supreme and universal power over the whole Church"; the college of   314–315
bishops

> together with their head, the Supreme pontiff, and never apart from
> him . . . has supreme and full authority over the universal Church. . . .
> The supreme authority over the whole Church, which this college
> possesses, is exercised in a solemn way in an ecumenical council. . . .
> This same collegial power can be exercised in union with the pope by
> the bishops while [they are] living in different parts of the world,
> provided the head of the college summon them to collegial action, or
> at least approve or freely admit the corporate action of the unassembled
> bishops, so that a truly collegial act may result (LG 22).

A special *ministry of unity* belongs to the pontiff of Rome as the successor of   221–223;
the Apostle Peter. He does not have this primacy above the Church, but   230–233;
within it as the head of the episcopal college. His authority is never   294–296
unlimited and absolute; it is tied to the basic structure of the Church, to the
gospel and the Church's Tradition, the sacramental and the episcopal
structure of the Church. The Roman pontiff is not to represent his
personal faith, but rather the faith of the Church, as binding. He is not to
repress or even to replace the authority and responsibility of the bishops
with his own authority, but rather to strengthen and defend them. The
First Vatican Council taught that the Petrine office was instituted by Jesus
Christ so that "the episcopate itself may be one and undivided", in order
to give it "a perpetual and visible principle and foundation of the unity of
faith and of communion" (DS 3050; NR 436; LG 18). The Petrine
office is a ministry for unity, a unity in the multiplicity of the local
churches. Through the Petrine office, the universal Church can speak and
act concretely; she finds in it at the same time her highest personal
representation. Something would be lacking to the Church and doubtless
to Christianity as a whole if this Petrine ministry did not exist; it is
something essential to the Church.

The two dogmas of Vatican I represent the conclusion of a long
historical development beginning with the revealed witness of Holy
Scripture. As Vatican II among many other events shows, the history of
the papacy did not end with Vatican I. That council in fact marked a new

beginning. We see more clearly since Vatican II that Jesus Christ has indeed given the Church an important center of unity in the Petrine office, but one that does not necessarily ground an administrative centralism and a uniformity. We must distinguish between the essential, permanent functions of the Petrine office and the many extended functions that have historically accrued to it, especially so far as the pope has been patriarch of the Latin Church. A resumption of full Church communion with the patriarchates of the Eastern church separated from Rome could leave to them in large measure their liturgical and disciplinary independence—as the example of the Eastern churches united with Rome shows.

We must recognize, of course, that the Church's truth and unity are expressed concretely in the Petrine office. So the Petrine office will always be a *sign of contradiction*. But this follows from the essence of the Church, which bears witness to the Incarnation of the Word of God. We encounter the same embodied concreteness immediately in the Church's proclamation and sacraments, which the ecclesiastical offices serve. We can now take up this theme in some detail. As we do so, the ministerial character of the Church and of its offices ought to become even clearer.

III

THE COMMUNION OF SAINTS:
THROUGH WORD AND SACRAMENT

1. The Church as the Communion of Saints

The Apostles' Creed adds to the confession of the one holy Church the
assertion, "I believe in . . . the communion of saints." This declaration,
which has formed part of the Creed since the fourth century, has roots in
the New Testament. It directs us once again to what is essential in the
Church. It asks us what the Church's life depends on and what is at stake.
The *original meaning* of this credal declaration is that the Church is a
community of what is holy. It exists because of a common sharing in the
goods of salvation, especially in the Eucharist. According to the New
Testament, the Church is built up by sharing faith in the gospel (Philem
6), by common celebration of the sacraments, especially the Body and
Blood of Jesus Christ (1 Cor 10:16), and by sharing in the needs of the
brothers (Rom 15:26; 2 Cor 8:4; Heb 13:16). The Church becomes reality
through the *word* of the gospel, through the *sacraments*, and through the
common *ministry* of love. The *eucharistic community* unites the Church
dispersed throughout the earth into *one* Church by participation in the one
body of the Lord.

266–269;
293–295

By sharing *in* what is holy, we are joined together as the communion
of saints. This *later meaning* emphasizes that *the Church is a community
(communio)*. Because there are offices in the Church, the Church is also
seen as a hierarchical community. But the confession of faith takes an
additional point of view. It sees the communion of saints as a communion
in which the whole people of God participates. It is a communion with
Jesus Christ (1 Cor 1:9), in the Holy Spirit (Phil 2:1; 2 Cor 13:13). It is a
communion with the Father and the Son (1 Jn 1:3, 6). Yet it is also a
communion in suffering (Phil 3:10), as well as a communion in consolation
(2 Cor 1:5, 7) and in future glory (1 Pet 1:4; Heb 12:22–23). Such
communion is both a gift and a task. Only if we live in the light and do the
truth do we have communion with one another (1 Jn 1:7).

The communion of saints encompasses the faithful of all peoples and
times. Through Jesus Christ and in the Holy Spirit we are united into one
community, not only with the faithful now living but also with the just of

253

143–144;
234–235;
336–337;
344–345;
347–350
all times. The communion of saints comprises *the Church on earth, the blessed in heaven, and the deceased in a state of purification*. Together they form the one body of Christ, in which all members answer for one another before God. So we not only honor the saints of heaven as shining examples of faith; we also invoke them for their intercession (DS 1821; NR 474). For the same reason, we pray for the deceased in a state of purification. Our unity with the heavenly Church is most intensively realized in the liturgy, when we celebrate together with all the angels and saints the praise of God's glory and the work of redemption (SC 104; LG 50–51).

> The communion of saints is the antidote and the counterweight to the Babylonian dispersal; it bears witness to such a wonderful human and divine solidarity that it is impossible for a human being not to respond to all others at whatever time they may live and wherever they may be called to live. The least of our acts echoes into infinite depths and makes all the living and the dead tremble (Léon Bloy).

We remember this communion of saints especially on the feast of All Saints (November 1) and on the memorial of All Souls (November 2).

224–230
The earlier and the later interpretations of the communion of saints are easily linked together. Since we have already discussed the second interpretation while speaking of the people of God, the body of Christ, and the temple of the Holy Spirit, we ought now to concentrate on the first, the original sense of this declaration. Originally it represented something more than an addition to the Creed of the Church. It extends the Creed by telling us how the Church becomes concretely the people of God, the body of Christ, and the temple of the Holy Spirit, and how she attains communion with the Father through Jesus Christ in the Holy Spirit. It tells us that the Church, as the communion of saints, is built up and realizes herself anew by communion in what is holy—by proclaiming the gospel, celebrating the sacraments (especially the Eucharist), and ministering in love.

2. The Word as Sacrament

2.1 The Salvific Meaning of the Word

Words are generally conceived as means for exchanging thoughts, information, or instruction. In the contemporary flood of words, we often grow weary of words and become dulled to them. Words without deeds are considered hollow and empty, even as insincere and dishonest. On the other hand, we often experience what the right word at the right time can mean for us and others, how it can brighten and change things. We all depend on such words of recognition, comfort, trust, encouragement, friendship, and love. A single word can often open a new world for us. Another person's inner world, the depths of his person, is accessible to us first and foremost through words. In the word, men communicate not only some *thing* to one another; they communicate themselves. The human word can be *active and effective*.

This is true in an incomparably higher measure for God's word. The Old Testament sees the word of God as a creative power that calls all things into being (Gen 1:3–2:4a) and that preserves them (Ps 147:15–18). This creative force of the word of God dwells most intensely in the personal "Word", the Son of God. "Through him all things came into being, and apart from him nothing came to be" (Jn 1:3). In salvation history, God reveals through his word not only who he is but also what he is and what he does for us in grace. In his Word, God acts as Savior toward us and in us. In salvation history the *word of God* is *a deed*; *it does what it says*. By his word, God himself is present to us in a living way, preparing and procuring salvation, pardoning, challenging us to choose and act. In his word, God himself meets us in his saving power. The word of God as deed is expressed in many places by Holy Scripture.

> For just as from the heavens
>   the rain and snow come down
> And do not return there
>   till they have watered the earth,
>   making it fertile and fruitful,
> Giving seed to him who sows
>   and bread to him who eats,
> So shall my word be
>   that goes forth from my mouth;
> It shall not return to me void,
>   but shall do my will . . . (Is 55:10–11).

Indeed, God's word is living and effective, sharper than any two-edged sword. It penetrates and divides soul and spirit, joints and marrow; it judges the reflections and thoughts of the heart. Nothing is concealed from him; all lies bare and exposed to the eyes of him to whom we must render account (Heb 4:12–13).

In the New Testament, the active and saving character of the word of God becomes most intense when *Jesus Christ* is described as the eternal Word

67–68;
134–137

become flesh in time. "Whatever came to be in him, found life, life for the light of men" (Jn 1:4). "Of his fullness we have all had a share—love following upon love" (Jn 1:16). In Jesus Christ, God's word has become not only audible, but visible. In the reading and proclamation of his word, God is abidingly, actively, and redemptively present in the Church (SC 7).

Because God's word has been spoken unsurpassably, definitively, and entirely in Jesus Christ, it remains *present in the Church* by the power of the Holy Spirit. The Spirit of truth who bears witness to and discloses the words of Jesus will remain with the disciples and be in them (Jn 14:17, 26). The Church has the commission from Jesus Christ to preserve faithfully the word of God issued once for all and to delve into it more deeply, in order to announce and expound it in a living way to all men. The Church claims the right to announce the word of God to all peoples always and everywhere, apart from any human power. The witness of the word of God is in principle entrusted to all Christians. The Apostles and those with them and after them who receive the task of proclamation are sent in a distinctive way to announce the gospel to all peoples (Mt 28:19–20; Mk 16:15). The Holy Spirit will remind them as they do so of all that Jesus said and did. The Spirit will lead them into the whole truth (Jn 14:26; 16:13–14).

Given the active presence of Jesus Christ in the Holy Spirit, the proclamation of God's word is not only about God, but "sent by God" and "standing in his presence" (2 Cor 2:17). It is not the word of man. It is of God (1 Th 2:13), "the power of God and the wisdom of God" (1 Cor 1:24), the Word of salvation (Acts 13:26) and of grace (Acts 14:3). Through this Word we are born to new life (Jas 1:18; 1 Pet 1:23). So the Apostle Paul understands himself as an ambassador "for Christ, God as it were appealing through us" (2 Cor 5:20). In the proclamation of the word of God, God himself is present through Jesus Christ in the Holy Spirit.

The Catholic understanding of the faith has always held fast to the salvific and gracious character of the word of God. In the liturgy, we have always celebrated the presence of Jesus Christ in the word. There were said to be two tables at the Liturgy, the table of the word and the table of the body of Christ (DV 21; PO 18). St. Augustine called the word an *audible sacrament*. Of course, this conviction attained its full importance only in more recent times. Lessons from the Reformation churches and church communities contributed to this. Vatican II clearly expressed its conviction of the importance of the word of God (LG 9; DV 1–10, 21–26; AG 9, 15). Pope Paul VI did so as well in his apostolic letter on evangelization in today's world: "Evangelization is the special grace and vocation of the Church. It is her essential function. The Church exists to preach the gospel, that is to preach and teach the word of God . . ." (EN 14). There

45–46;
176–177

224–225;
239–243
238–239

are many *reciprocal relations between Church and proclamation*. The Church arises from the proclamation of the gospel; she is the immediate visible result of it. The Church for her part is also sent in the service of proclamation. As bearer of the gospel, she begins by evangelizing herself.

> As a community sharing a common faith and a common hope which she proclaims and communicates to others by her life, and sharing likewise a common fraternal love, it is essential that she should constantly hear the truths in which she believes, the grounds on which her hope is based and the new command of mutual love (EN 15).

The Church is the guardian of the good news that must be preached. Finally, the Church, which has herself been sent and won for the gospel, sends out messengers of faith in turn, "not to preach themselves or their personal ideas, but rather the gospel" for which they have been engaged (EN 15).

If men announce the gospel of salvation, they do so under the commission, in the name, and with the grace of Jesus Christ. "And how can men preach unless they are sent?" (Rom 10:15). This *sending* belongs in principle to the Church as a whole and to all Christians. The whole Church is missionary, and the work of evangelization is a basic duty of the people of God (AG 35). It belongs especially to bishops, priests, and deacons as their first and most distinguished task. The proclamation of the gospel is never the individual and isolated action of a single person; it is rather *a most deeply ecclesial action*. Whenever someone announces the gospel in the name of the Church, which for her part does so in the name of the Lord, he is by no means absolute master of his proclamation of the faith. He cannot decide about it according to his personal standards and views. He must proclaim it in communion with the Church and her pastors (EN 60). 224–225; 239–243 219–222

The word of God, the gospel, enters individual lives in very *different ways*: through preaching, catechesis, or liturgical and sacramental signs, through books and magazines, or pictures and artistic creations, through the mass media, and not least in simple and spontaneous Christian witness in word and deed—the witness of life. The most concentrated form of proclamation is the homily; it is a part of the liturgy (SC 35) and so is reserved to bishops, priests, and deacons. If it is necessary and seems advisable, other forms of preaching are open to the laity on special commission from the bishop.

Proclamation must translate the message of the gospel, fixed once for all, into the language of the times, adapting it to the questions and difficulties of men. Proclamation always has a *dialogical structure*. Man is not the measure of the proclamation, but the one to whom it is addressed. 49–50; 217–218

Fundamental human rights, the dignity and the freedom of the human person, justice in human society, and the value and essence of the family, among others, also belong to the Church's task of proclamation. Finally, proclamation must use all the means at its disposal in any particular time, including schools, academies, and means of mass communication (CD 12–14; PO 4). What is decisive is that we announce nothing other than Jesus Christ and him crucified (1 Cor 2:2).

38–41   *2.2 Doctrine and the Magisterium of the Church*

The New Testament already presents the word of God as attested in the form of doctrine (Rom 6:17; 2 Tim 4:2; Tit 1:9). We find fixed doctrinal and confessional formulas in its texts. The responsibility for correct doctrine is especially entrusted to those who lead the Church as successors of the Apostles:

> Watch yourself and watch your teaching. Persevere at both tasks. By doing so you will bring to salvation yourself and all who hear you (1 Tim 4:16).

> Take as a model of sound teaching what you have heard me say, in faith and love in Christ Jesus. Guard the rich deposit of faith with the help of the Holy Spirit who dwells within us (2 Tim 1:13–14).

> In the presence of God and of Christ Jesus, who is coming to judge the living and the dead, and by his appearing and his kingly power, I charge you to preach the word, to stay with this task whether convenient or inconvenient—correcting, reproving, appealing—constantly teaching and never losing patience (2 Tim 4:1–2).

From such New Testament declarations has developed the Catholic *doctrine and practice of the Magisterium*. The task of the living Magisterium in the Church is to explain the word of God in a binding way. The Magisterium "is not superior to the word of God, but is its servant. It teaches only what has been handed on to it" (DV 10). The task of the Magisterium is "at the same time, to declare and confirm by her authority the principles of the moral order which spring from human nature itself" (DH 14). This Magisterium belongs to the bishops alone in communion

250–251   with the pope. It can be exercised in two ways. First, there is the *ordinary Magisterium*, when the bishops in communion with the pontiff of Rome—being one in faith and in mission however dispersed in the world—announce the faith with one mind. Second, there is the *extraordinary Magisterium* when the bishops united at an ecumenical council speak as

teacher and judge on questions of faith and morals, or when the Roman 250–251
pontiff, as head of the episcopal college, announces in virtue of his office as
the supreme pastor and teacher of all the Christian faithful a doctrine of
faith or morals in a definitive act (LG 25).

> With divine and Catholic faith, then, all that is to be believed which is
> contained in the written or traditional Word of God and presented by
> the Church in solemn decision or through ordinary and general
> doctrinal proclamation to be believed as revealed by God (DS 3011;
> NR 34).

When controversies arise that endanger the unity of the faith and of the
Church, the bishops have the right and duty of making binding decisions.
Where the bishops in universal agreement among themselves and in
communion with the Roman pontiff present revealed faith as definitively
obligatory, their witness is ultimately binding and *infallible*. The individual
bishop is not infallible; only the entire episcopal college in communion
with the Roman pontiff or the pontiff as the head of the episcopal college is
infallible.

Linguistically the *word "infallibility"* is not wholly unambiguous. It almost auto- 49–50
matically invokes notions of stainlessness, of perfection in every respect, or even
of sinlessness. To err, though, is human, as the saying goes, and as men the pope
and bishops are not excepted. For that reason, there have long been attempts to
replace the misleading and, for some, offensive word "infallible" with others.
Some speak of inerrancy, unerringness, or freedom from error. In substance, the
point is that with Jesus Christ the *truth of God has come into the world in a historically
unsurpassable and definitive way*. It is then promised forever to the Church on the
basis of the abiding presence of the Lord and of his Spirit. As the Church of the
living God, she is the pillar and bulwark of the truth (1 Tim 3:15). So it is the
fundamental conviction of all Christian churches and church communities that the
Church can never definitively fall away from the truth of Jesus Christ. Were this to
happen, falsehood would be victorious over God and his truth. Catholics believe,
of course, that this promise would remain vague if there were no *concrete voice for
this truth*, a way for it to become concrete in particular, binding declarations. The
Church must give her faithful the certainty that whoever accepts her word accepts
the truth. Otherwise the Church would be in danger of becoming a mere forum of
discussion; there would no longer be a community of witnesses that stands with
ultimate earnestness for the truth of faith. The Catholic Church is convinced that
this protector and this voice of the truth has been given to her in the Petrine office
as the head of the episcopal college and in the episcopal college in communion with
and in subordination to the Petrine office.

Of course, this conviction of faith must be understood correctly *in the larger
context*. There are three important points.

1. Properly speaking, *only God and his word* are infallible. The Church's Magis-

terium is unerring only in an interpretation, led by the Holy Spirit, of the definitive word of God and of the truths necessarily connected with it. The Church's infallibility reaches only as far as the revelation of God requires. It encompasses only questions of faith and morals, but not, for instance, political, scientific, or similar questions (LG 25).

2. The Magisterium stands *in the context of the infallibility of the entire Church* (LG 12). It does not receive its authority by "delegation from below". Still it is related to the Church's faith not only as determining that faith but also as invoking it as a criterion. In establishing the faith of the Church, the Magisterium must use every human means of discovering the truth. The assistance of the Spirit preserves it from error, but no positive inspiration or even new revelation is promised to it. When dogma teaches that such decisions by the Roman pontiff are irrevocable "from himself, but not from the consensus of the Church" (DS 3074; NR 454), this does not mean that the pope can detach himself from the faith of the Church. It merely means that his decision need not subsequently be ratified by a general council or by some other mechanism. In such decisions, the pope is assured, so to speak, of the assent of the Church. Such decisions remain factually in need of a comprehensive reception so that they may attain vital force and spiritual fruitfulness in the Church.

3. The exercise of the Magisterium by way of an infallible doctrinal decision occurs in relatively infrequent and *extraordinary cases*. The pope or a council must expressly make known when they are making such a decision; whoever asserts that such a decision is present must prove it in the individual case. Normally, the infallibility and inerrancy of the Magisterium are "embedded" in the everyday life and preaching of the Church, in her prayer, her liturgy, in the dispensation of the sacraments, and in brotherly help (LG 25). Thus, for example, the central and fundamental Christian truths of the Apostles' Creed have never been formally defined but were always believed and taught. This confers an irrefutable authority on the Creed even without formal definition.

The bishops and pope, then, are *authentic witnesses and teachers* of the gospel truth even when they do not speak in an ultimately binding and infallible way. The faithful must consent to a ruling presented in the name of Christ by their bishop and all the more by the pontiff of Rome in matters of faith and morals; they must adhere to it with religiously grounded obedience (LG 25).

224–225; 239–243; 175–177; 312–313   The bishops can fulfill their magisterial task only *in communion with the entire Church*. The whole people of God takes part in the prophetic office of Christ; all of the faithful receive the supernatural sense of faith from the Holy Spirit (LG 12). *Priests* take part in a special way in the prophetic office of Christ; they are coworkers in the preaching and teaching of the bishops (PO 4). The bishops also need, especially today, the collaboration of *theologians* for the exercise of their tasks. Theologians are to delve into the Church's faith in a scholarly way interpreting it according to the witness of Holy Scripture and the Church's Tradition and making it understandable to the times. Theologians stand on the foundation and under the norm of the Church's doctrine. They do need an appropriate freedom in the Church for the realization of their special task; this is what is meant by scholarly independence (CIC can. 809). The exercise of the episcopal Magisterium thus takes place in a varied exchange with the faithful, with priests, and with theologians. It depends not least on the liturgical-sacramental life of the Church.

3. The Sacraments as Visible Word

3.1 The Sacraments as Signs of Faith

We are body and soul. The body is animated and informed by a spiritual soul; the soul expresses itself in the body. Man's essence requires that he express in a bodily way his inner convictions, basic moral attitudes, moods, and feelings in words, images, symbols, and actions. Since God is a God of men, he bestows his life and love on body and soul. He speaks to us and acts in us through his word and through historical deeds (DV 2). Even the faith by which we respond to God is something more than an inner conviction or a matter of the heart. It expresses itself not only in words, but in images and symbols, in actions and rites, in songs and other works of art.

The sacraments are among these *sensible forms of grace* and of the love of God. As St. Augustine says, they are word become visible. They are also, as St. Thomas Aquinas tells us, *signs by which we confess our faith*. Vatican II says of the sacraments that they not only presuppose faith but also nourish, strengthen, and announce it; "for that reason, they are called sacraments of faith" (SC 59).

Today the *relation of faith and sacrament* is one of the main problems for pastoral ministry. In our parishes we frequently meet baptized persons who, so far as anyone can tell, are not believers. This situation undermines the whole structure of the sacraments, especially their relation to faith. This problem becomes more critical, leaving aside infant baptism, at first 276–279 confession, first communion, confirmation, and especially marriage. Can 318–319 the sacraments be given to non-believers? Without a minimum of inner openness for faith, a valid or a fruitful reception of the sacraments is not possible. So the pastoral task becomes that of strengthening weak faith. Both excessive rigor and laxity are equally forbidden. The importance of a living parish catechesis, especially of a thorough preparation for the sacraments, is clear.

Because the sacraments are the word become visible, there are *two elements*, bound together by an inner unity, in every sacramental sign. These are the sacramental word and the sacramental sign strictly speaking. The Letter to the Ephesians says of baptism that Jesus Christ surrendered himself for the Church "to make her holy, purifying her in the bath of water by the power of the word" (Eph 5:26). St. Augustine reduces this to a pregnant formula: "The word enters as an element, and there arises a sacrament." With sacramental actions in a narrower sense, words are spoken. In baptism, for instance, the priest says, "I baptize you in the name of the Father, and of the Son, and of the Holy Spirit". In the Eucharist, there are Jesus' words of institution. These sacramental words are even considered the soul of the sacrament (what is called the "form" of the sacrament). The sacramental sign strictly speaking consists not only of a bodily element—water, bread, wine, or oil—but also of an action— washing with water, eating the bread, anointing with oil. Sometimes there is only an action—the confession of sins in the sacrament of confession, the words "I do" in marriage. (These are called the "matter" of the sacrament.) The fact that word and sacrament belong together is also seen in that a liturgy of the word is normally part of the sacramental celebration except in an emergency. There are the liturgical greeting, readings from Holy Scripture, song, prayers, blessings, and a liturgical dismissal.

If one considers the structure of the sacramental sign somewhat more deeply, it becomes clear that sacramental actions take up basic human situations and represent them symbolically (the beginning of a new life, meals, a crisis of serious guilt, among others). These are situations in which man naturally asks about meaning, life, and salvation. The sacraments sanctify these basic human situations; they take them up into the mystery of Jesus Christ, his life and death, his Resurrection and exaltation, so that we might share in them. *The sacraments accompany one's whole life in all its important situations and stages.* Signs of faith, they are also signs of Christ by which he chooses to figure in our lives concretely, humanly, and integrally.

3.2 The Sacraments as Signs of Christ

The sacrament of God for men in which the grace of God has appeared in its fullness is Jesus Christ. *Jesus Christ* is *the primordial sacrament* of which all individual sacraments are unfoldings and embodiments. With the Apostle Paul, the Church knows herself to be only a servant of Jesus Christ and a custodian of God's mysteries (1 Cor 4:1). She cannot institute sacraments on her own authority. The *institution of the sacraments* can have its origin only in Jesus Christ, the one mediator between God and men (1 Tim 2:5). For that reason, it is the binding teaching of the Church that "all sacraments of the New Covenant have been instituted by Jesus Christ" (DS 1601; NR 506). This does not mean that Jesus explicitly established every sacrament during his earthly life. An explicit institution can also take place through the Risen Lord, as in the case of baptism, for instance. Neither must we think in every case of an explicit word or act of institution by Jesus. If the Church nevertheless affirms that all sacraments fulfill the intention of Jesus Christ, the reason is that Jesus Christ abides in the Church through the Holy Spirit in order to interpret his work of salvation, which has happened once for all, and to render it present. We cannot at all expect that Jesus Christ himself laid down all the details of the rites. It is enough if the general nature of the sacraments is founded in Jesus' whole saving work.

What was founded by Jesus Christ needs to be interpreted in the apostolic Tradition, which is kept alive and made present in the Church. *Without the witness of the Church* the institution of the sacraments by Jesus Christ, as indeed his whole proclamation and entire work, is inconceivable. It is not an embarrassment—indeed, it is appropriate—if the Church performed the individual sacraments from the beginning, but recognized them explicitly and clearly distinguished them from other rites only over the course of time. Thus the Church may not change the essence of the sacraments. It can and must elaborate the liturgical form of the sacraments and adapt it to the understanding of a specific time and culture (DS 1728; NR 519; SC 62).

All of this is particularly important in the question of the *number of the sacraments*. Each of the seven sacraments belongs from time immemorial in the life of the Church. The Orthodox churches agree in this practice with the Roman Catholic Church. But we first find an explicit summary and a related doctrine of the number of the seven sacraments in the twelfth century. Since then, it has been the explicit doctrine that "there are in the Church of Jesus Christ seven sacraments instituted by Jesus Christ: baptism, confirmation, Eucharist, penance, anointing of the sick, holy orders, and marriage" (DS 860, 1310, 1601; NR 928, 501, 506).

We should not understand this list in purely quantitative terms. The seven sacraments form an *organic unity* at the center of which stand baptism and the Eucharist. The Church's Tradition thus distinguishes between the two "major sacraments", baptism and the Eucharist, and the "minor sacraments", which aim to complete (confirmation) or restore (penance, anointing of the sick) the new life in Jesus Christ that is grounded in baptism and ordered to the Eucharist, or which serve the building up, in the order of nature and of grace, of the people of God that has its center point in the Eucharist (holy orders, marriage).

195–196;
204

The question about the institution and the number of the sacraments is one of the classic *denominational differences* between Catholics and Protestants. As distinguished from the Catholic Church, the Reformers recognize only two sacraments (baptism and the Lord's Supper), or at most three (with the addition of penance). The question of an explicit institution by Jesus plays a decisive role for the Reformers. Through modern New Testament research, however, it has become clearer that one cannot sharply separate the words of Jesus from the witness of the primitive community. Precisely in regard to the sacraments, the apostolic and the post-apostolic Tradition plays an important role. These insights have eased the problem of sacramental institution. Still, beyond the question of institution there are differing definitions of a sacrament. In consequence, the Protestant Churches count many of the actions that are held to be sacraments in the Catholic Church only as blessings (e.g., confirmation, marriage, ordination, anointing of the sick). Today, we can recall in common that Jesus Christ is the primordial sacrament, unfolded and brought near to men in the word of proclamation and in the different sacraments and blessings of the Church. This insight has led to a convergence of the points of view. But many of these important questions have hardly been well discussed ecumenically (*Evangelischer Erwachsenenkatechismus*, pp. 1124–25).

176–178

The relation of the sacraments to Christ is not limited to an initial institution. The Risen Lord abides near to us in and through the sacraments with his grace, his mercy, his reconciliation, and his new life. *Jesus Christ is the only true dispenser of the sacraments.* It is Christ, as St. Augustine teaches, who baptizes, consecrates, and forgives sins (SC 7). We encounter Jesus Christ himself in the sacramental symbols; the sacraments are a personal encounter with Christ. Pope St. Leo the Great tells us: "What was visible in Christ has passed over into the sacraments."

By being himself redemptively present in the sacraments, Jesus Christ makes present his work of salvation, especially his death and Resurrection, by which alone we attain grace and salvation. Through the sacraments, we are *taken into the paschal mystery of Christ* (SC 6). St. Thomas Aquinas explained that this inclusion in the mystery of Jesus Christ and his work of salvation has three dimensions. First, the sacraments are *memorial signs* of the work of our redemption, which has already taken place once for all.

289–290

Memory in the scriptural sense does not mean only a subjective recalling of an event, but also its objective re-presentation. In the liturgy, the antiphons for feast days sing in the present: "*Today* Christ is born", "*Today* the star led the wise men to the child in the manger", "*Today* the Holy Spirit appeared to the disciples under the sign of fire." As memorial signs, the sacraments are, secondly, *signs of salvation* that announce and bestow present salvation. In the liturgy, especially in the Eucharist, the work of our redemption takes place (SC 2). But the salvation now bestowed is only a pledge and anticipation of the eschatological salvation in the new world (SC 8). For that reason, the sacraments are, thirdly, *prophetic anticipations and signs of hope*. Our liturgy is the anticipatory celebration of the heavenly liturgy. In an antiphon of Corpus Christi, we hear all three dimensions of the sacraments: "O sacred meal in which Christ is our food—memorial of his passion, fullness of grace, pledge of future glory."

3.3 The Sacraments as Signs of Salvation

Both as forms of the word and of grace and as forms of encounter with Jesus Christ, the sacraments signify at once salvation and grace. The New Testament speaks of rebirth *from* water and the Holy Spirit (Jn 3:5), of redemption *through* the bath of rebirth (Tit 3:5), of purification *through* the bath of water in the word (Eph 5:26). The sacraments, then, not only point externally to salvation; *they contain and bestow the salvation they signify* (DS 1310, 1606; NR 501, 511; SC 59). By allusion to St. Augustine, the Council of Trent defines a sacrament as a "symbol of a sacred thing and the visible form of invisible grace" (DS 1639; NR 571).

The sacraments not only awaken and strengthen faith; they also bestow the grace they signify. They are not only means of faith, but also means of grace (DS 1605; NR 510; SC 59; LG 11).

Catholic doctrine goes further to say that the sacraments bestow grace *in virtue of the performance of the sacramental action* (*ex opere operato*) (DS 1608; NR 513). This formula is often misunderstood. It does not attribute a mechanical or magical efficacy to the sacraments. The true ground and power from which the sacraments have force is Jesus Christ's work of salvation; he is also their true dispenser (SC 7). The salvific efficacy of the sacraments presupposes faith. Indeed, the measure of grace we receive depends on our measure of openness and readiness as well as upon God's generosity. But faith does not produce grace; it receives it. It receives it through the sacrament as a form of encounter with Christ recognizable by signs. That is all that is meant by the phrase "*ex opere operato*". It does not express the whole of the Catholic understanding of sacraments and must be interpreted in the entire context of Catholic sacramental doctrine.

In what does salvation or the *grace of the sacraments consist*? In answering this question, we presuppose everything already said about the reality of redemption and grace. The sacraments bestow on us the love of God, in

185–187; 205–207

which the Father communicates himself to us through Jesus Christ in the
Holy Spirit. More particularly, we distinguish a double effect in the
sacraments: they give us a share in the office and mission of Jesus Christ,
and they also give us a share in his life. The *share in Jesus' office and mission* is
called the *sacramental character*. The term too is sometimes misunderstood.
It means that baptism, confirmation, and holy orders enable us to participate in the office and mission of Jesus Christ (DS 1313, 1609; NR 504,
514). Because they engage us definitively for Jesus Christ and his "cause",
we bear permanently their imprint and seal. Thus these sacraments cannot
be repeated. Through them, each of us is conformed in a specific way to
the priesthood of Jesus Christ. They engage us in the glorification of God
and in the salvation of man. This shows that the sacraments are not meant
merely for the private salvation of the individual, but always for the
salvation of the world and the public glorification of God as well.

*273–274;
279–280;
314–315*

Our participation in the mission of Jesus Christ can be exercised
correctly only if we also *participate in his life, death, and Resurrection*. All the
sacraments aim at enabling us to participate through sacramental grace in
the paschal mystery of Jesus Christ, so that we may be taken up into God's
life and love in the Holy Spirit through Jesus Christ. Every sacrament
bestows or strengthens this one grace in the particular way that befits the
specific sacramental sign, the human situation represented by it, and the
meaning of the particular sacrament. What we have said about the reality
of grace becomes concrete for the whole man in the sacraments.

*205–208;
270–272*

Because of this salvific meaning of the sacraments, it follows that they
are *necessary* to the faithful *for salvation* (DS 1604; NR 509). They are not
superfluous; neither are they a ceremonial embellishment or a mere
confession of brotherly solidarity. Being consciously and resolutely a
Christian requires the regular reception of penance and of the Eucharist,
along with the effort to live them personally in faith. While sacramental
practice is not the only criterion for a serious Christian life, it is an essential
one.

3.4 The Sacraments as Signs of the Church

Except in emergencies, all the sacraments are administered in the context
of a liturgical celebration. The sacraments take place within the liturgically
assembled and celebrating community.

The *liturgy* is not only an external performance of rites and ceremonies,
nor is it primarily concerned with instruction and action. In the liturgy,
Jesus Christ himself is acting; it is the expression of his priesthood. Jesus
Christ acts in the Church and through the Church. In the community that
preaches the word of God, renders thanks to God "with exultant and

sincere hearts" (Acts 2:46), celebrates the legacy of the Lord, sacrifices, intercedes, and hopes for the coming of the Lord, Jesus Christ is present. So the liturgy is the public worship of the whole mystical body of Jesus Christ, head and members. In it, the salvation of man is efficaciously signified through sensible signs, while God is glorified in a communal and public way (SC 7).

The chief reason why sacraments have their place in the liturgical celebration of the community is that *the Church in Jesus Christ is the universal sacrament of salvation* (LG 48, among others). As signs of Christ, the individual sacraments are also signs of the Church. On the one hand, the Church is built up through the sacraments; on the other, the sacramentally symbolic character of the Church is expressed in the individual sacraments. Jesus Christ and his salvation encounter us in the sacraments through the community of believers. This happens when we are taken up through the sacraments into the community of the Church (baptism) and made fully responsible members of the Church (confirmation), or when this membership is deepened and completed (the Eucharist) and a special mission in the Church is given (holy orders, marriage), or again when membership is fully restored after being disrupted by sin (penance, anointing of the sick). The sacraments are signs that express the redemptive meaning of the Church. They also build up the Church as the sign of salvation; through them, the Church grows and renews herself. In sacramental celebration, the Church is the communion of saints in both senses presented above: the community of men sanctified by the sacraments.

217–222; 222–224

The sacraments have a *communal character*. They are not private actions, but liturgical celebrations of the Church herself (SC 26). This holds in particular for the celebration of the Eucharist, the sign of unity and the bond of love (SC 47). So the faithful should not participate in sacramental celebration as mute spectators, but consciously, actively, and with spiritual benefit (SC 11, 14, among others). The communal character of the sacraments is clearly expressed so far as the celebration of the sacraments is a dialogue. Apart from the communion of the celebrating priest, no one can dispense a sacrament to himself; it is dispensed to him. For every sacrament, there must be one who administers, who performs the sacramental action under the commission and in the name of Jesus Christ, the one who alone administers the sacraments, and a recipient, who accepts the sacrament in faith.

The *one who administers the sacraments* must be explicitly sent and commissioned by Jesus Christ. For that reason, the administration of the sacraments is reserved—except in the cases of emergency baptism and the sacrament of marriage—to those with ministerial authority in the Church (DS 1610; NR 515). That is also why laymen must be commissioned by the bishop before they may distribute communion. Since the sacraments are signs and celebrations of the Church, the *validity* of the sacraments requires that the one who administers them perform the essential signs of the sacraments correctly, that is, in the way laid down in the Church, and that he further intend to do what the Church does (DS 1312, 1611; NR 503, 516). A baptism, for instance, that is not given in trinitarian form or a baptism in jest is not valid. The marriage vow "I do" is not valid when essential elements of the Church's understanding of marriage have been excluded. *Worthy administration* of the sacraments requires that the one who administers try to live what he performs sacramentally. The bishop says at the ordination of a priest, "Consider what you are doing, imitate what you perform, and place your life under the mystery of the cross." The valid administration of a sacrament does not require, however, the subjective holiness and orthodoxy of the one who administers it (DS 1612; NR 517). Various movements have tried, from the times of the ancient Church and until today, to make the validity of the sacraments depend on the personal holiness and orthodoxy of the one who administers them. These movements fail to recognize that the sacraments draw their strength not from the human holiness of the minister, but from the saving work of Jesus Christ. Jesus Christ himself is the true minister of the sacrament, and he can avail himself even of unworthy servants. Otherwise, constant unrest and uncertainty would arise in the community. The community of the faithful would always have to ask and investigate whether the priest were worthy; this would lead in turn to the formation of factions and the dissolution of church unity. All the major churches, even the Lutheran and Reformed ones, have decided for the objectivity of the church's mediation of salvation.

292–294   The *recipient of the sacrament* must possess a living faith and a believing readiness (disposition) for sacramental grace in order to have a worthy and *fruitful reception*. A sacrament received unworthily does not bring salvation, but rather judgment (1 Cor 11:27–29). We must prepare ourselves for the reception of the sacraments in the correct way, through reflection, prayer, and penance. An intention to receive the sacrament is necessary in any case for a *valid reception*. Under physical or psychological coercion, then, there is no valid sacrament. This is important, for instance, in the validity of holy orders and marriage. On the other hand, neither personal orthodoxy nor personal holiness is necessary for mere validity. The sacrament of penance is the only exception. So a baptized non-Catholic can validly receive the sacrament of marriage, and someone unworthy can validly receive holy orders, so long as both recipients do not directly, positively exclude the reception of the sacrament and its essential contents. It is clear that the sacraments are not magic or mechanical charms, but sacraments of faith.

3.5 Sacramentals

The sacraments are not only intermittent events in our lives. They must be prepared for and must take effect in the "liturgy of the world". The *sanctification of everyday life* happens first and foremost through the divine service of a life lived out of faith (Rom 12:1). To do this, men need signs as reminders of God and of God's blessing—especially in our industrialized, scientifically and technically rational world. Only by such signs can an atmosphere of faith be created in which we become conscious that our whole life is ordained to God and secure in him. Where such signs are lacking, Christian life is impoverished.

The Church has instituted sacramentals to be these signs. Sacramentals are *holy signs that are similar to the sacraments*. Unlike the sacraments, they were not instituted by Jesus Christ, but by the Church. They bring forth fruits of a spiritual kind, not by virtue of their performance (as in the sacraments), but by virtue of the Church's intercession and the cooperation of the recipient. Neither do they immediately bestow sanctifying grace;   206–207 rather they prepare us for it and express it. Through these signs, life's various realms and situations are sanctified (SC 60).

> Thus, for well-disposed members of the faithful the liturgy of the sacraments and sacramentals sanctifies almost every event of their lives with the divine grace which flows from the paschal mystery of the passion, death and Resurrection of Christ. From this source all sacraments and sacramentals draw their power. There is scarcely any proper use of material things which cannot thus be directed toward the sanctification of men and the praise of God (SC 61).

First among the sacramentals are the *blessings* for the different domains of life. They express man's need for blessing. Man longs for salvation, protection, happiness, and the fulfillment of his life. So men bless one another: they wish one another well. Above all, though, they hope and beg for blessings from God. God is the source of all good and of all blessing, in creation and in the history of salvation. Jesus Christ is the fullness of blessing. Holy Scripture tells us that Jesus "went about doing good works and healing all" (Acts 10:38); he embraced children and blessed them (Mk 10:16); he laid hands upon the sick (Lk 4:40); for those who heard him, he broke bread and blessed it (Mk 6:41). In Christ, Christians are blessed by God, the Father, "with every spiritual blessing in the heavens" (Eph 1:3). They are called at the same time to bless and to attain blessing (1 Pet 3:9). The Church mediates blessings under the invocation of the name of Jesus. Every benediction is a praise of God and a request for his blessing. For all benedictions, the true gesture of blessing is the sign of the cross. Benedictions thus presuppose at least the faith of the minister. This excludes any misunderstanding of benedictions as magical.

The best known, most ordinary blessing is also the best grounded biblically; this is the table blessing (grace before meals). The blessing of the weather and the petition for good conditions and the prospering of the fruits of the earth, the blessing of a house or a dwelling, the blessing of a journey, and the blessing of the sick, among others, also have great importance. Such benedictions are often linked with old customs, such as the blessing of wine on Midsummer Day, the blessing of throats on the feast of St. Blaise, the blessing of food at Easter, and the blessing of herbs on the feast of Mary's Assumption into heaven. The blessing of holy water that is used for other blessings (e.g., of Crucifixes and rosaries), and which we may also use in everyday life, reminds us of baptismal water and helps us to liberate the whole of creation from slavery (Rom 8:21), to fill it with new life in Jesus Christ. This is the clearest in the Sunday commemoration of baptism, the blessing and sprinkling of holy water (the *asperges*).

Certain blessings have permanent effects. Through them, persons or things are singled out from the profane realm and wholly consecrated to God and the liturgy. In these cases we speak of a *consecration*. There is a consecration of persons— distinct from the consecration of bishops, priests, and deacons—in the consecration of abbots, monks, and virgins. There is also a consecration of things: of churches, altars, and liturgical vessels, among others.

94–95;
126–127;
130–131

Exorcism is the act by which the Church asks officially and authoritatively in the name of Jesus Christ for protection from the attacks of the evil enemy and for deliverance from his power. Jesus himself practiced exorcism (Mk 1:25, among others). The authority and commission of the Church to perform exorcisms stem from Jesus Christ himself (Mk 3:15; 6:7, 13; 16:17). In simple form, exorcism is employed at baptism and at the consecration of holy water. The solemn, so-called great exorcism may be undertaken only with the permission of the bishop. In such an exorcism one must proceed with prudence and sobriety, in strict accord with the Church's criteria. In no case is exorcism a substitute for medical efforts.

The sacramentals and the customs often connected with them have significance in leading to the sacraments (especially the Eucharist), in adorning and explaining the liturgy of the sacraments, and in making them fruitful in everyday Christian life. But they themselves are never the center. This center remains the celebration of the sacraments.

IV

THE SEVEN SACRAMENTS

1. Baptism

1.1 Baptism: The Sacrament of Faith

After the outpouring of the Holy Spirit on Pentecost, Peter announced Jesus Christ crucified as Lord and Messiah. His hearers were struck deep in their hearts, and they asked him and the other Apostles, " 'What are we to do, brothers?' Peter answered: 'You must reform and be baptized, each one of you, in the name of Jesus Christ, that your sins may be forgiven; then you will receive the gift of the Holy Spirit' " (Acts 2:37–38). This text shows that from the very beginning, conversion to Jesus Christ was linked with baptism in his name. Baptism has always been the *entrance gate, and foundation of the whole of Christian existence* in the Church. Together with confirmation and the Eucharist, it is the sacrament of 278–279 Christian initiation, introducing and inaugurating Christian existence (SC 71).

The Church's Tradition of faith sees many Old Testament *prefigurations and foretokens of baptism*. The Church understands the hovering of the creative Spirit of God over the primeval waters, as well as the rescue of the clan of Noah from the waters of the flood and the rescue of the people of Israel at the passage through the Red Sea, as references to the reality and meaning of baptism. The primitive Church counted as fundamental Jesus' undergoing the *baptism of John*, when Jesus was proclaimed Son of God and Spirit-filled Messiah (Mk 1:9–11 par.). The baptism of John is, so to speak, God's final offer to Israel before the imminent day of judgment. What distinguished the *primitive Christian baptismal practice* from the baptism of John was that Christian baptism was performed "in the name of Jesus Christ". It not only promised deliverance from future judgment, but also bestowed a share even now in the salvation that had already appeared through the death and Resurrection of Jesus Christ, as well as through the outpouring of the Holy Spirit. Christian baptism is anticipated in the Old Testament and founded in Jesus' own baptism. It draws its strength from the death and Resurrection of Jesus as well as from the sending of the Spirit. It is dispensed *with the commission and on the authority of the Risen and Exalted Lord*.

"Full authority has been given to me
both in heaven and on earth;
go, therefore, and make disciples of all the nations.
Baptize them in the name
'of the Father,
and of the Son,
and of the Holy Spirit'.
Teach them to carry out everything I have commanded you.
And know that I am with you always, until the end of the world!"
        (Mt 28:18–20; Mk 16:15–16).

It follows that Christian baptism is above all a *sign of faith, that is, a sign of conversion, of the turning of one's life toward Jesus Christ, and of confession of him*. For that reason, since the time of the ancient Church the catechumenate preceded the baptism of adults. This was a long period of introduction into the faith and into a life lived according to it. Before the baptism of children, a baptismal conversation is to take place with the parents and godparents, who are later to introduce the child to the faith. At the baptismal celebration itself, the child to be baptized or the parents and godparents must renounce Satan, the evil one, and confess faith in God, the almighty Father, in Jesus Christ, and in the Holy Spirit. In response to this confession, baptism is administered "in the name of the Father, and of the Son, and of the Holy Spirit". Of course, it is not only faith that is necessary for the reception of baptism; but, baptism brings the *task of a lifelong growth and maturation in the faith*. As a sign of this, the community renews the baptismal confession every year at the Easter Vigil celebration.

1.2 Baptism: The Sacrament of New Life

The *sign of baptism* is washing with water and pronouncing the name of the triune God over the person to be baptized: "I baptize you in the name of the Father, and of the Son, and of the Holy Spirit." The water symbolizes purification and life. It expresses the double gift of baptism: *purification from sin and the gift of new life*. Baptism washes and purifies us from sin (1 Cor 6:11; Acts 22:16). It looses us from the disastrous fate common to all men under the power of sin, and it frees us from original sin and from all previously committed personal sins. Positively expressed, baptism is rebirth to new life (Jn 3:3, 5; Tit 3:5; 1 Pet 1:3, 23). It bestows justification and sanctification (1 Cor 6:11), it gives us the gift of the Holy Spirit (Acts 2:38; 1 Cor 12:13), and it gives sanctifying grace. Baptism makes us children of God and thus also heirs of God and coheirs of Christ (Rom 8:17; DS 1316; NR 531; LG 11). This new life takes effect in faith, hope,

108–114

191–204

183–187

205–207
206–208

and love, which are also infused in us through baptism. Because baptism bestows the light of faith, Holy Scripture also describes it as illumination (Heb 6:4; 10:32). For that reason, at a solemn baptism the baptismal candle is presented to the candidate: "Receive the light of Christ."

This sacrament's comprehensive importance for salvation implies the *necessity of baptism for salvation*.

> "The man who believes in it and accepts baptism will be saved; the man who refuses to believe in it will be condemned" (Mk 16:16).

> "No one can enter into God's Kingdom
> without being begotten of water and Spirit" (Jn 3:5).

The Church teaches that baptism is necessary for salvation only for those to whom baptism was announced and who had the possibility of deciding for it. Since God wills the salvation of all men (1 Tim 2:4–6), a man who lives according to his conscience and does the will of God as he knows it concretely, and who would certainly have desired baptism had he known of its importance, can attain salvation on the basis of such a *"baptism of desire"*. `217–220`

The forgiveness of sins and the gift of new life have been bestowed on us concretely in Jesus Christ. Baptism gives us a *participation in the mission and new life of Jesus Christ*. According to the New Testament, baptism is dispensed "in the name of Jesus Christ" (Acts 2:38; 10:48; Rom 6:3; Gal 3:27, among others). We are handed over to the Lord Jesus Christ in baptism and placed under his lordship.

Participation in the mission of Jesus, in his threefold office as priest, prophet, and king, is expressed at the celebration of baptism by the anointing with chrism, which is the sign of prophetic, priestly, and kingly dignity. Baptism grounds the *common priesthood of all Christians* (LG 10, 33; AA 3). Every baptized person should bear witness to Jesus Christ, making him present in his life, his family, and his profession. As Jesus Christ has done the work of redemption once for all, so we are placed in his service by baptism once for all. Baptism imprints a permanent, *"indelible spiritual mark"*, the "baptismal character", on the soul of the person baptized. The baptized person is dedicated once for all to Jesus Christ and is permanently called, sealed, and sent by him. The baptized person can indeed become unfaithful to his baptism through sin (or, in extreme cases, through apostasy) and so lose the new life bestowed in the Holy Spirit. But the calling, engagement, and imprint of Jesus Christ remain. For that reason, baptism is unique and cannot be repeated. `176–179` `239–243` `265–267`

The *participation in the new life of Jesus Christ* through baptism has been understood and interpreted by the Apostle Paul as *being taken into the death and Resurrection of Jesus Christ*. `159–161; 170–173`

> Are you not aware that we who were baptized into Christ Jesus were
> baptized into his death? Through baptism into his death we were
> buried with him, so that, just as Christ was raised from the dead by
> the glory of the Father, we too might live a new life. If we have been
> united with him through likeness to his death, so shall we be through
> a like resurrection (Rom 6:3–5; Col 2:12).

Because baptism takes us into the paschal mystery of Jesus Christ, his
death and his Resurrection, we Christians should be dead to sin and alive
for God. Baptism is the *foundation of the whole of Christian life as well as of
Christian death*. Because of baptism, we Christians are exhorted to become
297–301 what we are. Christian life must be a constant conversion and a constant
battle with the powers of sin; it is a continuous growth in new life, in faith,
hope, and love. One part of this growth is *asceticism*, the persevering effort
to lay aside everything that does not correspond to the Spirit of Jesus
Christ. Another is the practice of a Christian life, the endeavor to be
conformed to the image of Jesus Christ and to grow stronger in his power
(Phil 3:10; Rom 8:29; Col 3:9–10). As means to this, the Church's
Tradition points to fasting, praying, and alms-giving (Tob 12:8; Mt 6:1–8).
The life of the baptized person ought also to share now in a preliminary
way in the transfigured life of the Risen Lord; there should be experiences
of certainty, comfort, and joy, even mystical forms of the experience of
communion and friendship with God. A special expression of the new life
234–235 bestowed in baptism is a life lived according to the evangelical counsels, in
freely chosen poverty, as unmarried, and under obedience, according to
the rule of a religious community. The highest fulfillment of baptism and
at the same time the highest form of the imitation of Jesus is *martyrdom*, the
surrender of one's life for Jesus Christ and for one's brothers and sisters in
him. The Church Fathers spoke of martyrdom as a baptism by blood;
after baptism by water, it is the second immersion (Tertullian).

1.3 Baptism: Incorporation into the Church

Just as an individual man can live only in community, so the individual
Christian, who is reborn to new life in baptism, also needs the sheltering
218–220 environment of the whole people of God, the Church. Baptism has
always been understood as incorporation into the Church (Acts 2:41, 47,
among others; DS 1314; NR 528; LG 11). It is *the fundamental sacrament of
226–228 Christian initiation*. Baptism places us in a community of life with Jesus
Christ and incorporates us into his *body*. By being united through the one
baptism with Christ, we are also united in Christ with one another. Thus,
through baptism there arises the New Covenant people of God, which

transcends all natural boundaries of nations, cultures, classes, races, and sex. So Paul says,

> It was in one Spirit that all of us, whether Jew or Greek, slave or free, were baptized into one body. All of us have been given to drink of the one Spirit (1 Cor 12:13).

> All of you who have been baptized into Christ have clothed yourselves with him. There does not exist among you Jew or Greek, slave or freeman, male or female. All are one in Christ Jesus (Gal 3:27–28; Col 3:11).

> Live a life worthy of the calling you have received, with perfect humility, meekness, and patience, bearing with one another lovingly. Make every effort to preserve the unity which has the Spirit as its origin and peace as its binding force. There is but one body and one Spirit, just as there is but one hope given all of you by your call. There is one Lord, one faith, one baptism; one God and Father of all, who is over all, and works through all, and is in all (Eph 4:2–6).

Through the one baptism we are incorporated into the Church community in all times and all places. This is expressed concretely by our becoming part of the liturgical community, a community that may deserve "to be called by the name which is given to the unique people of God in its entirety, that is to say, the Church of God" (LG 28). As a rule, then, baptism should take place in the parish church as part of the celebration of Sunday—and, several times a year, within the eucharistic celebration itself. The baptism of adolescents and adults should be administered during the Easter Vigil so far as possible.

222–223

Since baptism is incorporation into the community of the Church, the *solemn liturgical administration of baptism belongs to ecclesiastical ministers*. In the ancient Church, baptizing was even the prerogative of the bishop. Only later was solemn baptism administered by priests and deacons as well. Since baptism is necessary for salvation, however, *in an emergency every Christian*—indeed every person, even an unbaptized one—can validly administer the sacrament, so long as one does so in the form and according to the intention of the Church (DS 1315; NR 530; LG 17). For the true celebrant of a baptism is Jesus Christ himself (cf. SC 7).

The ecclesiastical character of baptism also entails the *responsibility of the entire community* for the faith of the newly baptized person. Of course, special responsibility attaches to the godparents. Through baptism, all are brothers and sisters. This fundamental unity of all the baptized must be embodied more than naturally in mutual assistance and in the exchange of both earthly and spiritual gifts. The poor, the sick, the handicapped, and foreigners must occupy a place of honor in the community. Since ancient

Christian times, hospitality has been considered an important expression of our common union in Christ through baptism. In the Rule of St. Benedict, we read: "All arriving guests are to be received as Christ, for the latter himself will one day say: 'I was a foreigner, and you took me in.' " The baptized person, who is a stranger and a guest on earth and has no fixed abode, should be at home everywhere in the worldwide Church.

Through the one, common baptism, we are also united with baptized Christians who do not belong to the community of the Roman Catholic Church. As early as the dispute over heretical baptism of the fourth century and the Donatist dispute of the fifth century, the Church declared herself in favor of the validity of baptism administered in the correct form outside of the Catholic Church. Thus *baptism is the foundation of ecumenical communion* and of ecumenical endeavors to obtain a full communion of churches, which communion would be expressed finally in eucharistic communion. So Vatican II says:

219–220;
232–233

> The Church knows that she is joined in many ways to the baptized who are honored by the name of Christian, but who do not however profess the Catholic faith in its entirety or have not preserved unity or communion under the successor of Peter (LG 15).

> For men who believe in Christ and have been properly baptized are put in some, though imperfect, communion with the Catholic Church (UR 3).

> Baptism, therefore, constitutes the sacramental bond of unity existing among all who through it are reborn. But baptism, of itself, is only a beginning, a point of departure, for it is wholly directed toward the acquiring of fullness of life in Christ. Baptism is thus ordained toward a complete profession of faith, a complete incorporation into the system of salvation such as Christ himself willed it to be, and finally, toward a complete integration into eucharistic communion (UR 22).

Today it is clear that the baptism administered in the Orthodox churches, the Old Catholic church, the Anglican church, and in the major Protestant churches corresponds in intention and in execution to the baptism administered in the Catholic Church. All these baptisms are valid. For this reason, the conditional baptism once usually performed in the case of conversions from these churches is inadmissible. The baptism of Baptists, Methodists, Mennonites, the Moravian church, and Seventh Day Adventists is also recognized as valid. Validity is disputed in the case of the New Apostolic church and the Mormons. The baptism of Jehovah's Witnesses is surely not a Christian baptism according to the mind of the New Testament. The Salvation Army, Quakers, and Christian Science do not practice baptism.

1.4 The Question of Infant Baptism

We find adult baptism at the very beginning of the Church. It remains typical in the missionary regions of the Church. The baptism of young children becomes a problem or a practice only in the second generation. In the New Testament itself there are no direct witnesses for it. The New Testament, however, speaks several times of the baptism of a whole "house", of a whole family together with its servants (Acts 16:15, 33–34; 18:8; 1 Cor 1:16). It is possible that children were included in these cases. The first explicit and clear witnesses for infant baptism are found from the second century on. The baptism of young children has been a *practice* in the Church, both East and West, *from time immemorial*. Different popes and synods, above all the Council of Trent (DS 1514, 1626–27; NR 356, 544–45), have confirmed and defended this doctrine and practice.

In our century, there has arisen *new discussion about infant baptism*. As one argument against infant baptism, people often refer to the changed social situation. In the older Christian and denominationally uniform society—they say—the religious education of children was secured. In our pluralistic and secularized society, on the other hand, very many who are baptized as young children never grow up to a conscious and personal act of faith. Moreover, some see the baptism of young children as an attack on their individual freedom. For these and other reasons, many wish to postpone baptism to an age at which a young person can decide for himself.

To these critical objections against Church practice we can answer that the social situation has only an indicative value for the Church, never an ultimately normative one. The mission of the Church must indeed be realized under specific social conditions, but the Church may not submit to social norms. She must orient herself solely by the mission of Jesus Christ. Moreover, in regard to the second objection, a religiously and ideologically free education would be a complete illusion. Parents and educators mold and influence maturing children one way or the other, either through their faith or through their indifference, which would be expressed in an education supposed to be free and religiously neutral. Finally, one can ask whether today's questioning of infant baptism does not conceal an individually constricted understanding of the faith, one that no longer sees faith embedded in shared life and in the communal character of the Church. Indeed, does not the argument from a personal, autonomous act of faith misunderstand the faith as one's own work and as an achievement? Does it not overlook the gift character of faith and baptism?

Positively, *three points of view* can be advanced *in support of the practice of infant baptism*.

1. Christian existence grounded in baptism is free, unmerited grace with which God precedes all our actions and surrounds our lives from the beginning (1 Jn 4:10, 19; Tit 3:5). We have need of grace from the beginning because of original sin. This grace preceding all our actions and merit is particularly well expressed in infant baptism. The Church and

THE WORK OF THE HOLY SPIRIT

Christian parents would withhold an essential good from the child did they not bestow the sacrament of baptism shortly after birth.

2. Faith is related fundamentally to the community of believers and depends on it. Infant baptism articulates with particular clarity this dependence and inclusion in the sustaining community without which the child could not even survive. Through his parents and godparents, the young child is taken into the community of believers, which must answer for this child before God and men. That is also the reason a child may be baptized only if his later Christian education is guaranteed by parents or relatives. If this guarantee is not given, baptism must be prudently postponed.

3. Faith is not a single, discrete event but a process of growth. The baptized Christian is obliged to seek lifelong growth into Christ and into faith. The New Testament does not describe only the movement that leads from faith to baptism as its strongest form of embodiment (Acts 8:12–13; 18:8; 10:47, among others). It also describes the reverse movement by which those already baptized are reminded of their baptism and led ever more deeply into the baptismal reality (Rom 6:3–4; 1 Cor 6:9–11; Eph 5:8–9; 1 Pet 2:1–5). Finally, baptism is not only a sign of faith but also its source of strength. It is the sacrament of illumination. As such, it is just the beginning of a path, of a lifelong growth in faith.

All of this points to the need of a renewal in the *pastoral practice of baptism*. The entire pastoral effort consists in leading one to baptism and in developing the new life founded in baptism, both in the individual Christian and in the community. Baptismal practice in the stricter sense includes the adult catechumenate, the baptismal conversation with the parents and godparents (for infant baptism), pastoral ministry to engaged couples and newly married couples, and the fostering of responsibility in the whole community for the children's education in faith. The renewal of parish catechesis, by which maturing children are to be introduced to the faith and the life of the Church, is especially important (cf. *Gem. Synode, Schwerpunkte heutiger Sakramentenpastoral* 2–3). The sacrament of this growth is confirmation.

2. Confirmation

As with any life, Christian life begun in baptism must grow and mature. This process of growth is the fruit of God's grace. The sacrament of confirmation serves to strengthen and complete baptism. Though a separate sacrament, it is closely linked with baptism and is intended to
develop, strengthen, and complete what has been begun in baptism.

Vatican II reaffirmed that baptism, confirmation, and the Eucharist belong closely together as the three sacraments of Christian initiation (SC 71).

Baptism does bestow the Holy Spirit on us. One's whole Christian life stands from the beginning under the sign of the Spirit of God. Yet the *New Testament* itself describes a conferral of the Spirit by the laying on of hands that is distinct from baptism. The Acts of the Apostles tells us:

272–273

183–187

> When the apostles in Jerusalem heard that Samaria had accepted the word of God, they sent Peter and John to them. The two went down to these people and prayed that they might receive the Holy Spirit. It had not as yet come down upon any of them since they had only been baptized in the name of the Lord Jesus. The pair upon arriving imposed hands on them and they received the Holy Spirit (Acts 8:14–17; 19:6; Heb 6:2).

This passage tells us two things. First, the Apostles' laying on of hands united the relatively independent community of Samaria more firmly with the Church of Jerusalem, the center of unity. At the same time, the gift of the Holy Spirit was bestowed on the Samaritan Christians in a special way by the laying on of hands. These two motifs, *closer connection with the Church and strengthening through the power of the Holy Spirit*, were what later became important for the sacrament of confirmation.

The Church took up the distinction between baptism and the laying on of hands. Historically considered, the development has been quite complicated. While the East emphasized anointing, the West emphasized the laying on of hands. This laying on of hands was linked quite soon with an anointing; more exactly, it was considered to be contained in the anointing. Both the laying on of hands and the anointing originally formed one single action with baptism—or, as Bishop Cyprian (third century) said, a double sacrament. But while baptism was more and more administered by priests, confirmation was reserved in the West for the bishop. As the baptism of children became typical and dioceses grew larger, the Latin church of the West separated baptism and confirmation.

The history of the *sign of confirmation* has been rich and varied, but its meaning—the communication of the Holy Spirit—has remained constant. In connection with the renewal of confirmation by Pope Paul VI, which was encouraged by the last Council, it was decided in 1976 that confirmation would be administered by anointing the forehead with chrism while laying on the hand. At the same time, these words would be spoken: "Be sealed with the gift of God, the Holy Spirit."

Anointing with oil is an ancient sign. It signifies not only purification and strengthening but empowerment. The oil means strength, power, and splendor. It has been found since ancient times in connection with the coronation of kings and consecration of priests (2 Sam 2:4, 7; 5:3, 17, among others). So Jesus is the Christ, the One *anointed* with the Holy Spirit. Through confirmation, Christians—anointed ones—share more fully in the kingly and priestly authority of Jesus Christ and in his Messianic fullness of the Spirit. The *laying on of hands* symbolizes taking possession, but also blessing and commissioning. It says that the one being confirmed has been claimed completely for Jesus Christ and the Church; at the same time, a responsibility is conferred upon him. He is to spread and to defend the faith by word and deed in the power of the Holy Spirit and as a witness of Jesus Christ. He is thus to contribute to the upbuilding and growth of Christ's body, the Church.

The sign of confirmation points already to the gift of grace bestowed by the sacrament. First of all, confirmation lets us participate more intensely 240–241 *in the mission of Jesus Christ and of the Church*. It appoints us public witnesses of the faith and sends us forth to work responsibly in the Church. Since this takes place once for all, as with baptism, confirmation imprints an 265–266 *indelible spiritual mark* on the soul. This confirmation character is a sign of being taken permanently into the service of Jesus Christ. For that reason, confirmation, like baptism, can be received only once (DS 1609; NR 514).

The *gift of the Spirit in confirmation* is interpreted in the prayer that the bishop says while extending his hands, before the laying on of hands and the anointing with chrism. It belongs to the full form of the rite and contributes to the comprehensive understanding of the sacrament. The prayer says,

> Almighty God, Father of our Lord Jesus Christ, you have freed these Christians in baptism from guilt, you have bestowed new life on them by water and the Holy Spirit. We ask you, O Lord, to send the Holy Spirit, the Paraclete, upon them. Give them the Spirit of wisdom and of understanding, of counsel, of knowledge and of strength, the Spirit of piety and of fear of the Lord. We ask this through Christ, our Lord.

The Tradition of the Church has developed the teaching on the gifts of the Spirit to affirm that through confirmation "the Holy Spirit is given for the purpose of strengthening . . . so that the Christian may confess the name of Christ with courage" (DS 1319; NR 554). The Holy Spirit makes the confirmed person resemble Jesus Christ more perfectly. It strengthens him to give testimony to Jesus Christ for the edification of Christ's body in faith, hope, and love. Confirmation is the *unfolding, strengthening, and fullness of the Holy Spirit bestowed already in baptism*, together with a mission of responsible commitment in the Church for the service of men.

The original *celebrant of confirmation* is the bishop (LG 26). This reservation to the bishop, who holds the fullness of office in the Church, shows the closer connection of the confirmed person with the Church and the responsibility that the confirmed person takes on in and for the Church through his witness to Jesus Christ. If the bishop cannot come frequently enough to the individual parishes because of the size of his diocese, a priest commissioned by the bishop, usually one of his close associates, can also administer confirmation. In the case of serious danger, the parish priest or any other priest is authorized and obligated to confirm. The same holds for a priest who baptizes an adult or who admits someone already baptized into full communion with the Catholic Church.

For a long time, confirmation figured only slightly in the consciousness of Christians. In more recent times, there have been attempts to develop a separate *pastoral practice for confirmation*. Preparation for confirmation is the task of the entire community. It should take place as part of catechesis in small groups, supported by common experiences and tasks (days of recollection, weekend excursions, and charitable works, among others). The participation of suitable laymen is also helpful; the parents and sponsors (the same as the godparents, if possible) should also cooperate. Efforts should be made to ensure that at the end of the preparation each candidate for confirmation consciously and freely enrolls for it. The celebration of confirmation should take place in a solemn eucharistic liturgy. Those to be confirmed repeat and affirm before the whole congregation their baptismal confession. The sign of peace concluding the celebration of confirmation expresses the closer connection between the confirmed person and the Church. For that reason, the confirmed should be included in a living way in the life of the parish, especially through youth groups. The exercise of lay ministries in the parish should be reserved to the confirmed, who through confirmation are fully incorporated into the Church (*Gem. Synode, Schwerpunkte heutiger Sakramenten-pastoral* B. 1.2.6).

There is a special question about the *age of confirmation*. This is not a matter of dogma, but of pastoral judgment. In the first centuries, confirmation was given immediately after baptism, as it still is in the Eastern church. Even in the Latin church of the West, baptism, confirmation, and first admission to the Eucharist are joined together at the baptism of adults. In infant baptism, however, confirmation is postponed until a later age—according to canon law, until the age of discretion. Today many wish to restore the ancient unity of baptism–confirmation –Eucharist and hence advocate a confirmation age of about seven years. Others advocate giving confirmation to young adults, at an age when they are able to decide independently and definitively for Jesus Christ and the Church.

There are, though, good grounds for our present practice of administering confirmation at around twelve years of age. At this age, the child can already know and realize much of the importance of confirmation and therefore meaningfully ask for this sacrament. He begins to move away from the childish world, the faith of a child, and takes the first steps of a conscious faith. In his own way, he can and must be a witness for Jesus Christ. He can accept and follow as an obligation the chief commandment, to love God and one's neighbor. At this age, he can in his own way already take an active part in community life through youth groups and service groups. The most important form of participation is participation in the Eucharist. This is the high point and conclusion of incorporation into the Church.

3. The Eucharist

3.1 The Eucharist: Thanksgiving to the Father

The Eucharist is the *source and culmination* of Christian and ecclesial life (LG 11). The Acts of the Apostles tells of its place already in the primitive community in Jerusalem: "They devoted themselves to the apostles' instruction and the communal life, to the breaking of bread and the prayers" (Acts 2:42, 46). Especially on the first day of the week, the day of the Lord (Rev 1:10), the early communities gathered for the breaking of the bread (Acts 20:7; 1 Cor 16:2). The martyr-bishop Ignatius of Antioch teaches, at the beginning of the second century, that to be a Christian means to live "according to Sunday". A short time later, Justin Martyr provides a vivid description of the early Sunday eucharistic celebration: "On Sunday, though, we all hold a meeting in common because it is the first day on which God created the world through the transformation of darkness and primary matter, and because Jesus Christ, our Redeemer, rose from the dead on this day." The same is still true today. The Sunday eucharistic celebration is the most important expression of Christian life for the individual and for the community (SC 106). Of course, the eucharistic celebration on weekdays is also of great importance for both.

We have become newly conscious in this century of the Eucharist's central position. Through the renewal of the liturgy of the eucharistic celebration, which began under Pope Pius XII, was mandated by the Second Vatican Council (SC 47–49), and completed in 1969 by Pope Paul VI with the introduction of a new sacramentary, individual and active participation by the entire congregation has been substantially increased. The enhancement and renewal of the liturgy in our century is "a sign of the providential dispositions of God" and "a movement of the Holy Spirit in his Church" (SC 43).

In order to understand the core of the Eucharist, we must seek its origin in Jesus Christ, especially in connection with his proclamation of the Kingdom of God, his death, and his Resurrection. The earliest eucharistic practice of the Church goes back to Jesus Christ himself and is rooted in

him. In fact, there is a threefold *foundation of the Eucharist in Jesus Christ*. It
is prepared in the meal fellowships of the earthly Jesus, it is established in
his Last Supper on the evening before his death, and it is confirmed in
the Easter appearances of the Risen Christ in the context of the disciples'
meals.

The *meal fellowships* that Jesus held with his disciples during his earthly   129–130
life were foreshadowings and anticipations of the banquet of the last days
promised by the prophets—the heavenly marriage feast. They were also a
sign that those who had been lost were taken into the definitive community
of salvation. Here we see glorification of God and forgiveness of sins
bound closely together. The meals of Jesus were signs of the dawning
eschatological salvation (*shalom*), of new communion with God and with   155–156
one another. In contrast, the *Last Supper* that Jesus shared with his
disciples on the evening before his passion has a special character. What
the Lord accomplished in the night of his betrayal was something new.
While offering the prayers of thanks and praise, Jesus anticipated his
surrender to death "for the many" in the gestures of distributing bread
and wine and in the words accompanying and interpreting them. He also
let his disciples take part in that ritual. At the same time, he saw his
imminent death in the light of the final coming of the Kingdom of God: "I
solemnly assure you, I will never again drink of the fruit of the vine until
the day when I drink it new in the reign of God" (Mk 14:25). Jesus' words
at the Last Supper are confirmed through his *cross and Resurrection*. So Jesus
appeared to his disciples after the Resurrection once again at the meal   167–171
fellowships. This is described most impressively in the two disciples'
encounter with the Risen One on the way to Emmaus. They recognized
him as he broke bread (Lk 24:13–35, 36–43; Jn 21:1–14). In the primitive
community, this breaking of bread was considered the anticipation of
eschatological joy (Acts 2:46).

The New Testament texts about the Last Supper (Mk 14:22–25; Mt 26:26–29;
Lk 22:14–20; 1 Cor 11:23–26) raise many *historical questions* today, although we
cannot treat all of them here individually. None of these texts agrees literally with
the others. They already show traces of later liturgical features and of theological
reflection. Thus these texts witness to the fact that the primitive Church took up
the legacy of the Lord in a living way from the very beginning. But it would be
difficult to explain this without some basis in the Last Supper and in the commission
of Jesus. Even if they do not preserve uniformly the exact course of events and the
original wording of what Jesus said at his Last Supper, the Gospel reports cannot
be considered simply as a projection from the practice of the primitive community
back into the life of the earthly Jesus. The report in the Gospel of Mark clearly
bears features of an immediately historical narrative. Even the text handed on by
Paul harks back to a very old tradition found in the earliest communities. Above

all, the prospect of the final coming of the Kingdom of God (Mk 14:25; Lk 22:16, 18) is doubtless part of the Lord's original words at the Last Supper.

The following summary conclusions stand forth. The meals of the earthly Jesus, the Last Supper, and the eucharistic meals of the earliest community are enacted *under the sign of the coming lordship of God*. The eucharistic celebration anticipates the heavenly marriage feast (Rev 19:9). Thus every eucharistic celebration has an Easter character. We have celebrated it since the days of the early Church especially on Sunday as the day on which Christ rose from the dead (First, Second, and Third Eucharistic Prayers). The *Eucharist is an anticipatory participation in the heavenly liturgy and a foretaste of future glory*. It is a sign of the promise and the hope of a new, transfigured creation freed from all servitude. The Eucharist makes manifest and anticipates in signs what will one day *be* when God is all in all (1 Cor 15:28). Whoever eats of the eucharistic bread already has eternal life and will be raised up on the last day (Jn 6:54). Like manna in the Old Covenant, the Eucharist is food and provision for the journey of God's New Covenant people (1 Cor 10:3–4). But the manna in the wilderness was only the foreshadowing of the true bread of God, which has come down from heaven and gives life to the world (Jn 6:33). He who eats of this bread will never die (Jn 6:49–50, 58).

Because we celebrate in the Eucharist the Easter liberation from the power of death and that liberation's gift of a new, eternal life, the Eucharist is more than a mere meal. It is a "sacrifice of praise" (First Eucharistic Prayer; Heb 13:15). In it the one sacrifice of Jesus on the cross is re-presented; in it, future glory is anticipated. So Christians have called it *"Eucharist"*, *thanksgiving*, since the second century. In it we offer thanks and praise to God, the Father, for all the gifts of creation and of redemption. "Eucharist" means *salvation (shalom) and life in the worship and glorification of God*. We express this praise especially in the Preface and in the Sanctus. At the conclusion of the Eucharistic Prayer, it is gathered together in the great doxology:

> Through him, with him, and in him,
> in the unity of the Holy Spirit,
> all glory and honor is yours,
> Almighty Father,
> forever and ever.

The hymns, the vestments, the festivity and solemnity, the artistic creativity, and the decoration of the celebration of the Eucharist are also expressions of eschatological joy. Precisely today, when everyone seems so intent on achievement, utility, and success, feasts and celebrations free

348–352

288–292

of worldly goals are important signs of the new world for which we hope. We need to restore the meaning of Sunday, in the center of which should stand the celebration of the Eucharist. A truly festive celebration, something more than distraction and amusement, affirms the certainty that the power of evil and of death is overcome. The joy and thanksgiving at the Eucharist are directed to the passover of Jesus Christ, his passage through death to new life, in which we too are included. The Eucharist gives us courage and hope that we in all our weakness may hold out to the end despite sufferings and struggles. So the early Church prayed at the celebration of the Eucharist:

> Thou, almighty ruler, hast created all things for the sake of thy name; thou hast given food and drink for the enjoyment of men; to us, though, hast thou given spiritual food and drink and eternal life through Jesus, thy servant.
>   Above all we thank thee that thou art all powerful. Glory be to thee forever!

> Remember, O Lord, thy Church and redeem it from all evil and perfect it in thy love. And lead it home from the four winds, this holy one, into thy Kingdom which thou hast prepared for it.
>   For thine is the power and the glory forever.

> May grace come and this world pass away!
> Hosanna to the God of David. . . . Marána tha (come, O Lord).
> Amen (Did 10:3–6).

3.2 The Eucharistic Presence of Jesus Christ

The Kingdom of God announced and promised by Jesus has already become present in the word, work, and person of Jesus Christ. The anticipatory celebration of the Kingdom in the Eucharist takes place through the presence of Jesus Christ himself.　123–131

Jesus Christ is present in the eucharistic celebration in *many ways*. He is present in the celebrating community. "Where two or three are gathered in my name, there am I in their midst" (Mt 18:20). He is present in his word as well as in the person of the one who performs the priestly ministry. It is Jesus Christ himself who speaks to us, who invites us to the eucharistic meal, who acts in the Eucharist, surrenders himself to the Father, and bestows himself on us. But Jesus Christ is most present in the Eucharist when the eucharistic prayer of praise is spoken as a prayer of blessing over the bread and wine so that he becomes truly, really, and substantially present in virtue of these words under the eucharistic species　176–178; 262–264

(SC 7). This true presence of Jesus Christ is the heart of the Eucharist. The Eucharist's priority over all other sacraments follows not only from its bestowing the fruit of salvation upon us, but also from its rendering present in a special way the source of salvation, Jesus Christ himself.

The Church teaches that the true and real presence of Jesus Christ in the forms of bread and wine is secured by the words of Jesus: "This is my body", "This is my blood" (Mk 14:22, 24). "Body" in Semitic languages does not mean only a part of man, but rather the whole, embodied person. When we read "This is my body, which is for you" (1 Cor 11:24) or "This is my body to be given for you" (Lk 22:19), we see clearly that what is described is the presence of the person of Jesus Christ in his self-surrender for us. In a similar way, the word "blood" in Semitic languages means the vital substance of man. The blood "to be poured out in behalf of many" (Mt 26:28) is Jesus himself in the surrender of his life for us. By repeating these words spoken by the Lord on the evening before his death, the Church not only tells of the Last Supper; she also announces "the death of the Lord until he comes" (1 Cor 11:26). This proclamation is a solemn announcement that effects what it says. Repeating the account of the institution is a prayer of blessing over the bread and wine spoken in the name and in the person of Jesus Christ. Through it, *the body and blood of Jesus Christ, that is, the concrete embodied person of Jesus Christ, becomes present in his self-surrender for us under the forms of bread and wine.*

254–256

Jesus Christ's becoming present in the Eucharist is not something magical or mechanical. It takes place through a *prayer* directed to God, the Father, in the name of Jesus Christ *for the gift of the Holy Spirit* (a prayer called the *epiclesis*). Throughout his life Jesus did everything in the Holy Spirit; he offered himself above all as a sacrifice in the Spirit (Heb 9:14). Through the Holy Spirit Jesus is abidingly present in the Church and in the world. The eucharistic presence of Jesus Christ also takes place in the Holy Spirit. So the priest prays before saying the words of institution, "Let your Spirit come upon these gifts to make them holy, so that they may become for us the body and blood of our Lord, Jesus Christ" (Second Eucharistic Prayer).

69–72;
183–185

In the course of her history, the Church had several times to defend the real presence of Jesus Christ in the Eucharist and at the same time to explain it more deeply. In the *first and second controversies about the Lord's Supper* during the ninth and eleventh centuries respectively, the Church resisted a purely spiritual or purely symbolic understanding of the Eucharist. On the other hand, she also dissociated herself from a gross physical misunderstanding, such as that of the people of Capharnaum, who thought that one could receive Christ in the Eucharist in the way one eats natural bread (Jn 6:52). Faced with both misunderstandings, the Fourth Lateran Council (1215) taught the transubstantiation of bread and wine in the Eucharist. In the disputes with the Reformers in the sixteenth century, these questions were taken up again in a new way. *Luther* did indeed hold resolutely to the real presence of the body and blood of Jesus Christ "in and under the bread and wine" (the Great Catechism), as against the purely spiritual understanding of *Zwingli*. But he repudiated the Catholic doctrine of transubstantiation because of the conceptual problems connected with it, and he opposed the continuation of the presence of Jesus Christ outside the celebration of the Lord's Supper because the Lord's Supper was instituted for the use of the congregation. *Calvin* rejected the presence "in and under bread and wine" and taught that Jesus Christ, who had been exalted to heaven, is present at the reception of the Lord's Supper through the Holy Spirit. Only in our century has there been a certain understanding between the Lutheran and Reformed churches and so a mutual communion in preaching and the Lord's Supper (Leuenberg Concord). An *ecumenical rapprochement* but not full agreement was also reached between the Lutheran and Catholic doctrines. There is still no consensus on the question of the continuous presence of Jesus Christ.

Faced with the misinterpretations appearing in the course of history, the Church had to affirm the *true, real, and substantial presence* of Jesus Christ. At the same time, she had to say that this presence was a "mystery of faith" of a quite unique and incomparable kind. In order to hold fast both to the truth and to the mystery of the presence of Jesus Christ in the Eucharist, the Fourth Lateran Council (1215) and the Council of Trent (1551) employed the concept of transubstantiation (change in substance). In more recent times, Popes Pius XII and Paul VI have defended and confirmed this expression (DS 3891; NR 617).

> His body and blood are truly contained in the sacrament of the altar under the forms of bread and wine after the bread has been transubstantiated into his body and the wine into his blood through the power of God (DS 802; NR 902).

> The Church teaches and confesses "openly and without reserve that in the sublime sacrament of the holy Eucharist, after the consecration of bread and wine, our Lord Jesus Christ is truly, really, and substantially present under the form of those visible things as true God and man" (DS 1636; NR 568).

> Through the consecration of bread and wine, the change of the entire substance of bread into the substance of the body of Christ, our Lord, and of the entire substance of wine into the substance of his blood takes place. This change has been named transubstantiation (change of substance) aptly and in the true sense by the Catholic Church (DS 1642; NR 572).

The *doctrine of eucharistic transubstantiation* is not meant to be a rational explanation of the mystery of the Eucharist, which can be grasped only in faith. The doctrine is meant to protect the literal meaning in Jesus' words of institution against one-sided interpretations. The doctrine affirms that the true and substantial presence of Christ does not change the experiential appearances of bread and wine (size, smell, taste, and chemical composition, among others). So we cannot understand Christ's presence in the Eucharist spatially. Faith in the real presence of Jesus Christ in the Eucharist is not connected to the domain of what is accessible to natural-scientific investigation or to what is considered a substance in the natural sciences. Even natural things are more than one can grasp, measure, and calculate. The presence of Christ concerns the essence (substance) of bread and wine, which is not accessible to human experience. In the Eucharist, bread and wine lose their natural determination of being and meaning as bodily nourishment in order to receive a new determination of being and meaning. They are now reality-filled signs of the personal presence and self-bestowal of Jesus Christ. In the sensible signs of bread and wine there is embodied the self-communicating and self-bestowing love of Jesus Christ in such a way that under these forms Jesus Christ is present in his surrender "for us". The word "transubstantiation" insists that under the eucharistic signs of bread and wine a new—or, rather, *the* new—reality becomes present.

God's action in Jesus Christ has happened once for all. This is reflected in the *continuous presence of Jesus Christ* in the Eucharist outside the eucharistic celebration. The Catholic Church has always held fast to the continuous eucharistic presence of Jesus Christ. She has expressed her belief in the ancient custom of reverently preserving the elements remaining from the eucharistic celebration and bringing communion outside the eucharistic celebration to the sick (DS 1645; NR 574). The original and primary sense of the reservation of the Eucharist was the communion for the sick or viaticum for the dying. The distribution of holy communion outside the eucharistic celebration and the veneration and worship of the Lord abidingly present under the eucharistic species were added only secondarily. Among the forms of eucharistic piety outside the Eucharist there are eucharistic worship, eucharistic processions, especially on the feast of Corpus Christi, and private prayer before the most holy sacrament. These first spread in the Middle Ages. They have their meaning in the preparation and in the effects of the eucharistic celebration, not to say in communion itself (DS 1643; NR 573; SC 47). Understood in this context, these forms of eucharistic piety have a permanent importance in the Church (DS 1644). Thus they stand in need of cultivation and of revitalization in the life of every community and of every individual believer.

Thomas Aquinas beautifully expressed the central content of eucharistic faith in the famous Corpus Christi hymns *"Lauda Sion"*, *"Pange Lingua"*, and *"Adoro te devote"*. The latter (as translated by Gerard Manley Hopkins) says in part:

309–311

Godhead here in hiding, whom I do adore
Masked by these bare shadows, shape and nothing more,
See, Lord, at thy service low lies here a heart
Lost, all lost in wonder at the God thou art.

Seeing, touching, tasting are in thee deceived;
How says trusty hearing? that shall be believed;
What God's Son has told me, take for truth I do;
Truth himself speaks truly or there's nothing true.

3.3 The Eucharist: Memorial of the Sacrifice of Jesus Christ

The Kingdom of God that we anticipate in the eucharistic doxology and
that we now receive in the Eucharist as a foretaste has already dawned in
the Incarnation and in the death and Resurrection of Jesus Christ. The
presence of Jesus Christ in the Eucharist is not only the presence of his
person, but also the act of rendering present his work of salvation,
especially his sacrifice of the cross. That is what is meant when we speak of   157–160
the sacrifice of the Mass or of the *sacrificial character of the Eucharist*.

This sacrificial character is described in the *New Testament*, particularly
in Matthew's account of the words over the chalice: "For this is my blood,
the blood of the covenant, to be poured out in behalf of many for the
forgiveness of sins" (Mt 26:28). This declaration is very close to the Old
Testament story of Moses at the sacrifice of Sinai. He sprinkled half of the
sacrificial blood on the altar and half on the people, saying, "This is the
blood of the covenant which the Lord has made with you in accordance
with all these words of his" (Ex 24:8).

In order to understand these declarations more deeply, we have to see
that the Old Testament prophets and especially the New Testament
authors have fundamentally transformed the understanding of sacrifice as
it was understood in other religions. The Bible is not concerned with
external sacrificial gifts; these can be signs only of a personal surrender.
The Letter to the Hebrews has Christ say, upon his entrance into the
world, "Sacrifice and offering you did not desire, but a body you have
prepared for me; holocausts and sin offerings you took no delight in.
Then I said, 'As is written of me in the book, I have come to do your will,
O God' " (Heb 10:5–7; Ps 40:7–9; 51:18–19). Jesus does not offer the
Father some *thing* on the cross; rather, "he gave himself up as an offering"
(Eph 5:2). In contrast to the Old Testament, he does not offer many
sacrifices, but only a single sacrifice that holds once for all (Heb 9:11–28;
10:10, 14).

The Lord commissioned us to make present his one sacrifice in the
Eucharist: "Do this as a remembrance of me" (Lk 22:19; 1 Cor 11:24, 25).   264–265

By "remembrance" Holy Scripture does not mean merely recalling something to mind; it means the glorifying narration of God's great deeds, that become present here and now through the cultic celebration itself (Ex 13:3). In this way, Israel commemorated the deliverance from Egypt in the paschal meal. The New Testament memorial has an even deeper meaning. In the eucharistic sacrifice of praise through thanksgiving and under the signs of bread and wine, the Church commemorates liberation from the power of sin and death by the cross and Resurrection of Jesus. In celebrating the Eucharist, we proclaim the death of the Lord (1 Cor 11:26). In the Eucharist, Jesus' sacrifice of the cross, indeed his whole salvific work, becomes sacramentally present through word and sign.

The Eucharistic Prayer stresses this. Immediately after the account of the institution, the liturgically gathered community proclaims:

> Dying you destroyed our death,
> Rising you restored our life.
> Lord Jesus, come in glory.

And the priest says:

> Father, we celebrate the memory of Christ, your Son. We, your people and your ministers, recall his passion, his Resurrection from the dead, and his ascension into glory; and from the many gifts you have given us we offer to you, God of glory and majesty, this holy and perfect sacrifice. . . .

The *connection between the sacrifice of the cross and the sacrifice of the Mass* was in many ways no longer understood during the late Middle Ages; the understanding of the sacrifice of the Mass was further obscured by particular abuses. The Reformers were thus led to deny in principle the sacrificial character of the Eucharist. They thought that this doctrine undercut the uniqueness of the sacrifice of the cross; they thus called the Mass the greatest and most terrible abomination (Smalcaldian Articles) and an accursed idolatry (Heidelberg Catechism). The Council of Trent, which had to grapple with such massive attacks, succeeded in re-formulating the decisive central idea. The Council held fast to the uniqueness of the sacrifice of the cross. With the help of three concepts it expressed the relation of the sacrifice of the cross to the sacrifice of the Mass. The Sacrifice of the Mass is the sacramental *re-presentation, commemoration, and bestowal* of the sacrifice of the cross (DS 1740; NR 597). The Eucharist is not a new or independent sacrifice that replaces or somehow completes the sacrifice of the cross. It is the act of rendering sacramentally present the sacrifice of the cross, which has taken place once for all. "For it is one and the same sacrificial gift, and he is the same who now sacrifices through the

195–196

ministry of the priests and who offered himself then on the cross; only the manner of the sacrifice is different" (DS 1743; NR 599).

Today there are *ecumenical attempts* to remove the old polemics and misunderstandings in this question and to build up a mutual understanding. A renewed understanding of the biblical concept of memorial (*memoria*) as the act of rendering present a past deed of salvation has been helpful. This understanding, so central to the liturgical texts, was taken up anew by the Second Vatican Council (SC 47; AG 14).

The real ecumenical question is whether and to what extent the sacramental eucharistic act of rendering present the one unique sacrifice of Jesus Christ is also a *sacrifice of the Church*. In the Catholic understanding, Jesus Christ draws us into his sacrifice because we are his body united with him through baptism. Since the Christian community is placed by baptism   273–275 within the paschal mystery of Christ (SC 6), it can and should offer itself as a living and holy sacrifice (Rom 12:1; SC 48). So we pray: "May he make us an everlasting gift to you" (Third Eucharistic Prayer). In the Eucharist, the exalted Lord offers his sacrifice through the ministry of the liturgically gathered community and through its sacrifice of praise. The Eucharist is, "through, in, and with Christ", also a sacrifice of the Church. The sacrifice of thanks and praise by the gathered community is, so to speak, the sacramental form for the presence of Jesus Christ's one sacrifice. The Eucharist is the recapitulation, culmination, and fulfillment of the liturgy of Christian life; it is the highest expression of our worship of God as well as the source of the commitment of our lives to our brothers and sisters. This is possible only because we become in the Eucharist "one body, one spirit in Christ" (Third Eucharistic Prayer).

Because the sacramental act of making present the one sacrifice of Jesus Christ takes place within a liturgical celebration, the Eucharist is at once a sacrifice of praise and a *supplicatory, expiatory sacrifice*. It is observed "for the forgiveness of sins" (Mt 26:28). It wipes away daily sins and helps to avoid serious sins. The Eucharist can be an intercession for all. This practice of prayer is attested to in the ancient Church, not least in the ancient Christian catacombs. The eucharistic remembrance of the living and the dead continues in our own day. Every eucharistic sacrifice takes place within the "communion of saints". It can therefore be celebrated   253–255 representatively and as intercession for all members of the body of Christ. For the same reason, the Eucharist also commemorates the members of the body of Christ who have become partakers of heavenly bliss, the saints. If we celebrate the Eucharist in their honor, we do so by thanking God for the grace and glory he has bestowed on them. At the same time, we commend ourselves to their intercession and their protection.

3.4 The Eucharist: Sacrament of Unity and of Love

282–285   The celebration of the Eucharist, an anticipation of the heavenly marriage feast, is completed in the *eucharistic meal*. This aspect is clearer since the postconciliar liturgical reform. With the new position of the altar, which makes it possible to celebrate the Eucharist facing the people, the congregation can gather around the gifts as around a table. These spatial relations are symbols for the inner event of the Eucharist—the union of the individual with Jesus Christ and the union with one another in Christ.

  Reception of the Eucharist in communion brings about the *most intimate union with Jesus Christ*. When we consume the eucharistic species, Christ enters fully into us and we fully into him.

> "The man who feeds on my flesh
> and drinks my blood
> remains in me, and I in him" (Jn 6:56).

  What bodily food means for bodily life, the reception of the Eucharist does for spiritual life. It preserves, increases, renews, and delights (DS 1322; NR 566). Through communion fellowship with Christ, the new life of
299–300   grace is augmented in us, the diseases of sin are healed, and we are strengthened with the power to resist sin. At the same time, we receive in communion the pledge of heavenly bliss and of future immortality (Jn 6:54). So it is that we read in the Magnificat Antiphon of Corpus Christi, "O sacred meal, in which Christ is our food: memorial of his passion, fullness of grace, pledge of future glory" (SC 47).
267–269   Both the doctrine and the practice of the Church distinguish between *two ways of communion*. There is a simultaneously sacramental and spiritual communion, in which the body of Christ is received bodily and taken into the ready heart at the same time, and also a purely spiritual communion, in which there is union with Jesus Christ through the longing in faith for communion (DS 1648). Unworthy reception of communion by the sinner, whose heart is not prepared for union with Jesus Christ, works not salvation but judgment.

  For a spiritually fruitful reception of communion there must be an *examination of conscience* and a *careful preparation*. The Apostle Paul exhorts us:

> Whoever eats the bread or drinks the cup of the Lord unworthily sins against the body and blood of the Lord. A man should examine himself first; only then should he eat of the bread and drink of the cup.

He who eats and drinks without recognizing the body eats and drinks
a judgment on himself (1 Cor 11:27–29).

In the (Eastern) liturgy of St. John Chrysostom, the priest calls out to the
faithful before dispensing communion, "Holy things to the holy." A
Christian in the state of serious sin is obliged to receive the sacrament of
penance if possible before going to communion (DS 1646–47). So too any   300–304
celebration of the Eucharist begins with an act of penance for the forgiveness of everyday sins. Reconciliation with others is especially important
(Mt 5:23–24). Fasting before the reception of the Eucharist, the earlier
strictness of which has been much relaxed, also makes for worthy preparation. Whoever comes forward to receive answers the priest's words "The
body of Christ" with an "Amen". By this he says, "Yes, I believe; I am
ready in my faith to receive the body of Christ."

The reception of the Eucharist in communion is an *integral part of the eucharistic
celebration*. For that reason, the faithful should receive the body of the Lord after
the priest's communion from the same sacrificial celebration (SC 55). It is
emphatically recommended that the faithful receive holy communion in the
celebration of the Eucharist itself. For a good reason, however, communion can
also be given outside the eucharistic celebration. This is especially true for the
communion of the sick. A separate celebration of communion outside the celebration of the Eucharist, with or without a priest, should be limited to infrequent
cases of need.
    Historically there have been many changes in the *frequency of communion*. In the
early Church, Sunday communion was the rule. As a sharp decline in the
frequency of communion came about in the Middle Ages, the Fourth Lateran
Council (1215) prescribed communion once a year as a minimum. This ecclesial
law remains in force today (CIC can. 920). The Council of Trent, however,
wished the faithful to receive sacramental communion whenever they attended the
Eucharist. Pope Pius X introduced a radical change with his decrees on daily
communion (1905) and on the early communion of children (1910). They led to a
considerable increase in the frequency of communion. To be sure, a merely
quantitative increase in the reception of communion is not a meaningful pastoral
and spiritual goal. The goal must be the spiritually fruitful communion, for which
responsibility is assumed in faith. Its frequency will normally be connected with
the intensity of the rest of the Christian's religious life. For the great majority of
the faithful, Sunday communion will remain the pastorally practicable goal.
    Until the twelfth century, the usual practice was *communion under both species*.
In the thirteenth and fourteenth centuries, this practice gradually ceased. The
Bohemian Brethren and the Reformers traced communion under two species back
to a direct divine command and declared them necessary for salvation; the
Councils of Constance and Trent rejected this opinion with the argument that
Jesus Christ is wholly present under each of the two species (DS 1198–1200,

1725–34; NR 561, 588–95). The Second Vatican Council has again allowed communion under both species, without prejudice to the earlier dogmatic teaching (SC 55). It is permitted under special circumstances, for example, in religious communities or at occasions such as the baptism and confirmation of adults, nuptial masses, eucharistic celebrations at an ordination, viaticum, and spiritual exercises. With communion under both species, the sign of the eucharistic meal and its relation to the eschatological banquet in the Kingdom of God are much clearer. It is also more obvious that the New Covenant was formed in the blood of Jesus Christ.

The question of *communion in the hand or on the tongue* is not a fundamental problem. Up to the ninth century, it was usual to receive communion in the hand while standing. Reasons of reverence brought in the later practice of receiving it on the tongue. But communion in the hand can also be a sign of reverence. St. Cyril of Jerusalem shows as much when he likens the hands laid on top of one another to a throne ready for a king. We should not forget that we sin with the tongue just as with the hand or the heart. We should respect one another's decision in this matter.

The Eucharist signifies and effects not only the unity of the individual believer with Christ, but also the unity of all the faithful, the *unity of the Church*, in Jesus Christ. By taking part in the one eucharistic body of Christ, we are joined together into the one body of Christ which is the Church. "Because the loaf of bread is one, we, many though we are, are one body, for we all partake of the one loaf" (1 Cor 10:17). The Church Fathers saw the preparation of the bread from many grains and of the wine from many grapes as a symbol of the union of all the faithful in the one body of Christ effected through communion. Following St. Augustine, Church teaching describes the Eucharist as a "sign of unity" and as a "bond of love" (DS 1635; NR 567; SC 47; LG 26). St. Thomas Aquinas speaks of the Eucharist as the "sacrament of Church unity". It presupposes one's being within the unity of the Church, even as it signifies and deepens that unity.

Since the Eucharist is the sacrament of unity, the celebration of the Eucharist belongs to the entire assembled community. The faithful should not attend the celebration as mute spectators. They should *participate actively*. They should seek to understand the mystery of the Eucharist, to take part in the liturgical action consciously, devoutly, and actively, and to make the latter inwardly their own by offering themselves as a sacrifice to God (SC 48). From the doctrine that the Eucharist is the sacrament of unity it also follows that it can *be celebrated only by a validly ordained priest* (DS 802, 1771; NR 920, 713). The priestly office is a ministry of unity. Only the priest is authorized by his holy orders to speak the words in the name and in the person of Jesus Christ: "This is my body", "This is the cup of my blood." Besides the priestly ministry, there should also be,

229–233

226–228

232–233;
233–234

where possible, *other eucharistic ministries* at the celebration of the Eucharist —such as the ministries of deacon, lector, acolyte, and cantor. This unity of the priestly ministry and of the active participation of the community is expressed in the Eucharistic Prayer: "Father, we celebrate the memory of Christ your Son. We, your people and your ministers . . ." (First Eucharistic Prayer).

The eucharistic celebration of an individual congregation always takes place essentially in *communion with the entire Church.* The concrete criterion of communion in the Church is unity with the local bishop, who is himself united with the other bishops and with the Roman pontiff, the center of Catholic unity. This connection is expressed in the Eucharistic Prayer when the names of the local bishop and of the pope are mentioned. Whoever celebrates the Eucharist outside of this communion, cutting himself off and separating himself from it, turns altar against altar, as the Fathers say. Rupture of eucharistic communion is rupture of Church communion; conversely, *eucharistic and Church communion* go together indissolubly. The martyr-bishop Ignatius of Antioch warns us, "Be mindful to celebrate only one Eucharist." "Remain loyal to the bishop and to the presbyters and to the deacons. . . . Do nothing without the bishop!" "The eucharistic celebration that takes place under the bishop or one commissioned by him is dependable."

The eucharistic celebration presupposes *reconciliation and communion* within the celebrating congregation, even as it fosters them. We see this above all in the liturgical sign of peace. For the same reason, the eucharistic table fellowship in the ancient Church was extended into a community meal fellowship (*agape*). This custom is rightly being taken up again today in different forms according to different circumstances. The unity of the Church effected by the Eucharist is also a sign and an instrument of the unity of mankind. The Eucharist is *bread for the life of the world* (Jn 6:33). The Eucharist must take effect beyond the parish, in the world. We see this in the intercessions for all, especially for the needy, and also in collections for poorer parishes and for the poor of the world. These liturgical elements have been present in the Eucharist since ancient times. The celebration of the Eucharist prepares us and sends us out to the ministry of love and to deeds of reconciliation among all. We cannot share the eucharistic bread if we are not ready to share our daily bread as well and to advocate a just and fraternal order in the world. The Eucharist is the source of Christian ministry in the world.

From what has been said we can infer the answer to the difficult problem of *eucharistic communion between the separated churches and church communities.* Today we experience this separation at the table of the Lord as painful. The pain is acute

221–223

246–247;
250–252

231–233

217–222;
223–224;
227–228

232–234

for those who live in a denominationally mixed marriage or who are active in ecumenical circles. In fact, if the Eucharist is the sacrament of unity and of love, then separation at the table of the Lord represents a scandal that we must do all in our power to overcome. On the other hand, the Eucharist is not ours to command. As a legacy of the Lord, it is a "mystery of faith" that presupposes a common faith; it is a sacrament of unity tied to the unity of the Church. Where the common faith or the unity of the Church is lacking, a common participation at the table of the Lord is not possible in principle.

Yet since the Eucharist is both a sign of unity and a source of grace (UR 8; LG 3, 11), the Church can admit individual separated brothers and sisters to this sacrament when they are in danger of death or in other *states of serious need*. They must be unable to reach their own church and must request it on their own; they must also manifest the Catholic faith in relation to the sacrament of the Eucharist and be correctly disposed (CIC can. 844). In such difficult situations, one must weigh in conscience the aspects of the Eucharist as sign of full church communion and as means of salvation for the individual. In doing so, one must seek to avoid all scandal, which is entirely contrary to the essence of the Eucharist.

The question of *reciprocity* in admission to communion brings up additional problems. With the Eastern churches, which preserve a valid episcopal and priestly office, reciprocity is possible. For that reason, Catholic Christians for whom it is physically or morally impossible to receive communion in the Catholic Church may receive it in the Orthodox church (OE 26–28; UR 15). Since the Protestant churches and church communities have not preserved the original and complete reality of the eucharistic mystery because of the lack or the incompleteness of the sacrament of orders (UR 22), reciprocity is not possible (CIC can. 844).

Many Christians today have difficulties with this. But this painful situation cannot be solved by contrived liturgies or a merely pragmatic approach. Hasty solutions could take away any incentive to seek full church communion. Only serious effort and persevering prayer can help. We can overcome the problem at its root only by struggling to obtain unity in faith so far as humanly possible. If we have the strength to bear this painful situation in the spirit of prayer and penance, and if at the same time we do everything possible to take steps toward reconciliation, then we may hope that the grace of unity at the Lord's table will be bestowed on us in the not-too-distant future.

Ecumenical liturgies of the word, in which we as Christians seek unity, confess our common faith, and pray for one another and all men, help us on the way to eucharistic communion. Such ecumenical liturgies of the word cannot replace the Sunday eucharistic celebration. Still, they should belong where possible to the liturgical practice of every community (UR 8; *Gem. Synode, Gottesdienst* 5.2).

3.5 The Structure, Elements, and Parts of the Eucharistic Celebration

Understood most simply, the celebration of the Eucharist has two parts, the liturgy of the word and the eucharistic celebration proper. The two parts are so closely linked that they form a single liturgical celebration (SC 56). In the Eucharist, the table of both the word of God and of the body of the Lord is prepared (DV 21). A liturgical beginning and conclusion for the eucharistic celebration are added to these parts. The whole then takes on the following structure:

A. *The Opening*: entrance, greeting, general confession of guilt, *Kyrie*, *Gloria*, and opening prayer. This part introduces and prepares for the whole celebration.

B. *The liturgy of the word*. The core of the liturgy of the word consists of the scriptural readings with the responsorial psalm. The homily, the confession of faith, and the intercessions develop this part and conclude it. In the readings, which are interpreted by the homily, God speaks to his people and nourishes their life in the Spirit. Jesus Christ himself is present in his word in the midst of the faithful. The responsorial psalm is the congregation's response; in the Alleluia verse, the congregation hails the Lord present in the proclamation of the Gospel. In the confession of faith, the congregation assents to the word of God as heard in the readings and in the homily. In the intercessions, the congregation exercises its priestly office by praying for all men, especially for the needy.

C. *The eucharistic celebration proper*. This consists of three parts: the preparation of the gifts, the Eucharistic Prayer, and communion.

At the *preparation of the gifts*, bread, wine, and water are brought to the altar, accompanied by song and prayer.

The *Eucharistic Prayer*, the prayer of thanksgiving and sanctification, is the whole celebration's center and summit. The most important element is thanksgiving for the entire work of redemption, expressed most strongly in the Preface. In the *Sanctus*, the entire congregation unites itself to the song of praise sung by the heavenly powers. In the *Epiclesis*, the Church asks the Father to send the Holy Spirit upon the gifts so that they may become the body and blood of Jesus Christ. In the Consecration the body and blood of Christ become present under the forms of bread and wine through the words and actions of Christ. His sacrifice offered once for all on the cross is made sacramentally present. In the following *Anamnesis* (remembering), the Church commemorates the passion, the Resurrection, and ascension of Jesus Christ. Then it offers the sacrificial gifts to the Father through Jesus Christ in the Spirit. In the commemoration and intercession, it expresses its observance of the Eucharist in communion with the whole Church and the entire communion of saints. The closing doxology expresses the glorification of God once again in summary form. This is confirmed and concluded by the acclamation of the congregation.

Communion is introduced by the Lord's Prayer. The sign of peace and the breaking of the bread show that we partake of the one bread and are thus bound together in the one body of Christ. For that reason, the accompanying *Agnus Dei* also ends with the petition "Grant us peace." Communion itself ends with a concluding prayer, a petition for our fruitful reception.

D. *The conclusion*. The priest's greeting and blessing, then the dismissal, conclude the eucharistic celebration and send the participants forth to their everyday Christian lives in thanksgiving.

4. The Sacrament of Penance

4.1 Personal Penance

Through baptism and confirmation we become a new creation. Through the Eucharist we are united in the most intimate way to Jesus Christ and to one another. Nevertheless, we often experience in painful ways that we fall short in our following of Jesus Christ, that we even place ourselves in contradiction with what we as Christians should be and do according to God's will. Instead of letting ourselves be led by the Spirit of Christ, we often follow the "spirit of this world". Yet God's mercy is greater than all sin and guilt. He offers even those who have fallen into serious sin after baptism *another possibility for a change of life and for grace*. This is the sacrament of penance. The Church Fathers often speak of it as a second, toilsome baptism, a second plank of salvation after the shipwreck of sin.

The attitude toward the sacrament of penance is now in a *deep crisis*. There are many causes for this, including many misunderstandings and many unhappy experiences at confession. Above all, though, many today have difficulties in recognizing their own failure as guilt before God, as sin. Many do not even speak of personal sin any more. Too often we look for guilt and failure, if we do so at all, only in "the others", in our opponents, in the past, in nature, in our disposition, in the environment, or in circumstances. But when man no longer acknowledges his responsibility for himself and for his deeds, humanity itself is in danger.

123–125 This situation is all the more alarming because *Jesus'* call to conversion is at the center of his message about the coming Kingdom of God. According to Mark, the call to repentance belongs to Jesus' fundamental proclamation: "Reform your lives and believe in the gospel!" (Mk 1:15). Conversion and penance must be part of every Christian life. "Unless you change and become like little children, you will not enter the Kingdom of God" (Mt 18:3). According to Jesus, all need this conversion, even the just who think they do not need it. "If we say, 'We are free of the guilt of sin', we deceive ourselves; the truth is not to be found in us" (1 Jn 1:8).

When Jesus speaks of a conversion, he is thinking chiefly—and in the Old Testament tradition of prophecy—not of external works, such as penance in sackcloth and ashes with fastings, mortifications, weepings, and lamentings, nor is he thinking only of inner self-examination, reflection, and a change of opinions. All these can be meaningful forms for expressing a conversion. But Jesus tells us that we should not make a show of our fasting through a somber face and a gloomy appearance (Mt 6:16).

What is decisive in a conversion happens *in a man's heart*, in the center and the depths of his person.

> Yet even now, says the Lord,
> return to me with your whole heart,
> with fasting, and weeping, and mourning;
> Rend your hearts, not your garments,
> and return to the Lord, your God (Joel 2:12–13).

This conversion must take effect in doing good and in the concrete fulfillment of God's will, especially the demands of justice and love. There is no returning to God without returning to one's brothers and sisters. So the prophet exhorts us:

> Wash yourselves clean!
> Put away your misdeeds from before my eyes;
> cease doing evil; learn to do good.
> Make justice your aim: redress the wronged,
> hear the orphan's plea, defend the widow (Is 1:16–17).

For Jesus, just as for the Old Testament prophets and John the Baptist, penance is essential in a real conversion. It is *man's fundamental change of direction, a turning away from evil and turning toward God*. In this conversion, man must renounce the deceptive idols with which he thought to secure and fulfill his existence; he must seek the support and substance of his life in God alone. Conversion and faith are two sides of one and the same thing.

Of course, even the prophets encountered the dullness and hardness of man's heart. Any conversion requires that God bestow a new heart on man (Jer 24:7; 31:33). Conversion is not our work or our achievement. It is God's gift. It is the *grace of being allowed to begin anew*. God must first turn to man in gracious mercy before man can turn toward God. Our conversion does not mean bringing God around and conciliating him. On the contrary, it is always a response to God's preceding reconciliation. The definitive act of reconciliation happened when Jesus shed his blood "on behalf of many for the forgiveness of sins" (Mt 26:28). In Jesus Christ, in his cross and Resurrection, God has reconciled the world with himself once for all (2 Cor 5:18–19), establishing peace through the blood of Christ (Col 1:20).

Such a conversion happens fundamentally in *baptism*, which is the sacrament of changed life and of the forgiveness of sins (Acts 2:38). Baptism means a renunciation of evil and a turning toward the salvation that God bestows on us through Jesus Christ in the Holy Spirit. So baptism bestows on us once for all the new life in Christ, which must lead

271–273

to our resisting sin and living for God (Rom 6:6–14). Conversion or, as we also say, penance is thus a *constant task*; it characterizes the whole life of the baptized Christian. Of course, the Church early recognized that even the baptized succumb to temptation and fall away. She also knew, of course, that God is rich in mercy (Eph 2:4), bestowing the possibility of a new conversion on any sinner who is ready to change. St. Ambrose says that in the Church there are "water and tears: the water of baptism and the tears of penance". Since the Church as a whole is "at once holy and in need of purification, [she] follows constantly the path of penance and renewal" (LG 8).

The daily penance of Christians takes *many forms*. Holy Scripture and the Fathers emphasize three of them: fasting, praying, and giving alms (Tob 12:8; Mt 6:1–18). They also name reconciliation with one's neighbor, tears of penance, concern for the salvation of one's neighbor, intercession of the saints, and love. The living Tradition of the Church has added the reading of Holy Scripture and the praying of the Our Father. There are also other faith-inspired ways for carrying out a change in one's daily life—for example, change of attitude, common discussion about guilt and sin, gestures of reconciliation, brotherly confession, and brotherly correction. Even certain forms of leading a spiritual life, such as the examination of conscience, the monastic "chapter of faults", and discussion with a spiritual director, are forms of expression of penance. Nor should we forget the ethical consequences of a new orientation in life: change of one's lifestyle, asceticism and manifold renunciation, works of charity, and works of mercy, atonement, and reparation.

All these forms of everyday penance must come together in the common *celebration of the Eucharist*. It is the "sacrifice which has made our peace with you" (Third Eucharistic Prayer), since it is the re-presentation of the sacrifice of Jesus Christ offered once for all. Assisting at Mass and especially receiving communion bestow forgiveness for everyday sins and preserve us from serious sins (DS 1638; NR 570). We are reminded of this by the fact that the celebration of the Eucharist begins with an act of penance. There are also other liturgical forms for the forgiveness of sins. Examples are the penance service, reflection and prayer, intercession, the Church's liturgy of the hours, and reading and meditation on Scripture.

The *penitential seasons and penitential days* of the Church (Advent, Lent, Fridays) are special focal points of the Church's penitential practice (SC 109–10). These times are particularly suited for spiritual exercises, days of recollection, penitential liturgies, fasting, and charitable deeds.

All the forms of penance enable the sinner to let himself be formed anew by the Spirit of Jesus Christ and to express this Spirit both in a personal penitential attitude and in works of penance. Every form of Christian penance must be moved at least incipiently by faith, hope, and love. So they all share a *basic structure*. Its elements are insight into one's guilt, contrition for the deed committed or omitted, confession of guilt, willingness to change one's life (including making reparation of damages), asking for forgiveness, receiving the gift of reconciliation, thanks for the forgiveness imparted, and living a life of new obedience. We travel the road of penance not as individuals, but in community with all members of the Church. This ecclesial dimension is best expressed in the sacrament of penance, where personal penance is sacramentally concentrated.

4.2 Sacramental Penance

The Gospels tell us that Jesus forgave individuals their sins: "Your sins are forgiven" (Mk 2:5; Lk 7:48). He also gave this authority "to men" (Mt 9:8). The Church as a whole is to be a sign and an instrument of reconciliation. But this authority is given in a special way to the apostolic office which has been entrusted with the *"ministry of reconciliation"* (2 Cor 5:18). The apostle has been sent as an ambassador "for Christ, God as it were appealing through us. We implore you . . . be reconciled to God!" (2 Cor 5:20). The Church traces the authority to forgive sins granted to the ecclesiastical office back to the Risen Lord himself:

> "Receive the Holy Spirit.
> If you forgive men's sins,
> they are forgiven them;
> if you hold them bound,
> they are held bound" (Jn 20:22–23).

With Jesus himself, the forgiveness of sins always had a *communal aspect* also. Jesus reconciles sinners to God by taking them up into the meal fellowship with himself and with one another. The sinner isolates himself from God and from his brothers; through his sin, the community of God's people is disrupted and his own life in holiness is injured. That is why the sinner is excluded from full communion with the Church (1 Cor 5:1–13; 2 Cor 2:5–11; 7:10–13). He can no longer partake fully of the Eucharist, the sacrament of unity and of love. In penance, the person changing his life must travel again along the way by which reconciliation first came to him. He must reconcile himself with his brothers in order to attain a new communion with God. Conversely, through the forgiveness of God, we are, "at the same time, reconciled with the Church", whom we have wounded by our sins and who cooperates with our conversion through love, example, and prayer (LG 11). The communal structure and

293–296

ecclesial dimension of penance is best expressed in Jesus' words to Peter: "I will entrust to you the keys of the Kingdom of heaven. Whatever you declare bound on earth shall be bound in heaven; whatever you declare loosed on earth shall be loosed in heaven" (Mt 16:19). These words hold for the Church as a whole (Mt 18:18). The words *"binding and loosing"* mean that whoever is excluded (to bind is to banish) from the community is also excluded from communion with God. Whoever is taken up into the community again (the banishment is removed, "loosed") is also taken up by God into communion with him. *Renewed reconciliation with the Church is the way to reconciliation with God.* This was well expressed in the public penance of the ancient Church. So too the formula of sacramental absolution that has been obligatory since 1975 says, "Through the ministry of the Church, may God give you pardon and peace."

In its details, the sacrament of penance has had a long, complicated, and varied history. But the *basic structure of this sacrament* has always been twofold. Penance consists, on the one hand, of the acts of a changed life made possible by grace: contrition, confession, and satisfaction. On the other hand, it consists of the *action of the Church*. The ecclesiastical community under the leadership of the bishop and of the priests offers forgiveness of sins in the name of Jesus Christ, laying down the necessary forms of satisfaction, praying for the sinner, and doing penance on his behalf, in order finally to impart to him full ecclesial communion and the forgiveness of his sins. The sacrament of penance is at once a thoroughly personal, individual act and an ecclesial, liturgical celebration. So the Council of Trent teaches that the actions of the penitent in contrition, confession, and satisfaction are "as it were, the matter of this sacrament", while priestly absolution is its form (DS 1673; NR 647–48). The *fruit of this sacrament* is reconciliation with God and with the Church. It is often connected with peace and joy of conscience and with great consolation (DS 1674–75; NR 649).

We must still describe the individual elements of the sacrament of penance more exactly. For the penitent, *contrition* occupies the first place. Contrition is the "pain of soul and the detestation of sins committed, with the resolution to sin no more from then on". Contrition is called "perfect" when it is motivated by the love bestowed by God (contrition out of love). It has the power to forgive venial sins; it also brings forgiveness of serious sins when it is connected with the firm resolution to make a sacramental confession. Contrition is called "imperfect" when it is motivated by a consideration of the hideousness of sin or by fear of eternal damnation and other punishments (contrition out of fear). Such an unsettling of one's conscience can be a beginning that is later perfected by the gift of grace, especially by the imparting of the forgiveness of sin in the sacrament of penance. Of itself, though, contrition out of fear does not have the power to bring forgiveness of sins (DS 1676–78; NR 650–51).

Confession of guilt, even considered in purely human terms, has a liberating and reconciling effect. By confession, man owns up to his sinful past, assumes responsibility for it, and opens himself anew for God and for the community of the Church, thus opening the way for a new future. The Church teaches that confession is an essential and irreplaceable part of the sacrament of penance, by which the penitent subjects himself to God's gracious judgment (DS 1679, 1706; NR 652, 665). For that reason, it is necessary to confess those serious (or mortal) sins that the penitent remembers after careful examination of his conscience; the confession must adequately describe their concrete situation according to number, kind, and circumstances (DS 1707; NR 666). According to Church law, "all the faithful who have reached the age of discretion are bound faithfully to confess their grave sins at least once a year" (CIC can. 989). Although the confession of daily (or venial) sins, which do not exclude us from communion with God, is not necessary, the Church recommends it. This so-called devotional confession is a great help for personal formation of conscience and growth in the spiritual life. It should be included at least in the observance of the Church's penitential seasons.

In *satisfaction*, we make appropriate reparation for the damage caused by sin and for any scandal caused by it (e.g., restitution of stolen goods, restoration of another's good reputation). At the same time, satisfaction gives us practice in a new way of life; it is a remedy against weakness. Penance should correspond so far as possible to the gravity and kind of sins. It can include prayer, sacrifice and renunciation, service to one's neighbor, and works of mercy. Satisfaction is not some arbitrary act by which we earn forgiveness. It is rather the fruit and sign of a penance already effected and bestowed by the Spirit of God.

The *priestly absolution* in the sacrament of penance is something more 312–313 than a proclamation of the gospel of the forgiveness of sins or a declaration that God has forgiven sins. It receives the sinner back into full ecclesial communion. And so it is a judicial act, as the Church's teaching says, and belongs only to the one who is able to act in the name of Jesus Christ for the whole Church community (DS 1685, 1709–10; NR 668–69). The sacrament of penance is, of course, a gracious judgment in which God, the merciful Father, turns lovingly to the sinner through the death and Resurrection of Jesus Christ in the Holy Spirit. The confessor is equally judge and physician. He should act as a father and a brother. He represents Jesus Christ, who shed his blood on the cross for the sinner. That is why the confessor should proclaim and interpret the message of forgiveness for the penitent, should help him to a new life by counsel, should pray for him, do penance on his behalf, and above all bestow on him the forgiveness of sins in the name of Jesus Christ.

The new order for the "celebration of penance" (1974) provides *three forms of the sacramental penitential celebration*.

The celebration of reconciliation for individuals. Even this form should have a certain liturgical shape—a greeting by the priest, reading of a scriptural text, confession of sin, imposition of penance, prayer, priestly absolution, concluding doxology, and liturgical dismissal with priestly blessing. If pastoral reasons require it, the priest can omit or abbreviate some parts of the rite. The following parts, however, must always be preserved in their entirety: the confession of sin and the acceptance of the imposition of penance, the summons to contrition, the formula of absolution, and the dismissal. If there is danger of death, it is enough for the priest to say the essential words of absolution: "I absolve you from your sins in the name of the Father, and of the Son, and of the Holy Spirit." In practice, however, this renewed form of the sacrament of penance has not yet been generally implemented.

The communal celebration of reconciliation with confession and absolution of individuals. In this form, individual confession and individual absolution are connected with a common penitential celebration as preparation and as common thanksgiving. The individual confession is thus embedded in a liturgy of the word with scriptural reading and homily, common examination of conscience and general confession of sin, praying of the Our Father and common thanksgiving. This common celebration expresses more clearly the ecclesial dimension of penance.

The communal celebration of reconciliation with general confession and general absolution. This form is permitted only when there is grave necessity, such as danger of death. It can also be used when there are not sufficient confessors to hear the confession of individuals in a fitting way within an appropriate amount of time, so that the faithful through no fault of their own would have to go without the grace of the sacrament and holy communion for a long time. This form presupposes the resolution to confess serious sins individually as soon as possible. The decision on whether there is grave necessity belongs to the diocesan bishop, in consultation with the other members of the bishops' conference (CIC can. 961).

We should distinguish *penitential liturgies* in the narrower sense from these three sacramental forms of penance. The liturgies are an expression and a renewal of the conversion that took place at baptism. The people of God celebrates them in order to hear the word of God, which calls us to a change and renewal of life and which announces the redemption from sin through the death and Resurrection of Jesus Christ. A penitential celebration usually includes an opening (song, greeting, and prayer), readings from Holy Scripture (with interspersed songs or silences), a homily, a common examination of conscience, and a prayer for the forgiveness of sins (especially the Our Father). Sacramental absolution is not included. These penitential liturgies should thus not be confused with the celebration of the sacrament of penance. Still, they are very useful for conversion and purification of the heart. They can foster the spirit of Christian penance, help the faithful to prepare for their individual confessions, deepen the sense of the communal character of penance, and lead children to penance. Such services can bring forgiveness of venial sins when there is a genuine spirit of conversion and of loving contrition. They should therefore have a place in the life of every community, especially during the Church's penitential seasons.

4.3 Indulgences

The Church's doctrine and practice of indulgences is closely connected with the sacrament of penance. An "indulgence" is the remission of the temporal punishment due to sins, the guilt of which has already been forgiven. An indulgence presupposes a personal conversion, the reception of the sacrament of penance (if serious sin is present), and the reception of communion (in the case of a plenary indulgence). An indulgence is granted by the Church, from the treasury of the merits of Jesus Christ and the saints, to those who perform certain assigned works (such as certain prayers or visits to pilgrimage Churches).

The doctrine and practice of indulgences is difficult for many Christians today to understand. In order to understand it more deeply, one must grasp its historical roots and its greater context.

Generally speaking, there have been indulgences in the Church from the beginning. As regards details, indulgences have a long *history*. In the *ancient Church*, the intercession of confessors (those who had borne great sufferings in the persecutions) played a great role. Since the temporal punishments for sin were "served" in the ancient Church by punishments of a specified length, indulgences were often spoken of in terms of "days". In their present form, indulgences date from the eleventh century. Since the *early Middle Ages*, they have often been connected with certain works of piety—participation in a crusade, pilgrimages to holy sites, certain prayers or good works. Examples are the Portiuncula Indulgence, the Jubilee Indulgence on the occasion of a Holy Year, and the All Souls Indulgence.

Indulgences were also often connected with financial donations for ecclesiastical purposes. This led to great abuses, especially in the Middle Ages. These abuses were an occasion for the beginning of the Reformation. In consequence, the *Council of Trent* thoroughly reformed the practice of indulgences and eliminated   195–196
the abuses. It maintained in principle, however, that indulgences are exceedingly beneficial for the Christian people. It therefore condemned those who declared indulgences to be useless or who denied the Church the right to confer indulgences. The Council wished rather to limit indulgences according to the ancient, proven custom of the Church, and to exclude all acquisitiveness (DS 1835; NR 688–89). A doctrinal deepening of the teaching on indulgences and a practical *renewal for the present* were achieved by Pope Paul VI in his Apostolic Constitution on the Revision of Indulgences (1967).

For a deeper understanding of the *doctrine of indulgences* underlying the practice, one must first be clear that *sin has a double consequence*. Serious sin breaks communion with God and forfeits eternal life (the eternal punishment of sin). But it also wounds and poisons the union of man with God, as well as man's life in the human community (the temporal punishment of sin). Neither punishment of sin is "dictated" externally by God; both follow intrinsically from the very essence of sin. The remission of the eternal punishment of sin is effected in the forgiveness of the guilt and the restoration of communion with God. Yet the temporal consequences of sin remain. The Christian must strive to accept these temporal punishments of sin from God's hand in patient endurance of suffering, distress, toil, and finally in conscious acceptance of death. He should struggle to throw off the "old man" and to put on the "new man" through works of mercy and of love, as well as through prayer and different forms of penance (Eph 4:22–24).

The Church offers the Christian another path to tread in the gracious communion of the Church. The Christian who purifies and sanctifies himself with the help of God's grace does not stand alone. He is a member of the body of Christ. In Christ, *all Christians are one great communion*. "If one member suffers, all members suffer with it" (1 Cor 12:26). What is called the treasury of the Church or the treasury of grace is communal participation in the goods of salvation that Jesus Christ and the saints with the help of his grace have earned. In granting an indulgence, the Church speaks on behalf of the individual Christian with her authority to bind and loose as conferred on her by Jesus Christ. The Church authoritatively assigns the penitent a portion of the treasury of merits of Christ and the saints for the remission of sin's temporal punishment. In doing so, the Church wants not only to aid the individual, but also to spur him on to works of piety, penance, and love. Since the faithful departed who are in a state of purification are also members of the one communion of saints, we can support them by way of intercession as they suffer the temporal punishment for their sin.

In Paul VI's Apostolic Constitution mentioned above, the *essence of the treasury of the Church* is interpreted very fittingly. "It is not like a sum of goods which were amassed in the course of the centuries after the manner of material riches. Rather, it consists in the infinite and inexhaustible value that the atonement and merits of Christ, the Lord, have before God. . . . The treasury of the Church is Christ the Redeemer himself insofar as the satisfaction and merits of his work of redemption have their permanence and validity in him. Furthermore, the truly immeasurable, inexhaustible, and always new value that the prayers and good works of the Blessed Virgin Mary and of all the saints possess before God also belong to this treasury. They have followed in the footsteps of Christ, the Lord; by his grace, they have sanctified themselves and completed the work entrusted to them by the Father. Thus have they worked their own salvation and contributed also to the salvation of their brothers in the unity of the mystical body" (NR 691).

A particular problem is posed by what is called a *plenary indulgence*, which is the remission of all the temporal consequences of sin. If it is to be effective in this perfect way, it presupposes a perfect disposition of a kind very infrequently found, except when a Christian gives his whole life back into the hands of God, his Creator and Redeemer, in the hour of death. The sacrament of the anointing of the sick and the indulgence for the dying have their place here.

211–213;
253–255

347–349

5. Anointing of the Sick

Sickness and pain have always been among the greatest problems of human life. Sickness is more than a temporary disturbance of health; it affects most inwardly the whole man, body and soul. In sickness, man experiences his powerlessness and limitedness. He is torn out of normal life, is condemned to inactivity, and experiences how little we can control our lives. This experience leads to isolation, depression, worry, anxiety, and even to despair. On the other hand, sickness can help bring a person to a greater maturity. It helps us to attain deeper insights into what is superficial and transitory in our lives as opposed to what is of permanent importance. Still, the threat to life in sickness is an evil that man instinctively resists. Ultimately, sickness is a herald and reminder of death. The earthly life that is diminished and threatened in sickness is definitively taken from us at death. We first radically experience human frailty and limitedness in the face of death when it stands before us more clearly in sickness.

Holy Scripture sees in man's being threatened by sickness a sign that he lives in a world disturbed by sin, a world that has not been led back under God's full lordship. Nevertheless, the gospel refuses to see sickness as an immediate punishment for personal guilt. The Gospels tell us rather that *God wills life*. They depict Jesus as the great opponent and vanquisher of sickness (Mt 4:24; Acts 10:38, among others). The Gospels see in Jesus' healings of the sick a sign that God's lordship is dawning and that its coming brings salvation for the whole man, in body and soul. Holy Scripture tells us that God loves not only the healthy, but especially the sick, who can no longer achieve anything in the eyes of the world. He is particularly close to them. Jesus himself fulfilled the text of the prophet Isaiah: "It was our infirmities that he bore, our sufferings that he endured" (Is 53:4).

In the commission to "cure the sick" (Mt 10:8), Jesus passed on to his disciples his care for the sick. In the discourse on judgment, Jesus counts visiting the sick among the works of love for one's neighbor that decide a man's eternal destiny. Indeed, Jesus identifies himself with the sick (Mt 25:36, 43). The *obligation to visit the sick and to care for them* has had great importance in the Church's history. During antiquity and the Middle Ages, the Church attempted to follow Jesus' example and commission by way of hospitals, homes for the aged, nursing orders, charitable associations, and pastoral ministry to the sick. The Church never saw any opposition between medical care for the sick and spiritual care for them; the two belonged together. God wills the life of the whole man, body and soul. For that reason, doctors and all who devote themselves in any way to the care of the sick fulfill Jesus' commission in their own way.

The preeminent sacramental means of caring for the sick is the *sacrament of the anointing of the sick*. It is founded on Jesus' whole ministry for the poor. It is suggested more explicitly in the account of the sending out of the Twelve: "They expelled many demons, anointed the sick with oil, and worked many cures" (Mk 6:13). The practice of anointing developed in the primitive Christian communities, as the Letter of James tells us.

> Is there anyone sick among you? He should ask for the presbyters of the church. They in turn are to pray over him, anointing him with oil in the Name (of the Lord). This prayer uttered in faith will reclaim the one who is ill, and the Lord will restore him to health. If he has committed any sins, forgiveness will be his (Jas 5:14–15).

The *prayer* for deliverance from sickness has a long tradition stretching back into the Old Testament (Ps 6; 22; 28; 38, among others). Before his passion, Jesus himself struggled with his Father in prayer (Mk 14:36 par.; Heb 5:7). Jesus also taught his disciples to pray with childlike trust for all their needs and promised that they would be heard. The Church's prayer uttered by its official representatives in the name of Jesus may be certain of a special hearing. The symbolic gesture of *laying on hands* was practiced by Jesus himself with the sick (Mk 6:5; Mt 8:3; Lk 4:40). He entrusted it to his disciples (Mk 16:18), who certainly practiced it (Acts 9:12, 17; 28:8). By itself, this laying on of hands means different things. As a gesture of human and Christian devotion, as a sign of sympathy, of comfort, and of encouragement, it is a gesture of blessing that symbolizes the salvation bestowed by the sacrament. *Anointing with oil* can also have other meanings. For our particular context, what matters is that oil was a widespread remedy and cosmetic in antiquity, as it still is. So far as we can learn from the Gospels, Jesus himself did not anoint with oil, but he used other symbols, in some cases by touching the sick with saliva (Mk 7:32–33; 8:23; Jn 9:6). His disciples did anoint the sick with oil, even during his lifetime (Mk 6:13). If the primitive Christian communities took up this custom, it was not as some miracle drug that worked magically. The anointing is connected with prayer in the name of the Lord; it points symbolically to the deliverance and raising up of the sick person by God.

The two words *"deliverance"* and *"raising up"* here mean the healing of the whole man, body and soul. The Church can and should pray for the bodily health of the sick person as well. Part of this well-being of the whole man is the *forgiveness of sins*; sin means a turning away from God as the final salvation of man. The *elders*, the presbyters, are exhorted to visit, to pray for, to lay hands on, and to anoint the sick because the sick person is not on the margin of the community, but is rather united to the Church in a particularly intense way. The devotion and intercession of the community belong to him in a special way.

The *Church's Tradition* has richly developed the text from the Letter of James. The Tradition has seen it as establishing the sacrament of the anointing of the sick. This sacrament has, of course, undergone many far-reaching changes in the course of history. The most important was the practice of having the bishop consecrate the oil of the sick at the chrism mass on Holy Thursday. After this, there came the understanding (with the Carolingian period) that the sacrament of the anointing of the sick was a sacrament of the dying. It was "extreme unction", which was usually administered only to one in immediate danger of death. The faithful often took it as a death sentence. This cannot be described as simply an aberration, since sickness and death are so closely connected. Nevertheless, this development did curtail the original meaning as we encounter it in James (Jas 5:14–15). The Second Vatican Council has restored the sacrament's original and comprehensive meaning (SC 73–75; LG 11). In 1972, Paul VI enacted the renewal of the sacramental form, as encouraged by the Council, for the Latin Church.

Following the postconciliar liturgical renewal, the anointing of the sick is no longer confined to a "deathbed visit". Its context is visiting the sick in the spirit of the gospel and of pastoral ministry to them. The *recipients of the sacrament* are Christians in a dangerously weakened state of health because of grave illness or the infirmities resulting from old age. The sacrament may be repeated when the sick person, having regained his strength after a previous anointing, is again in serious danger or when further deterioration ensues from the same illness. The sacrament itself is administered in the context of a *liturgical celebration*. This includes an opening, a liturgy of the word, and a sacramental liturgy. In its renewed form, the sacramental liturgy corresponds exactly to the description in the Letter of James. It begins with a silent imposition of hands by the priest and with a praise of the consecrated oil that dates back to the fourth century. (If need be, it can begin with a consecration of the oil.) The sacramental sign is specified in Paul VI's Apostolic Constitution:

> The sacrament of the anointing of the sick is administered to those whose state of health is dangerously weakened, by anointing them on the forehead and on the hands with duly consecrated olive oil and saying the following words: "Through this holy anointing may the Lord in his love and mercy help you with the grace of the Holy Spirit. Amen. May the Lord who frees you from sin save you and raise you up. Amen."

The double anointing, on the forehead and on the hands, is meant to express that the sacrament is intended for the sick man in his totality as a thinking and acting person. The *sacrament's gift of grace* is fittingly

69–72;
183–187

symbolized in the anointing with oil; in Scripture anointing is a symbol of the gift of the Holy Spirit. Jesus Christ is the One anointed with the Spirit, the "Christ" without qualification. The true effect of the sacrament is the Lord's assistance and the help of the Holy Spirit (DS 1695–96; NR 697–98). It is the Holy Spirit who heals the diseases of the old creation, while sanctifying it and introducing the new. To this belongs the healing of the soul and, if God wills, of the body also (DS 1325; NR 695). The sacrament also removes sin and its consequences, if necessary and so far as the required contrition is present; it also raises up and strengthens the soul of the sick person through trust in divine mercy (DS 1696; NR 698). The Church commends the sufferer to the suffering and glorified Lord through anointing and prayer, so that the Lord may raise him up and deliver him. It exhorts the sick "to contribute to the good of the people of God by freely uniting themselves to the passion and death of Christ" (LG 11). The sacrament of the anointing of the sick leads to its end what was begun in baptism—conformation to the Lord's death and Resurrection. It completes the penance of Christian life and is the assurance of new life (DS 1694; NR 696).

According to the Council of Trent, the only *minister of the anointing of the sick* is the priest (DS 1697, 1719; NR 699, 703). It is the task of the responsible priest to prepare the sick person and those around him for the sacrament with the help of religious and laity. He should discuss the celebration of anointing in advance, leading all to a deeper understanding and to active participation. Only then should he administer the sacrament. As with the other sacraments, the sacrament of anointing has a *communal character*, which should be expressed in the rite itself. If the state of the patient allows it, the sacrament can be administered within a liturgy of the word or in the framework of a celebration of the Eucharist, after the gospel and the homily. With the consent of the bishop, the anointing of the sick may also be given to several sick persons at one time (for instance, in connection with pilgrimages of the sick or liturgies for the sick or occasionally in hospitals). Of course, the sacrament should not be administered indiscriminately to all older people beyond a certain age; it presupposes a dangerously weakened state of health. The deathbed visit, which was once the custom, during which the dying person was "provided" with the three sacraments of penance, anointing of the sick, and the Eucharist, should now take place only when someone falls unexpectedly into an immediate danger of death.

The sacrament to be given in the face of death is not the anointing of the sick but *holy communion* as viaticum and as pledge of our resurrection (Jn 6:54). Since the first general Council of Nicea (325), the Church has exhorted the faithful to receive the Eucharist as viaticum (DS 129). If possible, this should happen within a celebration of the Mass, at which the Eucharist should be administered under both species to the dying person and to those gathered around the deathbed. Those who can no longer take solid food may receive the Eucharist only under the form of wine. Before receiving communion, the dying person should renew his faith as he faces death, the same faith he (or his parents and godparents) once vowed at baptism and renewed at confirmation, the faith that he has reaffirmed every year at the Easter Vigil. It is fitting that the dying person be able to receive a plenary indulgence in the hour of death after a confession of guilt. Here what was begun in baptism comes to its completion—a participation in the death and Resurrection of Jesus Christ. Pastors, relatives, members of the nursing staff, but above all the seriously ill themselves should pay attention that the reception of the sacrament of viaticum is not unnecessarily postponed. The dying person should receive the Eucharist with full consciousness and join himself in faith and hope to the death and Resurrection of the Lord.

All the sacraments treated until now are given to all Christians for their own salvation as well as for the building up of the Church. Two further sacraments, holy orders and matrimony, serve primarily not one's own salvation but the salvation of others. They bestow a special commission in the Church and serve the natural as well as the grace-filled upbuilding of the people of God. They are a sign of salvation for the individual insofar as they bestow upon him the grace necessary for the exercise of his particular mission. The sacraments of holy orders and matrimony are also called the two *sacraments of a state in life*.

6. The Sacrament of Holy Orders

Jesus' proclamation was directed to the entire people of Israel. He announced the good news to all; he called all to follow him. From the great number of his disciples, though, he called the Twelve to a particular following, that they might have communion with him and share in his mission in a special way.

> He then went up the mountain and summoned the men he himself had decided on, who came and joined him. He named twelve as his companions whom he would send to preach the good news; they were likewise to have authority to expel demons (Mk 3:13–15; 6:6b–13).

The *special calling* of the Twelve did not result from their natural merits or personal achievements. Holy Scripture tells us very often of their dullness, inconstancy, and unfaithfulness. Their calling sprang solely from Jesus' *free election*. "It was not you who chose me, it was I who chose you" (Jn 15:16). Jesus' elective call is efficacious and creative. He gives what he asks; he *makes* those special disciples "the Twelve". His call is an *effective*

212–214; 243–244

calling to ministry. The end is a special *personal communion* with Jesus and a *mission* to preach and to heal the world of the power of evil. The one sent is like the one who sends: "He who hears you, hears me" (Lk 10:16; Mt 10:40; Jn 13:20). We see this representation especially when Jesus commissions his disciples on the evening before his death to make present again and again the redemptive surrender of his life unto death in the celebration of the Eucharist. "Do this as a remembrance of me" (Lk 22:19; 1 Cor 11:25).

After his Resurrection, Jesus confirmed this special calling and mission to preach, to baptize, and to forgive sins (Mt 28:19–20; Mk 16:15–16; Jn 20:22–23). He promised the Apostles his special assistance and sent the Holy Spirit upon them so that they might be his witnesses to the ends of the earth (Acts 1:8). As we have already seen, the New Testament attests that this mission to a special apostolic ministry continues in the Church. The Risen Lord continues to give his gifts of grace for the upbuilding of the Church by instating apostles, prophets, evangelists, pastors, and teachers, "in roles of service for the faithful to build up the body of Christ" (Eph 4:11–12).

Even in apostolic times, the sign of the conferral of office was a *laying on of hands* and prayer (Acts 6:6; 13:3). We meet this ancient gesture of blessing, of communicating the Spirit, and of conferring office in the Old Testament, when Moses confers office on Joshua (Num 27:15–23; Dt 34:9). It was practiced in ancient Judaism, especially in conferring office on the teachers of the law. In the New Testament's Pastoral Letters it is already presupposed as a valid Church practice.

> Do not neglect the gift you received when, as a result of prophecy, the presbyters laid their hands on you (1 Tim 4:14).

> Stir into a flame the gift of God bestowed when my hands were laid on you (2 Tim 1:6).

The essential elements of the sacrament of holy orders were already established in the New Testament; these were the laying on of hands accompanied by prayer for the gift of a special grace from God. In a developed form, these elements are found in Ignatius of Antioch, just after the New Testament period. In later Church Tradition, however, this sacrament was further developed; it had also to be defended several times against attack. We can see this at the Fourth Lateran Council (1215) 195–196 (DS 802; NR 920), but especially at the Council of Trent (1563) in answer to the Reformers (DS 1764–78; NR 706–20). The Council of Trent maintained that the sacrament of holy orders was instituted by Jesus Christ, that it mediates authority and grace, and that it may not be understood *only* as an induction into the office and into the *mere* ministry of proclaiming the gospel. In addition to defending the sacramental authority of absolution and of consecration, of course, the Council of Trent also stressed that all those active in pastoral ministry have the obligation of proclaiming the word of God. It even named the proclamation of the gospel as a bishop's preeminent task.

294–295;
303–304
257–262

From the earliest times following the New Testament period, Church offices have been transmitted in *three grades*: those of bishop, priest, and deacon. Because later the connection between priesthood and sacrifice was understood very strictly for a long time, it seemed questionable whether episcopal consecration, which does not confer an authority higher than that of "simple" priests in celebrating the Eucharist, was really a sacrament. This question was settled by the Second Vatican Council. The Council teaches "that the fullness of the sacrament of Orders is conferred by episcopal consecration" (LG 21, 26). It follows that bishops administer holy orders to others (LG 21, 26). The sacramentality of *priestly ordination* has never been disputed in the Church. The central task of the priest and the completion of his ministry has always been seen in the celebration of the sacrifice of the Mass (PO 2). The sacramentality of *diaconal ordination* was also taught unambiguously by the Council. The deacon is ordained "not unto the priesthood, but unto the ministry" (LG 29, 41). He is strengthened by the laying on of hands and "more closely bound to the altar" (AG 16) so that he can exercise his diaconal ministry more effectively. His tasks include liturgical ministries alongside the bishop or priest, administration of certain sacraments (baptism, distribution of communion, assistance at marriages) and of certain sacramentals (especially at Church burials), leading liturgies of the word and devotions, catechetical and homiletical proclamation, care of certain pastoral tasks in remote congregations (in the name of the parish priest and of the bishop), and the performance of social and charitable works (*Motu proprio* of Pope Paul VI, 1967).

243–245

246–247

Before the postconciliar liturgical reform there were still the so-called minor orders (porter, lector, acolyte, exorcist) and the subdiaconate. These had been considered only as sacramentals, especially since the Council of Trent, and were really only preliminary stages to diaconal and priestly ordination. In 1972, Paul VI replaced them with *"commissionings" for the "ministries" of lectors and acolytes* (servers at the altar). These ministries can also be conferred on laymen; they are no longer reserved for candidates for the sacrament of holy orders. The clerical state begins with diaconal ordination. The earlier tonsure is no longer practiced; there is, however, a separate rite for receiving candidates for the diaconate and the priesthood.

The detailed *form of the sacrament* of holy orders has had a long history. The imposition of hands and prayer were always performed. In the course of history, these were complemented with interpretative rites taken over in part from the Old Testament. In the case of diaconal ordination, these included the presentation of the book of the Gospels; in priestly ordination, there was an anointing of the hands and a presentation of the sacred vessels (chalice and paten). For consecration of a bishop, the rites included touching the book of the Gospels to the head, anointing the head with chrism, and presenting the episcopal insignia (ring, miter, and crosier).

In medieval theology, there was a widespread opinion that the essential signs of priestly ordination were the presentation of the sacred vessels (DS 1326; NR 705). It was first definitively established by the Apostolic Constitution of Pope Pius XII in 1947 that the essential sign of all three stages of the sacrament of holy orders is solely *the laying on of hands and a prayer within the ordination Preface*. The presentation of the sacred vessels and the other rites are from now on no longer considered necessary for the validity of diaconal, priestly, and episcopal ordination. They are, though, liturgical symbols interpreting the inner meaning of the laying on of hands (DS 3859; NR 724). This decision was confirmed by the postconciliar liturgical reform of the sacrament of holy orders by Pope Paul VI (1968).

176–178 The sacrament of holy orders bestows a *special participation in the office of Jesus Christ*, who is the one and only high priest and the one mediator between God and man (1 Tim 2:5). The man ordained is enabled to act in the performance of his mission "in the person of Christ", the head of the Church. Furthermore, he has a special share in the priestly, prophetic, and 257; pastoral office of Jesus Christ. He also has a *threefold ministry*. He is sent out 260–261 to preach and teach, to give the sacraments, and to lead the people of God entrusted to him. As in baptism and confirmation, this participation in the office of Jesus Christ is conferred once for all. The sacrament of holy 265–267 orders confers an *indelible spiritual mark* and cannot be repeated (LG 21, 28, 29; PO 2). A man who has been validly ordained can indeed be released from the obligations taken on at ordination when appropriate grounds are present, but strictly speaking he can no longer become a layman. The calling and mission he once received mark him permanently. So the word "laicization" is misleading. It means only that the man in question may no longer exercise his priestly activity; the sacramental mark remains, however.

The sacrament of holy orders bestows the *grace of the Holy Spirit* for the exercise of one's mission. Officeholders in the Church cannot fulfill their ministry correctly and fruitfully and be models for their flocks unless they have an inner conviction based on a special communion and friendship with Jesus Christ (1 Pet 5:3). They are not appointed as functionaries; they are witnesses whose witness cannot be detached from their persons if it is to be credible and fruitful. An ordained man is obliged by his ministry to strive in a particular way to lead a spiritual life. Such a life attains to holiness in a way proper to him, namely, through sincere and untiring exercise of his duties in the Spirit of Christ (PO 13). The grace of the Holy

Spirit enables the one ordained to reach the double goal at which his ministry aims: the glorification of God and the service of men.

Once ordained, a man does not stand alone; he is incorporated into a *community*. By their consecration, bishops are incorporated into the episcopal office, into the college of all bishops with and under the pope. Through their ordination, priests are incorporated into the presbyterate under the leadership of the bishop (LG 28; PO 7–8). Priests can exercise their ministry only in dependence on and in communion with the bishop. The vow of faithfulness they make to the bishop at ordination and the sign of peace given by the bishop at the end of the ordination liturgy show that the bishop considers them as his coworkers, sons, brothers, and friends and that they owe him love and obedience in return. Incorporation into the one presbyterate is also seen in the ordination when all priests present follow the bishop in laying on hands. The unity of the presbyterate is further shown at occasional concelebrations and in the collaboration and brotherhood among priests. The bishop says of the deacon at his ordination that he stands "at the side of the bishop and his presbyterate as a helper".
246–247; 250–251

In the Latin Church, episcopal consecration and priestly ordination carry an *obligation to celibacy*, the duty to live as unmarried and in perfect chastity. This obligation is not required by the essence of the priesthood, as the practice of the earliest Church and the tradition of the Eastern churches show. It must be seen in the context of the care for souls, the highest law of the Church. In the Latin Church, celibacy has been emphasized by different synods from the fourth century on, but it was first enacted as a general law only in the eleventh century. The Second Vatican Council approved and confirmed this law (PO 16). According to the Conciliar declarations, the obligation to celibacy is *appropriate* to the priesthood in several respects. As an unmarried state freely chosen for the sake of the Kingdom of heaven (Mt 19:12), it is a special sign of the imitation of Jesus, who himself lived as unmarried, and of undivided service for Jesus Christ and his "cause" (1 Cor 7:32). It is a sign of perfect self-surrender for God and men, of new life, and of the world to come, to which the priest has to bear witness in a special way.
320

This argument does not ignore the many difficulties of this law. The Council argues in the spiritual power of hope and from the conviction that the Lord will call for his Church a sufficient number of priests for ministry to the communities, if only the priests themselves and the Church as a whole earnestly ask for it. The shortage of priests in many countries must be an occasion to foster more initiative and responsibility in the communities themselves. If the present shortage of priests in many countries around the world is a symptom of a deeper and more comprehensive crisis, it cannot be eliminated in isolation by merely changing a law. This is clear not least in the fact that in our times, not only celibacy, but also marriage and the family have entered into a profound crisis. These three are deeply connected with one another, as we will show in the next section.

7. The Sacrament of Matrimony

7.1 The Essence of Matrimony as a Sacrament of the New Covenant

Marriage and family are counted among the most precious of human goods. Families are the basic cells of human society. "The well-being of the individual person and of both human and Christian society is closely bound up with the healthy state of conjugal and family life" (GS 47). Like other institutions and perhaps even more than they, however, marriage and family are now caught up in the comprehensive, far-reaching, and rapid changes of society and culture. There is both good and bad in this.

> On the one hand, in fact, there is a more lively awareness of personal freedom and greater attention to the quality of interpersonal relationships in marriage, to promoting the dignity of women, to responsible procreation, to the education of children. . . . On the other hand, however, signs are not lacking of a disturbing degradation of some fundamental values: a mistaken . . . concept of the independence of the spouses in relation to each other; serious misconceptions regarding the relationship of authority between parents and children; the concrete difficulties that the family itself experiences in the transmission of values; the growing number of divorces; the scourge of abortion; . . . the appearance of a truly contraceptive mentality (FC 6).

In this disquieting situation for the human conscience, the Church and all who are active in her proclamation must present anew the fundamental values of marriage and family. They must help younger people in particular, since these stand at the beginning of their path to marriage and family. The proclamation must disclose the beauty and greatness of their calling to love and to the service of life, opening new horizons to them (FC 1); through a new culture of the family, the proclamation must evangelize the now-developing culture from within and so contribute to a new humanism (FC 8). For all these reasons, the Church has often taken a position in recent times on questions of marriage and family. There are the encyclicals of Pius XI, *Casti connubii* (1930), and Paul VI, *Humanae vitae* (1968), the declarations of the Second Vatican Council (GS 47–52), and the Apostolic Letter of Pope John Paul II, *Familiaris consortio* (1981), which summarizes and develops all previous declarations.

The Christian understanding of marriage and family is grounded in the *order of creation*. God, who called man into being out of love, called him at the same time to love. Man is created according to the image and likeness of God (Gen 1:27), who is himself love (1 Jn 4:8, 16). "Love is therefore

the fundamental and innate vocation of every human being." No man can live without love. "Love includes the human body, and the body is made a sharer in spiritual love. . . . Consequently, sexuality, by means of which man and woman give themselves to one another through the acts which are proper and exclusive to spouses, is by no means something purely biological, but concerns the innermost being of the human person as such" (FC 11). The love between man and woman is part of man's likeness to God; it is a likeness of the unconditional and definitive love of   98–100
God for every man. The judgment "He found it very good" (Gen 1:31) holds for conjugal love as well.

The reality of sin has, of course, had a destructive and alienating effect   108–115
on the relationship between man and woman and on the transmission of life (Gen 3:7, 16). Yet God included marriage and family in the *order of redemption*. Already in the Old Testament, the covenant between man and   54–57
woman becomes an "image and likeness" of the covenant between God and men (Hos 1–3; Is 54, 62; Jer 2–3, 31; Ezek 16, 23). The covenant   134–137
between God and men finds its definitive, unsurpassable realization in Jesus Christ, who is God and man in one person and in whom God has definitively accepted every man. He is the bridegroom for God's New Covenant people (Mk 2:19); he loves the Church, his bride, and has surrendered himself for her (Eph 5:25).

Jesus' position on marriage is most clearly expressed in his words on divorce (Mk 10:2–9). Jesus was confronted with a controversy among the Jews on whether a man should be allowed to dismiss his wife. At first sight, Jesus' answer appears to sharpen the Old Testament law and so to saddle man with a heavy burden. In reality, Jesus refuses to enter into the dispute on the interpretation of the Old Testament law (Dt 24:1–4). He raises the question to a higher plane. He recalls God's original plan in creation. Certainly he knows of the hardheartedness of men that opposes the realization of God's will in creation. Yet now that the new creation is dawning in Jesus, God's first plan for creation becomes applicable again; indeed, through Jesus, it also becomes possible. Jesus' prohibition of divorce is not an external law to be realized only with difficulty; it is an expression of the New Covenant, a graciously bestowed new possibility for realizing the deepest meaning of the created and redemptive orders, a life lived out of love and faithfulness. We can say in summary that in Jesus' proclamation marriage belongs to the orders of both creation and salvation.

The Apostle Paul exhorts one to enter into a marriage "in the Lord" (1 Cor 7:39). Marriage is taken into the new being "in Christ" begun by baptism. For that reason, the New Testament domestic order sees marriage and family as the place of a particular Christian testing. The daily behavior of man and woman is to be oriented by love, faithfulness, self-surrender, and obedience to Jesus Christ (Col 3:18–19; 1 Pet 3:1–7; 1 Tim 2:8–15; Tit 2:1–6). The most important description of domestic order is found in the Letter to the Ephesians. The *covenant between man and woman in marriage* is there described *as an image of the covenant between Christ and the Church*.

> Defer to one another out of reverence for Christ.
>> Wives should be submissive to their husbands as if to the Lord. . . .
>> Husbands, love your wives, as Christ loved the church. He gave
>>> himself up for her. . . .
> "For this reason a man shall leave his father and mother,
>> and shall cling to his wife,
>> and the two shall be made into one."
>
> This is a great foreshadowing; I mean that it refers to Christ and the Church (Eph 5:21–22, 25, 31).

This passage doubtless reflects features of the prevailing understanding of marriage, according to which women were subordinated to men. Yet it also bursts through any patriarchal understanding of marriage. It speaks of the love and self-surrender of spouses and so of a mutual subordination. The text's most important declaration is not that the love and faithfulness between Christ and the Church is a model for marriage; it is that the love between man and woman in marriage is a sign that makes present God's love and faithfulness, which have definitively appeared in Jesus Christ and are abidingly present in the Church. "The marriage of baptized persons thus becomes a real symbol of that new and eternal covenant sanctioned in the blood of Christ" (FC 13).

The *Church's Tradition* found the sacramentality of marriage indicated in Holy Scripture, especially in the Letter to the Ephesians (DS 1799; NR 733). This doctrine is first found explicitly in the high Middle Ages (DS 1327, 1797–1812; NR 730, 731–46). It is not meant to make marriage into a mystery or to make it a reality totally dependent on the Church. The doctrine recognizes, rather, that marriage is a distinct created reality and that it is included as such in the order of redemption. A valid marriage is effected solely through the nuptial words ("I do"), the consent of the engaged couple, which is expressed in the form prescribed by the Church. According to Church law, nothing can replace this consent. Incidentally, the Church first developed a separate ecclesiastical form for contracting marriage in the Middle Ages; it first became generally obligatory and normative for the validity of marriage at the Council of Trent (DS 1813–16). Where only one public form of marital consent is observed, however, the couple can be dispensed for good reasons from the duty of ecclesiastical form.

Here, of course, there arises a new difficulty under today's circumstances. We cannot presuppose that all engaged couples who wish to be married in the Church

hold the faith of the Church when they receive the sacrament of marriage with
their "I do". The question of the relation between *faith and sacrament* becomes
particularly urgent in the case of marriage. Since the engaged couples have been
incorporated through their baptism into Christ and into the Church, it must be
presupposed that they assent at least implicitly to what the Church intends when
she celebrates a marriage. If, however, in spite of all pastoral efforts, they
explicitly and formally reject what the Church intends in the marriage of baptized
persons, the pastor must point out to them that it is not the Church but they
themselves who prevent the celebration for which they ask (FC 68).

261–262

The *sacramental sign* of matrimony is the free, personal act "by which the
partners mutually surrender themselves to each other" (GS 48). For that
reason, according to the most widely represented theological opinion, the
engaged couple give each other the sacrament of matrimony when they
declare their will to be married. This will is completed when the two
become one flesh (Gen 2:24; Mk 10:8), a union that encompasses all
domains of life.

The priest who assists at the wedding receives the words "I do" in the
name of the Church and pronounces the blessing of the Church upon the
spouses. His actions show that marriage is not merely a private affair for
the engaged couple, but a public sign of God's love and faithfulness. That
is clear already in Hosea 2:21–22, where right, justice, love, mercy, and
faithfulness are counted among the goods of the marriage covenant
between God and his people. The public *ecclesiastical form* for contracting
marriage, which is the usual one among Catholics, is no external formality,
no mere marriage certificate, much less an inappropriate entanglement of
state and Church. Neither does the public character of the marriage vows
take away their private origin in the immediate and wholly personal love
of the partners. The public character provides protection and recognition,
support and witness for the words "I do" and for a common life.
Conversely, the spouses are, for each other, their children, and the
Church, special witnesses of the salvation in which they participate
through the sacrament (AA 11). Matrimony forms a kind of domestic
Church, a Church in miniature (LG 11). Marriage and family not only
represent and express the essence of the Church; rather, they contribute
independently and actively to the building up of the Church. Marriages
and families are to be living cells in the Church and in the community.

222–223

Through the words "I do", by which the engaged couple give themselves to each other, they are taken in a special way into God's covenant
with men. It is God himself who unites them (Mk 10:9), so that from then
on they belong to each other before God, before each other, and before the
human community. The Church's doctrine speaks in this connection of

the *marriage bond* as the image of the inviolable covenant of God with men. Thus their covenant is not subject to their own designs nor those of the Church or human society.

263–265   As with every sacrament, the *grace of the sacrament of matrimony* consists of three things. Through their love and faithfulness, the married couple make God's love and faithfulness in Jesus Christ present. Second, they receive a share in that divine life; their "married love is caught up into divine love and is directed and enriched by the redemptive power of Christ and the salvific action of the Church" (GS 48). "Christian married couples help one another to attain holiness in their married life and in the rearing of their children. Hence by reason of their state in life and of their position they have their own gifts in the people of God (cf. 1 Cor 7:7)" (LG 11). Finally, Christian matrimony foreshadows the eschatological marriage, the joy and fulfillment of all reality in God's love (Mk 2:19–20; Mt 22:1–14; 25:1–13, among others). For that reason, celebrating marriage in the most solemn and festive way possible not only answers a general human and civil need; it makes good sense even in Christian terms as an anticipatory celebration of the eschatological marriage—an anticipation that awakens hope.

Of course, the mention of the eschatological marriage also reminds us that marriage belongs to the provisional order of this world (Mk 12:25; 1 Cor 7:25–38). It is not yet the definitive fulfillment. As a foreshadowing of the definitive goal,
234–235;   there is in the Church, besides the state of marriage, an unmarried state *freely chosen*
315   for the sake of the Kingdom of heaven (Mt 19:12). Whoever freely chooses to remain unmarried for the sake of the Kingdom of heaven is not as such a better Christian than the married person. Rather, he wants to enact symbolically a basic dimension of the common Christianity of all the baptized—the provisional character of all earthly orders and their orientation to the one thing necessary, the Kingdom of God. For that reason, the celibate wishes to be even now wholly and undividedly free for the Lord and "his cause" (1 Cor 7:32). Esteem for the freely chosen unmarried state undertaken for the sake of the Kingdom of heaven does not contradict the high value of marriage; rather, it presupposes the value of marriage and confirms it. If human sexuality were not considered a high value bestowed by the Creator, then its renunciation would also lose its meaning. Conversely, marriage only becomes a form of life truly chosen in freedom if there is also another officially recognized form of life. Marriage and the freely chosen unmarried state are two ways of representing and living the one mystery of the covenant between God and men. These two ways of life need each other; they stand and fall with each other. Vocations to the unmarried state are signs of healthy Christian marriages; the devaluation of the freely chosen unmarried state, on the other hand, necessarily leads to the failure to recognize the Christian values of marriage (FC 16). The present crises of Christian marriage, as well as that of the freely chosen unmarried state, mutually condition each other; they can only be resolved in a pastorally responsible way together.

7.2 The Essential Properties of Matrimony: Unity, Fruitfulness, and Indissoluble Faithfulness

At a Church wedding, the "I do" of the engaged couple is asked for and given in three forms. This shows that the "I do" has three concrete dimensions, each of which is of considerable importance for the validity of the marriage. It is a "Yes" to unity, to fruitfulness, and to indissoluble faithfulness.

The love of the married couple tends essentially toward a *unity of personal communion* that encompasses all domains of life. "They are no longer two but one flesh" (Mt 19:6; Gen 2:24). They are called to grow constantly in their unity through the faithfulness they enter by their marriage vows. "This conjugal communion sinks its roots in the natural complementarity that exists between man and woman, and is nurtured through the personal willingness of the spouses to share their entire life-project, what they have and what they are." This human communion is confirmed, purified, and completed by the communion in Jesus Christ bestowed in the sacrament of matrimony. It is deepened by common prayer and common reception of the Eucharist. "Such a communion is radically contradicted by polygamy . . . because it is contrary to the equal dignity of men and women who in matrimony give themselves with a love that is total and therefore unique and exclusive" (FC 19).

Fruitfulness is also an essential aspect of marriage. Conjugal love of its essence wants to be fruitful. The child is the fruit of a common love and is not an external or arbitrary addition to the mutual love of the married couple. The child makes real and fulfills that love. The service of life has been entrusted to married couples, even inscribed in them, at creation by God himself. "God blessed them, saying: 'Be fruitful and multiply' " (Gen 1:28). In their fruitfulness, married couples share in God's creative love; they are, as it were, coworkers of God, the loving Creator, and interpreters of his love. The fruitfulness of conjugal love is not limited, however, to procreation. It is extended and enriched in the fruits of moral, spiritual, and supernatural life that the parents transmit to their children in their upbringing. The parents are the first and the privileged educators of their children (GE 3). In this comprehensive sense, the fundamental task of marriage and family is to serve life (GS 50; FC 28). Older Christians who can no longer expect children when they contract marriage, and married couples to whom the blessing of children is denied, can still have a marriage that is meaningful in human and Christian terms.

The matrimonial mission today encounters a social and cultural situation in which it is difficult for many married couples to internalize the teaching of the Church and to live it out. The Church knows about the often burdensome and sometimes agonizing situation of many married couples and about the many difficulties of a personal and social nature. But she must place herself on the side of life, especially when faced with a prevailing mentality that is often inimical to life. The moral order was not created by the Church and does not depend on her judgment; it has been given to man, even inscribed in him, by God himself. For that reason, parents must ultimately make the decision about the number of their children in *responsible parenthood* before God. In doing so, they may not, of course, follow their own caprice; they must let themselves be led by a conscience that orients itself by the divine command and its interpretation through the Magisterium of the Church, according to which conjugal love must be open to new life. They must consider their own well-being as well as that of their children, those already born and those to be expected; they must consider the material and spiritual circumstances, the well-being of the whole family, of secular society, and of the Church (GS 50; FC 29–33). Particularly in the face of the above-mentioned difficulties, the *law of gradualness* applies to responsible parenthood. This law urges constant endeavor to overcome conflicting difficulties through discipline and moderation, through prayer and the regular reception of the sacraments (FC 34).

Finally, *indissoluble faithfulness* is part of the essence of conjugal love. It follows from the completeness with which the married couple give themselves to each other; any love deserving of the name is always definitive and can never be bestowed only "until further notice" or on a trial basis. The well-being of children also makes an unconditional and indissoluble faithfulness necessary for the spouses. God himself wills this at creation: "Therefore let no man separate what God has joined" (Mk 10:9). The deepest reason for this lies in God's faithfulness to his covenant, especially in Christ's indissoluble faithfulness to his Church, of which the sacrament of matrimony is both sign and fruit. The indissolubility of marriage receives a special firmness through the sacrament of matrimony. Especially today, one of the Church's most important and urgent duties is to present the value of indissolubility and of conjugal faithfulness. The Church must bear witness to the good news about God's definitive love and faithfulness for us, in which marriage participates and by which it is held and sustained. The Church proclaims this to those who consider it difficult, even practically impossible, to bind themselves to another person for the whole of life. The Church wants also to give recognition, help, and encouragement to those who often struggle, under considerable difficulties, to be faithful in marriage. We must also recognize the valuable witness of those married persons who, though abandoned by their partner, refuse to enter a new bond in the strength of faith and of Christian hope (FC 20).

Of course, the Church has had the painful experience from the very beginning that marriages between Christians can fail. There are situations in which the *separation of the spouses* must be accepted as the last resort, after every other reasonable attempt to save the marriage has proven futile. Separation is ecclesiastically possible; the Church community must help those separated to cope with their difficult situation and to preserve faithfulness (FC 83).

Many of those who get divorced enter into a new bond without a Church wedding. The situation of *divorced persons who are civilly remarried* must be judged justly. It makes a difference whether someone was unjustly abandoned in spite of sincere endeavors to save the first marriage or whether someone destroyed a valid marriage by his own serious fault. These Christians are not excluded from the Church in their difficult situation. The priests and the whole community, rather, should stand by them in attentive love so that they do not consider themselves as alienated from the Church, in the life of which they as baptized persons can and should participate. They can and should hear the word of God, take part in the celebration of the Eucharist, pray regularly, and cooperate in works of charity and in efforts to foster justice. "Let the Church pray for them, encourage them and show herself a merciful mother, and thus sustain them in faith and hope" (FC 84).

The Catholic Church maintains, however, in faithfulness to the words of Jesus Christ, that such a bond cannot be recognized as a sacramental marriage if the first marriage was valid and as long as the first marriage partner still lives. Since divorced persons who are civilly remarried are living in objective contradiction to God's order, Church practice does not admit them to communion as long as they live in full conjugal relations (FC 84). Difficult problems no doubt often result from this, not only for the Christians concerned but also for the pastors. It is not easy to reconcile faithfulness to the truth, to which the Church is obligated for the sake of love, with the tolerance and forbearance required by Christian love and mercy in a concrete difficult situation. Canon law can establish only a generally valid order; it cannot settle every individual case, many of which are often very complex. The paramount pastoral concern, of course, must always be that no error and confusion arise among the faithful with respect to the teaching and the practice of the Church on the indissolubility of marriage. Especially in our times, the Church must be an unambiguous sign in this question.

7.3 The Denominationally Mixed Marriage

A great number of Catholics live today in denominationally mixed marriages. Because of the constant shifting of broad sections of the population, denominationally mixed marriages are not at all an exception today; the attitude of many Catholics about them has also changed considerably in recent decades. A denominationally mixed marriage has many aspects; not all of them can be treated here. We will limit ourselves to a marriage between a Catholic and a Protestant. Information should be sought from one's pastor on the somewhat different regulations for marriages between Catholics and Orthodox Christians.

On the one hand, the denominational difference of the marriage partners can have an enriching, *vivifying effect* on their faith and on their marriage if both of them bring their own ecclesiastical heritage into the family, learn from each other, and so deepen and enrich their common life. On the other hand, the *difficulties* of a denominationally mixed marriage should not be underestimated. They result from a separation between the churches that has not yet been overcome and that is still painfully felt. Not only are there important differences in faith that have not yet been overcome, but also denominational prejudices and differing denominational mentalities. These can become a burden on the marriage and even lead to the alienation of the partners. These difficulties usually show themselves in child rearing and church attendance. Not infrequently, denominationally mixed marriages take refuge from such difficulties in a supposed neutrality. Religious questions are bracketed, which leads to the alienation of both partners and of their children from the churches.

An important difference between the separated churches is their *understanding of marriage*.

The churches agree that marriage represents God's order and stands under his blessing. But while the Catholic Church counts matrimony among the sacraments, Luther called it "an external, secular thing". He did not mean that marriage is something purely profane; he meant, rather, that marriage belongs, not to the order of salvation, but only to the order of creation. Following this presupposition, Luther had to deny the Church any competence in the canonical regulation of marriage and put the contracting of marriages into the hands of secular authority. Protestants consider a marriage contracted before a civil magistrate as valid before God and before the church; it is only confirmed by the church. For a Catholic, on the other hand, a marriage valid before God and before the Church comes about only through an ecclesiastical contract of marriage, except when one is explicitly dispensed from this "duty of form". For the Catholic Church, a wedding before a civil magistrate usually has consequences only in civil law. The differing understandings of the relation between the created and redemptive orders, between the Church and the world, as well as the differing notions of church in general, all reappear in the concrete differences about marriage.

In order to do justice to the changed circumstances and the ecumenical rapprochement that has recently occurred, the *canonical regulations* for denominationally mixed marriages were renewed in 1970 and then newly formulated by the 1983 Code of Canon Law (can. 1124–29). According to the new canon law, difference of confession no longer represents an impediment to marriage as it once did. The explicit permission of the competent ecclesiastical authority remains necessary, however, for contracting a denominationally mixed marriage. This permission presupposes that the Catholic partner declare himself willing to live as a Catholic Christian in his marriage, to bear witness to the faith, and to advocate to the best of his ability the baptism and the education of the children in the Catholic faith. Since, however, the education of the children is a matter for both parents and since neither partner should be given occasion to act against conscience, this obligation requires no more than doing what is possible in the concrete situation, according to the best of one's knowledge and conscience.

263–264

104–105;
195–196;
203–204;
215–216

The marriage should also take place in the Catholic form. If there are serious reasons against this, the bishop can dispense from this obligation. Of course, some public form of marriage must take place for the wedding to be valid, whether before a civil magistrate or in another church or church community. A religious form of marriage is normally to be preferred to a purely civil one. If the married couple wishes the pastors of both churches to cooperate at the wedding, this should be done so far as possible. Such a *"common church wedding"* does not, of course, represent a double wedding. The wedding takes place either in the Catholic form or in a non-Catholic form, with the pastor of the other church cooperating through prayer and blessing.

The changed ecumenical situation has led the churches in the last decade to foster a *common pastoral ministry* for denominationally mixed marriages and families. Its task is to help marriage partners find their way to a good marriage and to learn to live their marriage on the basis of the Christian faith. In addition, it should help to alleviate tensions between the ties of the marriage partners to each other and to their churches. A common ministry should encourage what is common in the faith of the marriage partners to become active and what is different to be respected. Such a common pastoral ministry of marriage support presupposes a climate of trustful collaboration between churches.

In relation to church attendance, the following principle should hold: each of the two partners should remain rooted in his faith and at home in his church according to his conscience. There should be regular attendance in one's own church and loving understanding when the marriage partner would like to participate in the Sunday liturgy of his church. On suitable occasions, though, denominationally mixed couples should also attend the liturgies of their churches together.

In no other sacrament does created reality become so immediately a sacramental sign of salvation as in matrimony. In no other sacrament, though, does such an overlapping and a tension come about between the old world, confused by sin, and the new world, which has appeared in Jesus Christ. The difficult pastoral situations we have discussed are signs of this interlacing. In individual cases, the two worlds can hardly be disentangled. The sacrament of matrimony points especially beyond the present age, between the coming of Jesus Christ in lowliness and his Second Coming in glory, to the heavenly marriage feast and a life in the world to come.

V

LIFE IN THE WORLD TO COME

1. What May We Hope For?

The last sentence in the Creed says, "We look for the resurrection of the dead and the life of the world to come." It is the Christian answer to man's deepest hope. Today this answer somehow seems both appealing and yet deeply foreign. It appeals to us as a *prospect of hope*. Hope is prototypically   15–17
human; no one can live without it. However, hope is different from mere optimism, which imagines that things will somehow work out. Hope reaches deeper and goes farther. It is an expectation that the bleak monotony and burden of everyday life, the inequality and injustice in the world, the reality of evil and suffering, will not have the last word, are not the ultimate reality. Hope believes that reality is open for something more. This expectation of a new possibility remains ambiguous. Especially today, anxiety about future threats spreads among many of us. The strongest objection against all purely this-worldly hope remains death. Mankind has always been unable to come to terms with death. Accordingly, all religions speak in some way of a hope beyond death. The question of what we may hope for is not, however, only a religious question; it is also a persistent question for human thought. It is inseparable from other questions: What remains? What holds? What is the meaning of life, of the world, of history? Why are we on earth?

But the last sentence in the Creed is, of course, deeply foreign to many people today. It provokes a *wealth of questions* as we ponder it. In theology, this last sentence has been developed in the doctrine about the "last things": death, judgment, heaven, hell, Purgatory, the resurrection of the dead, the Second Coming of Christ, the last judgment, the end of the world, and its re-creation. These themes show at once why the Christian Creed is so problematic for modern man. How are we to reconcile these declarations with our present notions of an evolutionary cosmos? The question "What may we hope for?" is very quickly transformed for us today into "What can we know?" Can we know anything reliable at all about a life after death? Is it not all reduced to a big Perhaps? Or are all these declarations only projections of our wishes and desires, mere empty consolations that hold us back from responsibility and joy in this world?

327

Many of our contemporaries think that musing on what they consider illusory hopes is less important than addressing the question: What can we do now? What can we do to assure and to increase happiness, peace, justice, and freedom in this world? Instead of a new life in the next world, they hope for a better life in this one.

Faced with such questions, Christian faith is challenged today to give an account of the hope that fills us (1 Pet 3:15). In order to begin such an account, we must first assure ourselves about the foundation of Christian hope. The point of departure and the *ground of Christian hope* are not just wishful dreams, projections, and speculations, not a cheap optimism with a happy ending, not the "principle of hope" (Bloch), and not a belief in progress, in evolution, or in revolution. We can speak in faith about our future only because this future has already begun in Jesus Christ. The fundamental conviction, the center of Christian faith, is that Jesus Christ is the first of those raised from the dead (Rom 8:29; 1 Cor 15:20; Col 1:18). *The basis and permanent measure of our hope is the Resurrection of Jesus Christ.* Everything that we as Christians can say about our resurrection to eternal life is only the unfolding and the extension of the fundamental declaration of our faith about Jesus Christ, his Resurrection and exaltation. Because we are united with Jesus Christ and his death through faith and baptism, we may also hope to be united one day with his Resurrection (Rom 6:5). St. Augustine says this very aptly: "Christ realized what is still a hope for us. We do not see that for which we hope. But we are the body of that head in whom what we expect became reality."

According to Holy Scripture, it is the *work of the Holy Spirit* to take the whole of creation into the new creation begun with Jesus Christ, and to lead it toward future transfiguration. That is why faith's declarations about the life of the world to come form the conclusion of the Creed's third part, which is devoted to the work of the Holy Spirit.

Our faith in Jesus Christ and in the workings of the Holy Spirit does not allow us to offer any *anticipatory report* about reality after death or a schedule of the events at the end of time. What Holy Scripture does offer is images and parables, which are something different from scientific hypotheses about the cold death of the cosmos or a pulsating universe. We must distinguish further between the binding content of faith in the biblical witness and its literary forms of expression. The declarations of faith are not meant to describe eternal life and the future world as one might describe objects in this world. Their purpose, rather, is to impart consolation, courage, and hope in regard to the world to come; they are meant to exhort us to a change of life so far as the judgment to come threatens whoever does not change. On the basis of the declarations in Holy Scripture, we cannot sketch a picture of the judgment day; nor can

170–173;
333–334;
336–338

183–187

125–126;
348–350

we imagine or conceive heaven or hell. The well-known artistic representations of heaven and hell, of last judgment and consummation, are not to
be considered unimportant; they can and should lead us to reflect. But
they cannot convey an objective representation. "Eye has not seen, ear has
not heard, nor has it so much as dawned on man what God has prepared
for those who love him" (1 Cor 2:9). If we as Christians talk about the
content of our hope, we must also be aware of the limitations of our
representations and concepts and of the linguistic poverty of our every
declaration. This does not detract from the certainty of Christian hope,   351–352
which is firmly grounded in God's faithfulness.

2. Death and Resurrection

2.1 The Christian View of Death

"In the midst of life we are encompassed by death." That is the beginning
of a hymn from the eleventh century. This hymn tells us that death is not
only medical and biological, not only the definitive cessation of our
cardiac and cerebral functions. Neither is death only the last hour, about
which no one knows when it will strike. *Death already reaches into this life.*
It determines and threatens life anew every day in a hundred ways.
Sickness, failure, and suffering are heralds of death; they are signs that we
ultimately do not control our own lives, which slip away from us and will
be finally taken from us in death. Death determines our whole life. It
determines it as finite, limited; life is only a certain space of time between
birth and death. "Seventy is the sum of our years, or eighty, if we are
strong" (Ps 90:10). So the hymn says: "O how fleeting, O how vain is the
life of men!"
     But this is only one side. The consciousness of death makes life not only
vain but also important and exciting. Because our life is limited, its time is
precious. It becomes important to "make the most of the present opportunity" (Eph 5:16; Col 4:5). Every hour could be our last. No moment
will ever return; each one must be turned to good account. Death is also
present in life in a positive sense. In the face of death, our life becomes
urgent, undeferrable, definitive. Without death, life would be a great
tedium; with death, it becomes a challenge, a decision here and now. It is
precisely by taking death seriously that we give life its meaning. The
Christian Tradition therefore calls death the *end of man's pilgrim state*. It
means that death is the final end of the possibility for shaping one's earthly

life and for working one's salvation by God's grace. That is why we must work while there is still time.

Life and death interpenetrate. Wherever death is repressed, wherever it is concealed, covered up, and made taboo, as often happens in our modern society, truly human life is also extinguished. Only the man who looks death in the eye and accepts it can live in a truly human way. But who can do that? What is the meaning of life in the face of death? What is the meaning of death for life?

The question about the meaning of both life and death already figures in the first pages of Holy Scripture. The first answer in Scripture is that God does not will death. *Death is a consequence of sin.* In sin, man wishes to reach for the tree of life himself, to grasp it arrogantly. He reaches too high and takes on too much. Instead of life he chooses death (Gen 2:17; 3:19). So Paul says, "Through one man sin entered the world and with sin death" (Rom 5:12). This does not mean, of course, that man in paradise would have gone on living his earthly life without end had he not sinned. In our finite world, life without death is not biologically conceivable. Yet the Bible is thinking not of biological or medical death, but of man's personal experience of death—death as a dark and absurd rupture, a breach, a painful loss filled with anxiety. Man's will to life resists this, rebels against it. God did not will *this* death. *This* kind of death is a symbol of sin, a sign of alienation from God, who is the source and the fullness of life. Because Holy Scripture sees death as a consequence of sin, it does not succumb to the temptation of making death heroic or of enthusiastically transfiguring its darkness. It sees the whole terror of death. In Scripture, death is the last enemy (1 Cor 15:26; Rev 20:14).

The fate of death, which was passed on to all through the first Adam's disobedience, is not decisive by itself for the Christian understanding of death. Even more important for the New Testament is the *saving death of Jesus Christ*, the new Adam, through whom even death, and precisely it, was vanquished. In an ancient hymn to Christ we hear: "It was thus that he humbled himself, obediently accepting even death, death on a cross!" (Phil 2:8). By free obedience, Jesus has defeated the power of death (2 Tim 1:10; Heb 2:14). Death in imitation of Christ is no longer simply a fate that overwhelms us against our wills. In our imitating Jesus, rather, death can be understood and accepted as an expression of the Father's will. Death has lost its sting (1 Cor 15:55). For that reason, the believer has passed over from death to life even now (Jn 5:24). The Preface of the Mass for the Dead expresses this *transformation of death* most clearly: "In him, who rose from the dead, our hope of resurrection dawned. The sadness of death gives way to the bright promise of immortality. Lord, for your faithful people life is changed, not ended. When the body of our earthly dwelling lies in

107–109

156–162

161–162

death we gain an everlasting dwelling place in heaven." Where death is accepted in faith and understood as a passage to eternal life, we can even speak with Francis of Assisi of "brother death" and be reconciled with it. We can even deliberately accept the martyr's sacrifice of life for the sake of the faith and the brothers.

In the Christian understanding of death, life and death belong together in a quite profound sense. Christian piety has derived from their conjunction the exhortation, "*Memento mori!*"—"Remember death!" This is not a summons to flee the world; it is an exhortation to order life and to pass through it in the right way. This saying does not suggest anxiety before death, but concern for a good death. The litany of All Saints also asks, "From a sudden death deliver us, O Lord." Behind such petitions there stands the insight that man should prepare himself for death and walk toward it consciously. Earlier ages urged a definite *way of Christian dying*. This was to happen in the circle of the family or community, and one was to be provided with the sacraments of the Church. In the late Middle Ages, there were special booklets entitled "The Art of Dying". In the modern world, by contrast, death has to a large extent become devoid of any art. Most of us die in the midst of advanced medical care, but therefore in the anonymity of a modern hospital—without human closeness and without spiritual preparation or accompaniment. The person dying is even more isolated because death is considered taboo. Life, of course, becomes banalized at the same time. It is high time that Christians learn to die in a way befitting their human and Christian dignity. Christian help in dying means above all that no one should die in isolation! We owe the dying especially the active, prayerful witness of our Christian hope.

2.2 Life after Death?

Medical research has made considerable efforts in the last decades to study the phenomenon of death. Accounts of people who lay in a coma and were then resuscitated have caused a sensation. The accounts of their experiences have made clear that dying is usually not experienced as painful and fearful, but as filled with joy and light. These stories may help in allaying many people's fear of dying. Nevertheless, they contribute nothing to the question of what happens in death itself or after it. Those who were "brought back to life" were not really dead. They stood on the boundary of death, but they did not cross over it.

Reflections by many philosophers lead us a step farther. Following Plato, some have tried to prove *the immortality of the human soul* demonstratively. Because the soul belongs to the realm of indestructible spiritual

97–98;
101–103;
335–337

23–24;
103–106

realities (the Platonic Ideas) and participates in it, they argue, it is essentially indestructible. Such arguments often reappear today in different forms. It can be shown that men long for life and happiness with a longing that cannot be quenched in earthly life. It has a dynamic that points beyond death. The longing, indeed the demand, for perfect justice, which is never fully attained in this life, poses again the question of life after death. Finally, the love that accepts another person absolutely says: you belong to me forever. Love cannot come to terms with separation by death; it must hope for a lasting, fulfilled communion. In the hunger and thirst for complete, whole, fulfilled, and perfect life, we meet the concept of the eternal. Eternity does not mean an infinitely long, and thus never-fulfilled life. On the contrary, it is the "simultaneous", complete, and perfect possession of unending life.

These human realities are pointers that make our hope for a definitively fulfilled life after death meaningful. Of course, such human considerations cannot provide ultimate certainty. Since death puts the meaning of one's entire life in question, an ultimate answer to it is only possible within the overarching context of the meaning of both life and death. For the Christian, this means that the answer to the question whether there is life after death can be given only by God, the Lord of life and the fullness of life. *A definitive answer is possible only in faith.* We must ask, then, what the witnesses of Christian faith say to us about life after death.

170–172;
336–338
336–337

The *Old Testament* originally understood life after death as a shadowy existence in a realm of the dead (*sheol*). There the deceased is cut off from life and excluded from the community of family, friends, and others; he lives in abandonment, isolation, and alienation. He is excluded especially from the people's praise of God. Of course, faith in the God who is the God of the living and not of the dead could not remain satisfied with this answer. Gradually, ever more clearly, the conviction grew that God is always faithful. Even if all other relationships are ruptured in death, the relationship with God remains. Various texts express this trust in unsurpassable ways:

> Yet with you I shall always be;
>   you have hold of my right hand;
> With your counsel you guide me,
>   and in the end you will receive me in glory.
> Whom else have I in heaven?
>   And when I am with you, the earth delights me not.
> Though my flesh and my heart waste away,
>   God is the rock of my heart and my portion forever (Ps 73:23–26;
>   49:16).

But as for me, I know that my Vindicator lives,
  and that he will at last stand forth upon the dust;
Whom I myself shall see:
  my own eyes, not another's, shall behold him,
And from my flesh I shall see God;
  my inmost being is consumed with longing (Job 19:25–27).

In praying these texts, it becomes clear that communion with God is stronger than the decay of the body, stronger than any earthly community. Communion with God is the only reality that lasts in death and beyond it. Even in the Old Testament, the center of biblical faith yields a conviction of life after death, at least among individual believers. This conviction is far removed from any notions conditioned by mythology or world views. It grows into the faithful confidence that Yahweh is not only the guarantor for his people at the end of history, but that he gives the individual a share in this future that not even death can cut off. There are no descriptions of the afterlife. It is enough for the Old Testament to know that *eternal life is God himself and being eternally accepted and loved by him*.

During the tribulations of the late Old Testament period, this hope increased. In the Book of Wisdom, the just man who is persecuted places new hope in God and gains courage to endure earthly circumstances by thinking of life with God. "But the souls of the just are in the hand of God, and no torment shall touch them. . . . For if before men, indeed, they be punished, yet is their hope full of immortality" (Wis 3:1, 4; 3:15–16; 15:3–4). In another branch of Judaism, there arose the thought of the resurrection of the dead (Dan 12:2; 2 Macc 7:9, 14; 12:43).

The *New Testament* too knows that God is "the God of the living, not of the dead" (Mk 12:27). For that reason, it takes up the Jewish notions to speak of entering into the bosom of Abraham (Lk 16:22) or into paradise (Lk 23:43). But the New Testament goes far beyond the Old. It bears witness that the life of God has definitively appeared in Jesus Christ. Jesus is the resurrection and the life (Jn 11:25; 14:6). Whoever hears the word of Jesus and accepts it in faith has already "passed from death to life" (Jn 5:24). "Whoever believes in me, though he should die, will come to life; and whoever is alive and believes in me will never die" (Jn 11:25–26). In the Gospel of John, Jesus promises us that we will be where he is (Jn 14:3). For Paul too, the definitive being-with-God, for which the Old Testament hoped despite death, becomes the hope for the definitive being-with-Christ (Phil 1:23), being-with-the-Lord (2 Cor 5:8). Paul speaks simply of those who are dead "in Christ" (1 Th 4:16). If the Old

170–173; 336–338

Testament saw God himself and eternal communion with him as heaven and eternal life, the New Testament makes this more concrete by saying that eternal life in heaven is *being definitively and completely in and with Christ*—and through him with the Father.

For both the Old and New Testaments, hope in the face of death and beyond death is not something added to the faith in God. Such hope is its ultimate consequence. When all relationships are ruptured in death, both Testaments hope in the faithfulness of God whom the New Testament sees as finally appearing in Jesus Christ. Man is essentially a cry for immortality and eternal life. But he cannot answer his own cry; doing so demands more than man himself can give. The answer can come only from the source and fullness of life. New life, man's immortality, is determined by his relationship to God; it is *existence coming wholly from God and wholly ordained to him*. This eternal life in Jesus Christ begins in faith, hope, and love even in the midst of this life; it is the strength to commit oneself to life. Eternal life finds its consummation in the vision of God face to face (1 Cor 13:12).

339–341   The encounter with God that takes place in death is also a *judgment* on man's life. "The lives of all of us are to be revealed before the tribunal of Christ so that each one may receive his recompense, good or bad, according to his life in the body" (2 Cor 5:10; Rom 14:10). Great theologians such as Augustine and Thomas Aquinas have explained that this judgment should not be imagined as an external judicial proceeding. It must be understood as a spiritual event. Faced with God's absolute truth as disclosed in Jesus Christ, a man will see the truth of his life. The masks will fall away; the distortions and self-deceptions will vanish. It will become finally clear to each man whether he has won his life or lost it. He will then enter either into life with God or into the darkness that is distance from God.

347–350   The *Church's Tradition of faith* needed a long time before it could formulate precisely the truth of the new and eternal life in God that is opened up to the individual in death. The linguistic poverty of our speech about a life beyond the bounds of death showed itself in this process. From the very beginning, of course, there was a clear point of departure and an unequivocal foundation for the emerging conceptual clarity: the *Church's practice of prayer*. The Church expressed its conviction of life beyond death very early in prayers for the dead and in commemorations of them during the celebration of the liturgy. There is evidence for these practices in the early Christian catacombs, for instance. They have been a constant element of the Church's life in the Mass, in burial prayers, and in rites for the dead. Such practices would lose all meaning without the conviction of life after death.

On the foundation of this lived Tradition of faith, the conviction that death means the separation of soul and body gained more and more ground. Whereas the body decays in death, the soul of the man who dies in the state of grace *is taken up into eternal communion with God*. This doctrine can be understood correctly only if we take seriously that the soul is not a part of man alongside the body, but is rather the life principle of the unified man in his totality. (In modern terms, the soul is his ego, his self, the center of his person.) With this sense, Pope Benedict XII solemnly declared in his doctrinal decision of 1336 that the souls of the saints enter heaven immediately after death and see God face to face; the souls of those who need purification enter heaven after their purification (DS 1000; NR 901–2; DS 857, 1305; NR 926; LG 49). This doctrine was both defended and further explained by the Roman Congregation for the Doctrine of the Faith in 1979. 331–332

> The Church holds fast to the continuation and the subsistence of a spiritual element after death that is endowed with consciousness and will, so that the "ego of man" continues to exist, whereby, of course, it lacks its full corporeality in the interim period. In order to name this element, the Church employs the expression "soul", which has become firmly established through the usage of Holy Scripture and Tradition.

There are numerous *objections* against this doctrine. In both our present picture of man and in Holy Scripture, soul and body are not two parts of man; rather, man is one in body and soul. Death affects not only the body, but the whole man. Conversely, eternal life would not be human were it not also intended for the whole man. In Protestant Christianity, the *doctrine of the total death of man* was often deduced from this. This doctrine says that the whole man dies in death and that he is recreated anew by God only at the end of time. The question then becomes how the identity of man can be preserved in this and the future life. Others speak of the *sleep of the soul* until the resurrection of the dead. If this doctrine means an insensibility of the soul, it contradicts the witness both of Holy Scripture and of the Church's Tradition, which expressed its conviction of life after death very early in its practice of prayer.

The assumption of a *re-embodiment* or a *reincarnation* of the soul after death in a new worldly life completely contradicts Holy Scripture and the Church's Tradition of faith. This doctrine is found in many non-Christian religions. In the modern period, it has entered in an altered form into Western culture. There are many reasons for this. Some of these are the notion of purification from the faults of one's previous life, the notion of just compensation for innocent suffering and renunciations in this life, but also the notion of being able to realize what could not be fulfilled in the short span of a single life. According to the Christian faith, no number of earthly lives could suffice for the purification and fulfillment of man. God alone and life with him are the holiness, justice, and fulfillment of man. 23–24; 103–106

101–104   Furthermore, according to the Christian conception, body and soul cannot be
             separated in such an extreme way that the soul could assume different bodies
329–330   without thereby losing its own identity. Finally, this life is taken with true
             seriousness only if it is understood as a unique chance for deciding with or against
             God—a chance that ends once and for all in death. This once-for-all quality
             of our earthly life corresponds to the once-for-all salvific deed of God through
             Jesus Christ, in which we permanently and definitively receive a share at death
             (Heb 9:27–28).

             With all due caution and reserve we can try to understand the *reality of the life of
             the deceased with God* somewhat more deeply if we reflect on the relation of body
101–103;   and soul. Since the soul is not a part of man alongside the body, but the center of
331–332   the person, the person of man enters into life with God. Of course, the body is not
             a mere part of man, but his person in concrete relation to environment and
             community, a relation to be thought of in such intimate terms that a "piece" of the
             world, our body, belongs to our personal reality. Against this background it
             becomes clear what the separation of the soul and body means: the cessation or the
             rupture of the previous relation to the environment and the community. This
162–163;   unrelatedness is expressed even in the Old Testament notion of *sheol*. To that
331–332   extent, the substance of the traditional notion of the separation of body and soul is
             thoroughly grounded biblically. For the believer, of course, there can be no
             absolute and total separation of body and soul, no full unrelatedness. A certain
             relation to the body and the world must be maintained, even if the relation remains
             incomplete and obscure in our experience. Faith confesses that the dead who live
253–255   with God remain united with us in Jesus Christ and in the Holy Spirit in the one
             communion of saints. We express this permanent unity in prayers for the dead.

             At this point, of course, it also becomes clear that Christian hope looks beyond
             the individual's communion with God to a common future for all, to a transformed
             corporeality in a transformed world, to the resurrection of the dead. The Church's
348–349   Tradition thus distinguishes between the *consummation of the individual* in death and
             the *consummation of mankind* and of all reality in the resurrection of the dead at the
             end of time.

2.3 The Resurrection of the Dead

God wills, calls, and loves the whole man, who is one in body and soul.
The whole man includes his relation to the world and to his fellow men,
which relation expresses itself in the body. The hope for bodily resurrection is not some later, foreign addition to faith in God. It too is an internal
consequence of faith.

170–172;   The *biblical witnesses* confess the future resurrection with firm faith but
331–333   do not describe the manner in which it happens. Faith's certainty grew
             from meditation on God in the midst of oppressive human experiences,
             especially in the period of the Maccabean martyrs. "The King of the world

will raise us up to live again forever" (2 Macc 7:9). "My brothers, after enduring brief pain, have drunk of never-failing life, under God's covenant" (2 Macc 7:36; Dan 12:2–3). We first find imaginative portrayals of the resurrection of the dead, as well as the reward of the good and the punishment of the wicked, in the so-called apocryphal literature (which does not belong to the Bible). These often-confused images developed from then-prevailing notions that can no longer be held today. Then, again, they are not necesssarily connected with faith in the resurrection. Indeed, they are contradicted by *Jesus' answer* to the Sadducees (Mk 12:24–27). These deniers of the resurrection of the dead presented to Jesus the case of a woman who had seven husbands. They asked him to which one she would belong at the resurrection of the dead. He answered, "You are badly misled, because you fail to understand the Scriptures or the power of God" (Mk 12:24). At the resurrection of the dead there will be no more marrying or giving in marriage; a different world will arise by the consummating, creative power of God. Ultimately, faith in the resurrection of the dead rests on the faith that God is "the God of the living, not of the dead" (Mk 12:27).

For the *earliest Church*, Jesus' Resurrection becomes the firm foundation for its faith in our resurrection of the dead (Acts 4:1–2; 17:18, 32, among others). Paul says, "If the Spirit of him who raised Jesus from the dead dwells in you, then he who raised Christ from the dead will bring your mortal bodies to life also, through his Spirit dwelling in you" (Rom 8:11; 1 Cor 15:12–22).

170–173; 333–334

In the *Gospel of John*, we discover an inner bond between the Eucharist and the future resurrection. Jesus says, "He who eats my flesh and drinks my blood has life eternal and I will raise him up on the last day" (6:54). Elsewhere, he says, "For an hour is coming in which all those in their tombs shall hear his voice and come forth" (5:28). Jesus himself is "the resurrection and the life"; he who believes in him will live, even if he dies (11:25).

When we read that those in the tomb will "come forth", that those who have done good will rise to life and those who have done evil will rise to judgment (Jn 5:29), we have *difficulty understanding* these things in modern scientific terms. But how else is the Bible to express the mystery of a future world and the resurrection of the dead except in the language and notions of its time? Many before us have had difficulties with the message of bodily resurrection. Indeed, the difficulties in the ancient non-Jewish and especially Hellenistic world were substantially greater than ours. To hope in the bodily resurrection was considered foolish and scandalous. When Paul spoke of it before the sages of the Athenian Areopagus, "some sneered, while others said, 'We must hear you on this topic some other time' " (Acts 17:32). Then as now, the question is, how are we to conceive this? How will it happen? Paul himself recognizes this question: "Perhaps someone will say, 'How are the dead to be raised up? What kind of body will they have?' " (1 Cor 15:35). It is obvious that this question becomes newly urgent within our modern world view with its link to the natural sciences.

Theologians have labored over this question, sometimes developing theories that seem strange to us today. *Two extremes* had to be avoided. On the one hand, there was a primitive *materialism* that thought we would reassume in resurrection the same matter, the same flesh and the same bones, as in this life. We know, though, that we replace our matter during this life in cycles of about seven years. The identity of the person from this life to the next cannot depend on a material identity. Paul also tells us that flesh and blood cannot inherit the Kingdom of God, because the perishable cannot inherit the imperishable. We shall indeed be the same, and yet we shall be transformed (1 Cor 15:50–51). "This corruptible body must be clothed with incorruptibility, this mortal body with immortality" (1 Cor 15:53). On the other hand, we may not understand this transformation purely spiritually in the manner of a worldless *spiritualism*. The resurrection produces a new corporeality, transformed and transfigured by the Spirit of God, bearing an essential (not material) identity with the former body. So the Fourth Lateran Council (1215) teaches that "all shall rise with the body that they bear here" (DS 801; NR 896). This mean between materialism and spiritualism can be called *spiritual realism*. It holds that in the end everything will be transformed and transfigured by the Spirit of God. We cannot picture that concretely. We know only that our world and our history will be the same, though in a quite different way. "So is it with the resurrection of the dead. What is sown is ignoble, what rises is glorious. Weakness is sown, strength rises up. A natural body is put down and a spiritual body comes up" (1 Cor 15:42–44). If with Holy Scripture we understand "body" to mean the relation to the environment and to community, a relation that is essential and proper to the human person, then bodily resurrection means that our relation to one another and to the world is restored in a new and fuller way. The resurrection of the dead is not merely a consummation of the individual, but the *consummation of all reality*. The whole world and its history will be filled by the Spirit of God at the end of time. Jesus Christ will then hand over his lordship to the Father, and God will be all in all (1 Cor 15:28). The longing of all creation, which "groans and is in agony even until now" (Rom 8:22), will be fulfilled. A new brotherly and sisterly community, a new solidarity will arise in this kingdom of freedom (Rom 8:21; GS 32). When this happens, everything that men have done in history will be brought in with the great

348–352

harvest of time. Everything done in love will be given a permanent place in the new creation. "Charity and its works will remain" (GS 39). It will then be manifest that God is the Lord of all reality—a truth now hidden and intelligible only in faith. God's glory will then fill all.

This is not a cheap consolation. It is an *exhortation* both *to commitment to life* and to battling against the powers of death, against atrophy or deformation of body and soul, against alienation among men, against everything that harms, profanes, or destroys life. The promise of the future life obligates us in the present. Hope in the resurrection of the body means that Christians have a responsibility for material creation; it too is destined for transfiguration. Perhaps this statement makes us pause. Will everything really enter into the Kingdom of God—even evil things? How will that satisfy our hope for a definitive justice?

2.4 The Coming of the Lord and the Last Judgment   178–180

The world and history as we experience them concretely are discordant and equivocal. Good and evil, deceit and truth are most often mixed together. The Gospels describe this situation with the parable of the weeds and the wheat (Mt 13:24–30). St. Augustine sees the whole of history from the beginning of creation to the end of time as a *conflict between the Kingdom of God and the kingdom of the world* or of the devil. The two kingdoms are radically different, but they overlap and are mixed together. The gospel is far from understanding history as a history of progress in which goodness, truth, and faith always gain ground. Such a naive optimism would contradict our entire historical experience. The New Testament itself expects an even fiercer attack by the powers of evil on the Church at the end of time (Mk 13:3–23 par.; 2 Th 2:1–3; Rev 12:13–18, among others).

The ambiguity of history and the power of evil in the world will not, however, be the last word; this is the conviction of both Old and New Testaments. The Old Testament awaits the *day of the Lord*. This is not some mere calendar day, but a day fulfilled by God, the day and the time when God's holiness and glory will become manifest. But this day is not to be sought with a superficial, optimistic complacency. The prophets await it as a terrible judgment. The prophet Amos says, with chilling clarity, "Woe to those who yearn for the day of the Lord! What will this day of the Lord mean for you? Darkness and not light!" (Am 5:18). But the Old Testament (especially in Hosea) also teaches that judgment means purification, a final deliverance and restoration for the people.

In the New Testament, the "day of the Lord" becomes the *day of Christ*. God has transferred judgment to Christ and has entrusted him with achieving the event of salvation. This day is thus called "the day of Christ Jesus" (Phil 1:6, 10; 2:16), "the day of the Lord" (1 Th 5:2; 1 Cor 1:8, among others), and the day of the "Son of Man" (Lk 17:24). The believing community expects the eschatological coming of Jesus Christ. Jesus' coming and appearance is called the *parousia* in the New Testament. This is badly translated as "Second Coming", which suggests an event that has already taken place once. In reality, this will be the consummation of what was begun in the Incarnation, cross, and Resurrection of Jesus Christ, the consummation of the work of Jesus Christ, and the definitive manifestation of his glory. The end of time will reveal that Jesus Christ is and was from the very beginning the grounding and central meaning of all reality and all history, the alpha and the omega, the first and the last, the beginning and the end (Rev 1:8; 22:13).

Because Jesus Christ is the original and final criterion, everything will be measured by him and against him at the end. Thus the New Testament proclaims him as God's *judge of the living and the dead* (Acts 10:42). The judgment of the individual and of nations is announced by grand images in the New Testament (Mt 25:31–46; Jn 5:28–29; Rev 20:11–15). We must, of course, remember that these images are not descriptions. They mean to tell us that everyone will receive in the end his rightful place and his true meaning from Jesus Christ. Every other power and domination will then be judged, dismissed, and deposed. Because Jesus Christ is the final criterion, this judgment will be a judgment of mercy for all those who trust in him. When Holy Scripture adds that God's judgment through Jesus Christ will be accompanied by the Twelve (Mt 19:28), the angels (Rev 3:21), and the saints (1 Cor 6:2), it means that those who are in Christ and live by him will be confirmed as the norm for his followers and secured in their rights.

The judgment on the last day means that *the definitive truth* about God and man, the truth that Jesus Christ is in his person, will become manifest in the end. Justice will triumph; right will be done for each (Is 9:11): the weak and oppressed, the humiliated and forgotten, the nameless victims of natural disasters and the obliterated victims of human ruthlessness and violence. The message of judgment is good news; it is an essential expression of Christian hope. Moreover, the future judgment is already at work in the present: for "whoever does not believe is already condemned" (Jn 3:18). Even now men are being divided on the basis of their good or evil deeds (Jn 3:18–21); this division will then be made manifest. The future judgment exhorts us to decision even now and to commitment here today.

For those who believe in Jesus Christ, the prospect of the Lord's coming is a *hope* for full redemption, for liberation from present anxieties and

333–335

compulsions. The coming of the Lord means the end of death and transitoriness. The believing community will then be able to take a deep breath after the tribulations of the last days: "Hold your heads high, for your deliverance is near at hand" (Lk 21:28). Paul is convinced that God "will strengthen you to the end, so that you will be blameless on the day of our Lord Jesus" (1 Cor 1:8). All who belong to the Church, the community of salvation, will be gathered from around the world (Mk 13:27). The Church herself will receive her perfected form after the removal of unworthy members (Mt 13:41–42); she will celebrate her marriage as the "bride prepared to meet her husband" (Rev 21:2), making her entrance into the city of God, the eschatological Kingdom (Rev 21:9–10). All the longing of the afflicted and persecuted community reaches out for that day: "The Spirit and the Bride say, 'Come!' Let him who hears answer, 'Come!' " (Rev 22:17).

The Bible musters richly figurative language to teach the faithful about future events that are not humanly imaginable. *Historically conditioned views and modes of expression*, which seem foreign to us today, entered into many portrayals of the *parousia*. In the great discourse on the last times (Mk 13), the coming of the Son of Man is described according to the prophecy in Daniel 7:13: "Then men will see the Son of Man coming in the clouds with great power and glory" (Mk 13:26). Still, the heart of this declaration is not an ancient world view, but the eschatological event effected by God, one to be experienced worldwide. "Apocalyptic" descriptions taken over from an ancient literary genre have influenced other portrayals, particularly 1 Thessalonians 4:16–17 and 1 Corinthians 15:52. If we read there of the angel's call and of God's trumpet, even of the rapture of the earthly community into the air, these are historically conditioned modes of expression that culminate in a perfectly valid declaration: "Thenceforth we shall be with the Lord unceasingly" (1 Th 4:17). From the range of images and from the differing descriptions, the permanent truth of faith stands out: Christ will come with divine power to judge the world and to take those who are his to himself forever.

    In the New Testament, there are many traces of the so-called *imminent expectation*. 125–127 This means that Jesus himself brought near the coming of the consummated Kingdom of God (Mk 1:15; 9:1; Mt 10:23). In his person, in his death, and in his Resurrection, the Kingdom of God has dawned in fact. The primitive community as well as Paul himself expected the imminent coming of the Lord (1 Th 4:15–17; 1 Cor 7:29; 15:51–52; Phil 4:5, among others). Indeed, the primitive community hoped anxiously and prayed for his speedy coming (1 Cor 16:22; Rev 22:20; Did 10:6). On the other hand, though, the New Testament also shows the experience of the delay in the Lord's coming (Mt 24:48; 25:5). Scoffers ask scornfully, "Where is that promised coming of his?" (2 Pet 3:4). In spite of this tension, no indication is found in the New Testament that there was any crisis about it. The primitive Christian hope did not entail a schedule. The message of Jesus and of the primitive community was meant to address men now and to confront them with a decision. The earliest Church always announced the returning Lord as coming, demanding, judging, and encouraging. In the certainty of hope, the accents could be placed differently. The central issue was always that unavoidable tension that exists between a decision in the here and now and a future that presses on but is not at our disposal, a future that can neither be predicted nor coerced. Even later Christian proclamation had also to endure this tension.

This realization is important for a correct understanding of the *signs of the coming of Jesus Christ* which are mentioned in the New Testament. These include grave tribulations such as wars, famines, earthquakes, and persecutions; the proclamation of the gospel throughout the whole world; apostasy and emergence of the anti-Christ (Mk 13; 2 Th 2:1–3). These are ancient notions that mean to exhort one to be wakeful and to encourage one to endure. No one can calculate the date of the Lord's coming from these signs. The New Testament clearly says, "As to the exact day or hour, no one knows it . . . only the Father" (Mk 13:32; Acts 1:7). He will come like a thief in the night, suddenly, when no one is counting on it (1 Th 5:2–3; 2 Pet 3:10). A glance at history shows clearly enough that we can always find these signs; they belong in different forms to the structure of this dying world. There have always been afflictions, wars, and natural disasters. The Church's missionaries have always attempted to push to the limits of the known world and have come up against anti-Christian resistance in doing so. The scriptural signs of the end have the function of exhorting us to constant wakefulness (Mk 13:33–37). For that reason, the Second Vatican Council aptly says: "We know neither the moment of the consummation of the earth and of man nor the way the universe will be transformed" (GS 39).

The *figure of the anti-Christ* was often particularly important for the eschatological interpretation of history. Who is this figure? According to the New Testament, the anti-Christ appears in the holy place. He "exalts himself above every so-called god proposed for worship", so much so that he "seats himself in God's temple and even declares himself to be God" (2 Th 2:4; 9–10). In the Bible's last book, the Revelation of John, the blustering, presumptuous, violent, and blasphemous beast from the depths is impressively described (Rev 13). These declarations have often played a fateful role in history. The ambiguity of history prevents us from making a sharp distinction now between the Christian and the anti-Christian and from personalizing the essence of the anti-Christian, thus identifying others as demonic. The temptation of the anti-Christian reappears again and again. Its essence is arrogance and pride, the will to power and success, which shows itself in violence, brutal oppression, egoism, envy, and hate, but also in deceit and the distortion of truth. In the First Letter of John, dangerous false teachers are also called "anti-Christs", embodiments of an anti-Christian spirit (1 Jn 2:18, 22; 2 Jn 7). In such false teachings, the anti-Christ is "in the world already" (1 Jn 4:3).

The *gathering of Israel* promised by the Old Testament is also often called a sign of the end. The Old Testament never understood this gathering purely politically; first and foremost it was the eschatological gathering under the obedience of faith. For that reason, it is important that Paul speaks of the eschatological conversion of Israel (Rom 11:25–32). Of course, there he does not speak of an eschatological sign but of the eschatological event itself. This event cannot be dated in history or undertaken politically. This century's gathering of Israel as a separate nation must be judged by Christians as a political and not an eschatological phenomenon, even if it is religiously motivated. The eschatological hope common to Jews and Christians is that all, including Israel, will recognize the one common Messiah at a gathering of the peoples in universal peace (shalom). According to Christian conviction, he has already appeared in Jesus Christ.

The conclusion from all of this is that *no direct eschatological interpretation of individual historical phenomena* can be deduced from the biblical declarations on the Second Coming and judgment.

The New Testament declarations on Jesus Christ's coming at the end of time as both judge and Savior of the world also have *practical meaning*. They exhort us to conversion and to discipleship here and now; they are meant to keep us wakeful, to give us consolation and hope. They tell us that the whole of history will one day come to an end. This end will not be emptiness, but fullness and consummation. In the end, truth, right, freedom, and life will triumph over deceit, violence, destruction, and hate. Thus understood, Christian hope is not the empty consolation of another world that shirks responsibility in this one; it is an encouragement to commitment in favor of right, truth, and love, already in this world. Still, the consummation of history is not possible "from below". No individual, no group, no class, no race can pose as the main actor in world history and pretend to precipitate the last judgment. Every this-worldly Messianism is rejected by the Christian. The Lord of history is God alone through Jesus Christ in the Holy Spirit. God will have the last word, a word of justice and mercy for all and for each individually.

177–179;
179–180;
208–210;
350–352

Christ's coming was an object of joyful expectation for the primitive Church, an event she awaited longingly. At her liturgical celebrations she cried, "Come, O Lord, come soon!" (1 Cor 16:22; Rev 22:20; Did 10:6). In later centuries, the day of judgment was seen more under the signs of fear and terror—as a day of wrath, tears, and lamentation. The tension between hope and confidence in eternal life, on the one hand, and wholesome fear and trembling before the real possibility of eternal damnation, on the other, cannot be avoided. With all due reservation and caution, we must ask once again: What is eternal life? What is meant by the life in the future world?

132–134;
281–285

3. Eternal Life

3.1 Heaven

In Holy Scripture and in the Church's Tradition of faith, eternal life in communion with God is described through many images: it is a heavenly marriage feast, life, light, and peace. When we talk of "heaven" in this connection, we echo the ancient world view, in which heaven was above the earth and the firmament. This spatial "above" was meant first and 92–93 foremost as an image of man's fulfillment and of *consummate beatitude*. We still employ this image today in our secularized language when we say, for instance, that someone feels as if he were in seventh heaven, or that someone enjoys a heavenly repose. For man, according to Christian faith, the state of definitive and consummate beatitude can only be God and communion with him. God alone suffices (Teresa of Avila). *Heaven is the eternal communion of man with God.*

The Revelation of John describes the blessedness of heaven by allusions to the Old Testament and in unsurpassable images:

> It was this that brought them before God's throne:
>   day and night they minister to him in his temple;
>   he who sits on the throne will give them shelter.
> Never again shall they know hunger or thirst,
>   nor shall the sun or its heat beat down on them,
>   for the Lamb on the throne will shepherd them.
> He will lead them to springs of life-giving water,
>   and God will wipe every tear from their eyes (Rev 7:15–17).

Elsewhere in Holy Scripture, the blessedness of heaven is said to be the *vision of God* "face to face" (1 Cor 13:12).

> Eternal life is this:
> to know you, the only true God,
> and him whom you have sent, Jesus Christ (Jn 17:3).

> Dearly beloved,
> we are God's children now;
> what we shall later be has not yet come to light.
> We know that when it comes to light
> we shall be like him,
> for we shall see him as he is (1 Jn 3:2).

Church teaching speaks of the vision of God (DS 857; 1000, 1305; NR 926; 901–2; LG 49). This means that God reveals to us in a gracious way the whole fullness of his life and his love. The whole depth of his truth and the unfathomable mystery of his reality stand resplendent before us as the ground, goal, and content of our own being, as our final fulfillment in meaning, our consummate happiness, and our eternal blessedness. The vision of God cannot be understood in purely intellectual terms; it includes *love, peace, and joy*. It is a participation in God's own blessedness and is the consummation of our present grace-filled being in Jesus Christ and the Holy Spirit. It is *perfect participation in the triune life of God*. But just as God is an unfathomable mystery for man, so is communion with him. We can neither make a schematic representation of that communion nor grasp it with conceptual exactness. "Eye has not seen, ear has not heard, nor has it so much as dawned on man what God has prepared for those who love him" (1 Cor 2:9).

Definitive communion with God does not happen in isolation; it also grounds the *perfect "communion of saints"*. Communion with Jesus Christ and with the angels and saints, communion with relatives and friends from our earthly lives, joy at the beauty of God's works in creation and history, joy at the victory of truth and of love both in one's own life and in the lives of others—all these belong to the blessedness of heaven.

Because heaven is the fulfillment and the crowning of life, the fruits of our earthly deeds and sufferings will also enter into its transfiguring eternity. The joy of heaven is also joy at a recompense received (Mt 5:12). In crowning our merits, God crowns the work of his own grace. Each will receive the recompense suited to him (Mt 16:27; 1 Cor 3:8). For this reason, there are differing degrees of heavenly blessedness. But just as small vessels can be as full as larger vessels (though the latter contain more), so everyone in heaven will be wholly fulfilled and wholly at peace in his own way. The one love of God poured out through the one Holy Spirit will unite all into the one body of Jesus Christ for the common glorification of God and his works.

103–106;
331–332

104–105;
205–208

253–255

202–204

3.2 Hell

Many people find the Christian conviction about hell problematic. They think that this life is hell enough. They say, hell is all the others (Sartre). Of course, it is more often ourselves. People speak of the hell of war, of Auschwitz and Vietnam, of the inferno of Hiroshima and Nagasaki, of the first circle of Stalin's hell (Solzhenitsyn). But the real question is whether one can conceive of a good God who mercilessly wills eternal torments in hell. How can one reconcile hellfire-and-brimstone sermons, which cause such anxiety, with the good and liberating news of the gospel? Does not the conviction of eternal punishments in hell mean giving up our Christian solidarity with all men?

Our first answer must be that no amount of subtle interpretation can hide the fact that not only the Old Testament but *Jesus* himself and the *New Testament* place the possibility of rejection before the eyes of the evil, the godless, and serious sinners (Mt 5:29–30; 10:28; 23:15, 33, among others). We read of eternal fire (Mt 3:12; 25:41, among others), of eternal punishment (Mt 25:46), of darkness (Mt 8:12, among others), and of wailing and the grinding of teeth (Mt 13:42, 50).

The *Church's teaching*, which has explicitly defended the eternity of the punishments of hell, stands on solid biblical foundations. The Church has condemned the doctrine, attributed to Origen (third century) and repeated since, that there will be a restoration (*apocatastasis*) of all creation, including sinners, the damned, and demons, to a state of perfect beatitude at the end of time (DS 76, 411, 801, 1002; NR 916, 891, 905; LG 48). How would human freedom and dignity be preserved if God were to bring all men home into his Kingdom at the end, even those who have firmly rejected him? The message of hell has a transforming effect on our lives; it brings earnestness and drama into our historical responsibility, especially if we cannot count in advance on reconciliation and expiation for all and for everything that we have committed or omitted.

We must, of course, understand the scriptural declarations about the eternity of hell correctly. These are not useless hortatory discourses; they are admonitions that challenge a man to make a decision. The consequences of a sinner's actions are held before his eyes not so that he may be punished, but so that he will change his life to find his way to eternal life. For that reason, neither Holy Scripture nor the Church's Tradition of faith asserts with certainty of any man that he is actually in hell. Hell is always held before our eyes as a *real possibility*, one connected with the offer of conversion and life. So understood, hell should remind us powerfully of the earnestness and dignity of human freedom, which has to choose between life and death. God respects man's freedom. He does not force beatifying communion on any man against his will. Neither does Holy Scripture leave any doubt that there are sins that exclude one from the Kingdom of God (1 Cor 6:9–10; Gal 5:20–21; Eph 5:5; Rev 21:8). We face a decision between life and death. Holy Scripture does not tell us, of course, whether any man has ever actually decided against God with ultimate finality and thus radically missed the meaning of his existence. Holy Scripture teaches us the *essence of hell* in images. When it speaks of the fire of hell, it is not to be understood in a grossly realistic sense. Much less should we think of sadistic tortures. But neither does a purely spiritual understanding do justice to the declarations in Scripture. The image expresses a reality of a much deeper nature. God in his holiness is a consuming fire for evil, deceit, hate, and violence (Is 10:17). Just as heaven is God himself, won for ever, so hell is God himself as eternally lost. The essence of hell is *final exclusion from communion with God* because of one's own fault. Because God alone is the fulfillment of man's meaning, the loss of God in hell brings the experience and the pain of ultimate meaninglessness and despair.

3.3 Purgatory

The doctrine of Purgatory was incipiently present in Judaism. It is found in the New Testament, however, only by way of allusion. The Church's Tradition rests scripturally on a saying by Jesus that indicates some possibility for forgiveness in the future world (Mt 12:32; 5:26), and a saying by Paul about the possibility of being saved "as one fleeing through fire" (1 Cor 3:15). But the real foundation for this doctrine is the *Church's practice of prayer and penance*. At the end of the Old Testament, prayer for the deceased is called a holy and pious thought (2 Macc 12:45). We find it practiced in the Church from the beginning—as is shown not least by the catacomb inscriptions (LG 50). This practice of prayer not only presupposes a life after death, but also a possibility for human purification after death. After the conclusion of his earthly pilgrim existence, man can no longer actively cooperate in his sanctification; but he can be cleansed and purified through suffering. The whole communion of saints can stand by his side in prayers, alms, good works, their own penance, and not least by celebrating the Eucharist in his behalf. This conviction first expressed itself in the practice of prayer and sacrifice for the dead; it was only gradually clarified into a doctrine about an intermediate state. The English "purgatory" merely reproduces the Latin "purgatorium", which means "place of purification" or "state of purification". 334–335

 The talk of purgatorial fire is an image that refers to a deeper reality. Fire can be understood as the *cleansing, purifying, and sanctifying power of God's holiness and mercy*. The encounter with the fire of God's love that takes place in death has a purifying and transforming power for the man who has indeed decided for God in principle but who has not consistently realized this decision and has fallen short of the ideal. Is this not the case with almost everyone? God's power straightens, purifies, heals, and consummates whatever remained imperfect at death. Purgatory is God himself as purifying and sanctifying power for man. We can understand the *doctrinal declarations of the Church* against this background (DS 856, 1304; NR 926). Most concisely, they affirm, "There is a place of purification, and the souls held there find help in the intercessions of the faithful, above all in the sacrifice of the altar which is pleasing to God" (DS 1820; NR 907).

The Eastern churches share with the Catholic Church the practice of prayer and sacrifice for the dead. But they have not undergone our process of doctrinal clarification. The *Reformers* entirely rejected the doctrine of Purgatory because they saw in the practice of prayer and sacrifice for the dead an implicit attack on the sole sufficiency of Jesus' sacrifice on the cross (CA 24). But even the Catholic doctrine exhorts us to be reserved: "Difficult and hair-splitting questions which do not foster edification and usually do not increase piety have no place in popular sermons before uneducated people." The bishops should therefore forbid whatever "only serves a kind of curiosity or superstition or looks like shameful gain" (DS 1820; NR 908). In spite of the firmness of this doctrine, then, there is a clear exhortation to be prudent and to reject naive or fanciful speculations.

Popular talk about the "poor souls" is justified so far as their "poverty" is understood to mean that they cannot be actively but only passively purified and sanctified. But they are not really "poor souls" so much as souls who experience the whole wealth of the mercy of God and who are a substantial step ahead of us in the realization of human hope and in nearness to God. Their pain before God's face is that they are not yet pure enough to be able to be wholly filled and beatified by his love. They suffer only the purifying pain of love. In this love, all members of the one body of Christ are united in solidarity. For that reason, Christians can answer for one another by prayer and penance and thereby complete for the body of Jesus Christ, the Church, "what is lacking in the sufferings of Christ" (Col 1:24). Of course, it is not as if Jesus Christ had not done enough for our redemption by his suffering and death. He did more than enough. But he lets us participate in the effects of his saving work so that we may do something on behalf of others for their salvation.

3.4 The New Heavens and the New Earth

124–130   As Christians we hope for the *Kingdom of God* that Jesus announced to us. It has already begun through Jesus Christ in the Holy Spirit; in the Church and in its sacraments, it reaches into our present at this moment. But it has
183–187;   *not yet* found its consummation. "In hope we were saved" (Rom 8:24;
205–208   1 Pet 1:3); as Christians we live between times. We await the consummated Kingdom of God in which God will be "all in all" (1 Cor 15:28), in

which all justice will be fulfilled and the freedom of the children of God finally manifested (Rom 8:19, 21), in which the Church too will stand "holy and immaculate, without stain or wrinkle or anything of that sort" (Eph 5:27). We still hope for the new heavens and the new earth (Is 65:17; 66:22; 2 Pet 3:13; Rev 21:1). "Yes, we know that all creation groans and is in agony even until now" (Rom 8:22).

The "life of the world to come" fulfills the hope not only of the individual believer but also that of the Church and of mankind, even of creation as a whole. Man's consummation in his body would not be possible without the consummation of the world; conversely, the world is created for man; it has meaning only as the place of human history and consummation. For that reason, the *consummations of man, of mankind, and of the cosmos* are indissolubly bound together *in one great and encompassing event*. Only because of this can we say that God is the Lord, light, and life of all reality. 336–337

We can speak of this fulfilled Kingdom of God only in *images and comparisons*, just as it is spoken of and affirmed in the Old and New Testaments, and above all by Jesus himself. The Old Testament prophets speak most strikingly of a great *peace (shalom)* in men and nature before the face of God. 125–126; 328–329

> They shall beat their swords into plowshares
>   and their spears into pruning hooks;
> One nation shall not raise the sword against another,
>   nor shall they train for war again (Is 2:4; Mic 4:3).

> Then the wolf shall be a guest of the lamb,
>   and the leopard shall lie down with the kid. . . .
> The baby shall play by the cobra's den. . . .
> There shall be no harm or ruin on all my holy mountain (Is 11:6, 8–9).

Jesus often describes the Kingdom of God in the image of the *marriage feast* (Mt 22:1–14). By this he means a close, joyful, and festive community of life and love. Finally, the Revelation of John uses the grand image of the *new Jerusalem*.

> I also saw a new Jerusalem, the holy city, coming down out of heaven from God, beautiful as a bride prepared to meet her husband. I heard a loud voice from the throne cry out: "This is God's dwelling among men. He shall dwell with them and they shall be his people and he shall be their God who is always with them. He shall wipe away every tear from their eyes, and there shall be no more death or mourning, crying out or pain, for the former world has passed away."

> The One who sat on the throne said to me, "See, I make all things
> new!" (Rev 21:2–5).

Besides the images that speak of peace, reconciliation, and salvation, there
are images of the *end of the world* in Holy Scripture. These have always
made a deep impression in all ages. We read that the sun and the moon will
turn dark, the stars will fall from the sky, the foundations of the world will
collapse, and the elements will dissolve (Mk 13:24–25; 2 Pet 3:10). Despite
their use of a historically conditioned world view, these images express
something true. The permanence of this world gives no ultimate security
to man; this world is transitory. What is more, it groans under slavery and
alienation because of sin; it yearns to be freed from it (Rom 8:21). The
form of this world, which is distorted by sin so that it often blinds and
seduces man, is passing away (1 Cor 7:31). St. Augustine explains, "The
form passes away but not the nature." Anxiety about the end of the world
is not the last word; that word is hope for the *re-creation of the world*
(Mt 19:28; Acts 3:21), for new heavens and a new earth. The new creation,
as distinguished from the first creation, is not a creation out of nothing. It
takes place within the first creation and so does not produce *a rupture and an
end, but rather the consummation of the world*. God is faithful to his creation.
Yet the redemption of creation is not only its prolongation, improvement,
progress, or evolution from existing reality. The transfiguration of all
reality when God's glory becomes universally manifest produces a critical
convulsion in the world's form.

The scriptural statements tell us nothing about the concrete way in
which the new world will come about. We cannot simply translate these
images. We can really only preserve them, remain true to them, and resist
reducing them to the language of our concepts and argumentations empty
of mystery. We may not place these images on the same level as our present
cosmological theories about the future of the universe, nor may we
confuse them with any this-worldly future utopias. The New Testament
expresses what is decisive when it says that *God will be "all in all"* (1 Cor
15:28). When God's glory is universally manifest, the creature's deepest
longing will be fulfilled and the free kingdom of the sons and daughters of
God will become reality (Rom 8:22–23). God's justice, life, freedom, and
peace, the light of his truth, and the glory of his love will then fulfill and
transfigure all. God's lordship and glory will be the ultimate reality
encompassing and beatifying everything.

Christian hope expects the consummation of man and of the world by
God's transforming power as an eschatological event that has already
begun irrevocably in Jesus Christ. We cannot construct the new world by
evolution or revolution, by being conservative or progressive. We cannot

even prepare it by establishing a "thousand-year reign" with a false appeal to Revelation 20:4–6. As God's deed, the Kingdom of God is *not a worldly utopia in a man-made future*. We must resist the old and always-new temptation of fanaticism, which wants to erect a theocracy on earth.

Still, our hope for the Kingdom of God is *not without historical consequences*. On the contrary, it first discloses to us the full meaning of time and of history. It addresses the futility of a technocratically planned and directed human future that can only generate emptiness, anxiety, and fear. The promises of the Kingdom of God are not indifferent to the horror and terror of earthly injustice and oppression. Relying on the strength of Christian hope and love, believers can and must anticipate even in this world, so far as possible, the reality of the Kingdom of God in however a fragmentary and sketchy way. They must be peacemakers and bringers of mercy, men who do not use violence, but who hunger and thirst for justice in poverty and purity of heart, and who even let themselves be persecuted for it (Mt 5:3–12). Their work of peace and of justice should be *the effect and prefiguration* of the consummate justice and definitive peace in the Kingdom of God (GS 78). Finally, Christian hope also brings responsibility for the world as creation and as an environment worthy of human beings. We must always distinguish hope for the end of history from hope within history, but we cannot separate them in principle. The Second Vatican Council teaches:

177–179; 208–210; 343

> We have been warned, of course, that it profits man nothing if he gains the whole world and loses or forfeits himself. Far from diminishing our concern to develop this earth, the expectancy of a new earth should spur us on, for it is here that the body of a new human family grows, foreshadowing in some way the age which is to come. That is why, although we must be careful to distinguish earthly progress clearly from the increase of the Kingdom of Christ, such progress is of vital concern to the Kingdom of God, insofar as it can contribute to the better ordering of human society (GS 39).

No human exertion, however great, can ever fulfill the whole thrust and scope of Christian hope. Because Christian hope exceeds all boundaries, its essence must lead to disappointment in purely human constructions. In this world, Christian hope will always meet with attacks, sufferings, tribulations, and persecutions. Nevertheless, the Christian who believes in the God of hope (Rom 15:13) does not need to be resigned to the disappointments of life and the setbacks and catastrophes of history. His hope is well grounded in the God who has definitively revealed and communicated his love to us through Jesus Christ in the Holy Spirit. For that reason, the Christian can affirm the closing verse of the *Te Deum*:

> In you, O Lord,
> I have placed my hope.
> I shall never be put to shame.

37–38   The "*Amen*" with which we conclude the Church's confession of faith in its liturgical forms expresses this trust and this hope. In Hebrew, the word "Amen" can be traced back to the same root as the words "to believe". The concluding "Amen" recapitulates the "I believe" at the beginning of the Creed. The "Amen" confirms it once again; it says "Yes, it is so", "I stand by that", "In this faith, my hope is firmly founded". In the New Testament, Jesus Christ himself is named "the Amen" (Rev 3:14). He is the ground, content, and goal of our hope. "Whatever promises God has made have been fulfilled in him; therefore it is through him that we address our Amen to God when we worship together" (2 Cor 1:20).

ABBREVIATIONS

AA   *Apostolicam actuositatem*: The Decree on the Apostolate of the Laity (1965)

AG   *Ad gentes divinitus*: The Decree on the Church's Missionary Activity (1965)

Apol   *Apologie des Augsburger Bekenntnisses*: Defense of the Augsburg Confession (1530)

CA   *Confessio Augustana*: Augsburg Confession (1530)

CD   *Christus Dominus*: The Decree on the Pastoral Office of Bishops in the Church (1965)

CIC   *Codex iuris canonici*: Code of Canon Law (1983)

DH   *Dignitatis humanae*: The Declaration on Religious Liberty (1965)

Did   Didache (Teaching of the Apostles)

DS   H. Denzinger/A. Schönmetzer, Enchiridion symbolorum definitionum et declarationum de rebus fidei et morum, Barcelona-Freiburg-Rome, 1979

DV   *Dei verbum*: The Dogmatic Constitution on Divine Revelation (1965)

EN   *Evangelii nuntiandi*: Apostolic Letter of Pope Paul VI on Evangelization in the Modern World (1975)

FC   *Familiaris consortio*: Apostolic Letter of Pope John Paul II on the Role of the Christian Family in the Modern World (1981)

GE   *Gravissimum educationis*: The Declaration on Christian Education (1965)

GS   *Gaudium et spes*: The Pastoral Constitution on the Church in the Modern World (1965)

LG   *Lumen gentium*: The Dogmatic Constitution on the Church (1964)

ME   *Mysterium ecclesiae*: Declaration of the Congregation for the Doctrine of the Faith on the Mystery of the Church (1975)

NA   *Nostra aetate*: The Declaration on the Church's Relations with non-Christian Religions (1965)

NR   J. Neuner/H. Roos, Der Glaube der Kirche in den Urkunden der Lehrverkündigung. Neu bearbeitet v. K. Rahner, K. H. Weger, Regensburg, 11. Aufl. 1983

OE   *Orientalium ecclesiarum*: The Decree on the Catholic Oriental Churches (1964)

PC   *Perfectae caritatis*: The Decree on the Up-to-date Renewal of Religious Life (1965)

PO   *Presbyterorum ordinis*: The Decree on the Life and Ministry of Priests (1965)

SC   *Sacrosanctum concilium*: The Constitution on the Sacred Liturgy (1963)

UR   *Unitatis redintegratio*: The Decree on Ecumenism (1964)

Quotations from the Documents of Vatican II are taken from the English translation edited by Austin Flannery, O.P., and published under the title *Vatican Council II: The conciliar and Post Conciliar Documents* (Northport, N.Y.: Costello, 1975).

The numbers in the margins are cross references to parallel or complementary statements. They should help to show the inner unity and the context of the various articles of faith.

GENERAL INDEX

Abba, 58, 64–65
Abel, 109–110, 115, 213
Abraham:
  as believer, 36, 54, 140
  calling of, 35, 36
  God's covenant with, 191–192, 193, 213
  salvation history and, 171
absolution, priestly, 303–304
Adam:
  disobedience of, 108, 111, 115, 133, 330
  Eve and, 140
  Jesus as, 104, 110, 158, 330
  original sin and, 111–112
"Adoro te devote" (Thomas Aquinas), 288–289
Albigensians, 49
All Saints, 254, 331
All Souls, 254
aman, defined, 37, 54
Ambrose, Saint, 144, 300
anathema, 49
angels, 92–94, 95
annunciation, 143, 145
anointing with oil, 279–280, 308–310
Anselm of Canterbury, Saint, 33, 133, 158
anti–Christ, 132, 195, 342
apocryphal literature, 337
Apostles:
  historical research on, 124
  Jesus' election of, 213, 311–312
  mission of, 170, 179, 237–238
  original witness by, 41–42
  threefold unity of, 231
Apostles' Creed, 39, 40, 253, 260
Apostolic Constitution (1947 A.D.) (Pius XII), 314
Apostolic Constitution on the Revision of Indulgences (1967 A.D.) (Paul VI), 305, 306, 309
Apostolic Council in Jerusalem, 49

apostolic succession, 239–240
Aristotle, 25
Arius, 68
asceticism, 274
Assumption of Mary, 151
astrology, 87
Athanasian Confession of Faith, 73
Athanasius, Saint, 68, 73
atheism, 21–23, 28, 116
Augustine, Saint:
  on Church, 227, 228
  on creation, 83, 106
  on earthly goods, 91
  on Eucharist, 227
  on faith, 38
  on grace, 201
  on hope, 328
  on justification, 191, 198
  on Kingdom of God, 107, 178, 339
  on love, 178, 206, 208
  prayer of, 187
  predestination and, 189
  on sacraments, 261, 262, 264, 265, 294
  on sin, 110–111, 350
  on triune God, 73
  on word of God, 256
Augsburg Confession (1530), 73, 195, 201
autonomy, 102–103
"Ave maris stella", 148

Babel, tower of, 110
baptism:
  candidates for, 219
  Church community and, 274–277
  Holy Spirit in, 227
  of infants, 277–278, 281
  passion of Christ in, 161, 214
  penance vs., 298, 299–300
  personal meaning of, 271–274
  as regeneration, 111

dogmatic Tradition and, 50
humanity and, 16, 24, 30, 31, 104
of Jesus Christ, 291
myths, 107–108

natural sciences, 79–81, 130
see also science
Nebuchadnezzar, King, 85
Nestorians, 135
New Covenant:
God's people of, 225–226
Holy Spirit and, 184
Jesus' death and, 155, 194
law of, 201
prophets on, 213
Newman, John Henry, 116, 208
New Testament:
on apostolic mission, 238–239
apostolic writings in, 41
on common faith, 40
on confession, 49
domestic order of, 317–318
Holy Scripture and, 42, 44
Jesus Christ as the Word in, 82
on knowledge of God, 26–27
on Resurrection, 165–167
revelation and, 34
on Son of God, 67–68
on unity, 48
see also Bible; Gospels; Holy Scripture
Nicene Creed (325 A.D.):
Apostles' Creed vs., 39, 40
on confession, 49
faith defined in, 68–69
on heaven and earth, 90
modern man and, 32
on prayer, 78
on Second Coming, 179, 180
text of, 10
Nietzsche, Friedrich, 21–22
Ninety–Five Theses on Indulgences (Luther), 195
nominalism, 203

offices, ecclesiastical, 229
Old Testament:
belief in, 37
covenant of, 205–206
creation in, 81–82

on death, 332–333, 334, 336, 339–340
great women of, 140
Holy Scripture and, 42, 44
Jesus and, 45, 57, 125
on knowledge of God, 26, 27
messianic hope in, 124, 125, 145
monotheism in, 60
realm of death in, 162
revelation in, 34
theme of justice in, 191–192
see also Bible; Holy Scripture
"On the Triune God" (Augustine), 73
order of prayer, 77
ordination, 268, 311–315
Origen, 346
original sin, 111–113, 277
Orthodox Church, *see* Eastern Orthodox Church

paganism, 49, 60, 173
"*Pange Lingua*" (Thomas Aquinas), 288
papacy, *see* Petrine office
parables, 33, 126, 192, 339
paradise, story of, 107–109, 115
parenthood, 97
see also families
parishes, 242
parousia, 340–343
Pascal, Blaise, 24, 105
paschal lamb, 158
patriarchs, 54, 56
Paul VI, Pope:
on anointing with oil, 279, 309
on Church errors, 211
on evangelization, 209, 256
on holy orders, 313, 314
indulgences reformed by, 305, 306
on Marian devotion, 145
sacraments and, 282, 287
Pelagianism, 110–111, 113
penance, 298–305, 347
Pentecost, 184–185, 214
Peter, Saint, 248–249, 251, 271
Peter Claver, Saint, 220
Petrine office (Roman pontiff), 247, 248–252, 258–260
Pilate, Pontius, 122, 154, 178

INDEX OF BIBLICAL REFERENCES